LEARNING DISABILITIES

Introduction to
Educational and Medical Management

LEARNING DISABILITIES

Introduction to
Educational and Medical Management

Compiled and Edited by

LESTER TARNOPOL, Sc.D.
City College of San Francisco
San Francisco, California

CHARLES C THOMAS • **PUBLISHER**
Springfield • *Illinois* • *U.S.A.*

Published and Distributed Throughout the World by
CHARLES C THOMAS • PUBLISHER
BANNERSTONE HOUSE
301-327 East Lawrence Avenue, Springfield, Illinois, U.S.A.
NATCHEZ PLANTATION HOUSE
735 North Atlantic Boulevard, Fort Lauderdale, Florida, U.S.A.

With THOMAS BOOKS *careful attention is given to all details of manufacturing and design. It is the Publisher's desire to present books that are satisfactory as to their physical qualities and artistic possibilities and appropriate for their particular use.* THOMAS BOOKS *will be true to those laws of quality that assure a good name and good will.*

Printed in the United States of America
N-1

Contributors

BARBARA BATEMAN, Ph.D. Associate Professor, Psycho-educational Studies, University of Oregon, Eugene, Oregon. Formerly: Associate Professor, De Paul University. Research Associate and Assistant Professor, Institute for Research on Exceptional Children, University of Illinois.

SAM D. CLEMENTS, Ph.D. Associate Professor, Departments of Psychiatry and Pediatrics; Director, Child Guidance Study Unit, University of Arkansas Medical Center, Little Rock, Arkansas. Project Director, National Project on Minimal Brain Dysfunction in Children, co-sponsored by National Institute of Neurological Diseases and Blindness, U. S. Public Health Service, U. S. Office of Education, and National Society for Crippled Children and Adults, Incorporated. Formerly: Assistant Professor, Department of Pediatrics; Co-Director, Child Guidance Clinic, University of Texas Medical Branch.

DOROTHY COLODNY, M.D. Member Attending Staff, County-University Hospital and Childrens Hospital, San Diego, California. Formerly: Senior Psychiatrist in Charge, Mental Retardation Unit, California Department of Mental Hygiene, San Diego. Certificate, Academy of Psychoanalysis.

SISTER EILEEN MARIE CRONIN, Ph. D. Chairman, Department of Education. Director, Ellen K. Raskob Learning Institute and Assistant Professor of Education, College of the Holy Names, Oakland, California. Doctoral Program in Curative Psychology and Pedagogy, University of Fribourg, Switzerland. Certificate, Pedagogy of Dyslexics, Word Blind Institute, Copenhagen, Denmark.

MARIANNE FROSTIG, Ph.D. Founder and Executive Director, Marianne Frostig Center of Educational Therapy, Los Angeles, California. Clinical Professor, School of Education, University of Southern California, Los Angeles, California. Formerly: Professor of Education, San Fernando Valley State College.

HELEN GOFMAN, M.D. Director, Child Study Unit, and Medical Director, Pediatric Reading and Language Development Clinic, Department of Pediatrics, University of California San Francisco Medical Center.

LESLIE WHITESTONE KNOTT, M.D. Clinical Associate Professor, Rehabilitation Medicine, Stanford University School of Medicine. Member, Medical Service Task Force, National Project on Minimal Brain Dysfunction in Children, Co-sponsored by National Institute of Neurological Diseases and Blindness, U. S. Public Health Service, U. S. Office of Education, and National Society for Crippled Children and Adults, Incorporated. Formerly: Medical Director, U. S. Public Health Service.

LEROY F. KURLANDER, M.D. Member Attending Staff, County-University Hospital and Childrens Hospital, San Diego, California. Formerly: Director, Child Guidance Clinic of San Diego. Assistant Professor, University of Southern California School of Medicine, Los Angeles, California. Certificate in Psychoanalysis.

STANFORD H. LAMB, Ph.D. Assistant Professor of Special Education and Co-Director, Communication Disorders Clinic, San Francisco State College, San Francisco, California.

LEONARD LEVINE, Ed.D. Director, Pupil Personnel Services, South San Francisco Unified School District. Formerly: Professor of Education, San Francisco State College.

JEAN LUKENS, M.S. Coordinator, Perceptual Development Program, Oakland Schools, Pontiac, Michigan. Cooperating Faculty, Wayne State University, Detroit, Michigan. Summer Faculty, University of Arkansas Medical Center, Little Rock, Arkansas.

RICHARD L. MASLAND, M.D. Chairman, Department of Neurology, Columbia University. Formerly: Director, National Institute of Neurological Diseases and Blindness, National Institutes of Health, Department of Health, Education and Welfare, Bethesda, Maryland. Professor, Psychiatry and Neurology, and Associate in Physiology, Bowman Gray School of Medicine, Wake Forest College.

PHYLLIS F. MASLOW, M.A. Research Coordinator, Marianne Frostig Center of Educational Therapy, Los Angeles, California. Doctoral candidate, University of Southern California.

VIOLET E. SPRAINGS, M.A. Director, Psychological and Educational Services, Diagnostic School for Neurologically Handicapped Children, Northern California, San Francisco, California. Assistant Professor, Psychology and Special Education, San Francisco, California. Doctoral candidate, University of California, Berkeley.

LESTER TARNOPOL, Sc.D. Faculties of Psychology and Engineering, City College of San Francisco, San Francisco, California. Research Director, Youth Leadership Training Project, Office of Juvenile Delinquency and Youth Development, U. S. Department of Health, Education and Welfare. Formerly: Professor of Mathematics, Loyola University at Los Angeles. Associate Professor of Metallurgy, University of Kentucky. Reasearch Associate in Geo-Physics, Harvard University.

NAOMI KERSHMAN ZIGMOND, Ph.D. Assistant Professor of Special Education, Boston University. Formerly: Instructor in Psychiatry, Harvard Medical School, Boston, Massachusetts. Assistant in Psychology, Department of Psychiatry, Massachusetts General Hospital, Boston. Consultant, U. S. Office of Education.

This book is dedicated to Muriel, Matthew and Daniel,
who motivated my inquiry into the field of learning disabilities.

Preface

O_N OCTOBER 15, 1966, the San Francisco Chapter of the California Association For Neurologically Handicapped Children (CANHC) held its
first symposium, *Learning Disabilities—Case Finding and Treatment,* in
San Francisco, California. Several of the papers in this book were based
upon those given at that symposium and constitute the core around which
the book was developed. The symposium speakers whose contributions appear in this volume are as follows:

Sam D. Clements, Ph.D., *The Psychologist and Case Finding*

Sister Eileen Marie Cronin, M.A., *Case Finding and Treatment: The
Teacher*

Helen Gofman, M.D., *The Physician's Role in Early Diagnosis and
Management of Learning Disabilities.*

Leslie Whitestone Knott, M.D., *Rehabilitation, the Community and
the Child with Learning Disabilities.*

Lester Tarnopol, Sc.D., *Introduction to Children with Learning Disabilities.*

On January 12 and 13, 1968, the San Francisco Chapter of CANHC held
its second symposium on learning disabilities at the California Scottish Rite
Memorial Temple, San Francisco, California. This symposium entitled
Children with Learning Disabilities — a National Dilemma provided
another group of papers for this book:

Sam D. Clements, Ph.D., *A New Look at Learning Disabilities.*

Jean Lukens, M.S., *Michigan's Perceptual Development Program.*

Richard L. Masland, M.D., *Children with Minimal Brain Dysfunction
— a National Problem.*

Lester Tarnopol, Sc.D., *Delinquency and Learning Disabilities.*

Naomi K. Zigmond, Ph.D., *Auditory Processes in Children with Learning Disabilities.*

In order to cover the topic of learning disabilities more adequately,
manuscripts were solicited from the remaining contributors to this volume
who had not been speakers at one of these San Francisco conferences.

The California program for educationally handicapped children was
the first state funded program for children of low normal to superior intelligence who were suffering from either a neurolgical or behavioral disability which substantially interfered with their learning in the ordinary classroom situation. Since funding started in 1963, the number of children in

this program has increased rapidly to 24,600 as of March, 1968. If funding and case finding continue at the present rate, there should be about 50,-000 children in this special program in a few years. This means that there are about 2,500 teachers now in the program and that there could be as many as 5,000 teachers, at the rate of one teacher per eight to twelve pupils. The number of administrators, supervisors and psychologists servicing this program could be expected to increase from the present estimate of about 500 to about 1,000.

Since the program for educationally handicapped minors grew so rapidly, very few school districts were able to find trained personnel to handle these various positions. And because the projected growth of the program appears to be geometrical, there is litle hope that many trained personnel can be secured in the near future. The universities and state colleges were unprepared for this growth and only a few schools of education have even developed the introductory courses for such a curriculum. The medical profession was likewise caught unprepared for the great rush of parents with their children wishing a work-up to determine if the children fitted one of the medical categories of the program.

In the face of this tremendous problem, the CANHC parents in those school districts where either the rapid program expansion or lack of program indicated the need for profesional training and increased communication among professionals undertook the tremendous task of putting on educational meetings, workshops and symposia on learning disabilities. The San Francisco symposia and a reading workshop were organized by the parents of neurologically handicapped children who had formed the San Francisco Chapter of CANHC. These conferences were primarily instituted to bring to the attention of professionals the new knowledge which was being accumulated on learning disabilities, and to encourage professionals to get acquainted with each other's work and to communicate with parents and each other.

Parents felt that pediatricians, psychiatrists, neurologists, psychologists, social workers and educators were rarely aware of the diagnosis "minimal neurological dysfunction" (in any of its many designations such as minimal brain damage, perceptual dysfunction, hyperkinesis, minimal central nervous system dysfunction, etc.) , and especially the relationship of this diagnosis to learning disabilities and educational remediation. This problem was well known to many parents because they had typically been shunted from pillar to post (professional to professional) in an attempt to get their children's conditions adequately diagnosed. And once having achieved a diagnosis, often after several years of trying, they usually found that no adequate services were available for either the children's or the parents' education.

A survey conducted by San Francisco CANHC disclosed that most often the mother was the first person to notice the child's problem, with school personnel cited in about 20 per cent and pediatricians in less than 15 per cent of the cases. Characteristically, parents complained that their pediatricians or psychiatrists were unaware of the existence of "minimal neurological dysfunction" and so preferred to ascribe the child's behavior to a disturbed mother-child relationship which they *had* heard about (even after an abnormal electroencephalogram and other neurological findings had been demonstrated in some cases). Also important to the parents was the fact that when a diagnosis of neurological dysfunction had been made medically, physicians generally were not aware of any special educational needs of these children, nor of the educational facilities which were available to the children.

Several school districts in California had recognized the need for special classes for children with learning difficulties over twenty years ago. By 1963, when the Waldie Legislation (Assembly Bill 464) was passed in California establishing special classes for Educationally Handicapped Minors with state compensation to the school districts for each child in such a class, several school districts already had a number of special classes operating. These classes had often been developed around the concept that learning disabilities were primarily related to emotional disturbance. The concept of organicity was a new one, not too well understood, and such ideas as neurological dysfunction, perceptual impairment, differential psychological diagnosis and prescriptive teaching were mere words.

It was clear that several things needed to be done. Many physicians had to be apprised of this syndrome and the need for remedial education. Communication among the various professions had to be promoted. More adequate special educational facilities for the children had to be developed within the public school system. CANHC symposia and workshops in various parts of California were designed to act as catalytic agents for these processes.

With the papers from the San Francisco symposia as a nucleus, a number of other manuscripts were solicited in areas not covered. In order to reach a balance between theory, research studies, administration and teaching methods, several new manuscripts were prepared and some recently completed research was acquired.

It was felt that a statement of the psychiatric implications of learning disabilities would be most important for this volume. Doctors Kurlander and Colodny have furnished a very moving, cogent description of their work and findings as psychiatrists with these children.

The work of the Marianne Frostig School in Los Angeles is well known in the field of learning disabilities. Because of the importance of an understanding of visual perception to the subject of learning disabilities, a manuscript was solicited and received from Dr. Frostig and Mrs. Maslow.

Miss Violet Spraings has developed a most extensive and intensive diagnostic test battery for assessing children with learning disabilities. I felt that it would be most useful for psychologists and others connected with this type of program to become familiar with her work. This test battery readily lends itself to the development of a prescriptive teaching program for children with learning disabilities.

The Illinois Test of Psycholinguistic Abilities has been recommended as part of the assessment test battery by many psychologists. In view of this fact, it was felt that a review of this test would be most appropriate. Dr. Lamb generously prepared a manuscript on the ITPA for this volume.

Dr. Bateman's research in the field of learning disabilities is well known. Her research on a gradual phonics versus a sound-symbol (phonics) method of teaching reading appeared to me to have many important implications for the programs for children with learning disabilities. I, therefore, have requested permission to reprint her important research manuscript in this volume which was granted. Both the research methodology and the results constitute a most valuable contribution to the field.

The Program for Educationally Handicapped Minors has been under state funding since 1963 in California. How this program is administered as well as the problems of administration which have been observed so far, should be of utmost value to others considering embarking upon such a program. Dr. Levine was prevailed upon to submit a manuscript based upon his experiences as the administrator of the excellent program for educationally handicapped children in the South San Francisco Unified School District.

I am most grateful to all of the contributors to this volume. It is hoped that this book will help others to develop new programs where they are needed and to improve the quality of many existing programs where the teachers and administrators have not yet had an opportunity to develop intensive in-service or other training.

LESTER TARNOPOL

Acknowledgments

T HE EDITOR WISHES to gratefully acknowledge the assistance received from a number of people in the preparation of this volume. Special credit is due my wife, Muriel, whose tremendous organizational ability and efforts made possible the excellent and important symposia from which many of the manuscripts were gleaned. She also read all of the manuscripts and offered a number of valuable suggestions and helped edit the material for typographical and other errors. Dr. Keith Beery read and made valuable suggestions concerning two manuscripts, "'Introduction to Children with Learning Disabilities," and "Parent and Professional Relations" which are gratefully acknowledged. All of the contributors were most cooperative in preparing their manuscripts for publication and their efforts are most sincerely appreciated. I am most grateful to Christine Gee for typing manuscripts for publication. Her tireless and meticulous efforts significantly reduced the work of preparing this material.

Permission to reproduce the following copyrighted material not accompanied by a credit line in the text is gratefully acknowledged.

Louise Bates Ames from her syndicated column of May 24, 1967.

William M. Cruickshank, *Children with Minimal Brain Damage: A Challenge to the Citizens of Pennsylvania.* Syracuse University Research Institute, 1965.

And from the following publications:

O'Reilly, R.: CANHC and the NH child. *California Parent-Teacher,* Sept., 1965.

Reitan, R. M.: Psychological assessment of deficits associated with brain lesions in subjects with normal and subnormal intelligence. In Khanna, J. L. (Ed.) , *Brain Damage and Mental Retardation: A Psychological Evaluation.* Springfield, Thomas, 1967.

Bateman, Barbara D.: Learning disabilities — yesterday, today and tomorrow. *Except. Child.,* Vol. 31, 1964.

Ferrier, F. E.: An investigation of the ITPA performance of children with functional defects of articulation. *Except. Child.,* Vol. 32, 1966.

Kass, Corrine E.: Psycholinguistic disabilities of children with reading problems. *Except. Child.,* Vol. 32, 1966.

Frostig, M.: *Frostig Visual Perception Program.* Chicago, Follett, 1964.

DeHirsch, K.; Jansky, J. J., and Langford, W. S.: *Predicting Reading Failure.* New York, Harper & Row, 1966.

Hardy, M. P.: The evaluation of communicative skills. *Proceedings 1967 International Convocation on Children and Young Adults with Learning Disabilities,* Pittsburgh, Home for Crippled Children, July, 1967.

Rabinovitch, R. D.: Dyslexia: Psychiatric considerations. In Money, J. (Ed.) : *Reading Disability.* Baltimore, The Johns Hopkins Press, 1962.

Silver, A. A., and Hagin, R. A.: Specific reading disability—an approach to diagnosis and treatment. *J. Special Ed., 1,* No. 2, Winter, 1967.

Olson, A.: Relation of achievement test scores and specific reading abilities to the Frostig test of visual perception. *The Optometric Weekly, 33,* July 14, 1966.

Eisner, V.; Goodlett, C. B., and Maynard, B. D.: Health of enrollees in neighborhood youth corps. *Pediatrics, 38:1,* 40, 1966.

McCarthy, J. J., and Kirk, S. A.: *Illinois Test of Psycholinguistic Abilities, Examiners Manual.* University of Ill. Press, 1961.

McCarthy, J. J., and Olson, J. L.: *Validity Studies on the Illinois Test of Psycholinguistic Abilities.* University of Ill. Press, 1964.

Sievers, D. J.; McCarthy, J. J.; Olson, J. L.; Bateman, B. D., and Kass, C. E.: *Selected Studies on the Illinois Test of Psycholinguistic Abilities.* University of Ill. Press, 1963.

We gratefully acknowledge the financial support of Ciba Pharmaceutical Company in co-sponsoring the symposia with the San Francisco Chapter of CANHC. Contributions were also gratefully received from the following co-sponsors: Archdiocese of San Francisco, Department of Education; Easter Seal Society for Crippled Children and Adults of California; Educators Publishing Service, Inc.; Junior League of San Francisco, Inc.; and United Cerebral Palsy of San Francisco.

L. T.

Contents

LEARNING DISABILITIES

Introduction to
Educational and Medical Management

PART ONE
BACKGROUND

Chapter 1

Introduction to Children with Learning Disabilities

LESTER TARNOPOL

CHILDREN WITH LEARNING disabilities stemming from minimal brain dysfunction have always existed. However, the nature of their dysfunctions is so subtle when compared with the blind, deaf, cerebral palsied, emotionally disturbed and mentally retarded that the problem has only been generally recognized for about two decades. In order to differentiate this more recently established condition from the others, it has been suggested that the term *learning disabilities* be used to indicate the various types of learning difficulties encountered by children with mild central nervous system dysfunction who are not mentally retarded.

Because the impairments associated with being blind, deaf, cerebral palsied, severely emotionally disturbed or mentally retarded are so readily discernible, national organizations have been devoting their energies to assisting children with each of these handicaps for some time. In most states, there are special provisions for the education of children with each of these different problems in public schools. However, since the learning disabilities associated with mild neurologic dysfunction are more subtle and are still being studied, only a few states have provided special public educational assistance to these children. And some states do not as yet have organizations concerned with the welfare of these children. For these reasons, it has been felt that a special designation is required to clearly distinguish this group of children who have previously been omitted from assistance, and for whom diagnostic and habilitative facilities are desired.

Johnson and Myklebust have suggested the term *psychoneurological learning disability* to distinguish the special group of children under discussion.[1] They point out that in cerebral palsy the common factor is motor involvement, in mental retardation it is generalized low mental ability, in the blind and deaf it is the sense which is impaired and in emotional disturbance it is a primary functional or psychological problem. In the case of a psychoneurological learning disability, it is the fact that all of these senses and abilities are adequate in the presence of a learning deficiency which characterizes the common denominator of this condition.

On the other hand, there are those who prefer an umbrella concept of learning disabilities. This group prefer to include in the concept of learning disabilities children suffering from an educational problem related to cere-

5

bral palsy, mental retardation, emotional disturbance, blindness, deafness, cultural deprivation, neurological dysfunction and any other cause.

Task Force One of the National Project on Minimal Brain Dysfunction in Children considered the questions of terminology and identification.[2] This committee was composed of nine physicians, two psychologist-educators and an agency executive. They managed to locate and list thirty-seven different terms used to designate the learning disabilities resulting from a neurological deficit in children of substantially normal intelligence. The terms were found to be of two types; those designating organic aspects of the problem such as "organic brain damage" and "minimal cerebral palsy," and a group which were related to a segment or consequence of the disorder such as "hyperkinetic behavior syndrome," "dyslexia" and "learning disabilities." This primarily medical committee adopted the term "minimal brain dysfunction" as best representing the disorder.

Task Force One based its terminology on the following premises:

"1. Brain dysfunction can manifest itself in varying degrees of severity and can involve any or all of the more specific areas, e.g., motor, sensory, or intellectual. This dysfunctioning can compromise the affected child in learning and behavior.

"2. The term *minimal brain dysfunction* will be reserved for the child whose symptomatology appears in one or more of the specific areas of brain function, but in mild, or subclinical form, without reducing overall intellectual functioning to the subnormal ranges (*Note:* The evaluation of the intellectual functioning of the 'culturally disadvantaged' child, though perhaps related, represents an equally complex, but different problem.) "

The term *minimal brain dysfunction* overcomes the major difficulties posed by many other designations of this syndrome, and it appears to be most advantageous for medical usage. In this term, *minimal* differentiates the condition from cerebral palsy and indicates the elusive nature of the symptoms, *dysfunction* covers damage as well as genetic, developmental or other deviations, and *brain* indicates the organ primarily involved.

Educators and parents often find the use of the term *brain* in the naming of the condition somewhat disconcerting. There is a feeling among some that brain damage gives rise to an irreversible learning disability. And the connotation of a dysfunctioning brain has many negative ramifications to the public just as do such terms as crazy, tuberculosis and syphilis. Therefore, many educators and parents seem to prefer a more neutral designation such as learning disabilities or educational handicap.

The term *educational handicap* was devised for use in California legislation which established by law the first state supported public school program for these children. Educationally handicapped children have been defined as minors "not physically handicapped or mentally retarded, whose learning problems are associated with a behavioral disorder or a neurological handicap or a combination thereof, and who exhibit a significant discrepancy between ability and achievement."[3] Thus these are children who have substantially normal intelligence or above and who are either emotionally or neurologically handicapped or both. Although no mention is made of genetic dyslexia, the concept of neurological handicap is undoubtedly meant to be broad enough in scope to cover learning disabilities of genetic origin. At the present time, this California law does not seem to include the educationally disadvantaged whose learning problems may be considered to derive from an impoverished environment. They are receiving special help in San Francisco, for example, in the form of smaller classes and a special reading clinic provided by federal funds. However, it appears that part of their educational problems can be attributed to emotional or neurological dysfunction in many instances so that many could also come under the California legislation for educationally handicapped minors.

SCOPE OF LEARNING DISABILITIES

It is estimated by the California State Department of Education that educationally handicapped (EH) children will ultimately be found to constitute about 4 to 5 per cent of the total school population. State funding assistance has been made available to local school districts which introduce programs for EH children up to 2 per cent of the school population (described in Dr. Leonard Levine's chapter). Some school districts have already exceeded the 2 per cent limitation on state funding and are financing the extended programs with local monies. It is estimated that there are now (1967-8) over 24,000 children in the program for Educationally Handicapped Minors in California and that this exceeds the number of such children serviced throughout the rest of the United States.

Early Diagnosis Important

In a syndicated column published May 24, 1967, Doctors Frances Ilg and Louise Bates Ames of the Gesell Institute of Child Development at Yale University made the following statement, "Within the next few years we hope that many public schools will recognize the fact that possibly as many (in our estimation) as one-third of the students are perceptually handicapped to some degree or other, and can and should be given specific help and training, within the school situation. Third grade is too late. By that time a child who is perceptually handicapped can be messed up good and plenty."[4]

Some prefer to use the term *perceptually handicapped* because it describes a major condition which seems to be at the root of many learning disorders. The Oakland Schools in Michigan use the designation perceptually handicapped in reference to their special classes for these children. This program is described in the chapter by Jean Lukens. Doctors Ilg and Ames made a very important point when they stated "third grade is too late." Recent research seems to confirm the concept that it is imperative to diagnose the condition early and start remediation immediately. A child whose learning disability is diagnosed before he starts learning to read in the first grade and who is given proper habilitative help has a very much greater chance of learning and avoiding emotional problems than a child diagnosed later followed by attempted remediation. *The earlier the diagnosis the better the prognosis.* Each year that a pupil with an educational handicap continues in school without an adequate diagnosis and special help, markedly decreases his chances for adequate educational recovery.

Several factors operate to reduce his chances. First, the disabled child develops incorrect habits of learning which become reinforced with use and so must be deconditioned while correct habits are substituted. For example, he may be practicing reading from right to left, down to up, and randomly on the page. Such bad habits will tend to persist even after he has learned to read properly and will tend to reappear in stressful situations. Second, as the result of his learning failures, the child may develop a poor self-image, becoming convinced that he is dumb and cannot learn like the other children. This tends to create a self-fulfilling prophecy type of situation because he may give up in the face of such overwhelming obstacles as perceptual distortions and difficulty learning and so not try to learn. Third, continuous failure is too much for anyone to cope with and creates an emotional overlay. Inability to progress like other children generally produces frustrations which generate anxiety and emotional problems which in turn further reduce his chances of learning. For these reasons, it is most important to diagnose children's problems early. Habilitation is much easier than remediation and markedly reduces the development of an emotional overlay.

Research seems to support the concept that it is important to diagnose and begin to habilitate children with learning disabilities as early as possible, preferably before they start to learn reading in the first grade. There are very few longitudinal studies completed from which we can draw conclusions. However, those which have been attempted seem to indicate that the percentage of children with learning disabilities who are habilitated is very high for those started by first grade and falls off for each year beyond first grade. It has also been noted that after third grade the rehabilitation rate decreases quite rapidly.

This general thesis also seems to be supported by recent research in another area of learning, performed in the South San Francisco Unified School District in California, by Rosenthal and Jacobson.[5] They demonstrated with controlled research that children's IQ scores can be increased significantly if the teacher is led to believe that the child has a high IQ regardless of his true IQ score. However, this only happened in the first and second grades. The experimental group in the first grade increased 15.4 IQ points more than the controls, while in the second grade the increase was 9.5 points. In the third to sixth grades no significant differential was noted. These results seem to indicate that learning patterns are established early and may become quite refractory by the third grade. This does not mean that poor learning habits cannot be replaced by good ones, but it does indicate that change becomes much more difficult to produce.

The Literacy Problem

It is not really known just how great the problem of illiteracy is. It has been estimated that half the world population cannot read or write. It is further estimated that about two-thirds of the world population would be considered functionally illiterate by the criterion of a fourth grade reading level. By this criterion, it is estimated that the illiteracy rate in the United States is in the vicinity of 10 per cent. By other criteria, estimates as high as 30 per cent are given for those with reading difficulties in the United States. The National Council of English Teachers estimated in 1962 that there were at least four million disabled readers in our elementary schools. In a lecture series at San Francisco State College during July, 1967, Dr. Ralph Rabinovitch, director of the Hawthorne Center in Northville, Michigan, stated that he believed 10 per cent of the middle class children were retarded in reading and that from 50 per cent to 70 per cent of the inner city poor were so retarded.

The problem of reading and functional literacy is a very recent one. A few hundred years ago, relatively few people could read whereas today in the United States it is rapidly becoming impossible to obtain work for the functionally illiterate. Thus, to be able to read has suddenly become vital to earning a livelihood and so to existence. This condition has introduced a new dimension into the reading crisis of our times.

Reading is a very recent human development. Consequently it has not acted as a determiner of survival in the evolution of man. Under the circumstances, it should not be too surprising to find a great many people who do not have the requisite innate visual and auditory perceptual skills to start learning to read at age six without special perceptual training. Bannatyne has pointed out that reading is the only activity which requires the eyes to move in only one dimension in regular scanning motions.[6] No wonder so many children have difficulty achieving this necessary lateralized eye movement.

Perhaps it is surprising that such a large percentage of the population are able to learn to read in the normal classroom and that so relatively few have genetic dyslexia (reading disabilities). Consider, for example, that about 7 per cent of the male population have some degree of genetic color blindness and about 4 per cent are quite color blind at least in the red-green modality whereas color blindness affects less than one per cent of women. Similarly, reading problems and perceptual dysfunctions seem to affect more males than females. Various ratios have been quoted. In the classes for the neurologically handicapped in California the ratio seems to be three or four boys to one girl. In the case of primary or genetic dyslexia, however, the ratio is said to be about twenty boys to one girl. Naturally, there has been speculation about the possibility that genetic dyslexia may be a sex-chromosome linked disability.

At any rate, since many more males than females have difficulty learning to read, and it is primarily the men who need jobs to support families and thus must pass employment tests, it has been suggested that books and other documents be made available to nonreaders on tape as recordings for listening and that much education should be carried on in this manner as a way of partially obviating the problem.

NEUROGENIC LEARNING DISABILITIES, HISTORICAL

Historically, H. C. Bastian, a British neurologist, is credited with first describing what may be referred to as *word-deafness* and *word-blindness*. In 1869, he described a patient who could hear well but was unable to recognize spoken words, and likewise a patient whose vision was adequate but who failed to recognize printed words. W. A. Morgan, also a British physician, described a case of congenital word-blindness in 1896. Although these and other neurological conditions affecting learning had been reported in the literature on different occasions, they did not become generally known. This was partly because their existence was denied by many professionals. Also physicians had very rarely considered their province to extend beyond medical diagnosis and mangement to the total child including his education. The concept of treating the total child is a relatively new one, and the necessary bridges to other disciplines such as psychology and education have not been sufficiently built. Although the value of multidisciplinary studies of children is generally agreed upon, not many such teams have been formed.

An understanding of the learning problems of children with dyslexia may have first been achieved in America by Samuel T. Orton, a neurologist and psychiatrist. He identified the syndrome of developmental reading disability in 1925 as different from mental retardation or brain damage, suggested a physiological cause for dyslexia and developed methods of remediation which were applied with favorable results to a great many disabled readers.

On the basis of studies of adults with traumatic injuries to the dominant brain hemisphere, which would usually be the left hemisphere for right-handed people and the right hemisphere for left-handed people, Orton made important deductions about the neurological meaning of language development problems in children who had no established brain injury. He also found that children with visual reading disturbances could see the print clearly and knew they were seeing letters and words which they could even copy correctly, but they nevertheless could not read the words. This condition, often referred to as *word blindness,* has now been recognized and described in many countries. Orton also described *word deafness* as existing in people whose hearing was adequate so that they were able to identify sounds correctly, but who could not understand the concepts being related in spoken language.

The learning characteristics of children with brain damage were first studied in the United States by Heinz Werner and Alfred Strauss, a psychologist and neuropsychiatrist, about 1940. Although their studies were primarily in the field of mental retardation, their findings often proved applicable to children with normal intelligence and stimulated others to investigate this field.

The work of Orton, Werner, Strauss and others has led to much research and to the diagnostic-prescriptive teaching approach to remediation. New insights into the problems of disabled learners were achieved by persuing medical, psychological and educational diagnoses of the factors which might be causing their problems. In this manner it was discovered that a group of sonsory perceptual disabilities were often related to learning disabilities. These were thought to be some form of neurological dysfunction causing either one or some combination of abnormalities of visual perception, motor coordination and auditory perception.

In 1947, Strauss and Lehtinen published a book which summarized the studies on minimal brain dysfunction for the preceding twenty years which was the first comprehensive presentation of this subject and is considered a classic work cited by most authors.[7] The turning point in the study of children with learning disabilities began at about this time and the following years saw a geometrically increasing incidence of research papers in this field. Twenty years of awakening interest in this child has led to the development of interdisciplinary diagnostic teams, special schools and special classes to aid in his progress. Many people have also become aware of the tremendous scope of the problem. Nevertheless, our total undertsanding of this problem may still be considered to be most rudimentary. There are only a few diagnostic teams relative to the numbers of children involved; only a few states have special classes for these children; only a few teachers are trained to teach these children, and very few teacher training institutions have taken hold and are doing research and training teachers. The demand, at present, very far exceeds the supply of trained professional personnel. That is why both professional and parent organizations are busily engaged in telling the story of the child with minimal brain dysfunction.

SOURCES OF LEARNING DISABILITIES

Eisenberg has suggested a provisional classification of the sources of reading retardation which should be the same for learning disabilities.[8] He suggests nine sources of retardation. Four sociopsychological sources of retardation are given as follows:

1. Defects in teaching.
2. Deficiencies in educational stimulation during the first six years of life.
3. Lack of environmental motivators.
4. Lack of motivation due to emotional factors.

Five psychophysiological sources of retardation are given as follows:

1. General debility due to malnourishment or chronic illness.
2. Severe vision and hearing losses.
3. Mental retardation.
4. Brain damage.
5. Genetic or congenital reading disabilities.

All reviews of the causes of reading disabilities tend to state this same group of factors with only minor variations. The differences tend to be primarily a matter of terminology rather than concepts.

This volume deals primarily with neurogenic learning disabilities and teaching methods most appropriate to the habilitation and remediation of these children. However, it should be noted that the learning difficulties manifested by this population are also found among many other children, and the methods of remediation and teaching will undoubtedly apply to these other children. Since some children may also have multiple involvements including any of those listed by Eisenberg, we remain cognizant of these possibilities both in terms of diagnosis and the implications for remediation.

The neurologically handicapped child has presented a serious diagnostic challenge to the professions of medicine, psychology and education. In most cases, the degree of impairment is such that the usual pediatric, vision and hearing tests do not disclose any abnormality. Thus, until recently this handicap generally remained undiscovered and the children's inability to learn was often mistakenly attributed to such things as laziness, neurosis, oversolicitous parents, too great parental pressure to learn, or other causes.

The emphasis developed over the past forty years on psychodynamic interpretations of behavior has led most professionals to conclude that the educational deficiencies which children exhibited were of environmental causation. Thus, it was usually concluded that since the most meaningful relationship was that between the mother and child, the child's learning problems must have been caused by deficiencies in this relationship. Since the child could not be conceived of as playing a determining role in this relationship, it followed that the mother was to blame! This type of thinking about the problem had three unfortunate consequences. First, it prevented many professionals from studying the child further to determine what *his* relationship might be to his learning problems. Second, it tended to generate a great deal of guilt and anxiety in the mother, effectively reducing her efficiency both in her emotional relationship with the child and her intelligent efforts to help the child with his learning problems. And third, it unfortunately tended to relieve professionals of the responsibility of investigating the effects of *their* advice and behavior on the child and his family.

The present emphasis on new approaches to both diagnosis of the child's learning disabilities and new methods of teaching him grew out of the failure of the child guidance movement to solve these and other problems. Years of proliferation of psychodynamically oriented mental health facilities saw our problems increasing rather than diminishing. In response to the increasing problem the practitioners called for more of the same type of mental health and educational facilities and practices which had failed to reduce the problem in the past. A few professionals saw the need to reevaluate the total approach to the learning problems of children and this gave rise to both the new theories and methods which are being tested. This subject is pursued at length in the chapter by Doctors Kurlander and Colodny.

Rabinovitch has had very extensive contact with children with reading disability and has conducted research both in their problems and remediation. Rabinovitch stated, "The reading process itself — including the crucial factors of sight vocabulary, phonetic recognition and analysis, and, in fact, the whole symbolization process — is minimally affected by emotional problems, but the application of intact skills is impaired by personality factors."[9]

Rabinovitch has indicated that a significant percentage of children referred to psychiatrists with adjustment or behavior problems have reading disability.[10] It was found at the Hawthorn Center (psychiatric clinic) that, for many boys, reading therapy was a necessary concomitant of psychiatric treatment. Rabinovitch states, "So often the school social worker or pediatrician refers the child with the hope, and even expectation, that the psychiatric clinic will find the learning problem to be due to an 'emotional block' and that through the magic of psychotherapy, perhaps limited to a few interviews, the child will be 'released' to learn adequately. Such unrealistic expectations have, unfortunately, been fostered in part by the attitude of some of our colleagues in child psychiatry and related fields who have been prone to over-generalize dynamic formulations." All of the evidence points to the conclusion that reading disability may be much more complex than was originally conceived. It appears that there are many different reading disability syndromes each requiring its own diagnosis and each different diagnosis may indicate the need for an individual remedial prescription.

Research Results

Silver conducted a dignostic study of 150 children with reading disabilities and a control group of thirty children from the same population matched for age, sex and IQ.[11] The experimental group ranged in age from eight-and-one-half to fourteen years, and in IQ from 81 to 123. These children had been referred to the Bellevue Hospital Mental Hygiene Clinic primarily for behavior problems and all had reading disability. Ninety-two per cent of these children were found to have right-left disorientation. However, mixed dominance was not found in greater proportion in the experimental group than the controls.

An arm extension test was found to distinguish 74 per cent of children with reading disability and none of the controls. In this test developed by Paul Schilder, both arms are extended with the eyes closed and the fingers spread. One hand tends to be higher than the other. It was found that the hand opposite the one used in writing tended to be raised higher in the children with reading disability. This was interpreted to suggest that clearcut cerebral dominance had not yet been established. In addition another 18 per cent of the reading disability group held both hands level indicating possible lack of dominance in either hand and therefore in either brain hemisphere.

Ninety-two per cent of the group with reading disability were found to have some visual-motor defects on the Bender Gestalt Test. On a visual figure-background perception test involving copying designs with marbles (Marble-Board Test), 92 per cent of the experimental group were unable to reproduce the designs on a second board. In addition, 50 per cent of the experimental group had defects of auditory perception measured by tests of word discrimination, auditory blending, sound matching and word meaning. On the Draw-A-Person Test, 80 per cent of the children with reading disability had deficits. Tactile tests revealed no significant defects in the experimental group. Silver concluded that 20 per cent of the children with specific reading disability had structural organic defects and another 70 per cent indicated evidence of other neurological and perceptual problems. Silver also concluded that 90 per cent of his experimental subjects showed signs of lack of clear-cut cerebral dominance.

DISTORTIONS OF VISUAL PERCEPTION

Children with neurogenic learning disabilities tend to exhibit one or more of three main types of deviations of function. They may exhibit distortions of visual perception, auditory perception, motor function, or any combination of these. Learning problems may also be related to the lack of integration among these functions, i.e., inability to translate a visual stimulus into correct motor activity as in copying letters. Rabinovitch believes that the "problem does not seem to be one in perception *per se,* but rather in the translation of perceptions into meaningful symbols that can be used in reading and related language functions."[10] Psychological tests have been developed to help determine the specific disabilities of each child in each of these several sensory modalities. Such tests permit a differential diagnosis of the child's specific learning disabilities. This knowledge permits an individual prescription to be developed for the teaching of each child.

At present, the neurological mechanism by which distortions of perception occur is not fully understood. Consider the way in which visual learning occurs in children. It is theorized that the infant first looking about him is unable to distinguish anything meaningfully and may not even know that everything he sees is not part of himself. He does not focus well and his two eyes operate independently so he perhaps sees a blur. The normal infant must learn to focus his eyes, coordinate them on the same subject, distinguish what is outside of him from himself, learn from experience both two and three dimensions, distinguish figure from ground, and since he sees everything upside down and backwards he must reverse the image. This process of learning to perceive visually appears to be a long slow one consuming many years of practice. Infants seem to require from three to six months of seeing their mothers' faces before they appear to be able to distinguish the human face and then they seem able to distinguish it only in full face but not in profile.

It is assumed that the reason the infant can eventually learn his mother's face is that it is constant; that is, it remains the same each times he sees it. However, not only must the face not change, but the infant's perception of the face must not change if he is to remember it.

Visual perception is clearly a learned process and probably continues throughout life. In the process of learning shapes, the infant feels them with his hands and mouth. Since the tongue is the most sensitive tactile part of the body, it is most useful for this purpose. He learns hard from soft, wet from dry, hot from cold in this same manner, thereby connecting what he sees with what he feels tactually. The learning of distances is accomplished first by reaching for objects near enough to touch and later by movement of the infant through space at the same time observing how things appear as he moves and how far he must move to reach an object. In this way, both the tactile and kinesthetic senses are used to learn visual perception.

In the course of learning such things as *b* from *d* and *was* from *saw,* many apparently normal children of age six get mixed up indicating that this process of object constancy is still maturing for these children. Thus the process of developing object constancy necessary for reading is maturational. On the other hand, it must be learned if it is to be grasped.

In the case of the child with minimal brain dysfunction who has a visual perceptual problem, often part of his problem stems from the fact that he has failed to develop object constancy. That is, each time he looks at something, it may appear different! If objects appear different each time he sees them, it becomes impossible for him to learn their shapes. One aspect of the perceptually handicapped child's job may be to learn how to see objects in the same way each time he looks at them so that he can learn to know them. Most often the reversals a child sees such as *was* for *saw* may be due to reading backwards, that is his eyes scan the word from right to left. This resolves itself into a laterality problem for such children and they must be taught to scan words from left to right only. On the other hand, some children actually may see some letters backwards as *b* for *d*. This may indicate visual perceptual immaturity or some other neurological dysfunction. Practice sensing the letters with several modalities as seeing, hearing and feeling, plus over-learning seems to help overcome this type of problem.

In one instance, a boy in a class for the neurologically handicapped printed *bog* for *dog*. After looking at his work he exclaimed, "Oh look! I made a *d* and it came out a *b*." Such a reversal could be due to either inadequate motor control or to poor integration of his visual perception and motor control. Teachers have observed that visual distortions do not tend to be constant. For example, some neurologically handicapped children who have learned to read tend to revert to distorted visual perception when they are tired or overanxious. They have also been observed to catch themselves making an error by observing that the word which was incorrectly read does not make sense in the context. Then they go back and struggle over the distorted word until they straighten it out and read the correct word. The use of cognitive processes to overcome this handicap makes it possible for some children of adequate intelligence to learn and to compensate for their perceptual problems provided the problems are not too great. The chapters in this volume by Dr. Frostig and Mrs. Maslow, Dr. Gofman, and Miss Spraings discuss visual perception and its relation to learning disabilities in greater detail.

MOTOR, BALANCE AND LATERALITY PROBLEMS

It has been observed that children with learning disabilities often may have motor and balance problems. They may have large or small muscle discoordination and laterality problems, such as distinguishing right from left. Such problems are generally considered to be related to neurological dysfunction stemming from possible damage, immaturity of function or other factors and may be used as indicators when present. It has also been observed that these children may also have difficulty writing, playing certain games and they may have social problems, sometimes quite severe.

There are a number of sets of physical exercises which are available to help the child develop small and large muscle control, laterality and balance. Those developed by Kephart, Barsch, Frostig and the Doman-Delacato exercises are well known. In many cases these exercises appear to be valuable in helping the child improve his muscle control, coordination and balance. Such improvement helps the child with handwriting and games, improves his self-image, and social acceptance. Laterality exercises help him determine right from left, up from down and front from rear.

A number of claims have been made which link motor, balance and laterality exercises with learning to read. Such exercises are included in most programs for children with learning disabilities. The exercises certainly seem to improve many a child's ability to do these exercises, as well as his motor control and coordination, laterality knowledge, ability at games, sense of balance and feelings of self-confidence. However, there is little evidence that ability to read is materially improved by these exercises. Because of the very great extent to which motor exercises are used in programs for educationally handicapped children, it is most important that the precise relationship between these exercises and learning be established by serious, rigorously controlled scientific research. If it is determined that some of this time could be better spent in programs more directly related to reading, this should be known and acted upon. This matter is discussed in greater detail in the chapter in this volume by Dr. Masland.

AUDITORY PERCEPTION

Many teaching programs for children with learning disabilities include both testing and remedial work in the areas of visual perception and motor deficits. However, they sometimes omit or slight the very important area of auditory perception and language development. Such programs neither include testing nor adequate remedial work in this phase of language development. This is a very serious omission since there are probably about as many children with auditory perceptual problems as there are with visual perceptual problems.

Sometimes a child will have a sufficient hearing loss in some part of the hearing range so that certain sounds dependent upon this range are difficult for him to distinguish. In such cases, the child requires remedial assistance of the type given to the hard of hearing. However, there are also children whose audiometer tests reveal no hearing loss but who nevertheless have serious auditory discrimination problems. Many people in special education believe that auditory problems are the most important ones in relation to language development and reading. It has been stated that blind children can learn reading and conceptual language skills much more readily than deaf children, on the average. It has been suggested, with some justification, that the majority of children with reading disabilities have a fundamental auditory processing problem perhaps in conjunction with a number of other deficits.

Delayed or retarded speech and language development has been postulated to be one of the most sensitive indicators of future learning and behavior disorders. The most usual reason for parents seeking professional advice concerning their preschool children seems to be related to anxiety over talking which leads them to question the children's hearing. Most of the children whom we are discussing who have minimal brain dysfunction and learning disabilities appear to have a case history of delayed or retarded speech and language development. This condition can, of course, be caused by many different factors such as neurological involvement, anatomic or physiological problems, emotional disorders and impoverished home learning environments.

Since speech and language development is well known as an indicator of possible future learning and behavior disorders, there appears to be little excuse for the continuing failure to identify these children and commence habilitation before the children enter kindergarten. Both the speech and language development and the motor and balance development of young children may be used for early diagnostic purposes and these developmental sequences should be familiar to every pediatrician along with a number of other parallel indicators such as hyperactivity, impulsivity, distractability and short attention span. The diagnosis of immature or defective visual perception probably cannot be undertaken quite as early. However, it is often found that the children evidencing delayed speech and language development also are found to have problems in the motor and visual perception areas.

Speech therapists can make an important contribution in auditory and speech habilitation for these children provided they themselves have had special training beyond the usual. It should be realized that helping children with learning disabilities requires a much more sophisticated approach than the usual speech and hearing training permits at present. The team of teachers required to work with children who have learning disabilities should generally include a speech, hearing and language specialist. Moreover, it is important that each child be tested by a team including the teacher, language therapist and psychologist. Their combined reports should be part of the total report studied by the admissions committee which decides on the child's placement. This committee should always include the authors of the reports.

Many children who have serious problems in auditory discrimination do not evidence any hearing loss on audiometer tests. Such children may have difficulty distinguishing certain vowel or consonant sounds such as *m* and *n*. Even more prevalent are disorders of auding. These children may have difficulty understanding or remembering what they hear in a temporal sequence or a sequence pattern. Characteristically, if given several commands in sequence, they may rush off and perform the first task and not remember the others. Thus, they would tend to do poorly on digit span tests or tests of rote memory of a series of nonsense syllables.

Just as with visual closure there may be a problem of auditory closure. In this case, the child has difficulty distinguishing a word when it is not clearly pronounced or when he only hears part of the word. This would make it difficult for the child to understand either different accents or slovenly spoken language. A child may even be unable to correct his own reading errors when he mispronounces a word because of failure to close on it.

Severe language disorders often involve problems of memory and recall. These are referred to as storage and retrieval disabilities. These disorders make it very difficult to learn language and when learned it may not be firmly established. Often such children have their most severe problems in the input system, fewer are more severely affected in their retrieval systems. For those children who have serious auditory involvement in these modalities, learning requires that all of their learning senses be simultaneously stimulated and that considerable repetition and overlearning be utilized.

According to Hardy both the clinical and research evidence which is being developed in this field support the concept that "the sensory systems are closely interlinked and that breakdowns in the management of intersensory information and the translation into motor output systems constitute a major problem in children with central nervous system dysfunction. These integrative dysfunctions seem to underly the more common language disorders."[12] Dr. Zigmond covers auditory perception and language pathology in her chapter in this volume.

CONCEPT FORMATION

One of the more difficult areas of training which has not yet been adequately explored is conceptualizing and reasoning disabilities. There are very few tests and remedial programs available for apparently bright children who have difficulty with concept formation. These children appear to have difficulty with comparisons, generalizations, judgments, classification and reasoning from given facts. They may fail to recognize that objects are the same regardless of size or form. Their difficulties may include grouping objects, pictures or ideas into categories, forming pictures or ideas into sequences, and judgments of size, distance, time, weight, direction, temperature, volume and texture. They also may fail to understand absurdities or to be able to make judgments in social situations.

Because of the fact that the field of learning disabilities is relatively new, most work has been done at the kindergarten and primary school levels of development. Reading has received the most attention. However, it will be necessary to develop both diagnostic tools and methods of habilitation in the areas of arithmetic and concept formation in order to present a more complete curriculum for the habilitation of children with learning disabilities.

TEACHING THE EDUCATIONALLY HANDICAPPED CHILD

For many years, professional educators have been urging teachers to teach each child according to his individual needs. Administrators and teachers have been told to develop their curricula and teaching methods with this concept in mind. However, the practical application of these precepts to a normal classroom has left much to be desired, in fact, as a general rule quite the opposite has prevailed in practice.

In some school systems, the principal takes pride in being able to look at the clock on his office wall and to be able to tell a visitor precisely what the children in each of his elementary grade levels is being taught at that very moment. Clearly, this lock-step teaching practice plus thirty to fifty pupils in each class are hardly calculated to permit treating each child as an individual. For those children who have any type of educational handicap, this system has often proven to be disastrous — they have failed to learn!

Besides large classes and the lock-step curriculum, there appear to be two further important reasons why the exhortations of the educators to teach to the needs of the individual child proved to be impractical. First, no real attempt had been made to determine the educational strengths and the weaknesses at the proper diagnostic level for each child; and second, to the extent that these factors could be determined, the special teaching methods required to meet these individual needs were generally not available. Perhaps for the first time in educational history it is becoming possible to give meaning to the concept of meeting the individual needs of children. This remarkable development is deriving to a great extent from studies of children with various types of handicaps. These studies are being carried out in the several areas of special education. Through research on how to teach the mentally retarded, emotionally disturbed, blind, deaf, neurologically impaired, genetic dyslexics and culturally deprived, a great deal is being determined about the process of learning. As a result, new insights are being achieved about how all children learn, including both the normal and abnormal. Consider one new teaching method, designated prescriptive teaching. In this method of teaching the educationally handicapped child it has been found useful to do two things. First, a differential diagnosis is made to determine his specific areas of perceptual dysfunction as well as his specific educational levels (reading, etc.) and second, an individual program is devised which utilizes his strengths, and both works around and strengthens his deficiencies. Diagnostic testing is discussed at some length in several places in this volume including the chapters by Dr. Clements, Dr. Frostig and Mrs. Maslow, Dr. Lamb, Dr. Gofman, Miss Spraings, Dr. Tarnopol, and Dr. Zigmond.

It is assumed that the child learns by receiving information through his senses. It is also assumed that almost everything the child learns can be introduced and reinforced through multiple senses. Thus, for example, five main sensory modalities may be used simultaneously to teach reading, spelling, writing and arithmetic. These modalities are visual, auditory, oral, tactile and kinesthetic. Some creative teachers are able to make use of the taste and olfactory senses as well. This theory of teaching appears to have many similarities with the Montessori and Fernald methods. However, the new methods differ in that they are based on more sophisticated diagnostic workups and a great many new teaching techniques.

Many educationally handicapped children are further impaired in their learning by anxiety and fears related to learning and classrooms. In order to cope with these problems and at the same time to increase learning efficiency, certain principles of good teaching are finding favor. The approach which is used with these children is first to establish their specific reading, spelling, writing and arithmetic levels. In each area, the teacher starts the child just below his achievement level so that success is insured. The educational process is set up so that only rewards and an absolute minimum of nonrewarding situations are encountered by the pupil. Punishment is generally avoided. The teaching method is so devised that the pupil has continuous success followed by rewards. Whenever the child fails, the teacher immediately drops the work back to within the child's achievement level so that he starts to succeed again and go forward. Thus, curriculums are developed wherein each child may proceed at his own pace and where he will have a minimum of failures and his successful efforts will be continually rewarded. These are the good teaching principles which are suggested for general use. Within this general framework a number of very different creative approaches have been devised.

Engineered Classroom

A teaching method developed by Haring and Phillips[13] and elaborated by Hewett[14] is referred to as the engineered classroom. This approach to teaching the educationally handicapped child is based upon the behavior modification model. In this model, the child is not viewed as being blocked in his learning by emotional conflicts, neurological impairment or other basic causes. Instead his level of academic and social functioning are observed and his behavior is modified to correspond with accepted academic and social standards by assigning carefully graded tasks within the child's ability level in a classroom which provides both structure and rewards in accordance with the well-known principles of operant conditioning developed by Skinner. The learning approach is based upon recognition of the facts that negative reinforcement causes some children to try less and fail more, and the longer children are permitted to maintain maladaptive behavior, the less possible their remediation.

Hewett has developed a hierarchy of educational tasks to be used in conjunction with the principles of operant conditioning which include the following:

1. The child must attend.
2. The teacher must stimulate the child by demonstrating something.
3. The child must respond to this stimulus.
4. The child must be rewarded for his correct response.

The teacher's job of demonstrating something means, in this case, that she must find out what the child is ready to learn and teach or demonstrate it. In order to help the teacher with this difficult but most important task, Hewett has arranged a developmental sequence of behaviors directly related to classroom operations and learning. These are the following:

1. The child's attention must be established (attention level).
2. He must become responsive to the teacher's demonstration (response level).
3. He must learn to attend and respond in proper sequence (order level).
4. He must develop an adequate amount of background knowledge to

be able to proceed to the academic and social learning levels (exploratory level).

5. He must become ready to function in the world of people to gain approval (social level).
6. He must develop mastery of academic material (mastery level).
7. He must become self-motivated to learn (achievement level).

Hewett suggests that children who do not have all of these qualities are social failures, and that they must have the first five levels of operation to start to learn in school. The method of teaching consists of first selecting a suitable educational task within the learner's ability level. Then a meaningful reward must be found for the individual child; the hierarchy of rewards being food, the teacher's praise, check marks which can be cashed in like savings stamps, and achievement satisfaction. One starts with immediate reward and goes to intermittent reward. Finally, the teacher must establish the degree of structure or control necessary for the child to accomplish the task.

In attempting to create a classroom design which will work with all children, the classroom is divided into sections. Each level on the hierarchy has a specific section of the room designated for its tasks and activities. The major sections within the room are an order center, an exploratory center and a mastery center. Children who are at the attention, response and order levels work in the order center. Children who are at the exploratory and social levels work in the exploratory center. Finally, those who are working at the mastery and achievement levels work in the mastery center. A number of such classrooms are in operation in California public schools. The concept of an engineered classroom has important theoretical and practical implications. However, at present, we have no research data comparing this teaching method with others. Until such research is forthcoming, we will be unable to assess the relative value of this teaching method for children with various types of disabilities.

Task Analysis and Methods Diagnosis

One of the common factors that many of the new habilitation and remedial programs seem to have may be termed task analysis. In order to help the child learn, the task which the child must perform is usually analyzed into its necessary components. Programmed learning, for example, is based upon a type of task analysis. The child's learning task is divided into small easily understood units which build upon each other to get across each new concept or unit of learning.

Hewett's engineered-classroom teacher must demonstrate something which the child is ready to learn. This means that she must have analyzed the tasks to be learned into learnable components and must start the child at his own level of understanding in this learning sequence. In order to assist the teacher with this difficult preparation, Hewett has divided both the room and the learning tasks into components which indicate the work to be done.

Prescriptive teaching, in order to be successful, must also use the principles of task analysis. Prescriptive teaching has been criticized as being insufficiently specific both diagnostically and in the remedial tasks to be performed once a diagnosis is made. Unfortunately, this has too often been the case. However, it need not be so. Useful differential diagnoses are possible to make using the tests presently available and with the continued development of new and better tests, diagnoses should improve. Also, a number of prescriptive teaching centers have had very good results with their methods indicating that some very adequate prescriptive teaching techniques are available. Analysis of those methods which seem to get results indicates that they often combine techniques for both working around and strengthening perceptual handicaps as well as the elements of task analysis in developing a program for each child.

The concept of methods diagnosis has also been advanced as a factor in teaching the handicapped. This means that the *method* which the teacher is using to teach vocabulary, numbers or concepts, etc., should be subjected to scrutiny and improved if found lacking. It is said that an average teacher generally states the principle or thing to be learned so that any child of good intelligence with no learning problems can grasp it. When some children fail, the teacher may say that they failed because they were less competent learners or they had insufficient ability.

The proposition has been enunciated that any child can learn any concept for which he has the necessary educational background or preparation if the concept is properly presented. Although the proposition is obviously a *non sequitur,* it implies an important concept. Namely, that we should stop blaming the child for his failure in school and start looking at the curriculum and the method of presentation. This proposition has been backed by demonstrating that children who could not learn from the usual teacher, could learn when the method of task presentation was properly analyzed.

In one instance, Siegfried Engelmann mentioned the following example: A teacher said she could not teach the concept *big* to a retarded child. She was asked to demonstrate how she taught *big.* The child knew tree, so the teacher went to a very big tree and embraced the tree while looking up at its bigness. She then said, "This big." To which the child replied, "No, this tree." Engelmann then demonstrated an approach which worked. He said, "This tree is big." Thus he stated what the child knew, namely, that it was a tree, then he introduced the concept that a tree could also be big. The child soon learned the meaning of *big* after several such examples. This is but a trivial example of something which has been demonstrated many times. Children who fail to learn often fail because the material was not presented so that they could understand it!

Prescriptive teaching, behavior modification, task analysis and methods diagnosis should all be part of every teacher's armamentarium. These are certainly proper subjects to be taught in schools of education. If these concepts and all of the new useful concepts which will be coming across the educational horizon could be incorporated into undergraduate or at least graduate courses within a reasonable time after their appearance, the teachers would be better able to cope with the rapidly changing conditions of modern society. In the past, it has taken each new concept about thirty years, on the average, to become course content. This condition can no longer be tolerated in a society where the amount of new research exceeds all previous knowledge in many disciplines about every ten years.

RESEARCH

There are a number of essential questions which remain to be answered by research. We need to know more about the origins of learning disablement, both with respect to factors within the child and teaching methods.

From the point of view of prevention, it is most important that the basic causes of minimal neurological dysfunction which give rise to learning disabilities be determined. At present, a number of possible causes have been postulated including the following: genetic; prenatal central nervous system damage from anoxia, disease, physical trauma, drugs taken by the pregnant mother, certain viral diseases of the pregnant mother, and malnutrition of the pregnant mother; brain injury during delivery which may be due to instruments, adverse effects of anesthesia, or the impact of too rapid or too long labor; anoxia immediately following delivery; postnatal trauma including disease, chemical abnormalities, high fevers, anoxia, physical injuries, malnutrition and encephalitis.

It has also been discovered that both premature infants and those born out of wedlock tend to include an inordinately high percentage with learning disabilities. Premature infants tend to have an immature nervous system and development, and it is believed that children born out of wedlock may have been traumatized by attempted abortion in some cases. Also, the incidence of minimal neurological dysfunction may be increasing in western society due to medical advances which save the lives of large numbers of both premature and otherwise damaged children who would not ordinarily survive. The contributions of chemicals in both the atmosphere and in preserving foods as well as the contribution of increased radiation have not as yet been assessed. Prevention of minimal neurological dysfunction will depend upon greater understanding of many of these factors.

From the point of view of the education of these children, there are several questions to be answered by research. First, what is the most efficient way to screen them? Second, what is the best test battery for purposes of differential diagnosis of the child's specific disabilities? Third, how deep and extensive is it necessary to go in developing a differential diagnosis for most efficient habilitation or remediation? Fourth, how many distinctly different conditions are we dealing with? Fifth, what is the relationship between each differential diagnosis and remediation? Sixth, what methods of habilitation work best with young children? Seventh, what methods of rehabilitation work best with older children?

These questions are prompted by seemingly contradictory results from many different researches. For example, Miss Spraings' extensive diagnostic test battery and the results achieved with children in the Northern California Diagnostic School For Neurologically Handicapped Children, which are discussed in her chapter in this volume, plus many other similar studies seem to favor the most specific possible differential diagnosis followed by prescriptive teaching. On the other hand, both Hewett's engineered classroom (previously mentioned) and Dr. Bateman's research on the intensive phonics approach to teaching reading (included in this volume) do not require extensive differential diagnosis to achieve their goals. Moreover, each of these approaches to teaching is quite different.

There is no doubt that prescriptive teaching based on differential diagnosis has helped many children learn, but teaching methods based on behavior modification also seem to be effective for some children and the sound-symbol method of teaching reading based on intensive phonics also claims much success. What we need to know is, which children are helped most by each of these and other different methods of teaching.

The "look-say" versus "intensive phonics" controversy which has been raging for about forty years has now become the "gradual phonics" versus "intensive phonics" dispute. The gradual phonics method of teaching reading starts by having the children acquire a sight vocabulary before teaching them the sound values of letters. The intensive phonics or sound-symbol approach starts by teaching the children the sounds of all of the letters and combinations without attempting to teach meaningful words. Then sound blending is taught which permits words to be read.

One problem is that many handicapped children have auditory perception problems and so have difficulty learning the sounds and blending. On the other hand, studies of reading conducted under the auspices of the

United States Office of Education, and Dr. Bateman's research, seem to favor the intensive phonics method for most children. However, it is said that no approach to reading is "teacher proof." In the various studies performed for the U. S. Department of Education, the differences in the results obtained by different teachers were said to be greater than the differences among approaches. It has been said that the differences among teachers is not their charm as many principals seem to think, but their skill in instruction. We will return to the subject of teacher training later.

As the chapter in this volume by Dr. Masland indicates, it is essential that research undertaken to answer any of the questions posed must be rigorous. Any research which does not meet all of the requirements for controls and rigor may produce spurious results. Any single nonrigorous or uncontrolled aspect of a research project makes it possible to obtain results which are false. Because of the difficulties inherent in this type of research, all of the variables which may affect the results are probably not possible to control. Consequently, the only alternative is to replicate each experiment many times, each time attempting to bring more variables under control. Statistical methods are also available for parcelling out the variables. It is also of utmost importance to perform longitudinal experiments over many years.

The difficulties inherent in research have never discouraged the researchers from continuing their work. However, people not specifically trained in research methodology have often been both discouraged and disparaging with respect to research efforts and the ultimate value of research. They often feel that it is not possible to study people in a meaningful way. The only succinct reply to these critics is that adequately trained personnel can do meaningful research in this field, and that there is *no* other known way of solving the problems posed. If educational research were to receive the tremendous financial subsidies which physical science research receives, many of the problems posed would soon be resolved. On the other hand, without rigorous research, these problems may never be resolved.

Lack of rigorous research tends to lead to fads. The method which gets the most favorable publicity is adopted. Which methods should be used tends to be determined not by the objective value of the method, but rather by the eloquence and authoritative stature of its supporters. Beacuse, in the past, this has usually led to the adoption of incorrect theories and wrong ways of proceeding, science has developed a series of controls against such subjective reasoning. These controls are part of the research methodology which make it possible to test all of the different theories and methods and to determine which can do the most for these children.

Engaging in research can help people think better and understand better what works for the children and what does not. Experience in industry, government and public and social agencies has indicated that, for best results, research should be done by the personnel who are most intimately involved in a change process. Thus, the school districts in California which had pilot research programs to educate these handicapped children before starting their district-wide programs seemed to know most about how to proceed. Those districts which either converted existing classes to classes for the Educationally Handicapped in California or which started their classes without simultaneous research encountered many problems which pilot programs obviated. Moreover, many teachers of the pilot research programs soon became the experts and consultants throughout the state.

There is a great deal of evidence to indicate that school districts accomplish most for the children by engaging in their own rigorously controlled research. Each school district which is large enough either to afford a research team or to have a qualified research director who can bring federal, state or foundation research funds to the district is well advised to engage in research. To the extent that the actual research is performed by personnel within the district who are to be part of any change process (such as the teachers, supervisors, psychologists and social workers), the new learnings will be implemented. It is well known that industry, government agencies and school districts have had expensive research performed for them by outside agencies and that most of these reports are collecting dust, unimplemented and filed away. This is very much less likely to happen when the research is performed by the persons who need to learn from it and who should implement it. It is well documented that the people who do the research learn the most from it and are most able to change and to implement the research findings. The school districts have a major advantage over all other agencies which might wish to do research on educating children. They have the children and teachers available in sufficiently large numbers generally, whereas professors are often severely limited in this respect.

TRAINING TEACHERS

It is said that in the physical sciences the amount of new knowledge gained in seven years now equals all of the knowledge previously acquired. Although research is not progressing at quite the same rate in the social sciences and education, nevertheless a similar situation probably obtains. Moreover, it is said that it takes about thirty years for a new concept to enter the textbooks. This means that by the time a student graduates and starts to teach, much of what has been learned is obsolete and in about ten years most of his previous learning may be obsolete. This would not be so bad if it were not for another, possibly more important factor. We tend to believe what we have learned and this fixes our perception so that *experience confirms these beliefs, whether or not the beliefs are right or wrong.* This is why involvement in action research is so important. This is a way of changing improper perceptions or incorrect beliefs.

Teacher training is done both in schools of education and in school districts' in-service training. Part of the job of every administrator and supervisor is training. This applies to any organization. In order to have meaningful in-service training, school districts will need to hire administrative personnel who have the scholarly background necessary for such training. This will represent a new departure for those districts which have been ignoring "knowledge of the field in depth" as a primary requirement for supervisors. Certainly, in the field of special education this requirement can hardly be ignored. It should not be ignored in other fields either, if school systems wish to do a creditable job of educating children.

Traditionally, educators have agreed that elementary teachers should best not be over-educated. Until recently, only two years of college was required of an elementary teacher. Today in California, five years of college are required to enter elementary education. However, only one course in methods of teaching reading seems to be required in many states. Yet, teaching reading is certainly the most important job of the primary teacher.

In order to solve all of the different teaching problems of the perceptually handicapped, the culturally deprived, and those children with both problems, a new breed of teacher will have to be developed. These teachers should best be recruited from among the very best classroom teachers with three years minimum experience with normal children. They should then receive several years of training in the special education of perceptual deficiencies, including the visual, motor, oral, auditory, tactile and kinesthetic sensory modes. They should become familiar with the latest behavior-therapy and motivational-reward systems. They should be familiar with all of the diagnostic tests used, their interpretation, and the habilitation and remedial methods which differential diagnosis suggests. The chapters by Sister Eileen Marie, Dr. Levine and Miss Lukens are devoted to teaching methods and problems.

After this extensive training, how shall we pay these master teachers? There is no way to compensate them within the current educational structure, except to make them administrators and thus to lose the value of all of their special training which is so badly needed in the classroom. The dilemma of education arises partly from the fact that there is no way to compensate specially trained, creative, master teachers. Yet these teachers are the *sine qua non* to the solution of the illiteracy problem. It may be necessary to establish a special salary scale for master teachers so that they can be retained in teaching.

The children we have been discussing have much in common with all other children. They have all of the basic needs for love, affection, achievement, ego-satisfaction and self-development common to all children. They are different in that they have a psychoneurological deficiency which prevents them from perceiving their environment and reacting to it in the same manner as most children. In general, they look very much like all other children. In terms of their specific abilities to learn, they exhibit differences. These apparently small differences tend to create severe learning problems for many of these children. If they are not provided an adequate learning environment, adjustment scars tend to develop which may impair them permanently. Qualified teachers are needed to serve these children. All of the skills of educational research must be brought to bear to develop adequate teacher training. The future of generations of children with learning disabilities who will grow up in our society depends upon the skills developed in their behalf.

REFERENCES

1. JOHNSON, D., and MYKLEBUST, H.: *Learning Disabilities—Educational Principles and Practices.* New York, Grune, 1967.
2. CLEMENTS, S.D.: *Minimal Brain Dysfunction in Children, NINBD Monograph No. 3.* Washington, Superintendent of Documents, 1966.
3. *California Administrative Code,* Article 27 of Title 5, Section 221a.
4. *Pittsburgh Post-Gazette,* May 24, 1967.
5. ROSENTHAL, R., and JACOBSON, L.: Teachers' expectancies: Determinants of pupils' IQ gains. *Psychol Rep, 19:*115-118, 1966.
6. BANNATYNE, A.: The Etiology of Dyslexia and the Color Phonics System. Mimeographed, 1966.
7. STRAUSS, A., and LEHTINEN, L.: *Psychopathology and Education of the Brain Injured Child.* New York, Grune, 1947.
8. EISENBERG, L.: Epidemiology of reading retardation. In Money, J. (Ed.) :*The Disabled Reader.* Baltimore, Johns Hopkins, 1966.
9. RABINOVITCH, R.D.: Personal Communication, December 4, 1967.
10. RABINOVITCH, R.D.: Dyslexia: Psychiatric considerations. In Money, J. (Ed.): *Reading Disability.* Baltimore, Johns Hopkins, 1962.
11. SILVER, A.A.: Diagnostic considerations in children with reading disability. *Bull Orton Soc,* May 1961.
12. HARDY, M.P.: The evaluation of communicative skills. *Proceedings 1967 International Convocation on Children and Young Adults with Learning Disabilities,* July 1967.
13. HARING, N., and PHILLIPS, E.: *Educating Emotionally Disturbed Children.* New York, McGraw, 1962.
14. HEWETT, F.M.: Educational engineering with emotionally disturbed children. *Exceptional Child,* March 1967.

Chapter 2

A New Look at Learning Disabilities

SAM D. CLEMENTS

A NEW LOOK AT LEARNING disabilities requires that we first take at least a quick glance at what now may be considered portions of the past.

In some respects, such a statement seems incongruous when we consider that the concept of learning disabilities, as we know it today, has a history of less than eight years. As is true with any new development, this brief history is marked with the battle wounds of confusion and controversy. This, however, is a predictable consequence when a concept is so potent that it poses a threat to tradition, challenges the comfort of custom, demands a reevaluation of past endeavors and jogs us into new ways of thinking and planning.

One of the major skirmishes has centered around the academic argument over terminology and definition. The National Project on Minimal Brain Dysfunction (Learning Disabilities) in Children — a collaborative program of the National Institute of Neurological Diseases and Blindness, the Easter Seal Research Foundation of the National Society for Crippled Children and Adults, the National Center for Chronic Disease Control of the U. S. Public Health Service and with the cooperation of the U. S. Office of Education is an attempt to gain clarification of this and other issues specific to this large group of exceptional children (estimated by many experts in the field to be 10% of the public school population).

The National Project developed a definition which encompasses the *symptoms* and *etiologic factors* of minimal brain dysfunction. It appears in the Task Force One document[1] and reads as follows:

"The term 'minimal brain dysfunction' refers to children of near average, average, or above average general intelligence with certain learning and/or behavioral disabilities ranging from mild to severe, which are associated with deviations of function of the central nervous system. These deviations may manifest themselves by various combinations of impairment in perception, conceptualization, language, memory, and control of attention, impulse, or motor function.

"These aberrations may arise from genetic variations, biochemical irregularities, perinatal brain insults or other illnesses or injuries sustained during the years which are critical for the development and maturation of the central nervous system, or from unknown causes.

"During the school years, a variety of learning disabilities is the most prominent manifestation of the condition which can be designated by this term."

31

This definition, with all the faults inherent in attempting to characterize and summarize a group of diverse children by means of a few words, has nevertheless served a useful purpose. It has been a boost to national thinking in this area and has helped us to focus our attention on this assortment of children and make them a target population for all-out concern. At the same time, this definition eliminates from the group other atypical children who are best described and labeled by other sets of words, and who are better served by different methods of management. It is the hope of the Project members that this definition will guide us toward designing the most efficient plan for amelioration of the difficulties of the MBD child.

Since a few educators have voiced their concern about planning educational programs based on medical description and diagnosis, and certainly, this is reasonable, the last sentence in the definition provides what has become the preferred educational term for these children, namely, "learning disabilities."

Educators and others have since penned a few similar definitions which they feel are more educationally-related and which attempt to dilute the so-called medical flavor of the Task Force One definition.

Of major current interest is the one up for adoption by the recently formed Division for Children with Learning Disabilities of the Council for Exceptional Children. It reads as follows:

"A child with learning disabilities is one with adequate mental ability, sensory processes, and emotional stability who has specific deficits in perceptual, integrative, or expressive processes which severely impair learning efficiency. This includes children who have central nervous system dysfunction which is expressed primarily in impaired learning efficiency."

Both definitions contain essentially the same ingredients. If we distill them, the same fundamental components will remain:

1. There exists in the general population a disturbingly large number of children who manifest varying degrees of deviation in learning and behavior.
2. These children possess average intellectual capacity.
3. These deviations result from subtle dysfunctioning of the central nervous system, particularly with regard to the reception, transformation and transmission of sensory data.

The unwritten implication of both definitions is that early identification, proper evaluation and the provision of appropriate educational programming is essential in order for the individual child to achieve the potential of which he is capable.

I would like to quote Dr. Richard L. Masland, Director of the National Institute of Neurological Diseases and Blindness:

"It is a fundamental tenet in this country that all men are created equal. It is an unfortunate fact that in some quarters this principle is being misconstrued to mean, also, that all children are created identical. Nowhere is the lack of identical endowment of children more clearly evident than in the varied capabilities which they demonstrate when faced with the defined academic requirements of our educational system.

"The increasing necessity for the mastery of academic skills for the achievement of an effective role in our present complex society is throwing into prominence the serious difficulties in learning experienced by a disturbingly large proportion of children. Whereas previously it was assumed that all such problems merely reflected a lack of overall intelligence — that is 'mental deficiency,' or 'mental retardation,' it is now recognized that in many instances, impairment of learning ability reflects some limited deviation of the intellectual processes. Under these circumstances, an individual whose overall intelligence may be normal or superior may at the same time experience difficulties in the mastery of intellectual tasks apparently requiring the use of some specific perceptual skill or intellectual process. Such an individual may fail to learn when taught according to techniques suitable for the average child, yet learn quite well when given special instruction which bypasses the intellectual block, or builds upon other perceptual or intellectual skills not ordinarily required for the mastery of the task.

"The variety of terms which have been coined for these conditions reflects our lack of knowledge regarding their nature. Some consider them manifestations of inherited traits. Others attribute them to subtle defects or injury of brain structure. Still others find psychological factors in home or school which are said to impair or inhibit the learning process. It is not adequately recognized that none of the above-mentioned factors can ever operate in isolation. The individual's performance today reflects the totality of his life experience. It depends upon the inherent genetic endowment of his brain, upon modifications of brain growth by illness or injury, and by the way in which his system has interacted with the emotional and perceptual stimuli to which he has been subjected.

"An acceptance of this thesis is essential if we are to accomplish the next step, namely a precise understanding of the nature of these innate deviations of intellectual performance, and of the instructional techniques which will obviate them. The cause will not be helped by those who are fighting to defend this or that old or new system of reading instruction. It will be helped only by those who recognize and appreciate the vast diversity of intellects, and who will seek to provide for each child the teaching experience which is appropriate to his way of learning."[2]

This, in part, is what a new look at learning disabilities reveals to us. It means a new respect for individual differences within and among children.

It requires that we differentiate the unique learning style of the individual child. It encourages us to seek new solutions to old problems.

For some of us, there have been fleeting moments of discouragement during these last eight years due to the fact that these elements were fundamental to the concept from the very beginning, but were ignored or obscured from the view of many professionals by the dust of the battle which they preferred to prolong. Unfortunately, in some parts of the country, parent groups were pressed into service and made to choose sides and defend positions designated by a few self-declared leaders from both the professional and lay ranks. All too often, the parents were caught between the lines, not knowing which way to turn, until they began to realize that the purpose of these maneuvers had never been made clear and were simply serving the selfish purpose of a few individuals.

No one can say it hasn't been exciting!

*　　　*　　　*

In a clinic, when working with a child and a family, one does not think about labels and definitions or spend time recounting "war" experiences.

What sort of thoughts do occupy my mind? I look at this youngster, regardless of age, and I think: Here is a child with most of his life ahead of him, and already things are off to a poor and painful start. The child is brought to us because he or she is transmitting certain behavioral signals which someone, usually parents, often teachers, physicians and others, receives and interprets as meaning that something is wrong. Parents come to us hoping for help and guidance. Most will do anything within their power to benefit their child.

I see in this child a living profile of deficits and strengths in intellectual functioning, emotional response, attentional factors, impulse control and relationship skills which are sufficiently divergent from accepted norms to pose a problem for learning and adjustment in his given environment. Likewise, the environment in which the child has developed is composed of a specific profile of demands and expectations which, unfortunately, do not always match the unique pattern of talents and areas of weakness of the particular child.

I remind myself that what I observe and measure in this child has been determined by a unique set of circumstances — *one that holds true for no other human being on the face of this earth*. His individuality has been prescribed by endless genetic variations which result in particular kinds of cognitive, sensory, motor and temperamental modalities with particularly imposed functional restrictions and potentials; by an endless variety of possible perinatal stress factors; by lags or variations in the maturational unfolding of the central nervous system; by possible interpersonal and/or sensory deprivations during critical periods of his development; and by an unrestricted number of other known and unknown determinants.

I begin to wonder if this child's individuality is understood, accepted and appreciated, but most importantly, will accommodations and adaptations be made for him as he proceeds through school, the one institution of our society through which each of us must pass. Has, will, or can the school become a saving resource for him? Or, will he, as is commonly done, be dumped into the academic mix-master and converted into something less than what he was at the beginning?

I caution myself that a diagnostic evaluation, even at the highest level of sophistication and refinement, can become but an empty and isolated activity unless implemented by programs of action. This means that I and my co-workers cannot confine our work to the four walls of the clinic. A portion of one's professional life must be spent working in the community, with schools, agencies, organizations and institutions in the planning and development of whatever programs are necessary and needed in order for this child to develop to whatever potential he possesses.

In our clinic, after a comprehensive multidisciplinary diagnostic evaluation is completed, and the results indicate that mild neurologic dysfunctioning is responsible for the child's areas of deficit in learning and behavior, then the term minimal brain dysfunction is used as the diagnostic formulation and in explaining and discussing the child's symptoms with parents. We are aware that the term is used to cover a wide variety of symptom combinations which manifest differently at various age levels. But, the reason for this term is simple. It emphasizes the fact that the major determinant of the child's faulty functioning is an organic one, and is not due to pernicious handling on the part of the parents.

The fact that thousands of these children come from good homes with normal siblings makes it untenable to postulate environmental or psychogenic factors as being the fundamental cause. Likewise, excellent academic achievement and the absence of perverse symptoms in thousands of known cases of children who have endured emotional trauma of every possible description, undermines a broad psychogenic hypothesis.

We are neither wedded to nor completely satisfied with the term minimal brain dysfunction as an all-encompassing category, in view of the fact that many different subgroups exist within this classification; probably as many as there are separate functions for the major circuits and structures within the brain. Eventually, as more knowledge accumulates, these will develop into clear-cut, perhaps mutually exclusive entities. There is much current research across the country which is probing deeper into the phenomenology of this varied group of children; and investigators are chipping at the edges of the newly emerging science of neuropsychology in the search for brain-behavior relationships.

In the meantime, the term *minimal brain dysfunction* as a diagnostic grouping is found to be most useful, both in the clinic and the research laboratory.

*   *   *

One natural but inhibiting factor relative to social action in the area of learning disabilities, and a contributor to the national dilemma, is the matter of its uneven development across the country. In some states, medical and health-related groups have guided its growth; in others, educators and public schools have set the pace. In other sections of the country, parent groups have provided the leadership. The moral is apparent when we consider that *progress has been slow where any one of these groups has acted independently of the others.* In other words, the most progress has been made in those communities and states where program development for children with learning disabilities has been seen as a joint responsibility of the total community. It is important to recognize that during this developmental period, leadership roles and responsibilities will change.

I cite as an example, the history of the learning disabilities movement in one of our south-central states. In its beginning six years ago, the parents' organization, with professional guidance, began a two-year program of public education. At this point, leadership was then transferred to the professional community; mainly medical and health-related groups who directed their efforts toward involving the state department of education, the teacher training institutions, and the public schools, particularly administrators and school boards. Major responsibility for the children was then assumed and is retained by the educators. The medical and health-related teams and the parents' organization now serve in the main as advisors, consultants and back-up teams to the educators and public schools. This system has worked well in this particular state. The number of trained teachers and public school programs for children with learning disabilities has increased dramatically. It is apparent that one of the techniques for winning this game is knowing when to toss the ball to another member of the team to put it into play.

*   *   *

One of the unfortunate circumstances in the field of learning disabilities has been this: He who makes the diagnosis *first,* tends to get the glory. Couple this with failure to follow through with needed services, or worse, assign this responsibility in cavalier fashion to others who were not involved from the beginning, and trouble begins to brew. In the recent past, the medical and health-related groups were, in the main, the ones who were first to make the diagnosis. I feel this state of affairs was partly responsible for most of the discontent which existed during the early years of the learning disabilities movement, particularly on the part of educators. Development was not only uneven geographically, but also among and within professional groups in local communities.

Frequently, the medical diagnostic report merely restates or confirms what an alert teacher already knows. Often, this confirmation is desired and requested by the educator. Thus, it serves a useful purpose.

But, *identification* of the child with learning disabilities and *cursory diagnosis* is relatively an easy task. The difficult part is fashioning and procuring an individualized educational program based on the unique profile of the deficits and strengths of the child, taking into consideration his innate individual differences, possible developmental discrepancies, learning style, etc. It should go without saying that educators are equipped and specifically trained to do this far better than other professional groups.

Confusion still exists in the minds of those who have failed to recognize that differences exist in the *objectives* of the "medical" diagnosis, as apposed to the "educational" diagnosis.

The main objective of the medical diagnosis is to demonstrate the existence of any causative factors of central nervous system functioning responsible for the condition and capable of amelioration or prevention. The educational diagnosis, on the other hand, involves the assessment of performance and capabilities. Its objective is to make possible the establishment of appropriate programs of educational management. *Diagnosis, be it educational or medical, must precede and prescribe treatment.* Its major function is to guide us in decision making.

So, although the diagnosis of the child with minimal brain dysfunction may be medical *or* educational, the treatment is, in the main, *educational*. The medical evaluation is essential to prevent the development or continuation of an unsuspected disease process. If and when this is a finding, then appropriate medical treatment is instituted.

A major contribution to treatment by the medical team is that of medication management. Most of these children *can* profit by the judicious use of certain special medications for control of specific symptoms, such as hyperactivity, hypoactivity, attention span, irritability, impulsivity, etc. Chemotherapy is beneficial when viewed as part of a comprehensive program in that the child can become more accessible for teaching — and the behavioral modification that can result make the child more socially acceptable, not only to others but to himself. And, this latter point is rarely mentioned and certainly underrated.

Looking ahead, the trend around the country now seems to be going in the direction of using the medical and health-related teams for two major purposes: one, for initial diagnostic *screening,* and two, as an ancillary team for the educators to use as part of the continuing care program when certain services, such as parent and child counseling and medical and medication management cannot be provided by school personnel.

The finer elements of educational diagnosis and treatment planning are left to the educators.

Since trained educational diagnosticians are in such short supply nation-wide, most schools which offer special services for children with learning disabilities are using the following as criteria for eligibility for these programs:

1. The child must have average or above intellectual capacity. In many schools the child must achieve an IQ score of 90 or above on *either* the Verbal *or* the Performance Scale of the Wechsler Intelligence Scale for Children.
2. The child must display a learning disability of significant proportion in one or more of the basic academic skills of reading, arithmetic, spelling and/or handwriting.
3. The child has one or more of the characteristics, other than the above common associated with the syndromes of learning disabilities, e.g., hyperactivity, deficits in expressive langauge, attentional difficulties, etc.

The child is then placed in a learning disabilities program, either of the resource room or self-contained classroom variety on a trial basis where prescriptive teaching is employed and adjusted to the child's needs. If progress is forthcoming during the trial placement, usually no less than a three-month period, then he continues in the program. If progress is minimal, then an additional trial period may be recommended, or further evaluation is done. The major ingredients of a successful program are flexibility, experimentation and ongoing evaluation.

*   *   *

Most of our efforts for the educationally handicapped child have focused on the elementary school age group. The trend is now to develop suitable programs for the older child — the junior and senior high school age groups. The possibilities for sound programs are endless and involve, for example, vocational preparation curricula as early as seventh grade and fortified by intensive training in the basic academic skills. Programs for the older child are being spearheaded, in the main, by educational groups.

On the other hand, the medical and health-related groups are concerning themselves with the preschool child, and in particular with the early detection of exceptional children and the institution of corrective management programs. Medical students, those who will soon be out in the field as private practitioners, and most often the professional person to whom parents will first come for help, are being taught the kinds of medical histories and the signs and symptoms in the infant and young child that places him at high risk for future learning and behavioral problems. They are learning how such children and their parents should be managed or referred during the preschool years.

Language, motor and other readiness programs are being developed for nursery schools and kindergartens. Public school kindergartens, in those states fortunate enough to have them, are being used as detection agencies for early identification of children with learning disabilities and early training procedures are becoming an integral part of their programs.

*   *   *

The learning disabilities movement is gaining such force across the country that in some quarters action is being considered to establish learning disabilities as a third major category on the national scene of education. Thus, since it encompasses such a large proportion of children and youth, it would maintain an intermediary position between general education and special education with an overlapping relationship with each, but holding an independent identity. It is true that our population of learning disabilities children holds much in common with both established levels of education, and at the same time is different from the population we think of as customary for either regular education or special education in the public school system. Whether or not such a far-reaching concept can be accepted by educators at the present time, I do not know. I do feel that the time is long past due for the total field of education to stop thinking of itself as merely two-faceted — regular education and special education — and the unfortunate inherent restriction which proclaims that "never the twain shall meet." Perhaps the child with learning disabilities is just what is needed to bring about this much needed change.

*   *   *

A new look at learning disabilities would have to include acknowledgement of the increasing level of sophistication and maturation taking place within the field. This is reflected in the increasing quickness with which we are able to recognize and reject the prima donnas, the dilettanti, the bandwagon jumpers, the leaders of cults and those who peddle programs of instant and lasting cure. As the market begins to flood with new teaching techniques and materials, we are becoming more discriminating regarding their usefulness and adaptability in the classroom.

*   *   *

No exceptional child has fired the imagination of professional people as has the child with learning disabilities. He has also created a great deal of discord. But now, eight years later, leaders in the field, even in disagreement, are speaking in softer voices; differences are narrowing, heads and emotions are cooling.

This child has acted as a catalyst in bringing together such groups as parents, educators, child psychiatrists, pediatricians, pediatric neurologists, child psychologists, optometrists, language pathologists, social workers, nurses, occupational therapists, physical therapists and others — if not yet working as well-oiled teams with a single goal, that of helping the children, then at least willing to sit, think, talk and work together.

And, this has come about not because this is just a new category of children. It has to do in part, I think, with the fact that such children are so easily salvageable, their potential is so good, and they have been ignored or misinterpreted for so long.

The national dilemma is turning into a national challenge, and with this change in orientation, the resolution of its many problems is at last in sight.

REFERENCES

1. CLEMENTS, S.D.: *Minimal Brain Dysfunction in Children: Terminology and Identification.* Washington, U.S. Government Printing Office, 1966.
2. MASLAND, R.L.: Forward to THOMPSON, L.J.: *Reading Disability — Developmental Dyslexia.* Springfield, Thomas, 1966.

Chapter 3

Parent and Professional Relations

LESTER TARNOPOL

ROLE OF PARENTS

PARENTS UNDOUBTEDLY HAVE the greatest emotional and intellectual investment in their own children's development, problems and future. This point need not be labored. As a rule, new services for handicapped children are obtained when parents demand them. Children with minimal brain dysfunction have followed the rule. There appear to be several reasons why parents are best suited to this function. First, only parents have a pervasive interest in the total development of their own children. Second, parents do not have to wait until someone decides that there are enough children exhibiting the disability to warrant special services before demanding help. Third, it has been demonstrated that both legislators and school boards tend to be much more responsive to the demands of parents than to professionals.

The alternative would be for the professionals to make the services available. Experience seems to indicate that they are much slower than parents to create change in the form of new services for several reasons. First, each professional may see only a few cases so that the incidence may appear minor to him. Second, often when a new concept first appears in the literature, many professionals cannot accept it since their mental sets only permit the syndrome to assume its previously learned meanings. This is no reflection on the professionals, it is a universal failing. Thus, although Morgan published his findings in 1896 and others thereafter discussed the problem in the literature, many authorities continued to claim that minimal brain dysfunction was not a problem of any scope. Third, the number of different professions involved, each of which must become acquainted with its own relationship to the problem, is very great and interprofessional communication is minimal. Fourth, the various professions are not organized to work together to get legislation or services in the manner in which parents can readily become organized for a single purpose. For these reasons, parents must assume a great deal of personal responsibility for getting whatever services their children need.

This general thesis has been echoed in a statement from Syracuse University prepared by Cruickshank at the request of a group of Pennsylvania citizens.[1]

"Although it is obvious that the so-called minimally brain damaged child has for many years been a part of the general child population, it has been

41

relatively recent that sufficient information has developed within the several professions which have a concern for such children to the point where some consensus has been reached. As late as 1935, research began to be developed in the United States which dealt with the psychological characteristics of these children, yet thirty years later this information is only just beginning to filter into the understanding and general practice of the professions involved.

"There are currently still great gaps in the knowledge about these children and there is some lack of unanimity regarding them. Incidence and prevalence studies are for the most part lacking. Parent awareness of these children has gotten ahead of professional awareness. Professional awareness is ahead of provisions for professional preparation of teachers, physicians, psychologists, and social workers, and it is also ahead of teacher education facilities and the availability of competent college professors to teach in this complex area."

Parent awareness of children with minimal neurological dysfunction has gotten ahead of professional awareness. Although this is a very difficult role for parents to assume, they have been forced into this position by the lack of diagnostic and remedial services available to their children.

Many parents also feel that there is an unfortunate lack of communication between professionals and themselves. They feel that they need to know everything possible about their child if they are to be able to assist him intelligently. On the other hand, physicians, social workers and psychologists are not accustomed to explaining their tests and other findings in great detail to parents. However, most of the parents who have been questioning the professionals very closely about their children are quite capable of understanding the test results and interpretations as they are generally professionals themselves. Perhaps for the first time, many parents are no longer content to accept the diagnoses and prescriptions of the various professions on faith. In the case of children with minimal brain dysfunction, parents have been misled too often and so have become severely questioning. The stories of these parents are well known to pediatric-neurologists and others, and appear to be so much alike that many have been recorded, and they play back like the proverbial "broken record."[2] It helps some neophyte parents of children with minimal brain dysfunction to listen to such recordings because they generally feel much relieved when they discover that they have not lost their senses since others have preceded them through the unbelievable nightmare of being tossed from one professional to another only to receive more improbable diagnoses and prescriptions.

Parents also complain of another type of communication failure between themselves and many professionals. They say that professionals often do not *listen* to either themselves or their children. What they seem to mean is that many professionals listen to them with a presumptive bias and so are unable to hear what is actually being said. Interestingly enough, the worst offenders often seem to be those who have had specific training in *listening* to clients.

The problem seems to arise from the fact that few people listen to what is specifically stated by the client. Instead the client's statements tend to be immediately subjected to interpretation based upon the clinician's "frame of reference." Thus, when the mother of an unusually hyperactive and impulsive child said, "I can't leave Joey alone to play outside because he might run heedlessly into the street," the clinician recorded, not the mother's precise statement, but "mother is overprotective." Fortunately for the child, this mother probably had both better instincts and understanding of the child than the professional, and so the child is still alive. What this parent desperately needed from the professional was advice and help in developing a workable program to train the child to become aware of danger and to act accordingly. This, of course, was not forthcoming.

Typically, the mothers of very impulsive, hyperactive children tend to be labeled as overprotective by clinicians who have had relatively little personal experience with the problems of daily living with these children. Fortunately for these children, most mothers have very strong feelings about the need to help their children. Mothers have pointed out that it is precisely this drive which has kept them searching for solutions to their problems; and what would have happened if they had not! Telling the mother that she is overprotective may make her feel guilty, but it does not help her solve the child's problems. Often there are other children in the family, and it is noted that the mother does not hover over the normal children.

Another common experience of some families has been a diagnosis of emotional disturbance followed by several fruitless years of play therapy. When this failed and the child's distress increased, one therapist turned to the parents who were now also in therapy and asked the rhetorical question, "Why does your child feel rejected?" In other cases, young severely hyperkinetic boys have been seen on a one-to-one basis by the child psychiatrist (as many as four sessions) and have been pronounced perfectly normal. This is one reason why children should also be observed in the home and play environments. In such cases, mothers have been questioned about their own anxieties, in view of the child's apparent "normality."

What the parents say they want and need is practical help in methods of working with their children. They want to know how to structure their home environments and specific methods of handling the child in the different situations which arise in the lives of these families. They would like to reach the practical level of functioning where meal time is no longer an upsetting, ulcer-producing situation, or a knock-down drag-out fight. This is the type of practical help they are asking for. And they also need some relief from these children. Agencies are needed to provide both baby-sitting and camping experiences for the children, both to aid in the development of the children and to preserve the sanity of the parents.

So far, help for these parents and children has been coming from several sources. Medication for the children, when it works, can be enormously helpful. The development of diagnostic facilities and teams, public school programs, special clinics, reading centers and full-time rehabilitation facilities have already helped a great many children and parents. An especially helpful program for families is described by Barsch.[3] He conducted a seven-year experiment in group counseling with parents of brain-damaged children which was found to be supportive, anxiety reducing and practically helpful. The parents were helped to perceive their children with greater understanding and to deal with problems more effectively. The parents were helped to recognize significant cues in the children's behavior and to aid the development of more adequate ways of behaving. Another program, helpful to parents, is the group therapy type program which some school systems have made available to their parents. These sessions may be held weekly with the school psychologist. In other instances, psychotherapists have rendered service as part of interdisciplinary teams. Doctors Kurlander and Colodny discuss the role of psychotherapy for both the child and parents in their chapter.

RESPONSIBILITIES OF PARENTS

Parents, too, have great responsibilities for the welfare of their children which they sometimes fail to assume. Many parents wait and take a "let someone else do it" attitude. If their physician or the school personnel do not observe their child's problems, they may make no independent effort to do so. When they become aware of the child's problems, they may wait for others to place the child in an appropriate rehabilitative setting without taking any positive action themselves. As a result, many children with learning disabilities have drifted through school with no special help and are educational, psychological and vocational casualties. Of course, this is also true of some children whose parents have tried very hard and unsuccessfully to get them help.

Some parents have such unrealistic or negative feelings about their children's learning disabilities and inadequate behavior patterns that they prefer to "hide the child." Fear of facing reality may prevent such parents from taking positive action in their children's behalf. Others hope that if they pay no attention to the problems they will go away. Often they are told by pediatricians and others to ignore the problems as they will disappear as the child matures. In the case of children with minimal brain dysfunction, this is a dangerous route to follow. Valuable time may be lost and could render rehabilitation most difficult.

Some parents seem to find it most difficult to accept the findings of an accredited team of diagnosticians when the diagnosis seems too drastic. This is not difficult to understand. However, if a diagnosis has been confirmed more than once by reputable teams of clinicians, the parents are well advised to assume the diagnosis to be valid, at least for purposes of taking positive corrective action. If the corrective action seems to help, this tends to validate the diagnostic findings.

Some parents appear to be too timid to express themselves directly to professionals. They may disagree with the professional but feel it is best to appear to agree and then simply to refrain from acting on the advice given. This may prevent the clinician from getting an adequate understanding of the case and so may encourage poor communication and misunderstandings. It may be better to keep communication channels open with free and complete discussion for the sake of the child. In some cases, the parents may fail to follow through with complete work-ups, prescribed medication, or structuring the home environment to the needs of the child. Clearly, such parents need understanding counseling to help them carry out their part of the prescription.

There are those parents who may simply be poor communicators. They tend to bring their impulsive, hyperactive child, or otherwise unusual behaving child into a new situation with new people without attempting to explain to the unsuspecting persons what to expect and what this behavior might mean. For example, parents have been known to start such a child in school or camp without explaining the child to the teacher or the camp director. Perhaps they hope that the child's behavior will go unnoticed or that the professionals will somehow "understand" the child's deviant behavior. This is not the best way to introduce the child to a new situation. People are generally more understanding if they know what to expect, and if the behavior has been explained to them. Otherwise, they may perceive the child in a completely incorrect way and be quite lacking in "understanding."

Finally, too many parents leave the work of getting services for their children to the few who join and work in parent organizations. They are too willing to permit others to assume the entire burden of responsibility. They are not willing to get out and work for their children's futures. Also, there are those who join a parent organization but fail to contribute in any meaningful way. Some are too willing to leave the burden of getting services for the children to those who are most willing to work and carry through on their assignments. And finally, there are many who lack the singleness of purpose so often required to get adequate programs and services for these children.

PARENTS CAN TAKE POSITIVE ACTION

In all probability, most parents of handicapped children go through periods of wanting to hide their children, guilt, denial, frustration, wishing someone else would do something, hoping it will go away and perhaps other defensive postures. Although this may be the pattern for many parents, it is not the pattern for all. There are, fortunately, many parents who recover from their initial reactions to frustration and the possible defense mechanisms which naturally develop in such situations. These parents begin to face reality squarely and proceed to take positive action on behalf of their children. They form organizations to work for legislation, parent education, public education, professional education and both private and public school classes for these children. These organizations are listed in the Appendix for the benefit of those who may wish such information.

As the result of the positive efforts of these parents and their professional friends, both state and national legislation has begun to be effected to aid in the diagnosis and education of these children. In many places, parents have resorted to banding together to start private schools to meet the special needs of their children which they felt the public schools were as yet unable to meet. By taking these various positive actions on behalf of their handicapped children, many of these parents have succeeded in turning despair and hostility into a creative outlet for their feelings. They gained not only programs for their own children, but self-respect and the knowledge that they had benefited many others as well. The educational and therapy programs developed for children with learning disabilities represent an important milestone in history. This marks a turning point in the philosophy of child guidance and in the child guidance movement itself.

In California, the California Association for Neurologically Handicapped Children, primarily a parent organization, not only helped effect the first state legislation making funds available to all California School Districts for special classes for Educationally Handicapped Minors, but they also have produced some very important films about these children. One, *Why Billie Couldn't Learn,* is a 42-minute, 16mm, color film depicting both the diagnosis and remedial procedures used in one California School Disrtcit.[4] Another, a 20-minute film, demonstrates various motor coordination and balance exercises used in another California School District.[5] These are both excellent films of the highest quality which are most highly recommended.

PARENTS FORM CANHC

The California Association For Neurologically Handicapped Children (CANHC) was formed to aid children with substantially normal intelligence who were educationally handicapped by virtue of minimal central nerevous system dysfunction. There were organizations helping and classes in school for the mentally retarded, the orthopedically handicapped, the emotionally disturbed, the blind, the deaf and the severely brain damaged. Another group of handicapped children was being distinguished which gave promise to become one of the largest groups, once adequate case finding was established. There were no special class or facilities for these children. This was the group variously distinguished by such terms as minimal brain damage, minimal cerebral dysfunction, minimal central nervous system dysfunction, hyperkinetic syndrome and others of similar import. The California Association For Neurologically Handicapped Children was formed statewide to help these children in 1963.

Perhaps the first major accomplishment of CANHC was in the legislative field. Assemblyman Jerome Waldie* of Antioch, California, had been interested by some CANHC parent founders in developing legislation for the education of these neurologically handicapped (NH) children. In 1963 the Waldie Bill, Assembly Bill 464, was passed in California which gave financial reimbursement beyond normal educational costs to any school district which set up a special program for educationally handicapped children including both the neurologically handicapped and the emotionally handicapped children of substantially normal intelligence. Dr. Robert O'Reilly, Ex-President of CANHC, stated, "This momentous legislation was written by a lawyer member of CANHC, guided through its tortuous legislative course by a CANHC salesman member and advocated in legislature hearings by a third CANHC member, a medical educator. Its legislative patron was Assemblyman Jerome Waldie of Antioch. This bill wisely provides for both NH and emotionally disturbed children, as the medical differentiation of the two disorders is not easily made. This is because emotional disturbances often develop secondarily in an NH child."[6] Since this momentous legislative step was taken in California, other states have been considering similar legislation some of which has already been passed.

Interest in the welfare of handicapped children must go beyond legislation. It is also important to engage in public education, case finding and research. Since both the case finding and education of neurologically handicapped children involve areas of controversy, the position taken by CANHC is to support whatever appears to be in the best interests of the children,

*Now United States Congressman.

which in this case logically refers to both the emotionally and neurologically handicapped children who are educated in special classes under the same legislative bill. CANHC's position is both eclectic and pragmatic. It is eclectic in that it does not favor any educational method over the others since none has proven to be effective for all children, nor has any method yet established itself as better than the others. It is pragmatic in that it favors that which works. Thus CANHC would like to see any method which has face-validity tested. That is, educational methods which by logical analysis appear to be valid deserve to be tested or used on an experimental basis. It is also considered that it is up to the proponent of any educational method to demonstrate by controlled scientific research the actual validity of his method. Thus, although face or logical validity may be acceptable for use in an experimental situation, final acceptance of any method must be based on scientific validation.

In 1966, Assemblyman Waldie stated in San Francisco that if CANHC had been formed two years earlier, the California legislation for the education of these children would have passed two years earlier in 1961 when it first appeared before the legislature and was defeated. The CANHC parents have continued their educational efforts on behalf of their children by means of symposia which have attracted national interest, workshops for teachers, pleas to boards of education for programs for educationally handicapped children and the production of movies demonstrating both the diagnosis and treatment of these children.

PARENTS SURVEYED

In 1965, a survey was made of the parents of children with learning disabilities in San Francisco who were members of the California Association for Neurologically Handicapped Children.[7] There were forty-four questionnaire respondents constituting about two-thirds of the parents. The results disclosed that mothers were most often credited with first noticing the children's problems. School personnel were cited in 18 per cent and pediatricians in only 14 per cent of the cases. Many pediatricians still seemed to be unaware of the syndrome and its learning ramifications. Each respondent listed only one child whom he considered as having a learning disability problem. Some parents have more than one such child but they apparently were not among those who replied to the mailed questionnaire. Boys outnumbered girls in this sample by a ratio of more than three to one. The children ranged in age from three to twenty, with about three-quarters of them between the ages of seven and twelve. Four years was the median age at which the problem was initially discovered. In more than 30 per cent of the cases, the problem was not discovered until the child began attending school.

Of the children in this survey who were subjected to formal diagnostic procedures, half received only one work-up and half more than one. The fact that only one diagnostic work-up had been performed did not necessarily indicate that the diagnosis was either complete or satisfactory. Dissatisfaction with diagnoses was reported by more than 25 per cent of the respondents. Psychologists and neurologists were most often involved in the diagnostic procedures, pediatricians and psychiatrists somewhat less often. Most of the children had received electroencephalographic (EEG) examinations. About half were reported as consistently abnormal while one-fourth were normal and abnormal at different times, and one-fourth were normal.

The most frequently cited diagnoses were neurological handicap and minimal brain damage. Almost half of the parents had not been told about their child's intelligence level. Half the children were reported to have IQ's in the normal range or better, two were listed as mentally retarded and one was referred to as a slow learner. Half of the children were described as having emotional problems and somewhat less than half as having perceptual-motor problems. Motor discoordination was diagnosed for approximately one-fourth of the sample. Epilepsy was noted in six instances and aphasia in four. Multiple diagnostic categories were often cited for these children.

Approximately 60 per cent of the school-age children with learning disabilities were found to be in regular classes and more than half of these received no special instruction in addition to their normal school work. About one-fourth of the children in regular classes also attended local private reading clinics which had been especially founded for children with psychoneurological reading disorders. Most of these children were receiving two hours of such tutoring per week. One child was receiving no instruction, having been dismissed from four schools as a behavior problem.

The majority of parents were dissatisfied with their children's progress in school. Less than one-quarter of the respondents found their children progressing satisfactorily. For the most part, the dissatisfied parents placed the blame on the unavailability of sufficient special classes in the schools and the lack of specially trained teachers.

Perhaps it would be instructive to read some of the parents' stories in their own words.

CASE OF JOHN AS RELATED BY MOTHER

A mother related her problems to the Board of Education in a letter which contained the following case history of her teen-age son, in part.

"My son was diagnosed three years ago at C Hospital as a victim of minimal brain dysfunction. I was also told that my only recourse was to prayer. Previously, long unavailing years had been spent seeking help from the professionals. 'You are too lenient.' 'You are too strict.' 'Give him more discipline.' 'Give him more love and less discipline.' 'Give him a good right to the jaw.' These were the words of advice generously doled out by the various pediatricians, neurologists, psychiatrists, social workers, counselors, and juvenile authorities. The boy looks normal, ergo, he is normal. What if his EEG tests were a little irregular? This proved nothing, but give him a little Librium® and Dilantin.® Three grand mal seizures did not prove he was epileptic and oxygen deprivation at birth was unimportant! Some professionals advised us to send him to a state mental institution. The forms were obtained. But he is not crazy. How could we?

"A day treatment center and neuropsychiatric clinic, after four months and one month respectively, said his problems were emotional in origin. I'm sure by then the emotional problems which had developed completely obscured the basic physical defect. A broken arm can be seen. Minimal brain damage is quite invisible to the naked Freudian oriented eye.

"My son's school record from kindergarten on is a complete disaster. 'What did you do in school to-day, my son?' 'The teacher had on blue earrings, and there was a bird singing in the tree outside my window.' 'But what did the teacher put on the blackboard?' 'I don't know mother, I was listening to the bird and looking at the teacher's pretty earrings. Can you get some earrings like hers?'

"My repeated requests that my son be put in a special class for slow learners were denied. And the denials made sense. My child was extremely bright, they said, and wouldn't fit into such a class. One counselor in high school, a gym teacher, put it in these words, 'Your kid is no slouch, he don't belong in no dummy class.' If he passes this term, he'll still have a year more of high school to graduation, and he's over eighteen.''

*　　　*　　　*

In this case, John's mother is obviously quite agitated, and with good reason. She has been attempting to cope with a very disturbed son for many years and to add to this tremendous burden, it appears that the professionals who have been consulted have only compounded her confusion with conflicting diagnoses and advice. It would probably have been much more helpful to this mother if most of those who wished to help her with advice had been able to realize that they did not understand this complex case and had simply said so. We are probably all too prone to give "helpful" advice when we would do much better to say, "I don't know," or when possible, "This is a complex matter which I don't fully understand. However, X team of clinicians specialize in this type of diagnosis. I suggest that you see them."

Of course, it is realized that the various professionals in this case might give a quite different version of this case history. At this point, we only have the mother's perceptions. At any rate, professionals could be much more careful of what they say to parents. Statements which may be construed to place the *blame* for the child's problems on the parents must be avoided. Such statements only produce immobilizing guilt in many parents and they certainly do not help the children. This mother's letter to the Board of Education may help other children, but action will not be taken in time to help her son in the public schools.

In the case of Tony which follows, the mother has her own recommendations.

CASE OF TONY AS RELATED BY MOTHER

"In November of last year, Tony at eight years of age, fell from a tree and received a concussion. He was admitted to the hospital that day. He was released two days later and upon reaching home began to vomit again. He was returned to the hospital that night and the following day an EEG was taken. Following this he was given elixir of phenobarbital. I do not know the dosage he was given while he was an in-patient. The neurosurgeon who was caring for him stated that day, that his EEG was 'wild.' He was sent home about five days later on phenobarbital, $\frac{1}{4}$ grain, three times daily. At that time he was returned to the care of his pediatrician. He continued to take this medication until the pediatrician felt it wasn't necessary. It had not affected Tony in any way, that is, he was neither more nor less active. It was discontinued in January. In April, about six months after the accident, a repeat EEG was taken. I was told at that time, by his pediatrician, that his EEG was like the first one, that is, it showed a dysrhythmia.

"At that time, in April, I made arrangements for Tony to attend a private reading clinic which specializes in the treatment of children with learning disabilities. This clinic takes the children twice a week for one hour sessions after a complete diagnostic work-up. The clinic asked for his medical record, and I requested the hospital to send one which would include particular attention to the results of the neurological work from his November fall. It might be interesting to know that the report, which I saw, stated that his EEGs were normal!

"At the reading clinic, Tony was seen by a neurologist who stated that Tony exhibited those neurological symptoms and 'soft signs' which are often found in children who have learning disabilities. The neurologist suggested that Tony be started with psychotherapy there, and he is being seen on a weekly basis. I believe that his lack of feelings of self-esteem have been intensified by failures in school and difficulties in his relationships with other children."

This mother is a nurse and she said that she followed the medical and educational progress of her child very closely. Two years later, a follow-up interview with his mother brought forth the following supplementary information. Tony had had five months of psychotherapy, once a week for fifty minutes, with a psychiatric social worker who was connected with the reading clinic and who knew a great deal about children with neurological dysfunction and learning problems as well as the emotional concomitants. Her statement continues.

"The psychotherapy was to make him amenable to learning. After five months, he started the remedial reading program. In one semester, his reading level increased from second grade to high third grade. The following October, at age ten, he was admitted to a class for the educationally handicapped in a public school in another neighborhood. This year, at age eleven, he was admitted to an intermediate class for the educationally handicapped in the public school in our neighborhood. He is doing work at about the high fifth grade level. He also has been attending class at a different private reading clinic two hours a week. The past few months at the reading clinic seem to have helped him calm down a great deal. They do both motor coordination and reading remediation at the clinic. They do lots of motor training which they call movement efficiency. They also photographed his eye movements to help study his reading patterns. They used a metronome to pace his spelling in order to slow it down and this seems to have had a positive effect as he was hyperkinetic. He is now reading near the fifth grade level and his hyperactivity is very much decreased.

"As the result of these experiences I have lost respect for many professionals. After Tony's fall, his pediatrician told me that I was hovering over him too much and he suggested psychotherapy for Tony. He said that I was overprotective. When Tony had difficulty learning in school, his teacher said he was a child who did not try. They need to become aware of neurological dysfunction and learning disabilities. And they must stop blaming the mothers for these problems in children."

CASE OF ANN AS RELATED BY FATHER

"As a preschool child, Ann was much like other children — she gave us no special problems. True, she was more restless than other kids, but there was nothing abnormal in her behavior. She was affectionate, curious, interested in lots of things, and had friends, many of them.

"But from the beginning, school for Ann was chaos. She was unmanageable in class — restless in an aimless way, out of her chair every few minutes, wandering around the classroom, oblivious to the class and the teachers, washing her hands, peering out the window, asking irrelevant questions.

"We didn't connect her damaging illness (encephalitis) at age one with this aberrant behavior, and didn't suspect that she might be brain damaged.

Neither did our doctors. Elaborate examinations at age five and at age eight revealed nothing. An EEG at age eight was negative.

"It was clear, said teachers and doctors, that Ann was a behavior problem, and that we the parents were at fault. Through most of Ann's first year in school, we consulted weekly with a school department psychologist. Public school came to an impasse. At age eight, she had six months with a tutor, who moved Ann's learning curve straight up. But the discipline was too rigorous for Ann. She began to have nightmares, crying spells and wet the bed. Two years in a private school followed. That, too, was a failure.

"When Ann was ten, we moved to S. Here she was put in an Opportunity Class. This was both good and bad. The teacher was charming and sweet tempered, and for the first time Ann didn't have to compete at school. She dearly loved her teacher and applied herself diligently to her lessons.

"But the lessons — there was the rub. While the Opportunity Class took a great deal of psychic pressure off Ann, this class was little more than a baby-sitting class, where the lessons had no particular meaning. Ann's teacher was charming but professionally inept, without any notion at all of how to work with children like Ann.

"Ann was in the Opportunity Class for three years — then moved on to junior high school, where she was once more thrown on her own resources, forced to compete in regular classes. She couldn't compete. She was a flat failure. The school administrators at junior high school were sympathetic to her plight, but had no place for her except in regular classes. The only special class was one for the mentally retarded, and Ann didn't qualify.

"It was while Ann was still in the Opportunity Class that she was brought into the Medical Center orbit for an evaluation, thanks to the efforts of personnel in the school department. It was at the Medical Center that we got the first realistic diagnosis.

"That was two years ago. Ann has been in the Medical Center Reading Clinic ever since. They did a lot for her, in spite of the fact that she goes to the clinic class only two hours a week. The first thing we noticed was a gradual improvement in Ann's morale. Nothing dramatic, just a gradual dropping away of some of her uncertainties. She began to approach her schoolwork with more confidence. Until then, Ann was still mired in the first grade primer. At home, she would struggle in anguish with her lessons, weeping bitterly, utterly stripped of confidence. Today, lesson time is still a time of anguish and frustration but with a difference. Now she doesn't give up. She persists, and she achieves.

"Today, in the 8th grade, she reads at about 6th grade level. At the same time, she is still a dyslexic, with specific problems of perception, and is still crippled in curious ways in her handling of words. She has a long way to go.

What Ann needs is more of the clinic type class and less of the pressure of regular public school classes, where much of the reading clinic's good work gets undone. She also needs a broader special curriculum. The clinic's classes are limited to reading.

"This year at school, Ann's grades are the best she has ever achieved. For the first time, she is actually competing. But the nervous strain is telling on her. While her morale is better now, she is still not equipped for this kind of competition. She is at the bottom of the pecking order, and feels alone and left out of things. The other children call her names like MR (for 'mentally retarded'), and this sort of thing has a devastating effect on Ann."

*   *   *

Both the cases of Tony and Ann allude to some of the serious problems which the children themselves have with others. Quite often other children call the handicapped ones names such as "mental" or MR with devastating effects on their egos. It is, of course, understood that these children behave differently. Nevertheless, at school every possible attempt should be made by the staff to explain their deviant behavior in a positive way to the other children and to tell the others how to act with them. Children who are different have generally been scapegoated by others, particularly by the poorly adjusted ones. It has been noted that the well-adjusted children seem to be able to accept deviant behavior in other children much better than disturbed children can. There are, of course, logical reasons for this probably related to the needs and defense mechanisms of disturbed children. A buddy system might be used successfully to reduce the problem, by pairing a handicapped child with a well-adjusted child.

These case histories also indicate that many of the parents of children with learning disabilities are both well educated and insightful. It has even been reported in the literature that the minimal brain dysfunction syndrome is a middle class syndrome especially prevalent among the children of the professional class. Most likely this appeared to be so because of the lack of intensive case finding among lower class children. Also professionals tend to be the most observant of their children's behavior and to question deviant behavior more than others.

These parents also seem to be aware of the effects of different educational practices on their children, much more so than these brief case histories report. Even though these particular parents are not teachers (many parents of educationally handicapped children are teachers), they are quite able to understand teaching methods and to assess the effects upon their offspring. Some of the parents have even gone much beyond the teachers of their children in studying the literature on learning disabilities and have attempted to help the teachers learn some of the new methods — not always successfully, unfortunately. It appears to be very difficult for many professionals to accept ideas from what they consider to be lay persons. When parents make suggestions from their real knowledge based upon intensive study of the research literature, many professionals become quite defensive and refuse to look into the new concepts proposed. On the other hand, some of the best diagnosticians and other professionals admit that they have become personally interested in these children and the research literature after being introduced to the concepts by intelligent parents.

PARENTS AND TEACHERS NEED INFORMATION

In order to do an intelligent job of handling and educating children with learning disabilities both parents and teachers need information. If parents are given an adequate picture of their children's problems and progress in schools and clinics, they will be able to do a more effective job at home with these children. Of course, some parents will need more help than others in understanding the data and in determining an appropriate course of action in the home environment. Most parents appear to be anxious to learn about their children and to cooperate in the habilitation or rehabilitation process.

At the same time teachers will also benefit from the same type of information. One of the greatest problems of teaching the handicapped has perhaps been lack of consistent and adequate diagnostic testing followed by regular, periodic retesting. Such testing informs the teacher about the child's strengths and weaknesses, it tells her in which areas the child no longer requires further remediation and in which he does. It also helps the teacher assess the value of different teaching methods used with the child. Too often, when the teacher is asked by parents about a child's progress, she can only give her subjective, qualitative opinion. On the basis of this type of evaluation, it is possible to continue to use inadequate methods and to make relatively little progress while *feeling* that the child is doing well. There is no substitute for regular quantitative testing!

Some schools do regular quantitative evaluations and send copies to the parents which are used as the basis for teacher-parent conferences. This type of testing and conference should occur each quarter or semester. Examples of evaluations provided parents by one private reading clinic are exhibited below. Each school can work out its own test battery and evaluation form. Beyond the tests shown in the forms below, this reading clinic also used the Wechsler Intelligence Scale For Children and a pediatric-neurological examination. These test results are not included in these reports. This clinic also felt that they were having good results from medication, so the neurologist often attempted to find a suitable medication whenever indicated by his findings.

The first reading evaluation by the Learning Institute gives the parents a very comprehensive overview of their findings and recommendations. It does not talk down to the parents, but rather assumes that the parents are fully competent to understand the analysis. This report is discussed with the parents before the child is started in the reading program. Such a report clearly defines the child's learning problems as they are understood from the testing performed by the institute personnel. It should be noted that the report is specific and quantitative in all learning modalities and that Bill's activities during testing are supplied in behavioral terms, not in psychodynamic inferences. Bill's initial evaluation follows.

LEARNING INSTITUTE

To: Bill's parents   Re: Bill
Reason for Referral: Difficulty with reading.   Age: 8-2

READING EVALUATION

Tests Administered:

        Peabody Picture Vocabulary Test
        Bond-Clymer-Hoyt Developmental Reading Test, Form LA
        Gilmore Oral Reading Test
        Huelsman Word Discrimination Test
        Wide Range Achievement Test, Spelling
        Wepman Auditory Discrimination Test
        Harris Tests of Lateral Dominance
        Keystone Visual Survey Test

Test Results:

Receptive Vocabulary	M.A.		8-3
	IQ		102
	Percentile		55
B-C-H	Basic Vocabulary	U.A.	1.4
	General Comprehension	L.A.	1.2
	Specific Comprehension	L.A.	1.5
	Average Reading	L.A.	1.3
Oral Reading	No score obtained		
Word Discrimination			1.4
Spelling			1.3
Laterality	Crossed Dominance		
Auditory Discrimination	Inadequate —could not concentrate		
Vision	Unable to get satisfactory cooperation. Test not completed. Ask for report if it has been done elsewhere.		

Behavior and Attitudes During Testing

Bill came in for testing without resistance but repeatedly blinked his eyes as if he was not at ease. He talked rapidly and often of unrelated things. He was concerned over doing well on the Peabody and asked, "Am I getting this correct?" When the words became more difficult he revealed his frustration by marking on the book with a pencil. He became more hyperactive and uncontrolled when the tests covered activities on which he feared failure. Being timed disturbed him and he attempted twice to turn off the stop watch. He needed encouragement to keep at the tests as he did not want to do the reading or spelling. He showed resistance to various activities. At times he was erratic in his behavior and appeared to be deficient in practical common sense and social restraint in regard to his own activities.

Bill resorted to physical complaints regarding his left arm and foot and also emphasized that he was tired and hungry when he wished the testing could be discontinued. He rationalized his difficulties on certain tests by such comments as, "This test is nutty."

Test Analysis

Bill scored in the normal range for his receptive vocabulary. His other test scores were fairly consistent in being at low first grade level. On the silent reading test the U.A. was given first. Because of some resistance to the reading test, it was decided to substitute the L.A. form for the rest of the test as it was closer to his reading level, and there would likely be less frustration and guessing. He achieved better on those subtests which had pictures to suggest clues.

On the word discrimination test, Bill revealed problems of vertical reversals reading *p* as *d* and horizontal reversal of *d* and *b*. Also he read *eggs* as *gess* indicating a sequence or transposal problem. He recognized that he was confused when asked to read the words aloud and said, "I'm mixed up."

Bill achieved one of his lowest scores on his spelling test at 1.3 grade level, as he only succeeded on two words *cat* and *go*. He also had considerable difficulty on the oral reading test so that he did not achieve above 1.0 for accuracy at a slow rate of reading. His principal difficulties were lack of an adequate sight vocabulary and lack of word analysis skills, so that he could not sound out common words. *Boy* was read as *ball, girl* as *good* and *ball* as *dog,* again showing confusion of *b* and *d*. Many words had to be pronounced by the examiner. He read slowly and laboriously, having to point to each word. When the second paragraph was apparently too difficult, he began to yawn, started turning the pages, wiggling and looking at his feet. The test was discontinued after this because of too many errors.

Bill had considerable difficulty on the auditory discrimination test. He showed less ability to concentrate than on the other tests; his mind appeared to wander, and he started playing with his clothes, even removing his belt and amusing himself with it. He scored in the inadequate range. However, this cannot be considered a valid test of auditory discrimination because of the lack of concentration. Also, a hearing test should be given later to rule out any hearing problem as he did not always repeat the words correctly when trying to sound them out loud.

Bill wanted so much to play with the visual screening equipment and it was so difficult to get adequate responses that this had to be discontinued. However, his desire to shut one eye during the vision test and during the eye dominance test on the Harris raises a question of coordination of his two eyes. He had relatively poor visual motor coordination on the tapping test and was not able to exert sufficient control to put only one dot in a square. He appears to have crossed dominance, preferring his right hand, left eye and right foot. His printing of his name showed poor motor control.

On Memory-for-Designs test he wrote 12 as 21 and 14 as 41, and also revealed some weakness of visual memory for remembering the designs.

Recommendations

1. An eye examination by an optometrist when his hyperactivity is under sufficient control that he can cooperate.
2. A hearing test and recheck on his auditory discrimination at a later time.
3. Continued efforts to find a medication which will enable him to concentrate and reduce his hyperactivity.
4. A teaching program at the clinic to help him with his visual perception deficiencies of position in space and spatial relationships, as well as visual motor coordination, to improve reversals, transpositions, sequence of letters and numbers and printing of letters.
5. Practice in auditory discrimination and associating of sound to letters as well as visual discrimination by using the letter box and also other kinesthetic methods to reinforce visual memory and auditory memory.
6. Help with developing a basic sight vocabulary and word attack skills.
7. Bill and his parents need counseling to help Bill handle his anxiety, defensiveness and frustrations which are revealed in various of his comments, and to help him develop control of his behavior in social situations.

*   *   *

The following four reports from the Learning Institute are quarterly reports of Bill's progress which were sent to his parents and were used as the basis of parent-teacher interviews. They are especially good because they are quantitative and the testing was done in each case by the teacher who worked with Bill. Thus both she and the parents were able to profit from the results of quantitative testing. Lack of such regular follow-up testing is one of the greatest deficiencies in some remedial learning programs. This applies to both private and public schools. Each school should work out its own report form. However, the things which report forms should have in common if they are to be useful are the following:

1. The testing and report should be done by the teacher.

2. The report should be quantitative.
3. The testing should cover all of the areas of the child's deficits.
4. The anecdotal report should be behavioral rather than inferential.
5. The report should be used in connection with a parent-teacher interview.
6. The evaluation should be done either quarterly or per semester.

LEARNING INSTITUTE

To: Bill's parents   Re: Bill
Deficiencies Noted on Admission: Hours attended: 26   Grade: 2
Visual-Motor Coordination — ocular control, handwriting, spacing of letters
Oral Reading — limited sight vocabulary
Silent Reading — comprehension, word recognition
Word Attack Skills — visual discrimination, auditory discrimination
Spelling — phonetic patterns, reversals, sequence of letters

Test Results for This Session:

	Grade Equivalent	
	Initial Tests — 2/66	*Final Tests — 6/66*
Word Discrimination	1.4	1.6
Oral Reading	0	1.4
Silent Reading	1.3	1.4
Spelling	1.3	1.8
Sight Vocabulary	49 Words	Inconsistent

Progress Report and Recommendations

Bill's Progress at this time cannot be measured accurately in terms of test scores. His performance varies with the amount of attention he is able to give at any one time. An inability to identify the correct sound with the printed symbol reduces fluency in oral reading and results in loss of comprehension.

Continued training is required in discrimination between letters (*m-w, n-u, b-d*) and sequence of letters within a word (*ilttle* for *little, pleh* for *help*).

LEARNING INSTITUTE

To: Bill's parents   Re: Bill
Deficiencies Noted on Admission: Hours Attended: 16   Grade: 2
Visual-Motor Coordination — ocular control, handwriting, spacing of letters
Oral Reading — limited sight vocabulary
Silent Reading — comprehension, word recognition
Word Attack Skill — visual discrimination, auditory discrimination
Spelling — phonetic patterns, reversals, sequence of letters
Vision: To be tested   Hearing: To be tested

Test Results for This Session:

		Grade Equivalent	
		Initial Tests — 6/66	*Final Tests — 8/66*
Word Discrimination		1.6	1.2
Oral Reading		1.4	0
Silent Reading	Word Recognition:	1.7	2.1
	Comprehension:	1.2	1.4
Specific	Comprehension:	1.4	1.3
Spelling		1.8	1.9
Sight Vocabulary		Inconsistent	Inconsistent

Progress Report and Recommendations

Bill's progress at this time cannot be measured accurately in terms of test scores. When he saw the tests, he said he could not do them, and even with encouragement, he gave up easily. Because he did not attend the last session, the subtest, comprehending specific instructions on the Silent Reading Test was not given. However, he showed a four months gain in word recognition.

During this session, Bill has tried very hard and would profit by returning.

LEARNING INSTITUTE

To: Bill's parents   Re: Bill
Deficiencies Noted on Admission: Hours Attended: 20   Grade: 3
Visual-Motor Coordination — ocular control, handwriting, spacing letters
Oral Reading — limited sight vocabulary
Silent Reading — comprehension, word recognition
Word Attack Skills — visual discrimination, auditory discrimination
Spelling — phonetic patterns, reversals, sequence of letters
Vision: To be tested   Hearing: Normal

Test Results for This Session:

	Grade Equivalent		
	2-66 Tests	3-67 Tests	Final Tests (6-67)
Word Discrimination	1.4	1.8	2.0
Oral Reading	0	2.7	2.9
Silent Reading	1.3	2.6	3.5
Spelling	1.3	2.6	2.6

Progress Report and Recommendations

Bill's self-image has improved so his confidence has increased.

Gain has been made in his ability to discriminate words. He still has difficulty distinguishing *u* from *n*, *l* from *k* and *f*, and *a* from *o*. He also has difficulty noting the small internal elements of a word, for example, *birtday* for *birthday* and *wantd* for *wanted*.

In oral reading no mistakes were made on the first and second grade paragraphs. Hesitation and need for examiner's help in pronouncing words was necessary on the third grade paragraph.

Bill's greatest gain was made in silent reading. Only two errors, *mean* for *meat* and *whole* for *whale* were made on the word recognition section. All comprehension questions attempted were correct.

Spelling should improve with an increase in phonetic skills.

Recommendations: Bill will profit from special help and should return.

LEARNING INSTITUTE

To: Bill's parents   Re: Bill
Deficiencies Noted on Admission: Grade: 3
Visual-Motor Coordination — ocular control, handwriting, spacing letters
Oral Reading — limited sight vocabulary
Silent Reading — comprehension, word recognition
Word Attack Skills — visual discrimination, auditory discrimination
Spelling — phonetic patterns, reversals, sequence of letters
Vision: To be tested   Hearing: Normal

Test Results for This Session:

	Grade Equivalent	
	Initial Tests — 6/67	Final Tests — 8/67
Word Discrimination	2.0	2.4
Oral Reading	2.9	3.0
Silent Reading	3.5	3.6
Spelling	2.6	2.8

Progress Report and Recommendations

A comparison of Bill's previous scores on quarter attendance indicates steady and solid improvement. This summer Bill made progress in all areas of instruction. He notices the small internal differences in words.

On the word discrimination test he spelled *cloub* for *cloud* and *cappage* for *cabbage*. In class he confuses *q-p-d* and *q-g*.

In oral reading no mistakes were made on the first grade paragraph and only one mistake, an omission, was made on the second grade paragraph. Hesitations and substitutions with some words pronounced by the examiner typified the third grade paragraph. The fourth grade paragraph was characterized by words pronounced by the examiner.

Silent reading has improved with an increase in word recognition. A gain was made in spelling. Bill is more sure of the short vowel sounds but this needs more reinforcement.

*   *   *

The role of the parent of a child with learning disabilities is most difficult, especially if the child is hyperkinetic and has serious social difficulties as is so often the case. An attempt has been made to suggest many things these parents can do to help their children and themselves. However, the most important help in the form of diagnostic work-ups, therapy and educational facilities will have to come from the professionals. The material presented has been designed to encourage professionals to help these parents and their children by indicating both the extent of their problems and some of the help which parents want.

ROLE OF PUBLIC SCHOOLS

The scope of the problem of children with learning disabilities is so tremendous that it can only be substantially reduced by massive efforts on the part of the public schools. It is generally agreed that more professional, competent teaching of these children tends to be done in the private reading clinics than in the public schools. This seems to be taken for granted. This was certainly the tenor of the case histories reported in this chapter. However, we are also cognizant of the existence of a growing number of very high quality public school programs for children with learning disabilities. Curiously enough, public schools generally have more money available than private schools for special education programs and the public school teachers are generally very much higher paid than the private school teachers. Thus the inability of most public school programs to equal the good private school programs for children with learning disabilities is paradoxical. Parents and professionals are becoming aware of this paradox and are urging school administrators to correct and restore the image of special education in the tax supported public schools.

To take their rightful place as leaders in the special education of children with learning disabilities, public schools should have the following:

1. Administrators with scholarly knowledge in depth of the field of learning disabilities.

2. Psychologists with broad clinical knowledge in depth of the testing of children with learning disabilities.
3. Teachers trained to give tests and to interpret test results who are also trained in individualized prescriptive teaching.
4. A continuous in-service training program for *all* personnel in this area of special education to keep up with the latest developments in the field.
5. Regularly scheduled parent conferences and participation in the program.
6. Training of *all* elementary school teachers in a broad spectrum of methods of teaching reading, spelling, writing and arithmetic.
7. Continuous rigorous research and evaluation within the public schools by their own *adequately* trained personnel.

In order to do a professionally competent job, public school administrators should seriously consider developing and using regular quantitative evaluation reports on each child which could serve the same purpose as the Learning Institute reports previously cited. If public school administrators build their programs for the educationally handicapped with the seven suggested points in mind and use evaluation reports on each child both to regulate the teaching of each child and in the parent-teacher conferences, there need be no reason for the public schools to take second place to the private schools in this field. This would best serve the interests of the public, and the public schools would certainly be able to take their rightful place as leaders in the field of the special education of children with learning disabilities.

In summary, parents have formed organizations to help children with learning disabilities because the professionals had abdicated this function. Educators, psychologists, pediatric-neurologists, psychiatrists and language pathologists are the professionals most closely involved in the diagnosis and habilitation of these children. Although some of these professionals have known of the problem for many years, they have not been organized to act. Thus, as a rule parents have appeared before boards of education to request classes and other services for their handicapped children. When parents have taken the lead, they have also exerted great pressure on professionals which has sometimes been met with strongly defensive reactions. When such defensive reactions have appeared, it was generally because the professionals had failed to read their journals and so were caught unaware of the new developments in the field of learning disabilities or minimal brain dysfunction.

The movement to recognize the existence of children of normal intelligence with learning disabilites is well launched. In several states, the public schools have accepted the responsibility of educating these children. California, which is the largest state in the union, has been the first to make state funds available to all local school districts for this purpose. The parents who formed the various associations to help these children and who gave unstintingly of their time and personal resources have initiated a movement which may well revolutionize the education of all children. Out of this development, individualized, child-centered teaching gives promise to become a reality.

REFERENCES

1. *Children with Minimal Brain Damage: A Challenge to the Citizens of the Commonwealth of Pennsylvania.* Syracuse, Syracuse U.P., 1965.
2. *A Lonely World.* Recorded by Media. Van Nuys, 1966.
3. BARSCH, R.: Counseling the parent of the brain-injured child. *J Rehab, 27:*1961.
4. *Why Billie Couldn't Learn.* Distributed by the California Association For Neurologically Handicapped Children, P.O. Box 604, Los Angeles, California 90053.
5. *Physical Education and the N.H. Child.* Same distributor as 4.
6. O'REILLY, R.: CANHC and the NH child. *California Parent-Teacher,* Sept. 1965.
7. TARNOPOL, L.: Unpublished survey of San Francisco CANHC parents. 1965.

PART TWO
PHYSICIANS' ROLES

Chapter 4

Children with Minimal Brain Dysfunction — A National Problem

RICHARD L. MASLAND

PART 1
A TERMINOLOGY PROBLEM

I AM NOT ENTIRELY happy with the term *minimal brain dysfunction* and I must say we have had a good many brickbats about the use of this term. It is a little different from saying "learning disability," and certainly the term *minimal brain dysfunction* is easily criticized. What do you mean by minimal? How big is little? What do you mean by dysfunction? Most of us do know what we mean by brain. Possibly this is the primary reason why some of us have adhered rather rigidly to this terminology. In the first place, it is not intended to be a diagnosis. There is not a disease, "minimal brain dysfunction." It is a condition or a symptom; but it is an entity in that it refers to a group of individuals with common disabilities whose disabilities require a program of management which is unique for that group of individuals. In this respect, the term has the same practical usefulness as a term such as *cerebral palsy* or *mental retardation*. These also are not diagnoses; they refer to the practical problem of providing services. There is another usefulness of this term *minimal brain dysfunction,* that is, to emphasize the fact that it is the child that is different and not the environment. We believe that there is a group of children who have deviations of the functioning of their nervous systems such that they do not react in the way the average child reacts to his environment and to environmental stimuli, and who, for that reason require approaches, methods of management, methods of training which are different and often unique for the individual child.

We have carefully avoided characterizing the cause. It is not desirable for the term *minimal brain dysfunction* to be equated with brain damage. In many instances, the child with a brain dysfunction has that dysfunction as a result of brain damage. But in many other instances we have no evidence that such damage has occurred. This is not the matter at issue. The matter at issue is the characteristics of the child which are different and the char-

Note: Presentation at the California Association for Neurologically Handicapped Children, San Francisco Chapter, Symposium on Learning Disabilities — A National Dilemma, January 12 and 13, 1968, at the California Scottish Rite Memorial Temple, San Francisco, California. Part 1 is an edited transcript of a tape recording. Part 2 was also presented at the 11th National Conference on Physicians and Schools (American Medical Association, Department of Health Education) La Salle Hotel, Chicago, Illinois, October 6, 1967.

acteristics of his learning opportunities and environment which should be different. Just where does the child with minimal brain dysfunction fit into the overall spectrum of the individuals in our community?

DISTRIBUTION OF INTELLIGENCE

If one considers a total population, and characterizes that population in terms of some standard intelligence test (a very unsatisfactory way of characterizing) you find that members of the population fall into a distribution curve (Fig. 4-1).[1] A major proportion of individuals will have average IQ scores and a smaller number will have either higher or lower scores. Now according to statistical theory, this should be a symmetrical bell-shaped curve. But it is not. Distributions for large populations show that there is a hump at the lower end. There are more individuals in the severely retarded group than there should be by the laws of chance. It has been postulated that those at the lower end are individuals who have suffered some spe-

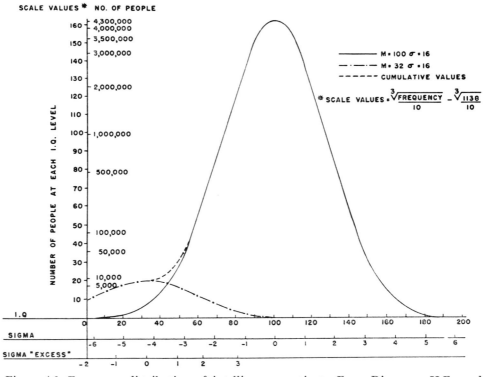

Figure 4-1. Frequency distribution of intelligence quotients. From Dingman, H.F., and Tarjan, G.: *American Journal of Mental Deficiency, 64* (6) :991, May 1960.

cific alteration or deviation in their intellectual capabilities. These are often spoken of as brain damaged, although included are also those with inborn errors of metabolism and other gross defects, some of which are developmental and some of which are genetic. Thus, within our population, we have a wide distribution in innate intelligence, if we can use that term, and we have superimposed on this a certain number of individuals who have had gross brain damage. But, where then do we find the child with a minimal brain dysfunction in this chart? We must look somewhere in the middle range, even up to and above the average level of intelligence, for the child with minimal brain dysfunction. Where is this child likely to come from?

Effects of Social Status

We have some rather interesting sociological data which may give us information regarding the compositon of the population in the normal range of intelligence. Figure 4-2 is from a study by Birch and Richardson of a large population in Aberdeen, Scotland.[2] They examined quite a group of children who were referred to them because they were considered by the community to be retarded in school. They divided these children into four groups in accordance with their family backgrounds. Those who were more privileged under category one and those who were least privileged under category four. Then they made an analysis of the intellectual capabilities of the four groups according to the percentage in each category who were found upon examination to have an IQ under 60. The interesting thing is that among those who came from the more privileged class, there was not a single child with an IQ above 60. The only children considered by the school system and by the community as being retarded or handicapped in school who came from this group were the ones with a severe impairment of intellectual capability. I take this to mean that when an individual has had superior social and educational opportunities, even though that individual has minor degrees of intellectual disability, he is able to get by in a community and he is not recognized as a retarded individual. Instead, his specific disabilities are overcome by special opportunity and special training to the extent that he is able to cope with the requirements of the school environment.

Multiple Intelligence Distributions

I would like to suggest that instead of having a single curve, such as the one in Figure 4-1, there are in fact many curves, many different populations of which for the purposes of this presentation I have selected two (Fig. 4-3). I have selected one group of children — one population, whose average IQ is around, say 120; and another population whose average IQ is around 80. The point I wish to emphasize is that within a given IQ range, for example from 70 to 90 (the individuals who are moderately retarded), there are included representatives of two populations — namely the average individual from the "retarded" population; and the "brain damaged" individual from the superior population. Thus, we have within any community, a mix of types of problems at any IQ level. At the low levels of IQ, we have a certain group of individuals whose basic constitutional capability is low and within this same range we may also have the severely brain damaged from other groups. At IQ levels of 80 to 100 will be included the average individuals of the lower population and, in addition, a number of individuals whose IQ should be higher but whose performance is impaired by some specific disability.

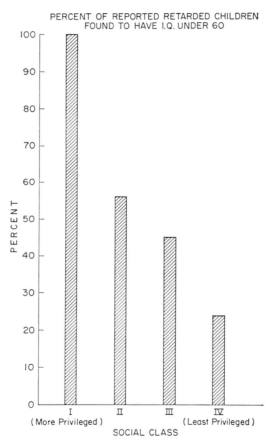

Figure 4-2. The relation of handicaps to social and obstetrical factors in all children living in one city. From H.G. Birch and S.A. Richardson, Academy of Cerebral Palsy, Dec. 1965.

Anoxia and Intelligence

There are a number of examples of the way in which this may take place. Figure 4-4 is a graph showing the follow-up IQ of a group of children who were asphyxiated at birth as compared to the distribution of intelligence among a group of control children.[3] You will note that the distribution curve for the asphyxiated children is shifted to the left. This is a graphical representation of two distinct populations.

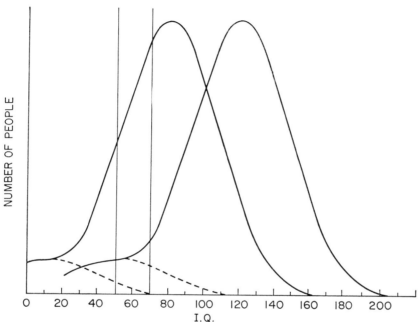

FREQUENCY DISTRIBUTIONS OF INTELLIGENCE QUOTIENTS IN TWO POPULATIONS

Figure 4-3. Frequency distributions of intelligence quotients in two theoretical populations.

Jaundice and Intelligence

Here are a similar set of bar graphs for a group of children who suffered from jaundice at the time of birth, (Fig. 4-5).[4] Exactly the same thing is observed. In this instance a comparison was made between a group of children who were jaundiced at birth and their siblings and you see that there has been a shift of the distribution curve of intelligence toward the low side on the part of those who suffered this insult at the time of birth.

Prematurity and Intelligence

These changes in intelligence quotient which have just been presented are rather modest in degree and the use of an intelligence test obscures a much more important problem. Figure 4-6 shows the results of the testing of a group of children who were premature at birth. The group under 2000

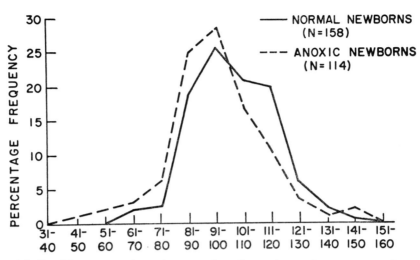

Figure 4-4. Intelligence quotients in normal and anoxic newborns at age three. From Ernhart, C.B.; Graham, F.K., and Thurston, D.: Relationship of neonatal apnea to development at three years. *AMA Archives of Neurology, 2* (5) :504-10, 1960.

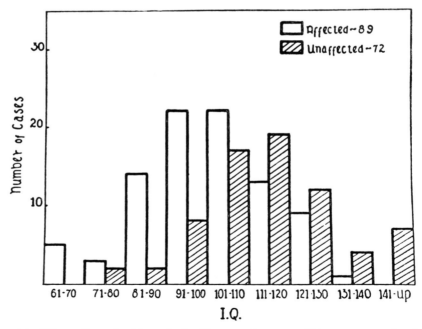

Figure 4-5. Effect of erythroblastosis fetalis on subsequent IQ — compared with unaffected sibling. From Gerver, J.M., and Day, R.: Intelligence quotient of children who have recovered from erythroblastosis fetalis. *Journal of Pediatrics, 36* (3) :342-48, 1950.

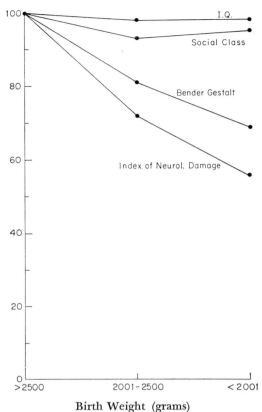

Birth Weight (grams)

Figure 4-6. Mean scores on measures of psychological development and associated variables by birth weight (gm)-white males. Scores converted to show impairment rating with score of the >2500 group taken as 100. After Wiener, G.; Rider, R.V.; Oppel, W.C.; Fischer, L.K., and Harper, P.A.: Correlates of low birth weight: psychological status at six to seven years of age. *Pediatrics, 35:3* (Part I) :434-44, 1965.

grams represented on the right are relatively small premature infants; and those over 2500 grams at the left are approximately normal sized infants. Thus, we have three groups of children: severely premature, small premature and normal. In this followup study the children were examined at the age of six.[5] The chart shows very little difference in the intelligence quotients of the children depending upon their birth weight. That is indicated by the very top curve. The various groups were deliberately matched for socio-economic background, so there was not a significant social class difference among the several groups. The significant difference between the children of normal weight and the small prematures was in a special performance test, a special test of certain perceptual skills, namely the Bender-Gestalt. In other words, these children who had suffered a neurological insult, as indicated by the bottom curve, suffered a specific type of disability as a result rather than an overall impairment of intelligence. Figure 4-7 is a more detailed representation of these findings.[5] This, I think, is in keeping with the results of the Scottish survey previously reported. In the case of the individual whose basic intelligence is good, the occurrence of brain damage does not lead to a picture of mental retardation, but it leads to impairments, much more specific impairments, of performance.

Specific Dyslexia

There are some other very interesting studies which I would like to mention in passing. The follow-up studies of a group of children with specific dyslexia, which is soon to be published by Margaret Rawson, provides some very interesting evidence as to the type of problem we are dealing with.[6] So far my talk would appear to be emphasizing the importance of brain damage, but I wish to reemphasize that we are talking of brain dysfunction, and in many of these instances we are not dealing with the results of a specific insult

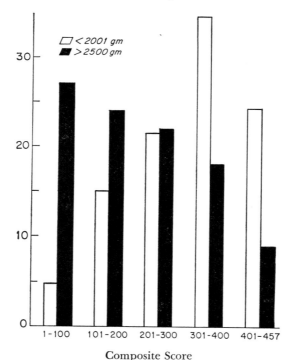

Composite Score

Figure 4-7. Comparison of two extreme birth-weight groups on a composite psychological score based on six variables: Stanford-Binet, Lincoln-Oseretsky, Goodenough, Bender-Gestalt, Speech Maturity, "Thinking-Mode." After Wiener, G.; Rider, R.V.; Oppel, W.C.; Fischer, L.K., and Harper, P.A.: Correlates of low birth weight: psychological status at six to seven years of age. *Pediatrics, 35:3* (Part I) : 434-44, 1965.

to the brain. A case in point is the group of dyslexic children on which Margaret Rawson has done a thirty- or forty-year follow-up. She made a comparison of the life histories of a group of individuals who were severely dyslexic in school as compared to their siblings and classmates. The interesting thing is that when the children were compared for IQ by the use of the standard school test, there was in fact an impairment of IQ on the part of the dyslexic children of about 20 points. Mrs. Rawson considers this to be the penalty that they paid for their disability in reading and writing in the standard intelligence testing situation. However, when the life histories of these two groups of individuals were compared, there was no difference in the performance of the dyslexic boys as compared to their nondyslexic associates. There was no difference in terms of academic achievement, in terms of business success, of marital success, or any other criterion that one could mention. Again these were individuals with a very specific limitation.

Twin Studies

I think we should not forget the importance of the inherited and constitutional element in determining an individual's intellectual capabilities, his strengths and weaknesses. Figure 4-8 is a study of resemblances between twins.[7] There are three groups of twins included: one group of identical twins reared together, one group of identical twins reared apart, and one group of nonidentical twins reared together. The graphs indicate correlations between the test scores of the twins in each group. Four different measures were used — the "dominoes" performance test, "Mill Hill" verbal intelligence test, body height and weight. Note that on three of these measures there is a very high correlation between the performances of the identical twins whether reared together or apart. Environment thus appeared to play little role in their similarities or differences. Only in respect to body weight did the nonidentical twins reared together show greater similarities than the identical twins reared apart. Apparently variations in environment do determine how much you eat.

Now one can quite properly say, "Well, these twins were not separated very early and maybe the environments were not so different." So I made a study in a slightly different way (Fig. 4-9) .[7] There were two types of separation which took place. One group of twins who were separated were cared for by relatives, presumably with similar attitudes and similar socioeconomic opportunities. However, another group of the separated twins were adopted, and many of them had not seen each other for years. When we compare their results on the dominoes test — the performance test which seems to characterize most precisely certain basic intellectual capabilities — we find that the differences we have plotted (here plotted as actual average difference in test

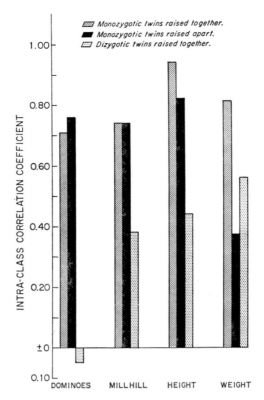

Figure 4-8. Resemblances between twins — Monozygotic twins raised together, Monozygotic twins raised apart, Dizygotic twins raised together. After Shields, J.: *Monozygotic Twins, Brought up Apart and Brought up Together* — An Investigation into the Genetic and Environmental Causes of Variation in Personality. London, Oxford University Press, 1962.

score) are exactly the same for those who were separated and raised by relatives as for those who were raised in a completely foreign home environment. The differences in the nonidentical twins are again of a completely different order of magnitude. A rather exhaustive review of the literature on this subject reveals these findings repeated over and over again wherever a scientific study of this sort is made. I think that we have to reckon with the fact that there are very important inherent differences in intellectual capability. I would like to suggest that these are not only differences in overall capability but they are probably in many instances differences in the specific way in which individuals handle information — the way they correlate information — and many other subtle differences which we are, at present, far too primitive to adequately comprehend.

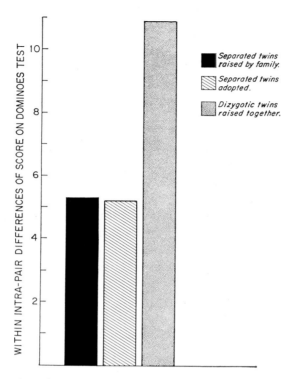

Figure 4-9. Effects of environment on twins performance test. After Shields, J.: *Mono-zygotic Twins, Brought up Apart and Brought up Together* — An Investigation into the Genetic and Environmental Causes of Variation in Personality. London, Oxford University Press, 1962.

INDICATORS OF LEARNING DISABILITIES

The important fact is that we are dealing with a group of individuals whose deviations from the average stem from many causes and they have many different patterns. However, regardless of these differences, they are very commonly manifested by delays in the achievement of certain expected performances. These provide landmarks or indications on which *we as a society should be able to recognize the child with a potential learning problem at a relatively early age and to provide variations in the environmental opportunities appropriate to his deviations in learning.* What are the usual indications? First of all, considering those individuals whose disability relates to brain injury, we very often find evidences in the history — the child who is premature or who has had difficulties in labor and delivery and a stormy neonatal course — the child with childhood meningitis or other serious neurological disability of childhood. Next, we are likely to have observed delays in crawling, delays in walking. The next milestone is language development and finally in the preschool child we are likely to have minor evidences of physical disability, clumsiness and evidences of incoordination. On more sophisticated testing, there may be delays of concept formation, or for example, delay in the establishment of right-left discrimination. (I won't digress into that great never-never-land of right-handedness versus left-handedness.)

Recently, the studies of Birch and his associates have suggested that there are other specific disabilities, such as delay in the establishment of intersensory correlative functions in the nervous system.[8] The fact that many of these deviations exhibit themselves as delays in maturation has led to a concept that these children have been held up at some stage in development. I think the concept of a maturational lag is a very important and a very sound one, and that many of the children with learning disabilities who are in the schools suffer from a delay in the maturation of a skill or ability essential in the learning process. My only concern regarding the use of the term *maturational delay* is that it implies, as does the term *mental retardation,* that if you run hard enough, maybe you will catch up. I think that the child with a maturational delay may catch up in his overall performance, but that most of the children with learning disabilities have deviations which are permanent. Even though these deviations may be obviated by the use of alternative methods of performance or through extensive training of essential skills, long-term follow-up indicates that most of the individuals who have had learning disabilities continue to have the deviations throughout their lifetime. Fortunately, many may also have other very powerful and effective strengths which may even make their overall effectiveness above average.

There are some interesting examples of such compensatory processes from other fields. People in the computer business have found that blind people are in many instances superior as programmers and as computer experts. There seems to be some compensation — some development of alternative methods of handling information, which make the blind person peculiarly skillful in this particular area of very complex intellectual activity. It may well be that some other individuals with more subtle disabilities have similar compensations through which they are superior in other respects.

PHYSICAL DEVELOPMENT THEORIES

The observation of these maturational delays and of related delays in physical development has led to the theory that in order for the child with a learning disability to advance, he has to recapitulate some of these earlier stages — that you have to correct the physical development before you can expect to advance in the more complex intellectual skills. I have been able to find very little theoretical or actual support for this theory. For example, I recently had the opportunity to examine a child who at the time of birth had suffered a complete transection of his spinal cord so that he was severely paralyzed from the shoulders on down. Here was a child who had not had the opportunity to use his lower extremities in any of the normal ways. Yet from a superficial examination, at least, there was no indication that this child's intellectual development had deviated in any way from that of the average child.

In spite of this, it is worthwhile to consider some of the specific studies which now have been accomplished for the purpose of determining the impact of physical training procedures on intellectual performance. Part 2 of this manuscript will consider visual perception, motor ability and intellectual functioning in detail.

PHYSICIAN'S ROLE

So far, I have been describing the problem of learning disabilities in educational terms. There is little question that in practical terms the major problem of the child with minimal brain dysfunction is the educational problem and the problem for the educator. But I have been asked, "Doesn't the physician have a role in this?" Certainly he does. In the first place, we should not be waiting until the child reaches school until we begin remediation and preparation for the school opportunity. The child who is likely to have learning disabilities can frequently be recognized even at an early age. The most likely and the most logical person to make this recognition is the physician. It is not easy for the physician to deal with this problem because the problems of the child with learning disability require tools which are not the tools of the physician. This means that the practicing doctor needs to know what the community resources are — to whom such a child may be referred for the special educational opportunities that he requires. The lack of such resources and the failure of the physician to be aware of those resources available are responsible for the two most common errors that doctors make in dealing with the child with minimal brain dysfunction.

What are these errors? The first, is to say, "Well, he looks all right to me. Just wait a few years. I think he is going to grow out of it." The second, the other extreme, is to say, "Your child is brain damaged and there isn't anything that can be done about it, so don't bother me." I think we can get away from these errors if we have in the community the resources available to help such children when recognized and if the physicians become knowledgeable about their existence and location. The second important task of the physician is to ascertain whether the child with a learning disability has other physical disabilities which may be remedied, particularly disorders of

vision and disorders of hearing. Certainly any child who has school disabilities should have the benefit of an exhaustive evaluation of these characteristics. Finally, every child should periodically be examined for the existence of
other physical ills such as thyroid disorder, or some of the more subtle disorders of metabolism which may impair his intellectual and emotional performance. The magnitude of the problem of providing essential services for
all children with learning disabilities is an almost overwhelming one. We
all have our contribution to make. The contribution of your society is one
of increasing significance, and I am honored to have had this opportunity to
participate in this inspiring occasion.

PART 2
VISUAL PERCEPTION AND MOTOR ABILITY

For many years it has been recognized and generally accepted that regular physical exercise is essential for good health in the adult and for proper
physical development in the child. Programs for active physical education
within the school system have been developed primarily for these purposes.
More recently, however, the possibility that carefully structured programs
in physical education may contribute more specifically to the education
process has received increasing interest. This interest probably stems from
several sources. First, there is increasing recognition of the fact that human
development is not an automatic process determined only by matters of
inheritance and physical growth. It is increasingly recognized that both
physical and intellectual development depend upon the continuing interaction of the organism with his environment. Proper environmental stimuli
are evidently essential for the maximum or even healthy development of the
individual.

Furthermore, works of Montessori, Piaget, Gesell and others have emphasized the orderly steps through which human development ordinarily
takes place. Both physical and intellectual skills evolve in regular progression
— a progression which in at least its grosser aspects is remarkably stereotyped
within the cultures where it has been investigated.

Growth and Development

From these observations of orderly progression has evolved the thesis that
delay at any one of these stages of development will of necessity impair the
evolution of the subsequent stages of this process. It therefore has been
postulated that it is not sufficient to provide training and remedial experiences at the later stages of the developmental process — it may be necessary
to retrace this process, working to achieve competence at lower levels of
development to lay the groundwork for the natural orderly process to take
place.

It is certain that human growth progresses through an orderly course. Body movement progresses from creeping to crawling to walking and running. Prehensile movements are at first gross. Recent studies of infant development suggest that the recognition of the hand as a useful object, then the use of the hand for prehension and exploration are learned activities carried forward under precise visual and sensory control.

Visual Perception

In the field of visual perception, the child appears first to recognize only the presence or absence of an object. Later differentiation is made on the basis of gross characteristics. Only by the age of six or seven does the individual develop the capability for differentiation on the basis of systematic exploration of many characteristics of surrounding environment. Right-left discrimination and the development of cerebral dominance are among the later stages of development.

The average individual proceeds in his development through orderly steps of this sort. The capability of an individual at each of these levels may be significantly influenced by environmental experience and training. In a highly competitive world, especially where maximum intellectual growth is essential for effectiveness, it seems inappropriate to leave such development to chance. At any rate, we have an obligation to provide for each individual the maximum opportunity for growth.

There remains however considerable uncertainty as to where our efforts should best be applied. Given a child of school age, we must ask ourselves the following questions:

1. To what extent does failure to develop at one "level" actually influence capability at higher levels of development?
2. To what extent will training improve capability at various levels of development?
3. To what extent will training at one level influence performance at other levels or in closely related areas of activity?
4. Under what circumstances is an educational effort properly directed specifically toward a desired skill, and when is it better directed toward the development of an essential underlying capability?

Unfortunately a limited number of data are available to provide precise answers to these questions.

TESTS OF CREEPING AND CRAWLING ON READING

Possibly we might consider first the most extreme possibilities. Specifically, to what extent will exercises directed toward the most fundamental physical activities — creeping and crawling — influence the more complex intellectual functions — reading and writing — in a group of "average" or "normal" children?

Table 4-I summarizes results obtained by Robbins in a controlled study to test this question.[9] His results fail to demonstrate that creeping and crawling exercises improved the school performance of this group of children. It should be noted that these were normal children with no defined areas of prior underdevelopment. Unfortunately the studies involved the comparison of whole classes in different schools, and exact controls were thus not established. Also, a three-month test may be inadequate.

TABLE 4-I
EFFECT OF THREE-MONTH SPECIAL PROGRAM ON READING SCORES

	Control	*Experimental*	*Nonspecific*
Pretest	2.15	2.43	2.18
Post-test	2.91	3.12	3.05
Gain	.76	.69	.87
% Gain	35	27	40

After Robbins, M.P.: *Exceptional Children,* 1966.

An almost identical study has been reported from the Wasco Union School District of California.[10] Three matched groups of fourth and fifth grade boys having mixed dominance were selected. One experimental group received mobility training as outlined by Doman-Delacato. The second experimental group received training which included measures specifically interdicted in the program recommended by Doman-Delacato. The third group served as a control. Training programs were carried on simultaneously thirty minutes a day for a period of five months. Analysis of the data disclosed no significant differences in the post-test scores of reading achievement or intelligence among the three groups.

EFFECT OF PHYSICAL EXERCISES ON IQ

A somewhat different study recently has been completed by Kershner, (Fig. 4-10).[11] It applied to a group of mentally retarded children in the Pennsylvania public school system. This study was established specifically to test the Doman-Delacato theory. The group of children ranged in chronological age from eight to eighteen years. The experimental group were given a highly complicated program involving training of movement, exercises in creeping and crawling, alterations of resting and sleeping posture, and the use of eye-patches to establish consistency of cerebral dominance. The control group were exposed to equivalent periods of time spent in nonspecific activities of games and activities solely designed to "give reason for the teacher to direct individual and group praise and encouragement." Activities included table play, building blocks, show and tell games, marching and rhythmic activities. The program was continued for a period of four months. Three hypotheses were tested with the following conclusions:

1. Can motor skills be improved by training?

The study revealed that the children trained under the Doman-Delacato regime showed greater improvement in creeping and crawling skill than did the controls.

2. Will motor training improve perceptuo-motor skills?

The study revealed that both groups had improved in perceptuo-motor skills, indicating that such skills can be improved by training, but that both regimes contributed to such learning.

3. Will improvement in creeping and crawling ability be accompanied by significant improvement in cognitive functioning as reflected in IQ gains?

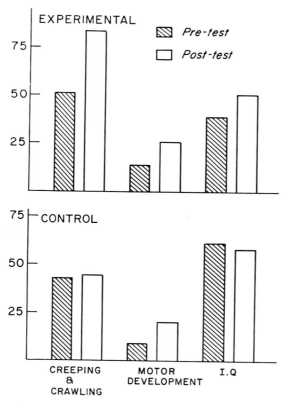

Figure 4-10. Evaluation of Doman-Delacato treatment of mentally retarded subjects. After Kershner, J.R.: An investigation of Doman-Delacato theory of neuropsychology as it applies to trainable mentally retarded children in public schools. Bureau of Research Administration and Coordination, Area of Research and Development, Department of Public Instruction, Commonwealth of Pennsylvania, May 1967, pp. 105 (mimeo).

The study revealed that the experimental group achieved greater gain in IQ (as measured by the Peabody Picture Vocabulary Test) than did the controls.

This study, which involved a total of twenty-nine children, appears to have important implications relative to the questions raised above. As a means for answering certain basic hypotheses however, it suffers from important defects. The training programs provided for the two groups of children differ not only in respect to the creeping and crawling activities, but in many other respects as well, including efforts to achieve lateral dominance and the use of various forms of sensory stimulation. It was thus designed to test a whole philosophy and program of education rather than a specific hypothesis.

Possibly a more serious flaw lies in the fact that the study dealt with a very limited number of children. The experimental and control groups originally differed considerably in respect to their intelligence levels — since the two groups were randomized and not matched. The two groups also differed materially in the age ranges involved, and presumably in the nature

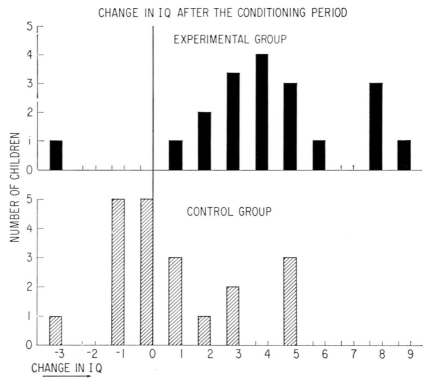

Figure 4-11. Physical training with regard to change in IQ. After Oliver, J.N.: *British Journal of Educational Psychology, 28:* 1958.

of their underlying disease. It is thus most difficult to draw broad conclusions from this limited sample.

A limited number of studies have attempted to assess in more general terms the impact of physical training programs on school performance. Figure 4-11 summarizes the results obtained by Oliver in comparing the school performance in a group of educationally subnormal children given regular physical training exercises as compared to a group who did not have the benefit of this experience.[12] The program involved a ten-week course of instruction. The children with physical training showed significant improvement in classroom performance.

However, the pitfalls of this type of experimentation are revealed by a subsequent study carried forward by Corder (Fig. 4-12).[13] A group of educable retarded boys were given a special program of physical education carried forward over a three-week period. Three groups of children were involved: an experimental group who received physical training; a group of "officials" who attended the training sessions but did not exercise, and a control group kept in the regular classroom.

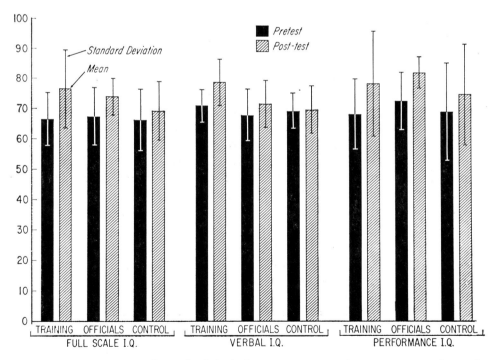

Figure 4-12. IQ means and standard deviations on pretest and post-test scores for training, officials and control groups. After Corder, W.O.: Effects of physical education on the intellectual, physical and social development of educable mentally retarded boys. *Exceptional Children,* 1966.

These studies reveal that although a physical education program provided specific improvement in physical prowess, the intellectual benefits achieved by a physical training program were shared by a group of "officials" who shared in the activities but not in the exercise. It appears that at least in this study much of the classroom benefit derived from the special physical training program was nonspecific in character and related to more subtle factors — possibly psychological, apart from the actual physical activities involved.

A similar study has been completed recently by Solomon and Pangle.[14] It involved forty-one boys enrolled in four public school special education classes in Nashville, Tennessee. Subjects ranged in age from thirteen years five months to seventeen years four months and their IQs ranged from 47 to 85. They were day students at these schools coming from an underprivileged community. Two groups received slightly differing programs of physical education. A third group received quiet games and the fourth group followed the school's daily routine which would have been followed by all of the groups had it not been for the special project being conducted. The training program was continued for a period of seven weeks. Children were tested before and after the training period for intelligence quotient, various parameters of physical fitness, and several criteria of personality development. They also were retested six weeks later to determine the permanency of any changes accomplished.

The study demonstrated that striking and persistent changes in physical fitness and capability were accomplished by this training program. There were no changes in intelligence quotient. There were no significant changes in the several psychological characteristics evaluated.

These several studies thus demonstrate that among mentally retarded individuals, physical fitness programs will improve physical fitness. The changes in performance and in intelligence quotient, when they occur, cannot be attributed directly to the physical training. They probably result from changes in motivation, interest and sense of adequacy.

PERCEPTUAL TRAINING AND READING

Let us turn then to the more general question. "To what extent will training in general perceptual skills lead to specific enhancement of reading ability?"

Interesting data were derived during the war from efforts to train military personnel in object recognition. An instrument called a "flashmeter" was developed to increase speed of object recognition. It proved a most effective means for rapid training of military personnel in the recognition of specific objects. These successes led to the belief that training in rapid recognition of objects might enhance reading skills and reading abilities.

A series of subsequent experiments however (see Fig. 4-13), have highlighted the limited applicability of the benefits of such training. Freeburne's studies were concerned with the influence of training in perceptual span and perceptual speed upon reading ability.[15] His subjects were college freshmen drawn from remedial reading classes. They were divided into three groups. Two groups were trained at word recognition by the use of a flashcard technique, the third served as a control. Of those who received training, one group were trained in speed of perception, the other in "span" or amount of material presented. These studies revealed that equal improvement of each skill could be accomplished by either form of training.

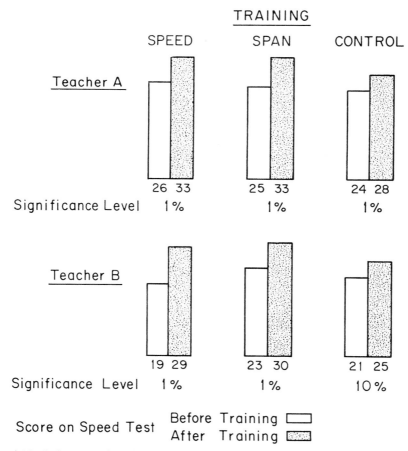

Figure 4-13. Influence of training in perceptual speed and span on reading ability. Significance of the differences between initial and final scores on flashmeter tests of perceptual speed. After Freeburne, C.M.: The influence of training in perceptual span and perceptual speed upon reading ability. *Journal of Educational Psychology, 40* (6) :321-352, 1949.

Thus, the graph presented indicates that improvement in "speed" performance was improved equally by either "speed" or "span" training. However, the control subjects of one teacher "A" made almost equal gains, possibly because of their brief learning experience during the testing sessions. Most significantly, however, there was no evidence that flashmeter training improved reading ability.

Similar studies by Gates compared the benefits of flashcard training with regular reading teaching in the classroom.[16,17] These studies revealed a remarkable specificity — the children trained with flashcards were quite effective at recognizing words presented in this fashion, but showed no increased facility in the recognition of words appearing on the printed page. Gates concludes that learning represents an adaptation to a very specific situation. Even in the case of a very complex task, there is little carry-over to apparently related abilities.

There is little question, however, that visual perceptive and perceptual motor skills are subject to training. Figure 4-14 shows rapid learning curves of individuals trained in rapid recognition of numerals, letters and combinations. In reporting his results, Dallenbach, working with second grade children, emphasizes that his *results differ from those of others who have worked primarily with adults,* and that *in his group of children a considerable transfer effect was observed.*[18] Thus, a group of his children given practice in the visual apprehension of numbers, digits and drawings showed modifications of performance lasting at least fifty weeks, and it was observed that the practiced children were superior to their unpracticed mates also in recalling and reporting correctly visual material of a different sort from that on which they have had their prior training (color instead of black and white, hetero-

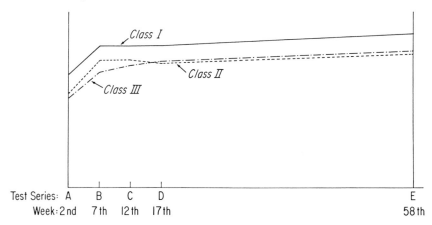

Figure 4-14. Effects of training in visual apprehension (period averages). From Dallenbach, K.M.: The effect of practice upon visual apprehension in school children. *Journal of Educational Psychology,* 5:390, 1914.

geneous instead of homogeneous, displayed for 30 instead of for 10 seconds, and demanding detailed description instead of mere enumeration). He concludes that the original work given the children had produced a training that not only persisted but also spread to some extent to other functions. Dallenbach noted that children who had received this special perceptual training were also superior in their regular classwork.

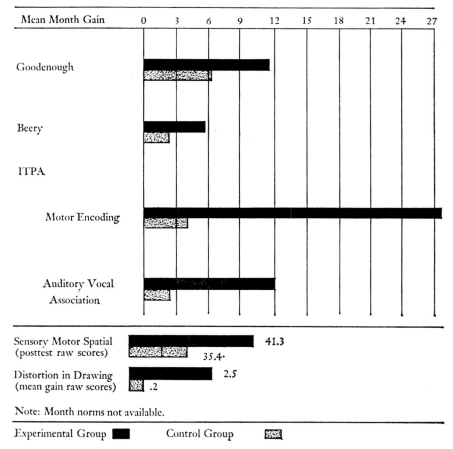

Figure 4-15. Representative mean gain scores for experimental and control groups. From Painter, G.: The effect of a rhythmic and sensory motor activity program on perceptual motor spatial abilities of kindergarten children. *Exceptional Children, 33*(2):113-16, 1966.

The effectivenes of perceptual motor training in improving perceptual motor skills also has been well demonstrated by Painter (Fig. 4-15).[19] Painter's studies involved an evaluation of a program of rhythmic and sensory motor activity involving the twenty lowest functioning children from a normal kindergarten. Half of the retarded group was given a special program of perceptuo-motor training. An equal number, matched for IQ, CA, MA and sex, served as control. Training was continued over a seven-week period. Following training, the experimental group showed marked improvement in the Goodenough Draw-A-Man-Test and in various elements of the Illinois Test of Psycholinguistic Abilities.

A related study by Chansky and Taylor shows similar results in a retarded group age eight to eleven years.[20] The experimental group received ten 1-hour instruction periods involving an organized program of building block construction. There was emphasis on proceeding from left to right, orderly progression, and completeness. The experimental group showed not only gains in discrimination of blocks, left-right-progression, and organization of work, but also significantly greater gains on the California Achievement Test and in Wechsler IQ.

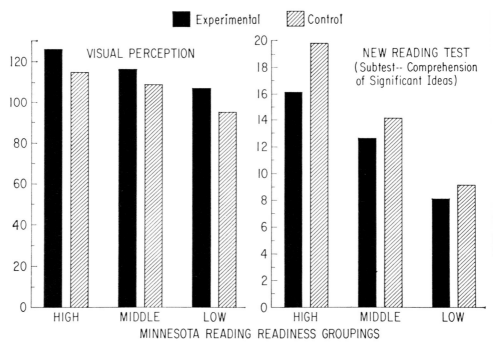

Figure 4-16. Results of perceptual training. After Rosen, C.L.: *Perceptual and Motor Skills*, 1966.

EFFECTS OF TRAINING RELATED TO AREAS TRAINED

In practical terms, the results of such perceptual motor training must be compared with the equivalent time which might be spent directed more specifically to learning problems. The results of Rosen suggest that for normal children time spent in perceptual motor training is less valuable than equivalent amounts of time spent in reading instruction (Fig. 4-16).[21] Rosen's study compared the reading achievement of children in twelve experimental classrooms who received a twenty-nine-day adaptation of the Frostig program for the development of visual perception with the gains made in thirteen regular classrooms enriched by an equivalent amount of time devoted to reading instruction. The results indicate that the children trained in perceptuo-motor skills gained most in perceptuo-motor skills. The children trained in reading gained most in reading.

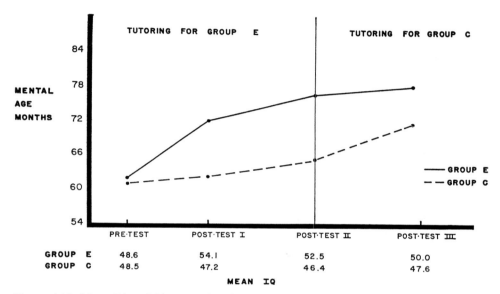

Figure 4-17. Mean Binet MA scores for the two groups during tutoring and nontutoring. From Gallagher, J.J.: *The Tutoring of Brain-Injured Mentally Retarded Children.* Springfield, Charles C Thomas, 1960.

Figure 4-17 indicates the remarkable improvement in language and learning performance in children with deficits which can be accomplished by properly implemented special education methods. The results of Gallagher with retarded, brain-injured, institutionalized children, in a carefully controlled study, document the extent to which a well-structured educational program can improve the intellectual performance of such a group.[22]

In regard to the less severely handicapped individual, results such as those reported by Schiffman indicate the improvement that can be accomplished by special educational methods directed toward a specific learning disability (Fig. 4-18).[23]

On the other hand, recent results of studies by Silver dealing with severe dyslexic children support the view that perceptual training directed toward a defined deficit will aid in the development of reading skills.[24] Preliminary results strongly suggest that in children who suffer disturbances of spatial orientation and concept formation, special training in visual and auditory perception will materially enhance the development of reading and learning skills.

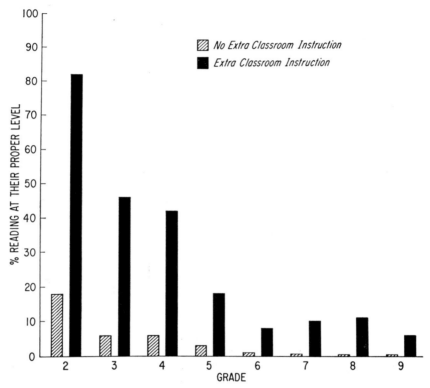

Figure 4-18. Percentages of corrective reading pupils reading at their proper level at end of 1960/61 year. After Shiffman, G.: Dyslexia as an educational phenomenon: its recognition and treatment. In Money, J.: *Reading Disability — Progress of Research Needs in Dyslexia*. Baltimore, Johns Hopkins Press, 1962.

From the limited number of studies available, it is difficult to derive firm answers to the questions which we have posed. However, certain general principles appear to apply. In general, learning is very specific. The more closely related to the ultimate task is the learning experience, the more directly beneficial will be the results. Thus, although there is no doubt that adequate physical training programs will improve physical fitness and even motor skills, it has not been proven that such training in the normal individual will enhance learning capabilities in the classroom. The evidence that perceptual motor training for the normal individual will enhance such specific learning as reading and writing is also equivocal. Results cited from Rosen's studies would indicate that under ordinary circumstances time is better spent in classroom efforts directed toward the subject matter to be learned.

The studies of Gilbert Schiffman, Archie Silver and others suggest, however, that where deficiencies exist, remedial efforts directed toward these specific deficits can be most beneficial.

There is a serious need for continued thoughtful research in this field. The evaluation of treatment is difficult and to date has suffered from several common errors.

1. Failure to select a homogeneous population for study.
2. Failure to test a specific form of therapy.
3. Failure to recognize and evaluate the impact of factors associated with but unrelated to the treatment program administered.

It is clear that there is no panacea for learning disabilities. It is equally clear that the ultimate answer lies in the development of educational methods based on a careful appraisal of the child's strengths and weaknesses. The essential need is to provide each child with an educational experience geared to his particular levels of competence and to extend this as quickly as possible to the specific tasks contained within the educational curriculum.

REFERENCES

1. DINGMAN, H.F., and TARJAN, G.: Mental retardation and the normal distribution curve. *Amer J Ment Defic, 64* (6) :991-94, 1960.
2. BIRCH, H.G., and RICHARDSON, S.A.: The relation of handicaps to social and obstetrical factors in all children living in one city. Presented at the American Academy of Cerebral Palsy, December 1 to 4, 1965, in Cleveland, Ohio.
3. ERNHART, C.B.; GRAHAM, F.K., and THURSTON, D.: Relationship of neonatal apnea to development at three years. *Arch Neurol, 2* (5) :504-10, 1960.
4. GERVER, J.M., and DAY, R.: Intelligence quotient of children who have recovered from erythroblastosis fetalis. *J Pediat, 36* (3) :342-48, 1950.
5. WIENER, G.; RIDER, R.V.; OPPEL, W.C.; FISCHER, L.K., and HARPER, P.A.: Correlates of low birth weight: psychological status at six to seven years of age. *Pediatrics, 35* (3:Part I) :434-44, 1965.
6. RAWSON, M.B.: Adult accomplishments of dyslexic boys: A follow-up study, in 1964-1965, of dyslexic and non-dyslexic students at The School in Rose Valley, 1930-1947. Hood College Monograph No. II, in preparation.
7. SHIELDS, J.: *Monozygotic Twins, Brought up Apart and Brought up Together — An Investigation into the Genetic and Environmental Causes of Variation in Personality.* London, Oxford U.P., 1962.
8. BELMONT, I.; BIRCH, H.G., and KARP, E.: The disordering of intersensory and intrasensory integration by brain damage. *J Nerv Ment Dis, 141* (4) :410-418, 1965.
9. ROBBINS, M.P.: A study of the validity of Delacato's theory of neurological organization. *Exceptional Child,* 1966.

10. FOSTER, J.M.: Effect of mobility training upon reading achievement and intelligence. *Res Resume,* 1965, vol. 30.

11. KERSHNER, J.R.: An investigation of the Doman-Delacato theory of neuropsychology as it applies to trainable mentally retarded children in public schools, Bureau of Research Administration and Coordination, Area of Research and Development, Department of Public Instruction, Commonwealth of Pennsylvania, May 1967, pp. 105 (mimeo).

12. OLIVER, J.N.: The effect of physical conditioning exercises and activities on the mental characteristics of educationally sub-normal boys. *Brit J Educ Psychol, 28:* 155-165, 1958.

13. CORDER, W.O.: Effects of physical education on the intellectual, physical, and social development of educable mentally retarded boys. *Exceptional Child,* 1966.

14. SOLOMON, A.H., and PANGLE, R.: The effects of a structured physical education program on physical, intellectual, and self-concept development of educable retarded boys. *IMRID Behav Sci Monograph* No. 4, 1966. (Nashville, Tenn., Peabody College Bookstore)

15. FREEBURNE, C.M.: The influence of training in perceptual span and perceptual speed upon reading ability. *J Educ Psychol, 40* (6) :321-352, 1949.

16. GATES, A.I.: Functions of flash-card exercises in reading—An experimental study. *Teachers College Record, 27:*311-327, 1925.

17. GATES, A.I.: A study of the role of visual perception, intelligence, and certain associative processes in reading and spelling. *J Educ Psychol, 17* (7) :433-445, 1926.

18. DELLENBACH, K.M.: The effect of practice upon visual apprehension in school children. *J Educ Psychol, 5* (1,2) :321-334, 387-404, 1914.

19. PAINTER, G.: The effect of a rhythmic and sensory motor activity program on perceptual motor spatial abilities of kindergarten children. *Exceptional Child, 33* (2) :113-116.

20. CHANSKY, N.M., and TAYLOR, M.: Perceptual training with young mental retardates. *Amer J Ment Defic, 68:*460, 1964.

21. ROSEN, C.L.: An experimental study of visual perceptual training and reading achievement in first grade. *Percept Motor Skills, 22:*979-86, 1966.

22. GALLAGHER, J.J.: *The Tutoring of Brain-Injured Mentally Retarded Children.* Springfield, Thomas, 1960.

23. SCHIFFMAN, G.: Dyslexia as an educational phenomenon: its recognition and treatment. In Money, J. (Ed.) : *Reading Disability — Progress of Research Needs in Dyslexia.* Baltimore, Johns Hopkins, 1962.

24. SILVER, A.A.; HAGIN, R.A., and HERSH, M.F.: Reading disability: teaching through stimulation of deficit perceptual areas. *Amer J Orthopsychiat,* 1967.

Chapter 5

The Physician's Role in Early Diagnosis and Management of Learning Disabilities

HELEN GOFMAN

INTRODUCTION—THE PROBLEM

IN OUR ENLIGHTENED SOCIETY, with laws against child labor, it may appear that today's children are provided with a carefree environment free of occupational hazards which permits them to grow to adulthood at a leisurely pace. It should be remembered, however, that our increasingly technical society has made going to school a compulsory job for at least ten to twelve years for most children. These children, therefore, make up a huge compulsory labor force, exposed to another type of *occupational hazard*, i.e., learning difficulty.

Today, the possession of a high school diploma is becoming the minimum requirement for adult productivity; it is increasingly difficult for a young person to get even the most menial job without it. Furthermore, the child's success or failure during his ten to twelve years of "compulsory labor" in school can have tremendous consequences on his self-image as an adult and on his feeling of self-worth as a citizen in our culture. The fact that our high school dropout rate nationwide is between 30 to 40 per cent[1] — and even in the affluent State of California at least 25 per cent of students leave public school without graduating — indicates that many of our young citizens are entering adult life with real questions in regard to their own self-worth and future productivity. There is failure somewhere in our educational production line, in terms of providing the final product demanded by our society.

There are many causes for these educational casualties. One common factor in most cases is the pupil's poor academic achievement, especially in reading and spelling. Studies throughout the United States have shown that as many as 30 per cent of our country's junior high and high school students are behind their peers in reading and spelling ability.[2,3] With dif-

Note: This material is based on presentations made at San Francisco Chapter, California Association for Neurologically Handicapped Children, Symposium on Learning Disabilities — Case Finding and Treatment, October 15, 1966, and Arkansas Association, 4th Annual Convention for Children with Learning Disabilities, April 29, 1967.

The training and clinical programs described are supported in part by the United States Children's Bureau (Grant 144), the Rosenberg Foundation, and the Junior League of San Francisco.

ficulty in reading and spelling there is hardly a subject in high school or junior high in which these students can achieve success — even shop courses require the reading of directions, writing reports and taking examinations.

Some examples of these educational casualties will illustrate the serious hazards experienced by some of our compulsory student labor force. These case illustrations summarize the combined efforts of our team at the University of California Medical Center who work together in the study of children with the complaint of "learning disorders." These team members, whose professional skills make possible these studies and the methods of approach to learning problems summarized in this chapter, should all be considered as contributors of this manuscript.*

The children whose problems are summarized in the following case examples were seen for a four-day evaluation (in the Child Study Unit at the University of California-San Francisco Medical Center) which included a pediatric history, physical examination, psychological testing, parent or family interview, neurological examination, evaluation of hearing, speech and language, ophthalmological examination and educational evaluation. Following a team conference, the findings were summarized and beginning plans for management were discussed with the parents and child. This four-day study is provided by the Child Study Unit as part of its training program for senior medical students and house staff in pediatrics and opthalmology.

CASE EXAMPLES

Case of Tony

1. *A teen-age nonreader:* Tony, age fifteen years nine months, in the ninth grade of one of the Bay Area high schools, was recently referred to our Child Study Unit by his English teacher who stated, "When I introduced poetry the first week by reading some aloud, Tony proceeded to explain e. e. Cummings' poem, "Portrait of Buffalo Bill" to the class. He seemed to have imagination, an aesthetic sense as well as well-developed inferential abilities. As long as we are engaged in oral work and discussion, Tony is part of the class. When we begin writing or reading, he puts his head down on the desk." She found that he was almost completely unable to read or spell. He had never been a behavior problem in school (perhaps this is one reason why he was not evaluated until so late in his school

---

*Mrs. Donya Harvin, Mrs. Eva Hitchcock, Mrs. Gladys Kassebaum and Dr. Keith Berry, psychologists; Mrs. Wilma Buckman, psychiatric social worker; Dr. Alan Leveton, psychiatrist; Dr. Leon Whitsell, neurologist; Dr. Richard Flower, speech, hearing and language consultant; Dr. Earl Stern, ophthalmologist, and Mrs. Alice Whitsell, educational consultant and director of the Pediatric Reading and Language Development Clinic.

career) and had been liked by his teachers because of his nice manners and willingness to cooperate. However, during the ninth grade he had been absent at least two days a week.

At the instigation of his English teacher, he was tested by the school psychologist. On the Wechsler Intelligence Scale for Children (WISC) * he showed the following profile:

Full Scale		IQ 77
Verbal Scale		IQ 79
		Scaled Scores
Information		5
Comprehension		7
Arithmetic		3
Similarities		10
Vocabulary		7
Digit Span		7
Performance Scale		IQ 80
		Scaled Scores
Picture Completion		6
Picture Arrangement		6
Block Design		7
Object Assembly		10
Coding		7

These scores would have placed him in the range of borderline intelligence. The psychologist noted that he was extremely fearful and reticent and agreed with Tony's English teacher that these scores probably did not adequately describe Tony's true potential. Further study was recommended.

Unfortunately, our clinic — as so many clinics in this country — has an enormous waiting list for evaluation of children with learning disorders. Although his appointments were squeezed in ahead of others, there was still a six-week wait. At the first appointment for his scheduled evaluation, he came accompanied by a security officer who had brought him from a juvenile detention home where he had been confined for two weeks after being picked up by the police for pulling a fire alarm under the influence of LSD. His mother joined him at the clinic.

Tony came from a home broken by divorce from an alcoholic father when he was two years old. His mother, whose English was limited, still has a communication difficulty in Spanish as well as in English. She was the sole support of her three children — Tony was the middle child, with an older sister and younger brother. After the divorce, his mother took the children to her home in Nicaragua and returned to the Bay Area when Tony was six years old and ready to start first grade. He could speak only Spanish and began his job of learning to read not only with the handicap

---

*The WISC subtests will be described in more detail later in relation to the case of Mark.

of specific difficulty in visual and auditory functions and small motor coordination which was still apparent at age fifteen, but also with the added
handicap of having to learn English. This latter is not unusual in many
urban communities in this country. After his learning difficulty in the first
grade was noted, he was placed back in kindergarten, but again he had great
difficulty the following year with reading and writing in the first grade.
Despite this difficulty he was promoted each year and was considered by the
school to be a dull but earnest student. In Sylvia Richardson's words,[4]
this boy represented an example of a sizeable number of children who are
"smuggled through our school system" with disastrous results. Tony's
mother, because of her poor English and her own difficulty with reading
and spelling, was unable to help him. In her bewilderment and frustration,
she constantly accused him of being lazy with his school work — although
she stated that he was not lazy about jobs around the house.

Tony became progressively more embarrassed by his reading and spelling difficulties and began to stay home on days of tests because, to quote him,
"I felt sick at the thought of sitting in class, unable to write anything on
paper when all others around me were writing answers and looking at me
just sitting there." He tried to hide his reading and spelling problems from
most of his friends — a difficult job when you consider how we are sur-
rounded by signs, none of which Tony could read. Tony, like most teenagers, had heard many fantastic tales about the effects of LSD. As he said,
"I was partly curious, but also I heard it was a mind-expander and some of
my friends who know about my trouble reading said maybe it would help
me with my reading. So I tried it. But it did not help and I had a bad reaction."

On testing with the Wide Range Achievement Test (WRAT), he obtained the following levels:

WRAT	Grade level
Word Recognition	1.9
Spelling	1.8
Arithmetic	5.0
Actual Grade Level	9.6

His confusion in two-dimensional spatial relationships and left-right orientation is illustrated by his reading "drib" for "bird" and "bees" for
"seed."

His confusions and inconsistencies in spelling were quite evident (Figs.
5-1 and 5-2). It would have been impossible for Tony to read or fill out
the simplest forms which are usually necessary in applying for a job, a
driver's license, etc.

He showed severe problems in visual-motor function (Bender Visual-

The baeg eny a big Said

Figure 5-1. Tony, 15 year 9 month ninth grader. Attempt to print from dictation, "The bird ate a big seed."

The bert a eny a gis died

Figure 5-2. Tony's attempt to write from dictation "The bird ate a big seed."

Motor Gestalt Test — 9-year level), in auditory discrimination (significant errors at the 6-year level on the Wepman Auditory Discrimination Test), and in visual memory. His small-motor coordination was very poor. He impressed the five members of our staff who saw him as an intelligent boy in his oral conversation, in contrast to his low scores on formal testing.

Demoralizing experiences in connection with his reading and spelling problem continued for Tony, even during his weeks in the detention institution. School classes were provided for the inmates and Tony described his classroom difficulties. The first day the teacher asked Tony to take his turn reading aloud from the text book on American History. Tony tried but, of course, found the task almost completely impossible. He stumbled, made wild guesses and was finally permitted to sit down, after becoming completely embarrassed by the snicker and ridicule from his peers. Tony stated he thought the teacher must have seen how difficult reading was for him, and he "couldn't believe it when the next day the teacher asked me to read out loud again. I just couldn't go through that again and when I refused he sent me to my room and I lost all my privileges because he said I wasn't cooperating." Until Tony's reading disorder was explained to his probation officer and teacher, Tony was regarded as uncooperative and, therefore, a likely candidate for assignment to a correctional institution under the California Youth Authority.

Tony's recent behavior was interpreted as representing a desperate cry for help. Rather than being sent to a California correctional institution, which his probation officer stated could provide little help for reading problems — one of the primary needs of many of these delinquent boys, he was allowed to stay at home on probation with the provision that he receive special teaching and counseling. His high school provided counseling and a more suitable curriculum, and he was enrolled in one of the classes of our Pediatric Reading and Language Development Clinic, where he was seen for three hours per week along with two other teen-age boys with similar reading and spelling difficulties. These classes were established to demonstrate to our doctors-in-training what could be done to help children of average or above-average intelligence who have specific problems in reading and spelling and thereby impress these future physicians with the importance of the role of early diagnosis. These classes are taught by teachers with special training in specific learning disorders.*

Since Tony and other students like him have experienced almost overwhelming failure in the school situation, the philosophy of the teachers in our Pediatric Reading and Language Development Clinic is to try to provide as much success as possible initially. This is done by beginning work at the level where the student can be successful. Frequently this is many grade levels lower than anyone has suspected. This philosophy also involves, at first, making use of the student's relative strengths in the teaching situation.

Tony had been attempting to memorize whole words visually in connection with reading and spelling and had no word-attack skills. Therefore, during his first lessons, an attempt was made to teach him to include an auditory approach in trying to read and spell words that were new to him. For example: after making the auditory association to the written symbols "ou" and adding consonants to this vowel combination, Tony was able at the end of the first week of classes to write the sentence shown in Figure 5-3. Although some errors were evident in this written work, it represented a big step for Tony in expressing himself on paper.

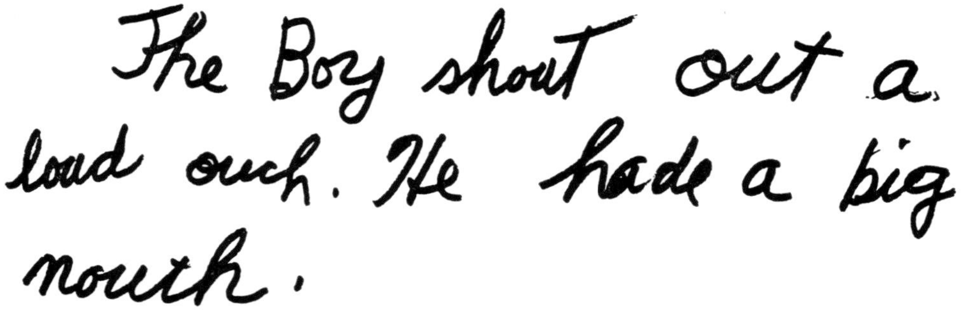

The Boy shout out a. load ouch. He hade a big nouth.

Figure 5-3. Tony's written work after three hours of special teaching.

Figure 5-4 is an example of Tony's written use of prepositions in a sentence, after approximately thirty-six hours of help. Two weeks later, after about five more lessons, Tony arrived early for class one morning. His teacher, Mrs. Whitsell — who is responsible along with Tony for these ex-

*The major support for this Clinic comes from the Junior League of San Francisco.

amples of his progress — noted that he had picked up a *National Geographic Magazine* and was leafing through an article on the war in Vietnam, looking at the illustrations. She asked Tony to choose his favorite picture from the group. From the series, most of which were action-packed war photographs, he chose one of three smiling Vietnamese children playing in a sampan on the bank of a quiet river. Tony was unable to read the caption, so Mrs. Whitsell read it to him:

> In a moment of serenity, while tides of terror rise and fall around them, Vietnamese youngsters play in a sampan. Strife seems far away; yet the deadly war inflicted upon the country by the Communists may destroy their village and snuff out their lives at any time. For the future of innocents like these, Americans fight and die in Southeast Asia.

She suggested that Tony write the caption for the photograph in his own words. Figure 5-5 is his version, done completely on his own except for assistance in spelling *Vietnamese.*

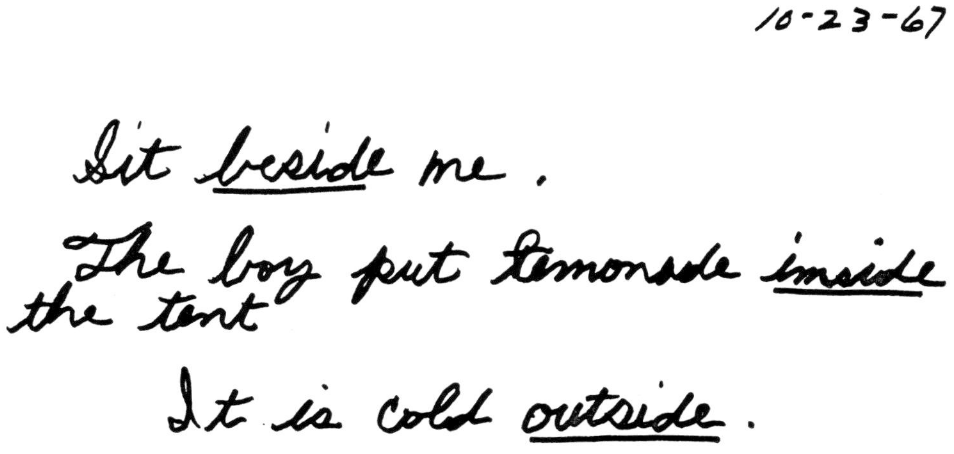

10-23-67

Sit beside me.

The boy put lemonade inside the tent

It is cold outside.

Figure 5-4. Tony's written work after thirty-six hours of special teaching.

After about forty hours of help, he was able to read at the beginning third grade level, e.g., "Jim Forest and Dead Man's Peak"[5] with good speed, accuracy and comprehension. He had also responded to the teaching of words and phrases basic for existence in our literate society, such as DO NOT ENTER, EXIT, YIELD, PED XING, DANGER.

Tony's teachers in high school are now more understanding of his specific learning problems. He attends class regularly and has had no further difficulty with the police. Without the evaluation and help for his reading and spelling problems, it is not difficult to imagine a different outcome for Tony.

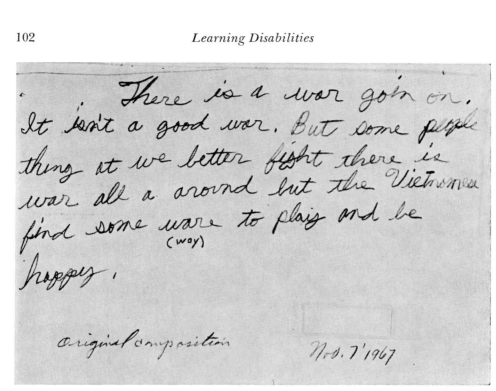

Figure 5-5. Tony's paraphrasing of the caption accompanying a photograph from the *National Geographic Magazine.*

Case of Roger

2. *Twelve-year-old boy with difficulty in spelling and handwriting.* In contrast to Tony, Roger, age twelve and a half years, came from a stable, academically oriented family. At the end of the first semester in the seventh grade, his pediatrician referred him to the Child Study Unit for evaluation because "he is striving to maintain the standards expected by his family at great cost to himself, because he is so conscientious. He is quite capable of doing his work but it takes him a very long time and exhausts him emotionally. I do not know that he has a reading disability but I am extremely suspicious that this is his problem."

His mother described Roger as a pleasant, well-adjusted child who had difficulty in handwriting and spelling since he first started kindergarten. As a preschooler, he showed normal development except for difficulty with small-motor coordination — he never enjoyed or did well in coloring or drawing. Roger also showed some difficulty in reading and received remedial reading help during the elementary grades. His mother felt that Roger's good oral work, excellent vocabulary and especially his high motivation had helped him get along in school until the seventh grade, at which time he began to receive very poor grades because of his "atrocious handwriting" and poor spelling. He became very discouraged with his teachers' continual complaints about his written work. Just prior to our evaluation, he had repeatedly stated, "I'm stupid" and seemed about ready to give up.

On the WISC he scored the following:

Full Scale	IQ 118
Verbal Scale	IQ 126
	Scaled scores
Information	11
Comprehension	15
Arithmetic	11
Similarities	17
Vocabulary	19
Digit Span	12
Performance Scale	IQ 106
	Scaled scores
Picture Completion	11
Picture Arrangement	17
Block Design	11
Object Assembly	10
Coding	5

With a scaled score of 10 being average for each of the subtests, it was evident that Roger was functioning considerably above average on many of the verbal subtests and that, in comparison to his high verbal subtest score, he showed relative weakness in the performance subtests and a severe weakness in the subtest "Coding."

On the WRAT he scored the following:

WRAT	*Grade level*
Word Recognition	5.6
Spelling	5.1
Arithmetic	5.0
Actual Grade Level	7.5

On the Gilmore Oral Reading Test he was able to read paragraphs at 7.0 grade level in accuracy, 9.8+ grade level in comprehension, but only 4.5 grade level in speed.

An example of his poor handwriting and spelling from dictation is shown in Figure 5-6. With his slow reading rate and great difficulty in written work, this very intelligent boy was spending most of his time on homework and receiving little success or gratification.

Roger's difficulties with two-dimensional figures, e.g., the Bender Visual-Motor Gestalt Test (Fig. 5-7) are illustrated by his attempts to copy them (Fig. 5-8). Using the Koppitz scoring, his reproductions are more like those of an eight and one-half-year-old. Although Roger was beyond the age norms for the Frostig Developmental Test of Visual Perception, his poor

small-motor coordination was quite evident in his attempts to draw lines
from left to right in this hand-eye coordination task (Fig. 5-9).

His difficulty invisual memory for two-dimensional figures is illustrated
by Figures 5-10 and 5-11, where he was shown the example for ten seconds
and then asked to draw it from memory. Note his rotation of figures and
errors in sequencing.

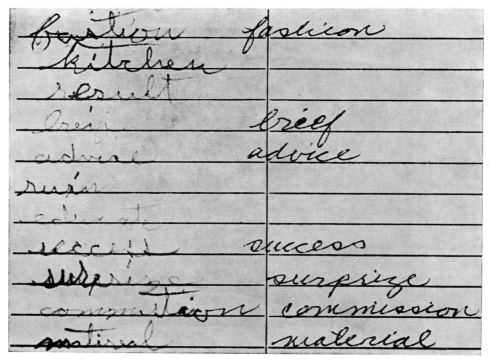

Figure 5-6. Roger, age 12 and 1/2 years. Spelling from dictation.

It was our impression that, due to the remedial help he had received in
reading, his excellent verbal ability and his good motivation he had compensated fairly well for his specific reading disorder, and that he needed
most help and understanding for his spelling and writing difficulty. Roger
also had great difficulty with beginning Spanish, despite getting up every
morning at six of his own volition to study it for an hour and a half. The
foreign language requirements in junior high and high school often present impossible obstacles for these students who have partially compensated
for their specific reading disorder in their native tongue.

Roger was allowed to drop Spanish. With a better understanding of his
genuine difficulty with spelling and handwriting, despite his superior verbal intelligence, his parents and teachers were able to become more sup-

portive and helpful. A six-week summer session between the seventh and eighth grade in our Pediatric Reading and Language Development Clinic was of some help in improving his spelling and handwriting (Fig. 5-12).

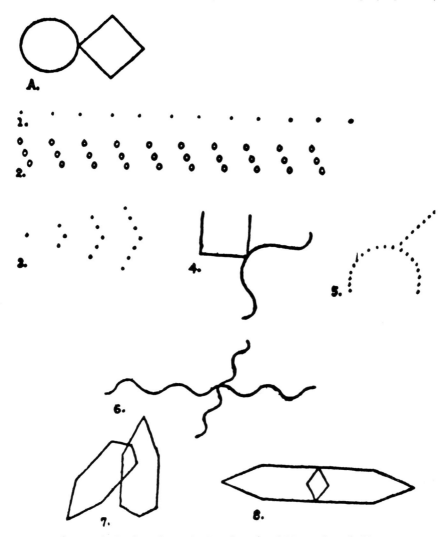

Figure 5-7. Designs from the Bender Visual-Motor Gestalt Test.

Roger is now a junior in high school. His parents report that considerable effort has had to be directed each year in trying to achieve understanding from his teachers in regard to his difficulties in handwriting and spelling. If Roger is heavily penalized for these difficulties, as happened in science, a subject he especially enjoys, he becomes discouraged, upset and does poorly.

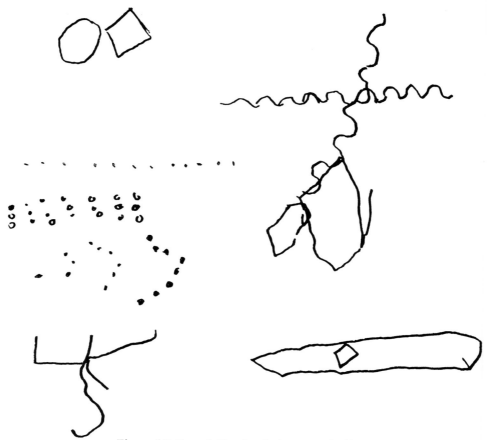

Figure 5-8. Roger's Bender design reproductions.

If his problem is met with understanding, as when some of his teachers allowed oral or taped examinations instead of written tests, he does very well. Unfortunately, there are a number of junior and high school teachers who cannot be convinced that poor handwriting and spelling in an intelligent student can be caused by anything other than carelessness, laziness or emotional problems.

UNDERSTANDING LEARNING DISORDERS

These boys are examples of children with specific learning disorders. They each show achievement in reading and spelling that is far below their overall mental abilities. At least 5 per cent of school children have this problem[6] which is related to the demands of our culture, e.g., reading and writing disability. In a nonliterate culture they might experience few problems.

From these examples it is evident that the intelligence quotient (IQ) alone is certainly not enough to describe a child's learning difficulty or to assist in planning his educational program or home management. The various strengths and weaknesses in specific functions of his central nervous system must be understood.

How could these boys have been detected, diagnosed and treated earlier? How could we have prevented these children from becoming "school battered?" The blame should not be put entirely on the school; the medical profession should also bear its share. Pediatricians are specialists not only in their knowledge of childhood disease, but also in their knowledge of growth and development — and this should include emotional and mental growth and development. Medical education has been tardy in training physicians in this area of childhood medicine and in applying this knowledge to assist the school system in the prevention of problems such as those experienced by Tony and Roger.

One approach in understanding children's learning difficulties is to consider the requirements for the task of learning to read, write and spell and to compare these requirements with the behavioral development and cognitive functions which the individual child brings to the task.

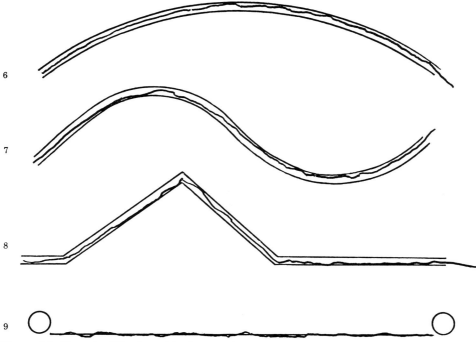

Figure 5-9. Roger's difficulty with the test for Eye-Motor Coordination from the Frostig Developmental Test of Visual Perception.

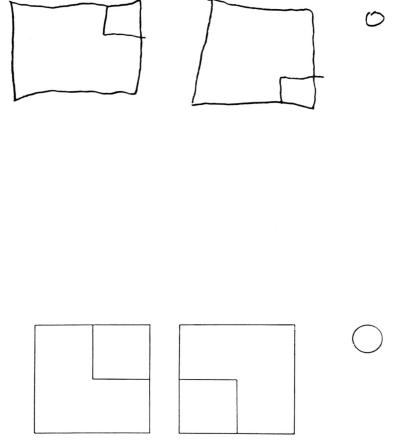

Figure 5-10. Roger's difficulty in visual memory for two-dimensional spatial relationships from the Benton Visual Retention Test.

BEHAVIORAL PREREQUISITES FOR LEARNING

The child should be able to do the following:

1. Sit still.
2. Attend to incoming stimuli.
3. Sort visual, auditory and tactile-kinesthetic stimuli from the background of distracting sight, noise and movement in a classroom.
4. Maintain some measure of impulse control.
5. Tolerate some frustration.
6. Wait a reasonable time for gratification.

These abilities are a blend of the child's developing central nervous system function and his reaction to the environment, so that lack of these abili-

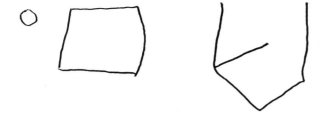

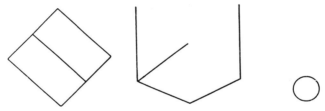

Figure 5-11. Roger's difficulty with memory for two-dimensional spatial relationships and visual sequencing (Benton Visual Retention Test).

This century is one of changing climate, it is changing due to the excess of CO_2. There are larger amounts of coal and gas. When the sun heats the CO_2 it becomes warmer. If the burning of gas and coal continues the climate will change.

The Polar region will melt and flood the coast line and the land mass will lessen. With the great population explosion we can't afford it.

Figure 5-12. Roger's improved written expression after six weeks of special remedial help. Note typical errors in spelling of *climate, burning* and the confusion of *m* and *n* in spelling *mass.*

ties may result from both. The child may not have been taught to manage these prerequisites or his developing central nervous system may make this teaching by the parents unusually difficult. Susan Gray[7] describes the enormous problem which the "culturally disadvantaged" preschool children in her study had in figure-ground discrimination in relation to their environment. Their overcrowded one or two room houses may present a clutter of disorganized visual and auditory stimuli (e.g., a deaf grandmother with the television on very loud, while children and mother are shouting to be heard). These children, as well as the child who has difficulty in attending and sorting out stimuli on the basis of central nervous system dysfunction, may find attention to auditory, visual and tactile-kinesthetic cues from the teacher difficult in the usual bustle of the elementary grades.

The physician who sees preschool children should evaluate from questioning the mother and personal observations in the waiting room and office the child's activity level, attention span, impulse control, ability to wait for gratification and frustration tolerance. If the child has unusual difficulty, he may be more vulnerable to school difficulty and may require help before he is subjected to the stresses of an ordinary first grade (or before he stresses the teacher!).

CENTRAL NERVOUS SYSTEM FUNCTIONS INVOLVED IN LEARNING

The physician should be aware of the role of the central nervous system involved in learning to read, write and spell. He has the first opportunity to check these functions, as he follows the child prior to school entrance, and he can play an important role in seeking consultation in the evaluation of central nervous system weaknesses and in alerting the school and parents to the child's special needs.

We are just emerging from a period when learning difficulties in the child of average or above-average intelligence have been considered to be mainly emotional in etiology. Until recently, many physicians, psychologists and educators seemed to forget that the brain is a thinking organ as well as a feeling organ.

What functions of the central nervous system are involved in learning to read, write and spell? An effective method of presenting these requirements to our doctors in training and explaining this process to parents is to expose them to the task which the first grader faces in learning to read and spell, by making up a new alphabet so they can re-experience opening a primer for the first time (Fig. 5-13).

The child has the task of associating his spoken symbol system (spoken language) with a written symbol system (written langauge). His mastery of spoken language, therefore, is of primary importance in this new printed and written language learning.

Language development. A vulnerable child may be one with delayed speech development, speech difficulties, different mother tongue, different dialect from that of the teacher (e.g., the child who says "disaball" for "this is a ball" may have much confusion when asked to associate his spoken *giant word*[8] "disaball" with the four individual printed words "this is a ball." In our evaluation of several thousand patients with learning difficulties in recent years, delay or deviation in language development constituted the most important factor in learning disorders in children.

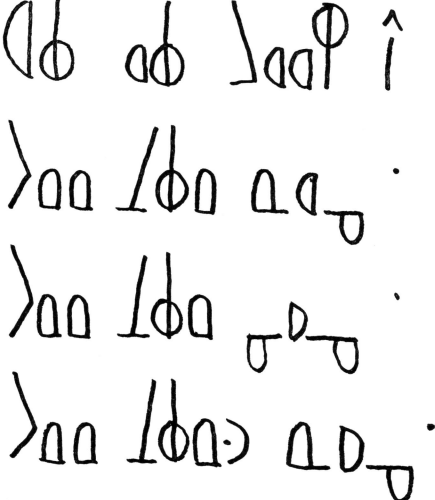

Figure 5-13. Mock alphabet.

Visual perception, visual sequencing, spatial relationship, left-right discrimination. The child must be able to perceive small differences in two-dimensional spatial relationships. If the example in Figure 5-13 in our new alphabet says:

> Oh oh look!
> See the dog.
> See the pig.
> See them dig.

one may easily confuse the symbol sequences for "dog" and "pig" and "dig" because of the similarities of our *new* alphabet symbols for *d, b, p, g* and for *o* and *i*. Our own alphabet presents the same confusion, e.g., *d, b, p, g, q, 9* and *6* are all variations of the theme of the vertical line and circle. There are many more confusing spatial relationships; in fact, the lower case letters of our alphabet seem almost perversely designed to create confusion in two-dimensional relationships, e.g., *m, n, h, u, c, e,* etc.

Auditory discrimination and auditory sequencing. The child must also associate the sound with the symbol and, therefore, perceive small differences in sounds in the beginning, ending and middle of words. Some children have great difficulty in distinguishing the difference, for example, between the vowels in *pin* and *pen* or the last consonant in *spend* and *spent.*

Visual and auditory memory. The child must store these two-dimensional spatial relationships of written symbols, their associated sounds and their sequences in those parts of the brain concerned with memory, so that when he is asked to recognize or spell a given word he can recall the shapes and sounds of the individual symbols in their proper sequence.

Small motor coordination, gnosis, praxis, left-right discrimination. Through the functioning of the motor and sensory neurons involved in controlling the small motor coordination of his fingers, the child must be able to push a pencil in many different directions on paper to reproduce these shapes in proper sequence.

Auditory, visual and tactile-kinesthetic tracking. In order to teach pupils to read, write and spell, teachers must explain the task to their pupils via verbal directions, visual examples, and tactile-kinesthetic demonstrations. Children vary in their ability to follow and remember these sequences. One of the most common problems which we have observed is the difficulty of some children to remember a verbal explanation, i.e., process a sequence of auditory verbal signals (auditory tracking), especially if it is lengthy and involves remembering several different chores. For example: "Now children, get out your lined paper and your pencils; print your names in the left hand corner, and the date in the right hand corner. Now, copy the whole list of words from the board and put a line under only the words that begin with *b*." By the time the teacher finishes the explanation, the child has forgotten the beginning of the instruction, so that he either completes only part of the task, distorts it, or sits in utter confusion, becomes disturbed and sooner or later disturbs the class and the teacher.

There is a great variation among children in their readiness for these complicated tasks of learning to read, write and spell. Considering that pediatricians feel, for example, that the onset of walking alone may range from nine to sixteen or eighteen months, it seems strange that professionals who deal with learning have decided that all children at the magical age of six years should be ready to cope with this much more complicated human task. Many studies[9-14] confirm the wide variation in the abilities of six-year-olds in the functions enumerated.

CASE EXAMPLE

A first grader with a specific learning disorder. Mark illustrates the problem of the young child with specific weakness or dysfunction in some of the central nervous system functions involved in early school learning. He came to the Child Study Unit at the age of six years eight months, halfway through first grade, at the suggestion of his school nurse who wondered if he needed glasses since he was unable to distinguish many of the letters from each other.

His teacher commented on his poor coordination in copying figures, "He can't remember numbers and words from one day to the next. Although he understands number concepts, e.g., fourteen, he can't recognize the number when he sees it written." This is illustrated by an example of some of his first grade arithmetic work (Fig. 5-14). His teacher also noted, "He is polite and seemingly cooperative, but sometimes I can't get through to him. He seems immature and, in some of his mannerisms, he is more like a three-year-old. He does try hard."

The fourth of five children, Mark was delivered in our hospital at term after seventy-eight hours of ruptured membranes and a pregnancy complicated by symptoms of pre-eclampsia. The nurses in the nursery noted generalized fine tremor and rigidity of his legs on the third and fourth days postnatally. His development was within normal limits: he was walking at fifteen months (later than his siblings), and using sentences at eighteen months. He had moderate trouble with allergies which caused frequent absences from kindergarten. He was babied because of this, especially by a Spanish-speaking spinster aunt who lived in the home. Mark spoke both Spanish and English on entering school.

His older brother and sister and three maternal cousins also had reading difficulty. His mother and sister had mild speech deficits. His mother reported that Mark was beginning to be upset with his difficulty in reading and writing and cried because some of his classmates teased him about being stupid. Recently, to his mother's consternation, he had asked her what MR meant after his peers had used this term applied to him.

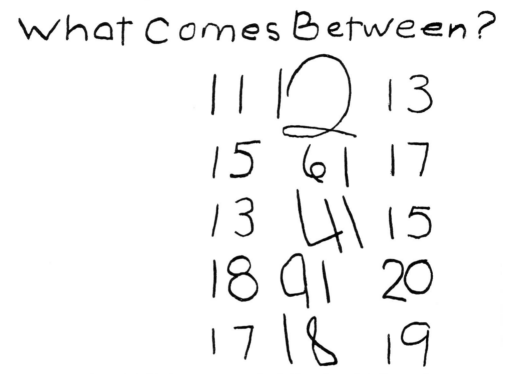

Figure 5-14. Mark, 6 years 8 months. Arithmetic work in first grade.

His physical examination was within normal limits, except for the neurological findings. He had a clumsy, pigeon-toed gait with asymmetrical arm swing, mild athetoid movement of the right upper extremity, striate posture of the left upper extremity, bilateral finger agnosia, faulty position-sense in fingers and toes, poor left-right discrimination. On the Lincoln-Oseretsky Motor Development Scale[15] (a standardized research instrument made up of tests of posture, rhythm and large and small muscle coordination) he scored below the fifth percentile for his age. He was unable to walk a line backward, stand on one foot, stand in heel-to-toe position, or to perform fine finger movements.

On the WRAT he was unable to recognize any words and very few letters. His attempts at spelling are shown in Figure 5-15. Note his difficulty in spacing his name. He was unable to spell any first grade words. The "word" on the right was his attempt to print *and*. On psychological testing, using the WISC, he achieved a full scale IQ of 92 (within the normal range). If this IQ number were all that his teacher heard about him, she might conclude that his learning difficulty was due to an "emotional block." Knowing Mark's IQ in no way clarified his problem; we were interested in his strengths and weaknesses as evaluated by the various subtest scores.

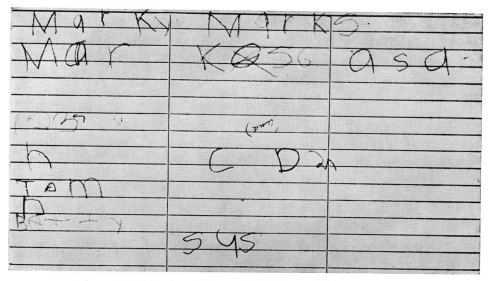

Figure 5-15. Mark's spelling on Wide Range Achievement Test.

The WISC is divided into two main parts — the Verbal Scale composed of six subtests that require only verbal answers to verbal questions with no hand manipulation or writing necessary, and the Performance Scale composed of five subtests that require a minimum of verbal explanation and verbal response. When we examined Mark's Verbal and Performance scores, it was apparent that he showed more weakness on the Performance than on the Verbal Scale. WISC scores for Mark at age six years eight months were as follows:

Verbal Scale	IQ 101
Performance Scale	IQ 83
Full Scale	IQ 92
Verbal tests	*Scaled scores*
Information	11
Comprehension	11
Arithmetic	10
Similarities	14

Vocabulary	9
Digit Span	6
Performance tests	*Scaled scores*
Picture Completion	10
Picture Arrangement	7
Block Design	9
Object Assembly	8
Coding	4

The individual subtest scores suggested strengths and weaknesses of the various abilities being tested. A scaled score of 10 is average, so that if Mark had earned a scaled score of 10 on all subtests, he would have achieved an IQ of 100. A very rough comparison can be made between this average IQ of 100 and the average scaled score. For example, in the first verbal subtest (Information) consisting of such questions as: "From what animal do we get milk? How many pennies in a nickel? Who discovered America? etc.," Mark achieved a scaled score of 11. If we were to assess his intelligence *only* by how much information he had accumulated in comparison to a cross section of children his age *in this culture,* he would have earned an IQ of roughly 110. Looking at the other subtests, we can see that Mark was also within the average range in Comprehension (a series of questions assessing social judgment), Oral Arithmetic and Vocabulary (defining the meaning of words). He was superior in Similarities (his ability to categorize or abstract, e.g., "How are a cat and a mouse alike?"). On the subtest Digit Span (his ability to repeat a series of numbers both forward and backward) he demonstrated a severe weakness with a scaled score of 6. This subtest suggested a weakness in auditory attention or immediate auditory recall. Some weakness in visual memory may also have been indicated, since visual memory assists in recalling a series of digits backwards. When we reviewed Mark's subtest scores of the Verbal Scale, he showed great variation — comparable to a variation in IQ from *about* 140 to *about* 60, depending on which intellectual function we were trying to assess.

He also showed varying strengths and weaknesses on the Performance Scale, from 10 to 4, with his greatest weakness in Coding, a test of eye-hand coordination involving visual perception, visual memory and small motor coordination. Thus, from Mark's score on the WISC subtests, certain weaknesses appeared that deserved further study. The low score on Digit Span raised the possibility of difficulty in auditory attention and auditory and visual memory for sequences. The low score on Picture Arrangement also suggested some difficulty with visual sequencing. The very low score on Coding suggested difficulty in visual perception, and/or visual memory, and/or small motor coordination and/or their integration (visual motor coordination). The Bender-Gestalt Test (Figure 5-7) provided further evaluation

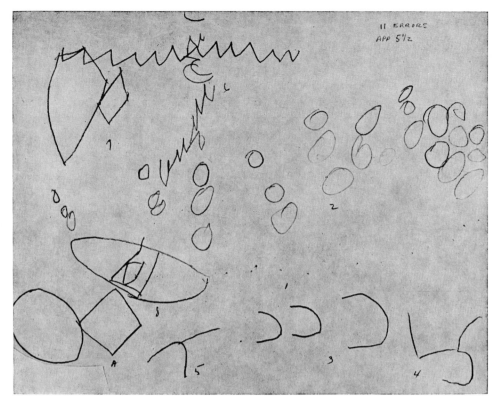

Figure 5-16. Mark's Bender design reproductions.

of visual perception and eye-hand coordination. The two-dimensional figures were presented separately on cards and Mark was asked to copy them just as he saw them — no speed or memory was required for this test. Mark's difficulty in perceiving and reproducing two-dimensional spatial relationships was evident from his reproductions (Fig. 5-16) which were at about the five and one-half year level. His Draw-A-Person was also immature (Fig. 5-17). Further study of his difficulty in visual-motor function is illustrated by some examples of his performance on the Frostig Developmental Test of Visual Perception. Mark showed his poor small motor coordination in his attempt to guide his pencil without going outside the boundary lines (Fig. 5-18). In Figure 5-19 (finding one just like the one in the box), his confusion with two-dimensional space was shown by his choice of mirror images for the flower and the block. Even with a series of dots to help him, Mark had difficulty reproducing two-dimensional figures (Figs. 5-20 and 5-21).

We now begin to understand his difficulty in coping with the complicated two-dimensional spatial relationships of letters and words. On further

testing, Mark showed severe weakness in visual memory and auditory tracking but good ability in auditory discrimination. Thus Mark, despite his
overall normal intelligence, had severe weaknesses in visual perception, visual memory, motor coordination and auditory tracking.

Mark was enrolled in one of our classes at the beginning of the summer
session after completing first grade.* Figure 5-22 is an example of his

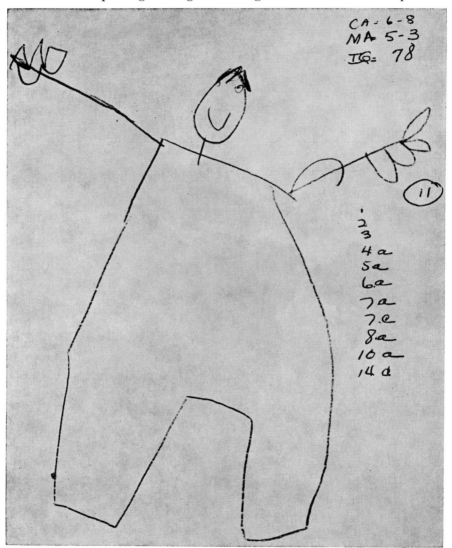

Figure 5-17. Mark's Draw-A-Person.

*The examples of Mark's progress are made possible by the efforts of Mrs. King Sams,
remedial teacher, University of California Pediatric Reading and Language Development
Clinic.

struggle with a series of *ap* words. Six weeks later he appeared much more sure in his use of the pencil in printing (Fig. 5-23). When he reached the third grade, Mark was reading at grade level at high second grade speed. His spelling, as so often true with these children, lagged behind at 2.3 grade level on the WRAT. Figure 5-24 is an example of Mark's beginning mastery of cursive writing. At the age of nine and three-quarters years his Bender reproductions showed improvement over his previous testing (Fig. 5-25), but scored two years below his chronological age. His great difficulty in visual memory for two-dimensional figures is illustrated by an example of his attempts to copy the geometric forms from the Benton Visual Retention Test from memory (Fig. 5-26).

Mark will continue to need understanding and help as he proceeds through the upper grades and faces more demands for expressing himself with the written word. He is still a cooperative hard-working boy with an air of self-confidence. The observations of his teacher and school nurse of his early learning difficulty enabled Mark to be evaluated and understood before too much harm was done. The physician should also play a role in early recognition of learning difficulties.

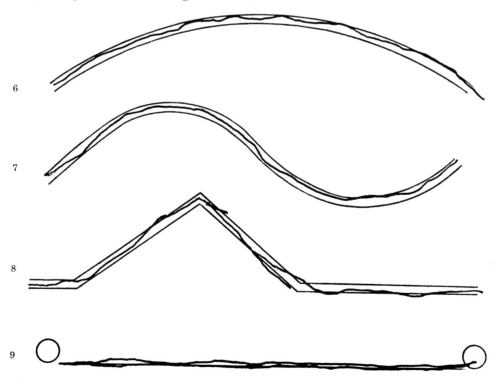

Figure 5-18. Mark's difficulty with the test for Eye-Motor Coordination from the Frostig Developmental Test of Visual Perception.

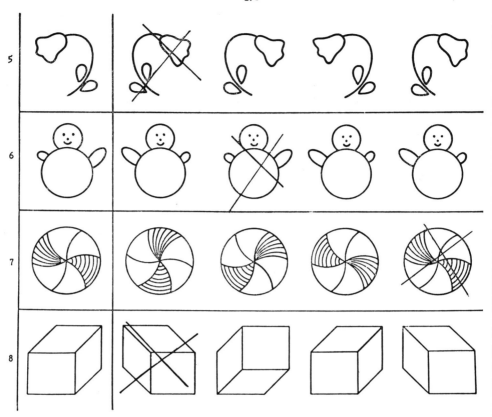

Figure 5-19. Mark's difficulty with the test for Position-in-Space from the Frostig Developmental Test of Visual Perception.

PHYSICIAN'S INDEX OF SUSPICION FOR LEARNING DISORDERS

The weaknesses in the various central nervous system functions involved in learning language skills may be on the basis of developmental deviations in the central nervous system from genetic origin, or due to insults during the prenatal or perinatal periods, or during infancy and early childhood. In the medical history, particular attention should be given to possible clues to central nervous system dysfunction. The physician should develop an *Index of Suspicion* from the following clues, no one of which will lead to a diagnosis of *specific learning disorders,* but the total profile of which will be significant:

1. *Sex.* Males are more vulnerable but, obviously, this alone will not lead to learning disability.
2. *Family history* of reading, spelling or speech disorders.

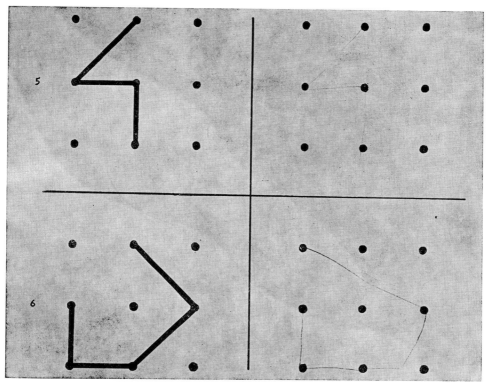

Figure 5-20. Mark's difficulty with the test for Spatial Relations from the Frostig Developmental Test of Visual Perception.

3. *Illness* or *difficulty* of the mother *during pregnancy,* including spotting, bleeding or toxemia.

4. *Birth history,* including prematurity, prolonged or precipitous labor or unusual delivery, perinatal anoxia.

5. *Neonatal course,* including sucking ability and general activity compared to that of siblings: a history of poor sucking, excessive sleeping, apathy or increased irritability may indicate deviation in central nervous system function.

6. *Developmental milestones* in comparison to siblings, especially *speech development* and large and small *motor coordination.* A significant number of children who have had a history of delayed speech development also have had difficulty in academic language skills.[16] Many children with learning difficulties have associated problems in large muscle coordination, a history of awkwardness and clumsiness as preschoolers and, at school age, poor ability in those sports which require skilled coordination, e.g., baseball. Even

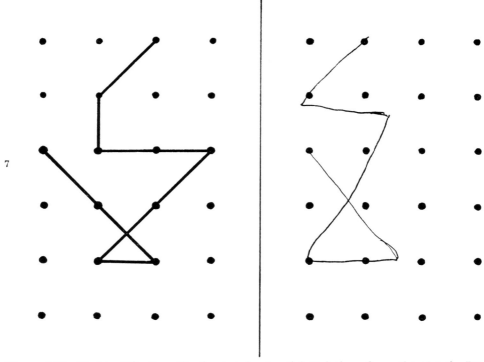

Figure 5-21. Mark's difficulty wtih the test for Spatial Relations from the Frostig Developmental Test of Visual Perception.

greater delays are usually apparent in small muscle coordination when the parents note the child's awkwardness and/or disinterest in coloring, cutting, tying shoes and using eating utensils.

7. *Illness or accidents* that could cause *central nervous system insult or injury* (central nervous system infections, severe dehydration in infancy).

8. Associated with learning problems and central nervous system dysfunction may be a group of symptoms which make up the *hyperkinetic syndrome*. Children with this syndrome are usually brought to the physician as behavior problems. Their symptoms of hyperactivity, distractibility, short attention span, emotional lability, cyclic behavior, low frustration tolerance, poor impulse control, overreactivity to excitement, temper outbursts and clumsiness make them difficult to live with or even to tolerate in the doctor's office. Relatives and neighbors often make the parents feel as though they are to blame for the child's behavior which makes them appear and feel failures as parents. It is easy for them to become resentful

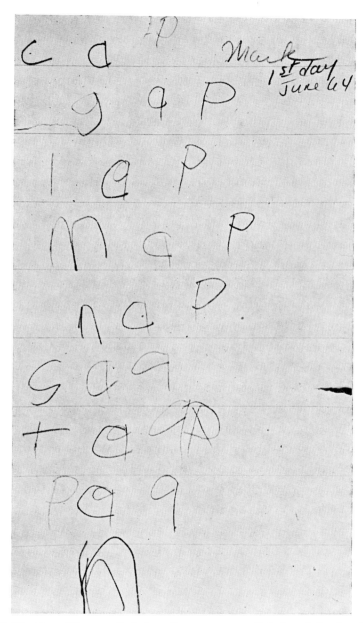

Figure 5-22. Mark's spelling on first day of summer remedial class following his completion of first grade.

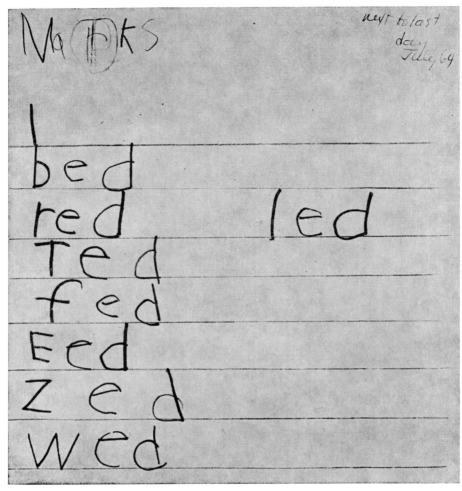

Figure 5-23. Mark's spelling after six weeks of summer remedial class.

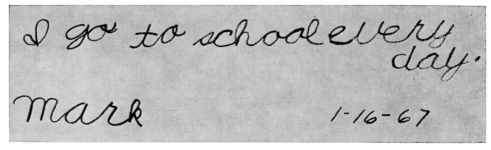

Figure 5-24. Mark's beginning mastery of cursive writing (9 years 8 months of age).

of the child with resulting poor parent-child relationship. When this type of child enters school, he often disrupts the classroom and adds to the parents' resentment and anxiety. These parents need sympathetic help rather than the criticism which they often receive from professionals.

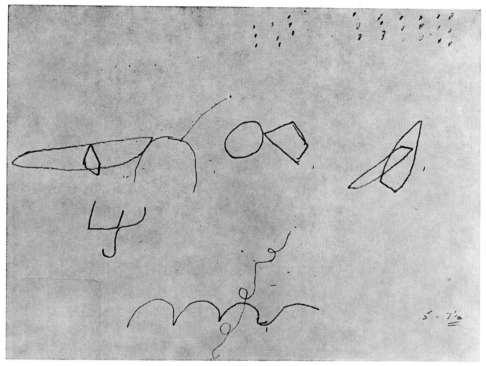

Figure 5-25. Mark's Bender design reproductions at age 9 years 8 months.

The following factors are not necessarily specific to learning disabilities, but may severely increase the problems for the child with a learning disorder:

9. *Chronic illness and physical handicaps.* These may cause the child to miss much school and get behind in his learning and school work. He may begin to dread school and make destructive use of his illness in a vicious cycle of increased symptoms and increased school absence.

10. *Unrecognized seizures.* Petit mal and psychomotor seizures, especially, may often masquerade as inattention, day dreaming, temper outbursts and bizzare behavior.

11. *Cultural factors.* Different native tongue or dialect, different behav-

ior standards, poor nutrition, insufficient rest and frequent changes of school can present severe handicaps.

12. *Dysfunctional home environment.* Especially poor communication in the family and disturbed relationship between parents.

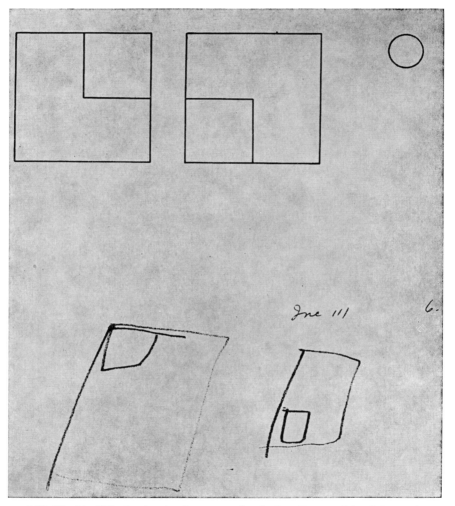

Figure 5-26. Mark's difficulty in visual memory for design, Benton Visual Retention Test.

PHYSICAL EXAMINATION

Special attention should be given to the following:

Vision. It is the opinion of most ophthalmologists that although visual and ocular difficulties seldom cause difficulty in learning to read,[17] poor visual acuity, strabismus and astigmatism may contribute to fatigue and slow rate in reading.

Hearing. The possibility of a *fluctuating hearing loss* should be considered if parents or teachers complain that, at times, the child seems to have difficulty in listening. The child with a *high frequency hearing loss* and difficulty in hearing the high frequency consonants, such as *s, t, p,* may be commonly misdiagnosed because he can hear low frequency tuning forks, most environmental noise and the vowel sounds of speech. These children are frequently accused of not paying attention.

Speech and language. Since language development is the fundamental basis for learning to read, write and spell, the early assessment of the child's speech and language development is most important. If a child is not using any words by the age of two years a developmental assessment and an evaluation of his hearing should be made. If his speech is not reasonably intelligible to the immediate family by the age of four years, a comprehensive evaluation — including psychological testing and hearing and speech evaluation — should be made. It is easy for the physician to be unaware of a speech or language deviation, since many children are reluctant to talk in the doctor's office. A careful history from the parents may alert the physician to this important developmental deviation.

Motor coordination. Observation of the child as he dresses and buttons his clothes, and his use of paper and pencil, can be most informative. A preliminary assessment of his visual-motor coordination can be made by asking him to do the following:

> Draw the best man he can
> Copy a circle already drawn (at age 3 years)
> Copy a + in imitation (at age 4 years)
> Copy a square (at age 5 years)
> Copy a triangle (at age 6 years)
> Copy a diamond (at age 7 years)

Hopefully, the time will come soon when children with potential learning disabilities can be detected and evaluated before they even start kindergarten, so that their deficiences can be understood and special help given before they experience even half a year of failure.

MEDICAL MANAGEMENT

Some children with the hyperkinetic syndrome show dramatic improvement on special medication, particularly that which appears to enable them to screen out multiple stimuli and attend to one. In our experience, the first drugs of choice are the amphetamines, the second Ritalin®, with the dosage tailored to the requirements of the individual child.

One of the most important aspects of medical management for all children with specific learning disorders concerns help for the maligned parents and teachers who have the daily task of working with them. Almost all the parents of the children in our Pediatric Reading and Language Development Clinic have been made to feel at fault for their chldren's learning difficulties, especially for their hyperactive behavior. In their frustration and bewilderment, parents easily become defensive, place all the blame on the teacher and may work against, rather than with, the school system.

They need much help in understanding their child's specific problem. Frequently, the child may be seen by the pediatrician, the neurologist, the psychologist, the hearing and speech consultant, or the psychiatrist, and the parents are confronted with confusing and conflicting information that leaves them utterly bewildered. It is essential that someone tie this information together and present it in a meaningful way to the parents as well as the classroom teacher. It is not unusual for evaluation reports to end up in the files of the school psychologist or school guidance personnel, with the teacher unaware that the child has been studied.

Who should help parents understand the child's problem? Whoever can do it best. It might be the school psychologist, the principal, the teacher, the physician, or the school social worker. It would be to the child's advantage if they all could. In our pediatric training program we try to train tomorrow's physicians to do this.

As special programs for these children are developed in the school system, it is essential that parents understand the program and cooperate with the school. Without parent cooperation and support any program is doomed to failure. We have found regular parent meetings to be of great value in the Pediatric Reading and Language Development Clinic.

Our aim is to rear children to become productive adults with a feeling of worth and some value to society. From our experience in seeing children with school problems, however, *it appears that our society has devised an educational system that defeats this purpose for many children and creates much frustration and anxiety in dedicated teachers and parents.* We talk of the importance of respect for the individual and yet our democratic educational system is not able to practice this. Democratic education does not mean the same and equal teaching for all. Considering the complexity of the brain and the almost infinite interconnections required for integration of its functions,[18] it would not appear reasonable to look for a single lesion as a cause for learning disorders or a single teaching method as a cure.

In recent years, we have heard heated declarations from proponents who support their own panacea for these educational problems. Individual strength and weaknesses in learning must be understood and methods developed to meet them. But we lag badly. Since Sputnik there has been increased emphasis on achievement and excellence. This *may* be fine for the excellent, but the all too frequent ruthless competition for grades results in little or no reward for less-than-excellent students. We see parents, especially from suburbia, who panic if their child does not get top grades.

The pressures put on some children today are horrendous, especially those with learning problems on the basis of real weaknesses in central nervous system functions involved in learning to read, write and spell, who are constantly told by teachers, parents and sometimes physicians, "You could do better if you tried." This slogan follows them wherever they go. These children say they do try, but cannot do better. In their discouragement with failure, they develop defenses familiar to us all — they clown, misbehave, become belligerent or apathetic and develop an "I don't care" outward appearance. Their teachers and parents suffer too. Perhaps we need to reevaluate our long range aims and educate ourselves and parents in understanding human differences, individual strengths and weaknesses, instead of trying to force children into a system where they have little chance of success.

The future of any nation is directly related to the optimal development and education of its children. It is tragic that our affluent society is still unable to meet the needs of so many of our future citizens, and that so many of our children continue to be subjected to the occupational hazard of failure in their job of going to school.

Some children can learn to read and write at perhaps age three years, others need much more readiness training and much special assistance in the early years of school. Yet, parents (and the child) are often made to feel great failures if the child is not in step with the "norm" in all abilities. We are all trying to march to a system that needs changing. Our efforts should go toward changing the system so that the varying developmental rates and intellectual strengths and weaknesses can be evaluated and individually met in educating our children.

REFERENCES

1. Schreiber, D. (Ed.) : *Guidance and the School Dropout.* Washington, D.C., Project: School Dropouts, National Education Association, 1964, p. 267.
2. Neisser, E.: *School Failures and Dropouts.* Public Affairs Pamphlet #346, New York, Public Affairs Committee, 1963.
3. Eisenberg, L.: Reading retardation: I. Psychiatric and sociologic aspects, *Pediatrics, 37:352,* 1966.
4. Richardson, S.: *Learning Disabilities: An Introduction.* Palo Alto, Charles Dorsey Armstrong Memorial Foundation Seminar on Dyslexia, May 1966.
5. Rambeau, J., and Rambeau, M.: *Jim Forest and Dead Man's Peak.* San Francisco Harr Wagner, 1959.

6. GALLAGHER, J.R.: Specific language disability (dyslexia), *Clin Proc Child Hosp, 16:* 3, 1960.

7. GRAY, S.: *Overcoming Learning Handicaps Imposed by Deprivation.* Pre-School and Early School Enrichment Conference, Berkeley, U. of Calif. Extension, March 1966.

8. BEREITER, C., and ENGELMANN, S.: *Teaching Disadvantaged Children in the Pre-school,* Englewood Cliffs, Prentice-Hall, 1966, p. 34.

9. DE HIRSCH, K.; JANSKY, J., and LANGFORD, W.: *Predicting Reading Failure.* New York, Harper, 1966.

10. JOHNSON, D., and MYKLEBUST, H.: *Learning Disabilities.* New York, Grune, 1967.

11. CLEMENTS, S.D.: *Minimal Brain Dysfunction in Children, Terminology and Identification.* Washington, D.C., NINDB Monograph No. 3, U.S. Dept. Health, Education and Welfare, 1966.

12. BATEMAN, B.: Learning disorders. *Rev Educ Res, 36:*93, 1966.

13. ILG, F., and AMES, L.: *School Readiness.* New York, Harper, 1966.

14. FROSTIG, M.: The needs of teachers for specialized information on reading. In *The Teacher of Brain-Injured Children: A Discussion of the Bases of Competency.* Syracuse, Syracuse U.P., 1966, p. 87.

15. SLOAN, W.: The Lincoln Oseretsky motor development scale. *Genet Psychol Monogr, 51:*183, 1955.

16. GOFMAN, H.; FLOWER, R.; BUCKMAN, W.; HITCHCOCK, E.; HARVIN, D., and LEIB, S.: *Follow-up Studies of 'Normal' Children with Delayed Language Development.* Report to Western Society for Pediatric Research, Portland, Ore., November 1965.

17. BETTMAN, J.; STERN, E.; WHITSELL, L., and GOFMAN, H.: Cerebral dominance in developmental dyslexia. *Arch Ophthal, 78:*722, 1967.

18. MASLAND, R.: Brain mechanisms underlying the language function. *Bull Orton Soc, 17:*1, 1967.

APPENDIX

Tests Used	Reference
Bender	BENDER, LAURETTA: *Visual Motor Gestalt Test. New York,* The American Orthopsychiatric Association, Inc., 1946.
Benton	BENTON, ARTHUR L.: *The Revised Visual Retention Test,* New York, The Psychological Corporation, 1955.
Frostig	FROSTIG, MARIANNE: *Developmental Test of Visual Perception.* Palo Alto, California, Consulting Psychologists Press, 1963.
Gilmore	GILMORE, JOHN V.: *Gilmore Oral Reading Test.* New York, Harcourt, Brace & World, Inc., 1951.
Koppitz	KOPPITZ, ELIZABETH M.: *The Bender Gestalt Test for Young Children.* New York, Grune & Stratton, 1964.
Wepman	WEPMAN, JOSEPH: *Auditory Discrimination Test.* Chicago, Language Research Associates, 1958.
WISC	WECHSLER, DAVID: *Wechsler Intelligence Scale for Children.* New York, The Psychological Corporation, 1949.
WRAT	JASTAK, J.F., BIJOU, S.W., JASTAK, S.R.: *Wide Range Achievement Test, Reading, Spelling, Arithmetic from Pre-School to College.* Wilmington, Del., Guidance Associates, 1965.

Chapter 6

Psychiatric Disability and Learning Problems

L. F. KURLANDER *and* DOROTHY COLODNY

CHILDREN WITH LEARNING DISORDERS are fortunate if they have no associated problems of behavior; they are fortunate and rare if they have no secondary problems of feeling. Such disorders of behavior and feeling are often mistaken by parents and professional workers for primary problems of emotion and regarded as though they were entirely interpersonal in origin. It is important to identify the many kinds of learning problems, largely because if this is done, not only academic failure but psychiatric symptoms may be avoided. Even later when such symptoms are present, relief of the learning problem itself may be the most explicit and economical treatment for them.

Child psychiatry since Freud has developed a traditional and very strongly psychoanalytic bias, which seems to be changing, though rather slowly. It first recognized, then emphasized almost exclusively, the importance of the family constellation in the growth of emotional health in childhood. The pioneers, Anna Freud, Bowlby, Spitz, Allen, Erikson and many others fostered a humane and sensitive style of concern with the child's subjective experience and the parents' experience and interaction with the child. Both diagnosis and treatment were oriented toward these issues. The atmosphere of the Child Guidance Movement in the United States has been one of enthusiastic belief that emotional trouble, that is to say, anxiety and unhealthy defense against it, could be understood and even cured if it was viewed as the product of unconscious motivation. If the young patient could be helped to see and oppose his unacceptable drives, and if at the same time parents could be led to acknowledge and modify their unconscious mistakes, children should get well. The evidence for this process has been questioned by students of scientific method, but it is true that when such treatment has been practiced by kindly and civilized therapists, certain symptoms are often diminished. The strength of this point of view has been that, at its best, it is very respectful of the individual and his feelings, and it is a gentle and poetic philosophy. Its weakness has been a tendency to stagnation and dogmatism; a failure to integrate new knowledge of child development, especially in the study of biological differences; and a reluctance to explore the psychological processes which are precursors of the level of symbolism at which psychoanalytic theory operates. At its very worst, it is therapeutically nihilistic and fixes blame on parents whose children do not respond to its methods.

This trend has greatly influenced medicine, education and the social sciences. Exclusive emphasis on family dynamics and opposition to medical and educational management of psychiatric disorders was once scientifically progressive, but now represents a lag, sometimes a hindrance to the care of troubled children. It is frequently hard for us to develop new ideas without an atmosphere of controversy, and we focus on the argument rather than the child, line up in terms of the interest in learning *or* in emotion instead of trying to define the fascinating interactions. In the field of learning disability, we may deny the genuine emotional pain.

In the years since Schilder and Bender first noted the organic signs of mental illness in children, there has been rich and exciting exploration of the neurophysiological basis of emotional disorder. For years, the characteristics of the post-encephalitic behavior disorder in children was known — that the affected child was restless, irritable and explosive. It was also known that drugs and delirium produced symptoms which, in an undrugged and healthy child, would be called "functional." But in the past two decades, the students of less drastic brain damage have slowly documented the classic triad of minimal neurological handicap (hyperactivity, distractibility, impulsivity) which so often accompanies and compounds learning trouble. The disabling handicaps of perception have been catalogued and methods of retraining developed. Cognition and how it can be improved has been studied. Variations in temperament and deviations in developmental patterning have been recorded. It has been shown how failures in formal learning processes affect the development of socialization. Correlations between certain metabolic disturbances and behavior and learning have been made, such observations as transient disruption of behavior in porphyria, permanent failure of learning and social behavior in phenylketonuria. The causes of disabilities are not always clear, but many etiological elements have been indicated; to the likelihood of many different prenatal and postnatal insults is added the probability of some genetic patterns in learning handicap. Our nomenclature has changed with our concepts; at present, *minimal brain dysfunction* is the official term for various combinations of neurological deviation which produce difficulty in learning and behavior.

Child psychiatry, as a discipline, has always acknowledged the glaring cases of gross neurological disorder related to known neurological disease. The American Psychiatric Association nosology includes "chronic brain syndrome with behavior disorder." But for statistical purposes and on medical insurance forms, we are still obliged to choose whether a child suffers from an "organic" disorder of the classic sort or a "neurotic" disorder with quite different traits. It used to be rather simple to compare the two blandly: the "organic" symptoms had little interpersonal meaning; the "neurotic" disorder was accorded complicated and causal motivation. Doctors, teachers, social workers, parents felt obliged to determine whether failure to read was "organic" or "emotional," a "learning block" or a "learning disability." Generally the organic handicaps were considered fixed and untreatable and probably this was an additional reason well-meaning adults were reluctant to attach the diagnosis to an innocent child. The emotional disorders allegedly responded to appropriate psychotherapy.

Some years ago, it was noted that many children with authenticated minimal cerebral dysfunction were first seen in psychiatric consultation for symptoms which had been always regarded as "neurotic." We called these manifestations "pseudoneurosis" and tried to define the differences in causation, significance and requirements between the two. The true "neurotics" presumably had intact central nervous systems. We assumed they were reacting to external pressures, mainly poor child-rearing practices, by internalizing their problems as intrapsychic conflicts, expressing these in turn by symptoms with symbolic meaning. We then believed that they required psychotherapy, with insight as its goal, for them and for their parents, as well as more permissive handling at home and at school. The "pseudoneurotics" by comparison, we thought, suffered mainly from neurological malfunction and their awareness of it, as well as their secondarily disturbed family relationships; they expressed their primary biological anxiety and secondary interpersonal anxiety in symptoms which were superficially much like those of the other children. But we thought they needed a very different kind of help. Instead of permissive insight therapy, we prescribed for them external guidance, medicine, tutoring, reinforcement for their disorganized physical and mental patterns and, for their parents, education and consultation, rather than actual psychotherapy.

This has proved to be a somewhat misleading contrast, trapping us into an arbitrary dichotomy. The old belief that a child's psychiatric ailment was either a neurotic one with complex psychodynamics or an organic one in which the symptoms were without much meaning did, it is true, shift slightly with our apparent sophistication, to a statement that the disorder was a neurotic one with certain dynamics or an organic one with very different ones.

We are in trouble with this new contrast because we see fewer and fewer "pure" neurotics. As our index of suspicion of some kind of neurophysiological dysfunction rises and as we apply the same diagnostic tests to all the children we see, we find that a high percentage of our patients prove to show some of the indications we had previously confined to the organic side. That is, they show some lifelong undue vulnerability to anxiety, some striking peculiarity in developmental history, some minor neurological signs, some characteristic irregularities on psychological testing, some measurable or at least discernible disability in communication skills. If we take the trouble to look, a surprisingly high number display gross perceptual or conceptual deficit or marked disinhibition, though it is true this may not be the parents' presenting complaint. By now, we have rather sheepishly concluded that it is wiser to stop talking about real and false neurosis and to say instead that whenever a child appears with any significant psychiatric symptom, we must consider the possibility that it may mask a treatable neurological handicap.

Even the word "mask" is a little imprudent. Anna Freud taught us long ago that, except in acute panic states, we do not observe anxiety directly but only the psychological defenses against it. We do not see the wind but the trees as they bend before it. Psychological symptoms are all outward signs of an inner feeling of helplessness, whether it is caused by the strength of the Freudian "instincts" or the weakness of perceptual or cognitive skills.

Children are appropriate subjects for psychiatric investigation if they have obvious excessive anxiety or if they express their anxiety, even normal amounts of it, deviously or in abnormal ways. But we must note that a certain kind of unacceptable conduct is not the result of anxiety but the direct consequence of the impaired skills; we need not consider these as "emotional problems" or "psychological" but as disturbances of *behavior,* due primarily to the cerebral dysfunction. Psychiatrists and those oriented to psychological thought have been taught a code of meaning and motive to apply, a bit uncritically, to certain kinds of behavior. For instance, hyperactivity means "flight from relationships"; hypoactivity, "withdrawal into fantasy"; destructiveness, "hostility"; tics, "hidden wishes"; failure to read, "block against learning"; and depression, "anger against the self." But there are alternatives which to many of us sometimes appear more likely. Hyperactivity may simply express immaturity of the nervous system; hypoactivity may be a lack of motor and interpersonal skills; destructiveness may be a random combination of hyperactivity, poor motor skills and poor judgment which comes from delayed ability to abstract. Tics may be pure motor overflow under any kind of stress. Failure to read is often either developmental delay or some degree of dyslexia. Depression may be frank awareness of present and potential biological failure.

At times, this approach may seem absurd in its simplicity. A bright child's failure to understand a command may be literal failure to comprehend language in certain circumstances. It is not necessarily a power battle with the parent of the same or opposite sex, or hostile negativism. If we realize that behavior is at all times dependent on complex, fluctuating bio-chemical processes and electrical circuitry, we need strain ourselves no further than to remember that it is possible to short a circuit or blow a fuse. It is true that this kind of behavior does not often appear alone without secondary distortions of feeling, since children learn early to interpret their own behavior in the same idiom as do those around them.

Relative freedom from anxiety depends on intact bodily equipment and reasonably high self-esteem, a sense of adequacy in the physical and social world. Ideally, a child develops his powers in an orderly sequence: motor, sensory, perceptual, cognitive, with interpersonal development as a reflection and parallel of these. If a child's motor skills are immature and unstable, if his image of his world is inaccurate or fluctuates, if his grasp of language or ideas does not meet the expectation for his age, he suffers most of the time from an awareness of imminent danger; first he may fear falling down physically, later falling down in his parents' eyes, last falling down in his own eyes. This consciousness of personal inadequacy was called "castration anxiety" by early psychoanalysts who realized, with great sensitivity, that a child can suffer intensely from his own deficits, whether real or fancied; he compares himself with others, even with adults; he often fears he will be punished for his shortcomings. Rightly or wrongly, he feels unlovable and unloved.

The processes of coping with anxiety have been well described in many places, especially by Freud and Anna Freud, Sullivan, Horney, Lois Murphy, etc. The techniques by which humans unconsciously keep out of awareness a sense of unlovability, failure, danger to the self are exceedingly ingenious. These same processes, we now realize, are invoked whether the anxious feeling of helplessness is based on real handicaps or those imputed to a child by parents who seem to ask too much of him. These mechanisms, however, do not always work. We consider them neurotic if they perpetuate rather than relieve anxiety. Often, although a device may temporarily distract a child or his parents from his real fear or his real disability, it does not do this well enough; it takes too much energy, it is in itself too disabling. These are the mechanisms we call "neurotic symptoms," which perform a service at too high a price and substitute one kind of unhappiness for another.

To confirm a suspicion that true disabilities may underlie or coexist with neurotic symptoms, one is obliged to diagnose them all precisely, using the best instruments available. This requires a careful study of each patient's constitution and each patient's life, an attempt to discover the stresses bearing upon him and to estimate the relative pressures of each and how long they have been operating. We must explore the family background, looking for a history of similar and related complaints and the current family atmosphere, seeking the attitudes of the patient toward himself and others and others' attitudes toward him. We must put parents sufficiently at ease so they can tell us fully and truthfully the story of the patient's conception, prenatal and postnatal development and his course in the family, school and neighborhood. We must try to define his diffuse temperamental tendencies. We must separate, if possible, troubles caused by real mishandling or real mental illness or real ignorance or hatefulness in parents from troubles due to secondary interaction of a child with basically wholesome parents who are upset and confused because their good and honest efforts have failed. We must sort out the child's primary weakness, his failure to develop skills properly and at the proper time, his tendency to perceive partly and to react wholly, his inner sense of inadequacy due to failures in performance, achievement and comprehension from his difficulty due to damaged self-esteem and his attempts to hide it from himself and others.

So long as we do not assume that the presence of a disability or the existence of family distress is the cause of all the observed data, the diagnostic procedure may be brief or extensive. Most children in trouble are entitled eventually to history, physical examination, psychological testing and evaluation of academic skills. But sometimes a diagnostic shortcut and a therapeutic trial is justified if we do not mistake it for a definite answer.

Psychiatric examination is a relatively unstructured procedure and is done differently by every doctor. Its goal is to note the sources and expression of the child's anxiety. One observes the terms on which he deals with his own physical equipment, with a stranger and with a social situation. We watch his motility, his tempo, his speech, mood, his apparent intellectual skills, his ability to receive communication and reply; we especially seek out indications of what this child is doing to put himself at ease and how he presents himself to a representative of the outside world. We encourage him to reveal as much as he can of his feelings about himself and others and notice if he cannot do this, or if he confides too easily. We take a sample, so to speak, of his thoughts and feelings. We make a particular effort to observe what defenses against anxiety he demonstrates or reports, and we must be willing to take his complaints at face value, at times, without being too symbolic or too clever. Since we are primarily physicians, in this examination we try to answer the fundamental medical question: where and how much does it hurt?

The physical examination should, in addition to thorough general steps, include a search for the minimal and shifting signs which are known to accompany disorders of learning. The classical neurological examination does not suffice, and many children with severe handicaps are given clean bills of health by excellent neurologists who are not especially interested in minimal cerebral dysfunction. We are told, "There is no evidence of disease," and this is true. But we are not looking only for disease processes or even evidence of past brain damage. Instead, we are seeking conditions which prevent optimum functioning now. At times, this part of the study is done most usefully by a pediatrician or psychiatrist or family doctor who is willing to look for the "soft" signs and to apply some simple but very meaningful paper-and-pencil tests.

Often psychological testing is a more sensitive tool for this purpose than clinical examination, if the psychologist is well informed and the tests are chosen and reported correctly. Many children are tested for IQ and cleared of handicap because the numerical average of the many abilities tested is reported as a simple score. This is very misleading. What is needed is a profile displaying the scatter of the child's abilities, the inconsistencies between one skill and another, the incompatibility between verbal and performance skills or fluctuations among them. This is what causes adults to be puzzled by the child and the child to be puzzled by himself. His perceptual abilities must be tested and clues sought that he may be compensating with undue effort for an old visual-perceptual handicap or else that he has compensated for the visual handicap while still showing difficulty in sorting out auditory or other stimuli. Estimates are needed of the child's ability to attend, concentrate, form abstractions and any hint of his cognitive style should be mentioned, for we are greatly concerned with his ability to organize the raw material of his world. An educator's estimate of his academic skills, apart from his underlying ability and potential, is of the greatest use. This should include more than whether he can read aloud at grade level but should be an estimate of his efficiency and style in listening, speaking, reading and writing and an opinion whether he has perhaps modified his own dyslexia with too much fatigue and emotional strain.

For a time, it seemed that a machine could answer our questions, but the electroencephalograph was given undue importance in this area since it cannot rule learning handicaps in or out. When other data suggest a localized lesion or a true disorder of consciousness, then an EEG is essential. It can be diagnostic or lifesaving. But its value to us depends on the skill and point of view of the neurologist who reads the tracing and how the reading is applied to the total problem.

When the results of the foregoing tests are coordinated, they should be conveyed to the parents and to the child. One must gauge the meaning of a handicap to each person. Parents may be relieved at the thought that the child has a remediable disorder to which we can give a name. This may be a great comfort after self-accusation and criticisms of poor mothering or fathering from relatives or neighbors or the child himself. To other parents, the idea of a defect is a very wounding thought; they prefer to be blamed rather than to see themselves the blind transmitters of a genetic taint, or helpless before the biological facts of neurological disease or individual differences. They may have some need to blame each other as part of a conflict in which this child is very incidental. They may, with great difficulty, yield the notion that the child himself is quite free to change his ways if he would try harder. Or they may feel very guilty at the discovery that they have been punishing the child for behavior beyond his control.

The child himself, from an early age, has some opinions on this subject. Like his parents, he has his entrenched or preferred way of regarding his problems. He may see himself as bad, dumb or both; or as mistreated. He may insist that he is failing on purpose or is destructive intentionally, since he too can be frightened by the thought of helplessness before his handicaps. He needs to know that though he has a disability, it can be helped; though he is to be blamed no longer, he still has a responsibility to help himself. We cannot expect this of him unless we can promise him more kinds of aid than he has had before. He needs to be told quite bluntly, if it is true, that he is not stupid and is not crazy; that, like everyone, he has weaknesses, and his are connected with learning and self-control. He often has picked up strange notions about why his head is being examined, tested, wired. One can usually explain the truth without frightening any child who can understand language at all.

If we discover that the actual disability is minor, compared to the secondary complications of failure and resentment in parent and child, this must be stated just as clearly. Those parents who feel too immature to give sufficient emotional support to their children have, in recent years, become quite knowledgeable about "brain damage" and "neurological handicap" and can use this means of denying their other difficulties. It is possible to offer a remedy for the minor handicap and the major disturbed relationship with a minimum of rancor and blaming. One wonders sometimes if we need insist so strongly that parents verbally acknowledge their error so long as they are willing, even without confession, to work toward change. Often, if one can first modify the child's minimal hyperactivity, or even tantrums normal to his age, the parent can become surprisingly frank and helpful.

We are constantly reminded that anxious parents and children must be reassured. Reassurance, particularly for the adolescent with defects, does not consist in perpetuating the myth that nothing is wrong. If we do this, he distrusts us because he knows better. He does not, however, know *enough* better. Until we tell him that he perseverates, and what this is, he thinks he is stubborn; till we tell him about his dyslexia, he believes himself globally stupid. If we conceal the fact that his brain may be subject to lapses of attention or electrical storms, he has reason to fear he is "losing his mind."

When the patient has appeared in our office because of specific neurotic symptoms, displaced fears, obsessions, etc., both he and his family need to be told the nature of the phenomena. We need not conceal the fact that some children are more prone than others to anxiety, from whatever cause and to symptom formation when their lives exact too much from them. They can be taught to recognize their own symptoms (such as tics) and to scrutinize their lives and limit their burdens just as a gardener with a backache knows when he must put down his hoe. One need not spend years waiting for the patient or his parents to stumble on these truths in a prolonged, undirected, psychotherapeutic experience when we have the benefit of the recorded experience of doctors and patients before us.

Treatment must await a diagnostic conclusion. *We find no usefulness in the practice of drifting into open-ended psychotherapy and waiting for a diagnosis to become apparent.* Scientific medicine has learned the dangers of haphazard application of a single treatment before diagnosis, whether it is an antibiotic or psychoanalysis. But for the child with learning disability and his parent, the diagnostic procedure and the diagnosis itself may be the most curative experience of all. Being taken seriously, questioned rather than reproached, included in the project of investigation, informed of our goals, seems to relieve them of the feeling that the purpose of the study is to fix blame. And since neither need be accused at the expense of the other one, parent and child can afford to be on better terms from the start. They can be shown in each other's presence how very hard life has been for all of them. Both can be enlisted in a battle against the handicap, rather than encouraged to complain about each other.

If a specific learning disorder has been identified and a remedial class or good tutor is at hand, it is often worth a trial of this one relatively simple measure alone. With improvement in performance, many anxieties lessen and secondary symptoms sometimes subside without further treatment. Many times, of course, the associated abnormalities of attention and motility prevent the best use of remedial education. Then medication is the second resource. Usually at this point, someone — parent, teacher or family doctor — challenges the wisdom of "suppressing" the psychological symptoms with drugs before they are completely understood and "worked through." The question remains controversial but we see it as a measure which allows a child and those around him to experience him as less restless, demanding and explosive, and this appears to us to be an absolute good. No one has ever proved conclusively that insight (for which weary acquiescence is often mistaken) is the only cure for the painful symptoms of anxiety.

In young children, if the symptoms can be controlled by drugs while maturation is allowed to take place, the drug can many times be discontinued later and the child maintains his gains since, in addition to whatever reorganization has happened in the nervous system, the new picture of the child's personality will persist in his own and his parents' mind. Even if he does continue to need a tranquilizer or psychic energizer for some time, it can be prescribed in carefully supervised nontoxic doses and relieves as much suffering, we think, as insulin or penicillin. The passion of advocates and opponents of medication in psychological disorders of children is an enthralling subject on which a good deal has been written elsewhere. What the child himself thinks of this medicine is interesting, too, but should be no more decisive in choosing his treatment than what he thinks of other necessary drugs. If he is not encouraged to play games and drive wedges among adults about it, he usually can recognize and reports its effects, good and bad, and can be enlisted in deciding the best drug and dosage.

Because so much of his learning and social trouble is related to awkwardness and motor disability, any legitimate program of physical training which reinforces the child's physical strength, coordination and directionality is good for him if it is done in an atmosphere which acknowledges his special needs and does not make grandiose promises. Swimming, dancing, judo, bicycling, etc., all can be helpful when adapted to the child's current level of functioning.

Patterning in his life at home and in school with routine and protection from overstimulation is necessary. Special classes for the educationally handicapped are growing as many states acknowledge that money is better spent early for remediation than later for correctional homes and hospitals. Parents can learn from the special teachers a great deal about managing their children at home.

Psychotherapy is a last and expensive resort. We have described it in the past in a form we thought specific for the child with neurological handicap. Now we are beginning to think that the specificity is less for cerebral dysfunction than for the social attitudes we see today in most parents who have any trouble at home: a difficulty in knowing and transmitting the nature of childhood and its graded demands and privileges; parenthood and its privileges and responsibility; a real failure in feeling their right to authority, however loving and appropriate; an incapacity to provide what Rappaport has called an "ego bank" for the emotionally indigent child. Generally, of course, the overactive "organic" child must be shown that neither his doctor nor his parents are afraid to set limits; in spite of some muttering, he usually welcomes this. He needs a chance to speak openly about his troubles but here, too, he must be shown, both in treatment and at home, that repetitive complaints do not improve communication, are not welcome and need not be his permit for special privilege. We have seen the conventional rule of psychotherapy ("permission to say anything at all though physical attacks are forbidden") increase anxiety and lower the self-respect of both patient and therapist. One cannot urge strongly enough that, whatever his underlying pathology, no child should be permitted to abuse an adult, though he is free to describe how he feels, which is quite another thing.

One fact is clear to all; if a child's suffering is related to bad living conditions, we must try to improve them. If he cannot learn in school, no amount of talk will restore his pride till he can be helped to learn. If he is really blocked (this is uncommon), he must be helped to see that his fears are inappropriate or less appropriate than they may once have been. If he has true disability, he needs retraining of the most specific sort and at as elementary a level as the disability lies.

If his trouble is in "organically driven" behavior, this too is out of the province of the "talking cure." Time, medicine, training and understanding are the treatment of choice.

If his symptoms are neurotic defenses against anxiety, we try to alleviate the anxiety by making it unnecessary. Here the measures mentioned may possibly suffice.

But if his problems include the overall difficulties in living, which so many neurologically compromised children display, he may need from parent or therapist a special kind of help. This is the child who, instead of, or in addition to academic troubles, has chronic trouble in knowing how to live and talk with other people. He exhausts his parents, fights constantly with siblings, is the butt of playmates and classmates; he fails to recognize danger signals in human relations; he cannot gauge the emotional climate enough to come in out of the rain. We once called this incapacity "a lesion of intuition," thinking that the other needs of these children took precedence over the smooth learning of social techniques. But tests of the children and recent research in cognition more convincingly suggest that real immaturity of conceptual and language skills have made it hard for some children to learn patterns and meanings of human interaction exactly as it made it hard to learn arithmetical meaning or to understand proverbs. This child has a defect of social perception, like his impairment of visual perception, and equally he has a hard time learning more complex skills which depend on the simpler ones. He lacks self-awareness in the social sense, as he lacks a stable body image. Appreciation of this specific disability by parents and teachers can help them both to offer concrete instruction in social behavior and to protect the children from disaster while time allows them to mature.

Psychotherapy can be valuable to this kind of child. It need not be intensive or prolonged. It should simultaneously help child and parents, and sometimes brothers and sisters, to realize the meaning of the information we have obtained and to readjust their feelings about the child, his problem and their responsibilities. It emphasizes facts, rather than inferences — *what* the members of the family are doing, rather than *why* they are doing it; *what* misunderstandings have arisen rather than *why* anyone should misunderstand. For the family, it is important to validate their experience of the child's troubled functioning and how disagreeable this can be; for the child we must confirm our knowledge of his discouragement before we can show him how to operate differently. Because his disability so often includes a tendency to think too concretely for his age, we must teach him in a most literal fashion how to stay out of trouble, how to acknowledge his limitations, how to allow and encourage others to treat him better. This is unlike our old technique which focused on changing motives and assumed that if the heart were pure, the mind would know how to think. Many observers have noted that the neurologically handicapped child is singularly sweet, forgiving, guileless, lacking malice. It is not his motives but his machinery which does not work. He needs less to be inspired than instructed. And as in any psychotherapy, it is important for the patient and his parents to know what are the real issues in his life and to discourage vigorously the irrelevant and misleading symptoms, the denying, the boasting, the complaining, the accusing, the demonstrating.

Parents do not need treatment unless they, themselves, have a definable and treatable disorder. But they need a good deal of explanation, interpretation, help in understanding and help in management and some forthright help with their feelings about the child. Parents who have suffered a great deal of frustration and anger are often afflicted with a special kind of paralyzing guilt which makes it hard for them to restrain or punish a child when he may need it. These parents need a good deal of support in learning what is to be fostered and what prohibited in their child, what they should accept or ignore, and what symptoms should really alarm them. The child must know that we confer with his parents and essentially what is going on. With his tendency to disorientation, he is quite unable to deal with secret alliances or what he may feel as divided loyalties. The actual therapy can be achieved in many ways, depending on the patient's needs and the therapist's style. But simplicity and directness are essential.

The children whose needs are least likely to be met are those whose disabilities are hidden beneath accretions of secondary symptoms or whose symptoms are so dramatic and frightening that our attention is misdirected to them alone. We can cite three categories to which we should be alert, though there are many more. But we know how often the disabilities are overlooked of these three types — the gifted, the "school phobes," and the adopted children.

The gifted child with dyslexia or hyperactivity is constantly referred to psychiatrists with the assurance that since his IQ is so high, any school failure or behavior disorder must be the result of "emotional blocking." Many times, of course, he has not been tested at all and then, because his relative disability drops him only into the average range, he is regarded as a child of average endowment and disturbed behavior. Even if his disability is noted, he is often disqualified for remedial classes if his achievement is not sufficiently impaired in comparison to his classmates. He suffers particularly by the frequent reproaches from teachers and parents that if he is able to achieve in one subject, he should be able to do so in another; if he can perform well one day, it is proof that he should be able to excel every day. This ignorance of the discrepancies and fluctuations in the skills of such a child provokes resentments which may easily be compounded into real problems of motivation. Usually, the gifted child can grasp the nature of his learning patterns when it is explained to him and can choose very sensibly whether to devote his efforts to correcting a defect or to develop other skills and avoid the failures. He responds well to most modalities of treatment, if his emotional problems have not lasted too long or if his parents are not too frightened by the concept of disability to allow us to help it.

The "school phobes," better called "school refusers," divert us with the severity of their suffering and with their conspicuous family pathology. Every child psychiatrist sees a number of children every year who unaccountably refuse to go to school, claiming physical illness, unsupported by medical findings, or unbearable anxiety as an excuse. In most cases, some glaring abnormality of family life is present, usually the need of one or both parents to keep the child at home, for company or babysitting, or as a buffer in marital discord, or simply to take the parent's mind off his own troubles. Treatment for acute school refusal is simple and it works — medication for anxiety, administrative pressure on child and parents to cease truancy, psychological exploration of family interaction. Because the first two measures often relieve the symptoms and the third activity is so fascinating, we are tempted to go no further. But since we have begun to request adequate psycho-educational testing (not just the usual Stanford Binet administered for school placement), it becomes clear that added to forces keeping the patient at home, are motives driving the child away from school. Usually these are learning problems. Boys are likely also to have coordination and impulse troubles on the playground. Girls show social immaturity and fear of delinquent classmates. But when we test carefully their psychological equipment and academic skills, we nearly always uncover some impairment of reading or listening, as well as considerable irregularity in inter- and intratest scores.

Case Histories

Lydia, for example, is a thirteen-year-old whose younger sister has a hereditary ailment causing periods of illness and intense family concern. Lydia is attractive, charming, considered bright. Her parents value academic success. When she refused to go to school, she cited her dismay at the wild conduct of several classmates. Her parents were convinced that her symptoms, including weakness and nausea, were a play for the attention usually accorded her sick sister. Lydia was returned to school in the usual manner. Mother was shown the ways in which she had guiltily condoned the patient's behavior. But only subsequent careful testing demonstrated that Lydia's surface charm concealed rather dull intellect, deficient verbal skills and a "profound" reading disability. Nothing else had explained for us why this seemingly bright child could not reject the delinquents easily and join the group of academic achievers.

———

Billy is an eight-year-old boy who balked at parochial school and stayed home fretting about "germs" and washing his hands red and raw. It is true that his father was in mortal danger in a war zone overseas. His mother was very worried. But Billy, in third grade, had never learned to read at all. His colorful complaints distracted those around him from the handicap which would ruin his future to symptoms which were really irrelevant. He improved only when he was first encouraged to express his fears for his father and his humiliation in himself, then helped to channel his energies into learning basic skills in a way which permitted him some success.

*   *   *

Adopted children appear in our offices in much higher proportion than in the general population. It has been suggested that adoptive parents are unduly concerned about their children or that previous contact with an agency has prepared them to seek help earlier or more willingly, but the presenting problems are really no less serious than those of other families. The complaint is generally about learning or management problems, though it may be any other kind of maladjustment or unhappiness (depression, hysteria, suicide attempts, etc.). On examination and testing, we find a high incidence of all the forms of cerebral dysfunction. We can speculate about the cause: whether a child's origin, in an undesired pregnancy, produced the prenatal insult of attempted abortion; whether the mother's nine months of anxiety had an adverse physiological effect on the fetus; whether the traits we see are genetic and the same learning disability and impulsivity in our patient existed in his parents, leading them into sexual delinquency which produced the child. Our attention has often been directed to the adoptive parents' ambivalence about the adoption and the child and to parental anticipation that the child would reproduce his natural parents' sins. But, whether or not these speculations can be sustained, and if so, whether these conflicts are the cause of the present trouble, the children themselves seem to respond only to specific treatment if at all. The parents need special reassurance because so often at the time of the adoption they were urged to regard the infant's mind as a blank slate on which it is their responsibility to write a successful life story. The child surely benefits from a chance to express his thoughts and feelings about his origins. But most of all, they all need to know what qualities are part of the child's present constitution, what can be done to make best use of them, and how he can be taught to learn better.

If this highly vulnerable population could be explored early and systematically and helped sooner, much suffering of an especially poignant sort could be avoided. If the risks could even be acknowledged more frankly in advance, possibly hyperactive or slow learning children would have a better chance of spending their lives with parents best suited to loving and helping them.

There are other groups of children which we can call "high risk" groups, tentatively now, more accurately later, as data on this subject will be gathered in more scientific prospective studies. Meanwhile, one can only comment on the impressions of those who have taken the histories of children with obvious present disability. One should suspect learning problems in a child with a sibling who is neurologically handicapped, mentally retarded or epileptic; in a child who has any congenital anomaly, however minor, or a sibling with an anomaly; in a child with a story of a difficult pregnancy or delivery, with an Rh problem, even if no transfusion was required; in a premature child. One should follow with interest a baby who is colicky, hypertonic or who has feeding or eating patterns in any way unusual; a baby who is a rocker or headbanger; one who has had even one febrile seizure. One must not lose interest in a child with a developmental delay even if he seems to outgrow it; the late walkers, shoelace tiers, bike riders, and especially the late talkers, often reappear as late or handicapped readers. The clumsy, restless or habitually miserable child may show a spurt of good cheer when he starts off to school only to meet a defeat in first grade efforts to read and write. The child with a history of chronic or repeated illness, even if it is not life-threatening or severe, and especially the child with the "allergic diathesis" seems to have a high likelihood of trouble; whether because his many high fevers did "damage" or because of the developmental effects of chronic malaise or transient hearing loss or lowered attention, one can only guess.

Here are examples of some children brought for psychiatric care because of symptoms which are very classically "neurotic" and whose families and doctors believed their problems to be purely "emotional," but who proved to have, in addition, considerable evidence of cerebral dysfunction.

Case Histories

Tom, age ten, was brought for emergency consultation because one morning he told his parents he had been preoccupied with thoughts of suicide all night. Both parents were intelligent and well educated. Both were oddly reluctant to have the child examined, each later confiding his conviction that he would be blamed for this trouble. Tom had been tested in school, found to be intellectually gifted, with a score of 145 on a Stanford-Binet. His poor grades were attributed to his "emotional problems." Both at home and school, Tom was noted to be physically restless, constantly talking, irritable, demanding, complaining, hard on himself and those around him. He easily became preoccupied and indecisive over any issue; he could not decide what to wear in the morning; he often ruminated about religious questions. In second grade, he had been retained for "immaturity." In spite of this textbook picture of obsessional trends, depression and suicidal preoccupation, it seemed a good idea to explore further. Developmental history unearthed an account of mother's single, unexplained convulsion shortly before Tom's birth. Tom was colicky and tense as an infant, had many colds and fevers. His moods shifted fast in childhood. Even recently, he was less chronically depressed than chronically anxious and unsettled. On examination, he was attractive, friendly, charming, a little too ingratiating and confiding. He was verbally brilliant. He was clearly highstrung and described his constant feeling of uncertainty, asking, "Do grownups have this much physical and mental tension?" He confirmed the story of suicidal thoughts but said he really did not wish to be dead, he was just not sure how he could stand feeling as he did. He denied minding his school failures, but his eyes filled with tears as he did so. The psychologist administered a Wechsler Intelligence Scale for Children and a full battery of projective tests. On the WISC he did not score quite so high as on the Binet, and there was a good deal of intratest scatter. Bender-Gestalt showed evidence of only partial compensation for visual-motor handicap. Even on the Rorschach, patterns of biological anxiety were more striking than the depression and obsessional defenses against it, which were reported, but noted to be quite ineffectual. Neurological examination noted some minimal weakness of motor skills on one side, mixed dominance and poor visual tracking. EEG was moderately abnormal. Tom's academic skills were very uneven. Though he read at grade level, his spelling and handwriting were several years retarded. His auditory-perceptual skills were effortful and inaccurate. His attention was fitful. Tom was handled by emergency assurance to the parents that he was less a present suicide risk than a personal and educational one. They were surprised to discover that his difficult personality did not seem to be all their fault. Tom's gross anxiety was modified, though not totally relieved, by medication. He was enrolled in a class for academic remediation. He was seen for a few sessions, and so was his mother, for discussion of his problems and the ways in which he and his family must control his restlessness and misery. Improvement was marked, but not spectacular, and it is understood by all that Tom does not have a disease but a certain kind of constitution, with many gifts, some disabilities and some terms to make with the world. He is an interesting example of the child who could easily have been treated for obsessional neurosis alone or even hospitalized as a suicide risk.

––––––

Linda was fourteen when seen first, but she had a two-year history of brief contact with several psychotherapists and refusal to cooperate. She was brought because she refused to touch any object previously handled by her father, whom she insisted she hated. If the word "father" was said, she said "mother." As more and more of her home became "contaminated," her activities became more limited. She ate alone and sparingly. She refused to wash in the family bathroom. She had always been a docile child but no threat modified this behavior. She was not psychotic; she herself knew that what she did was irrational. Her parents long-standing marital conflict was well served by Linda's symptoms, since they each blamed the other for them. The symptoms limited Linda's social life; she was a very pretty, but quite immature adolescent and she was thus spared social anxiety. A prolonged period of intensive psychotherapy, with interpretation of Linda's relationships, her fears, her jealousy, her ambivalence toward both the hated father and the beloved mother, changed nothing. When attention and treatment shifted to her poor coordination, her incompletely compensated perceptual defect and her faulty conceptual skills, she functioned better in school and fought her battles at home more normally. When her brilliant older brother and precocious younger sister were included in a family conference and learned that Linda was not merely spoiled but handicapped, they were able to give her a little support. This girl displayed all the characteristics of obsessive-compulsive disorder in a form which could be more permanently disabling than a frank psychosis. We are convinced that in a happier, more secure, less competitive family, her disabilities would have taken quite a different style of expression. Nevertheless, the symptoms could not be reversed or relieved by psychotherapeutic intervention, as we have so long been taught. Instead, it seemed as though when Linda's own resources were strengthened and her own mental processes better organized, she was able to reorient her own patterns of thought and action.

———

Wendy presented an equally recognizable picture of a child with anxiety reactions. At age eleven, she was referred by her pediatrician because of "emotional problems." She was chronically fearful and tearful and had episodes of terror focused on fears of dying or the death of her loved ones. She was one of two daughters and was noticeably overshadowed by her more competent and attractive older sister. She had a lifelong history of overreacting to stimuli; of responding to difficulties by apprehension and clinging to her mother. She resembled her mother in appearance and in her reactions, patterns of misery and anxiety. Examination showed her to be a fragile, tense, sniffling child, complaining and worrying aloud. She saw life as a succession of miseries, discomforts and disappointments. She herself was unable to focus on her actual disabilities in this welter of anxious experience. But testing indicated poor coordination, excessive motor overflow, poor visual-motor skills, poor reading ability with very inadequate word-sounding skills. Psychological tests showed average intelligence but confirmed the visual-perceptual handicap, and projective tests indicated anxiety, feelings of worthlessness and impaired interpersonal relationships. Reading appraisal showed a spelling handicap and a year's reading retardation.

There is no question that Wendy had anxiety attacks and that they were expressed in an interpersonal idiom. One must choose whether to include in the causation of her helplessness to deal with surges of feeling, her lifelong experience of all these other tested inadequacies.

———

Timmy, age eight, was a boy whose parents were worried about his restlessness, hyperactivity and emotional immaturity. He was a bright child and had always made excellent grades in school, but he was "too intense," cried easily and was clumsy. When he was a tiny child, he would have delirium and visual hallucinations whenever he had a high fever. Examination showed him to be earnest and bright but restless and very conscious of his restlessness, though he was not at all aware that the abuse from class-mates about which he complained was related, as the teacher reported, to his constant awkward bumping and pushing. Though he was bright on testing, there was a discrepancy of 21 points between his high verbal skills and low performance score on the WISC. He could not recall information in sequences. His figure drawings were vague in outline, drawn in profile, large-eyed and characteristic of interpersonal disturbance. This is a child who could be classified as having a personality pattern disturbance with intermittently paranoid ideation. It would be only too easy to regard him as psychotic during a delirium and after a few episodes to think of him as a mentally ill person. He was able to discuss his restlessness a little more with encouragement and eventually, after a period of suspicion and conflict, to notice that he was better controlled physically and less provocative to his playmates if he took his pills regularly.

———

Randy was seen by us first when he was four years old. His adoptive parents were alarmed by a bizarre preoccupation with female feet, which he liked to observe and stroke. At the time, this was regarded as a purely psychological disturbance related to his jealousy of his newly acquired baby sister. The symptoms subsided with reassurance and very firm handling on the part of the mother, who wisely insisted that all females in the house keep their shoes on in Randy's presence. In brief psychotherapy, he was en-couraged to play freely except in this one way. After a few visits he was dis-charged, symptom free. He reappeared at age eight with complaints by his parents that he was restless, impulsive, mildly disobedient. His attention span was relatively brief and his hearing appeared to fluctuate with his bouts of allergy. On psychological testing at this time, he displayed severe perceptual disability in a setting of otherwise superior skills. Projective test-ing showed a personality expectionally sound except for some areas of im-maturity. No characteristics of neurotic patterning were seen, though they were carefully sought. Reading skills were good but deviant in their pat-terning and it was thought that Randy was compensating for marked audi-tory, as well as visual difficulties. It is hard to know the relationship between his previous psychological crisis and the second set of symptoms, except to comment that this child had unusual fragmentary ways of perceiving hu-mans when he was small and continued to have trouble with perceptual or-ganization of other material. The last time the child was seen, the emphasis had again shifted. At age ten his academic performance, with help, had im-proved, but his social skills were unsatisfactory to his rather demanding mother. Randy found it hard to please her, though he was willing enough to do it if he were told how rather simply. It is our impression that his development is generally a bit irregular and he is contending with more than a deviation in his infantile sexual life, though this is one time when such a deviation was actually documented by ourselves.

———

Eleven-year-old *Larry* was referred by a school conselor who was acquainted with his history of constant minor delinquencies and family despair since he started school. This child had been seen by a succession of psychological specialists and pediatricians, all of whom observed that his parents were rejecting, father demanding, mother cold. Brief trials on insufficient doses of ineffectual drugs had proven to them that medication had nothing to offer him. The child seemed unresponsive to psychotherapy, incorrigible by military school. At times he achieved impressively in school, especially in his intermittent artistic efforts. He was reported to read avidly, mainly during classroom instruction. Mother wondered if he had a conscience at all. The diagnosis of "psychopath" was entertained. The school psychologist was the first to note the wide scatter in his psychometric testing and the clinical picture of poor attention, hyperactivity and failure of controls.

Larry's parents, it is true, were totally defeated by him and no longer could speak of this child with love. They feared him and feared for him. They recognized his bad judgment. They were sensitive enough to know they were held accountable by the community for their son's destructiveness, minor thefts and insolence.

On examination, Larry was an attractive and disarming child, using his charm to conceal his anxiety, his restlessness and the real defects in his sequential and logical thought. He seemed very confused about his own identity, his age and his proper privileges; both literally and figuratively, he did not know his place. He read fast and often well, but his reading was uneven and approximate. He admitted that the books he read so ostentatiously were only the simplest fiction and he avoided his textbooks. Projective tests showed him to be quite unable to deal with conceptual material or to really know right and wrong in a framework suitable to his age and the hazards to which his age exposed him. Psychological diagnosis at the time was "Situational Reaction to Neurological Handicap, with the trend of his reaction, partly because of limited parental support, in the direction of psychopathy or psychotic breakdown." Though a relative reading disability and a specific perceptual handicap were found, there was so much evidence of negativism that remedial help at the time was contraindicated. This is the child with cerebral dysfunction who has compensated to some extent intellectually but not at all emotionally or socially. The label "psychopath" will probably fit him better in a year or two. One wonders whether his parents could have helped him more if they had been less burdened by their own guilt and others' accusations during the early years when he was simply a hyperactive and difficult child. If he had shown franker learning problems, he might have received specific help sooner and more willingly. As it is, one can simply reinterpret the data to the family and to the child, hoping that he can consider some new views of himself than that he is doomed and had better be tough. Perhaps his parents can see Larry as infantile, rather than criminal, and protect more than punish. We can offer some medicine for the poor controls, knowing that this is a very partial answer. The school can be encouraged to follow up on their accurate observations, with hope that maturation of Larry's conceptual skills will construct for him a delayed conscience before the Courts must act. Psychotherapy for Larry must be intermittent after all the previous disappointments, for he regards it as just more entrapment and beside the point. Working through his parents, if their own discouragement will permit it, may be the best plan, since even if the child's course cannot be altered greatly now, his parents need not feel solely responsible.

*   *   *

It is not quite time to say there is no "neurotic" child at all or that constitutional deviation must exist with any psychiatric trouble. It is important to maintain our interest and our techniques for observing interpersonal and intrapsychic experience. But we surely have a responsibility to identify any form of disability if it offers an avenue for specific and effective help. If a neglected disability persists, the best efforts to remove secondary symptoms will never succeed fully. Even a disability which our present knowledge cannot correct or which may be found too late for correction does far less psychological harm if it can be defined and acknowledged than if it produces a nameless, pervasive anxiety. If the handicap can be approached first by the least expensive, most practical and available measures, the more costly, time-consuming psychotherapy can be reserved for those who can respond to nothing else or to nothing else without psychotherapy, too. In this way, our limited psychiatric resources will go further.

The general public, educators and doctors in the future will probably be familiar enough with the indications and symptoms of learning problems, whether or not they are concealed by psychiatric symptoms, so that they will find the deviant child early and spare him and his family much anxiety and pain.

REFERENCES

1. ALLEN, FREDERICK, H.: *Psychotherapy with Children.* New York, Norton, 1942.
2. BAX, MARTIN, and MACKEITH, RONALD: Minimal cerebral dysfunction. National

Spastics Society Medical Education and Information Unit in Association with William Heinemann, Medical Books, Ltd., London, 1963.

3. BENDER, L.: The psychological problems of children with organic brain disorders. *Amer J Orthopsychiat, 19:*404-415, 1949.

4. BENDER, LAURETTA: *Psychopathology of Children with Organic Brain Disorders.* Springfield, Thomas, 1956.

5. BOWLBY, JOHN: *Maternal Care and Mental Health.* Geneva, World Health Organization, 1951.

6. BIRCH, H.G. (Ed.) : *Brain Damage in Children: The Biological and Social Aspects.* Baltimore, Williams & Wilkins, 1964.

7. CLEMENTS, SAM D.: Some aspects of the characteristics, management and education of the child with minimal brain dysfunction. Arkansas Association for Children with Learning Disabilities, Inc., 1966.

8. CLEMENTS, SAM; LEHTINEN, LAURA, and LUKENS, JEAN: *Children with Minimal Brain Injury.* Chicago, National Society for Children and Adults, 1964.

9. CLEMENTS, SAM D.: *Minimal Brain Dysfunction in Children.* U.S. Dept. of Health, Education and Welfare, 1966.

10. Committee on Nomenclature and Statistics of the American Psychiatric Association: *Diagnostic and Statistical Manual of Mental Disorders.* American Psychiatric Association, Washington, 6, D.C., 1962.

11. CRUICKSHANK, WILLIAM (Ed.) : *The Teacher of Brain-Injured Children.* Syracuse, Syracuse, 1966.

12. DENHOFF, E., and ROBINAULT, I.: *Cerebral Palsy and Related Disorders.* New York, McGraw, 1960.

13. EDGINGTON, RUTH, and CLEMENTS, SAM D.: Indexed bibliography on the educational management of children with learning disabilities. Chicago, Argus Communications, 1967.

14. EISENBERG, L.: Psychiatric implications of brain damage in children. *Psychiat Quart, 31* (1) :72-92, 1957.

15. ERIKSON, E.H.: *Childhood and Society.* New York, Norton, 1950.

16. FLOWER, RICHARD; GOFMAN, HELEN, and LAWSON, LUCIE (Eds.) : *Reading Disorders.* Philadelphia, Davis, 1965.

17. FREUD, ANNA: *The Ego and the Mechanisms of Defense.* New York, Int. Univs., 1946.

18. HELLMUTH, JEROME (Ed.) : *Learning Disorders.* Seattle, Special Child, 1965-66, 2 vols.

19. KNOBLOCH, H., and PASAMANICK, B.: Syndrome of minimal cerebral damage in infancy. *JAMA, 170* (12) :1384-387, 1959.

20. KURLANDER, L.F., and COLODNY, D.: 'Pseudoneurosis' in the neurologically handicapped child. *Amer J Orthopsychiat, XXXV* (4) :733-738, 1965.

21. KURLANDER, L.F., and COLODNY, D.: Panacea, palliation or poison: the psychodynamics of a controversy. *Amer J Psychiat,* June 1965, vol. 121, No. 12.

22. LEVENTHAL, THEODORE, *et al.*: Therapeutic strategies with school phobics. *Amer J Orthopsychiat,* Jan. 1967, vol. XXXVII, No. 1.

23. LEVI, AURELIA: Remedial techniques in disorders of concept formation. *J Special Educ,* 1966, vol. 1, No. 1.

24. MONEY, JOHN (Ed.) : *Reading Disability.* Baltimore, Johns Hopkins, 1962.

25. MURPHY, LOIS, and ASSOCIATES: *Personality in Young Children.* New York, Basic Books, 1956.

26. SILVER, ARCHIE: Behavioral syndrome associated with brain damage in children. *Pediat Clin N Amer,* August 1958, pp. 687-698.

27. SOLNIT, ALBERT J., and PROVENCE, SALLY A.: *Modern Perspectives in Child Development.* New York, Int. Univs., 1963.

28. SPITZ, R. A.: *'Hospitalism' in the Psychoanalytic Study of the Child.* Finichel, O. (Ed.), New York, Int. Univs., 1945.

29. STRAUSS, A., and LEHTINEN, L. E.: *Psychopathology and Education of the Brain Injured Child.* New York, Grune, 1947.

30. THOMPSON, ALICE C.: *Educational Handicap.* Los Angeles, Associated Clinics, California State College, 1966.

31. WITMER, HELEN LELAND, and KOTINSKY, RUTH: *Personality in the Making.* New York, Harper, 1952.

Chapter 7

Rehabilitation, the Community and the Child with Learning Disabilities

LESLIE W. KNOTT

ABOUT SIX MONTHS AGO a mother accompanied by her six-year-old twin daughters entered my office seeking help. As she was unfolding her story, I noted that the two apparently normal little girls were having considerable difficulty in sitting quietly; they began annoying each other, frequently interrupting the mother and distracting the conversation in general. To ease the problem I made available colored chalk and a blackboard, pads of paper and colored pencils, all of which were promptly put to use — each for a short period of time. They soon spotted a stapling machine on my desk which, with permission, was vigorously operated to the point of becoming jammed. The mother reprimanded the children on occasion and did manage to continue her story. The children's activities in my office and the mother's story fitted nicely together.

It seems that the mother was able to manage these children fairly well during preschool years. When the children entered school, however, it was not long before they were removed from the classroom because of the teacher's inability to cope with their short span of attention and their hyperactivity. The mother was eventually informed that the children's behavior suggested minimal brain dysfunction. She came to my office for the purpose of finding out where she might acquire the specialized medical attention to check on this possibility and, if confirmed, where she might obtain appropriate medical attention. With equal concern she raised questions as to ways and means of providing an education for these children. She also wondered what might be the eventual outcome in the years ahead.

As the mother continued the discussion of her children's future, it became quite clear that appropriate medical attention alone would probably not meet the entire needs of these children. The physician's part in the overall management would be only a segment of a broad spectrum of services likely to be needed by the family and the children themselves. Whether or not these children and others like them achieve a satisfying and productive life within the limits of their ability hinges on the understanding and attitudes not only of the physician but of the parent, sibling, friend and neighbor, school and civic agencies, religious organizations and, finally, employers. In short, it is the attitude of the community at large and the services which it is willing to provide that help to make the difference between success or failure as a minimal brain dysfunction child progresses to adult life.

Before discussing our community at large, I should like to digress for a moment and comment on what we know about the eventual outcome of children who are the victims of minimal brain dysfunction (MBD). Here, unfortunately, objective data are not available, and we can rely only on the impressions of the relatively few professional personnel who have had the opportunity to follow these children over a period of years. These impressions indicate that behavioral and learning disorders so characteristic of MBD will persist through the early school years, but many, if not most of them, show a predictable decline in the major clinical problems of distractibility, hyperactivity and perseveration as they approach the teen years. Irregularities in visual-motor coordination, psychological tests, and even reading problems may improve as the child approaches adolescence. Some claim that MBD children as adults are indistinguishable from the general population and adapt well to the adult world; the one exception is coping with changes in routine living.

Others, however, are not as optimistic in their impressions. In a sizeable number of MBD children, learning disorders will persist to some degree and reading difficulties will continue throughout life. Problems in concept development, symbolic formation, organization of thinking, and tendencies toward concrete thinking may well continue into adulthood despite improvements in some of the major clinical problems of childhood. Impressions in one clinic indicate that a majority of these children present evidence of damage to the processes of inhibition and self-control and are, therefore, more apt to become character problems, criminals, addicts, alcoholics or borderline-adjusted people. Some studies suggest that MBD may be a forerunner of certain psychoses, either as a direct result of the underlying brain disorder or as a secondary effect of the social and learning disabilities imposed by the damage.

Regardless of whichever of these two views prevails, it seems clear that during the early, formative and school years, most if not all MBD children and their parents require in varying degrees a relatively large number of services to assist in meeting the needs of the child relative to medical care, family living, training and education and social relationships. The emphasis on adequate services during the early years may be all-important, as Dr. Edward Lis of the University of Illinois and his staff point out, ". . . the long-term adjustment appears to be determined not so much by the severity and frequency of symptoms originally associated with the diagnosis of MBD but by the degree of acceptance of the child's limitations and the family's ability to set realistic goals and levels of expectation for him. Moreover, families who are able to create a favorable emotional climate and consistently support the child's efforts to master his developmental tasks at his own rate of maturation, add a therapeutic dimension of significant magnitude which we feel is often the difference between a basically successful and an unsuccessful outcome."*

A similar belief is expressed by Dr. Raymond L. Clemmens of the University Hospital in Baltimore in stating, "The importance of parent attitude, educational management and other psycho-social factors seem to have a great bearing on the determination of the outcome."*

This is not meant to imply that services during childhood only are the total answer. As previously indicated, an appreciable number of MBD children may continue to have problems and may require assistance extending well into adult life, especially in the realm of social behavior and vocational interests.

With these views in mind, we are better able to make some assessment of what the community can and should offer to meet the lifetime needs of the MBD child. It is obvious that in any given child it is difficult to predict the kind and quantity of future service that may be needed or when it will be needed. The important point is the availability of adequate service, if and when the need arises.

MEDICAL CARE

The first and foremost need is for family physicians or pediatricians who are aware of MBD and are schooled in its diagnosis and management. Not all physicians agree as to the existence of the diagnostic entity of MBD. Some believe it is more a psychological than an organic problem. Nevertheless we cannot disregard behavior disorders and learning disabilities and must make every effort to determine the cause of these conditions. Whether the physician attributes the cause to organic or other factors, he will still be responsible for providing general, as well as specific, medical care to the child and advice to the parents.

Through his leadership and guidance he will attempt to alleviate any anxieties or possible sense of guilt on the part of the parents and help them to adopt a realistic approach to the management of the child. Obviously, he cannot be all things to the MBD patient or his parents, but will judiciously seek the assistance of medical consultants, other professional personnel and appropriate community resources when they are indicated. Ideally he will remain as team leader and coordinator of these services, at least until the situation becomes stabilized.

---

*Personal communications to C. Arden Miller, M.D., Chairman, Task Force II, Medical Services, Minimal Brain Dysfunction — National Project on Learning Disabilities in Children.

A child's hyperactivity, distractibility and perseveration are likely to complicate any medical treatment rendered to the child and call for greater than ordinary understanding on the part of a consulting physician or any related health profession involved. The child's family physician may at times be required to impart such understanding to other doctors called into consultation. Likewise, the child, in the course of his development, will encounter other persons, some of whom may lack knowledge or understanding of MBD, e.g., teachers, clergy, law enforcement personnel, welfare workers. Here again, the physician may be asked to assist the parents in providing an explanation of the child's behavior.

The earlier that adequate medical attention is sought and a diagnosis established, the greater are the chances of avoiding misunderstanding and mismanagement of the child by the parents and his siblings. The physician, then, can serve as a keystone, not only in managing the child's illnesses but also in wisely utilizing other community services that may be indicated.

Not infrequently parents do not know where competent medical advice can be obtained, as for example, in the case of the mother mentioned in the introduction to these remarks. If the child is under the care of a pediatrician or a family physician, it would be advisable to consult him first. If he should feel inadequate to evaluate the child, he or the parents may inquire at the local medical society headquarters for the names of physicians who are familiar with learning disabilities in children. The probabilities are that the several physician names suggested would include one or more pediatric neurologists whose interests center on neurological handicaps in children. The pediatric departments in medical schools may serve as another source of information. It is quite possible that the medical school sponsors a special clinic for children with neurological problems and, at times, specifically for children with learning disabilities. Such clinics are established, for example, at the schools of medicine at the University of California in San Francisco and at Stanford University in Palo Alto.

OTHER PROFESSIONAL PERSONNEL

In many instances the physician will have utilized the clinical psychologist, the audiologist and speech pathologist in arriving at a diagnosis and overall assessment of the child. The same professional disciplines can make valuable contributions in the long-term management by providing supplemental therapy when it is indicated. Periodic testing or evaluations will also be necessary to determine the child's progress in the course of growth and development. Other professional medically related services helpful to overall management are those provided by the medical or psychiatric social worker and the vocational counselor; their contributions will be discussed later in this presentation.

If the physician refers the child or the parents to any of the nonmedical professional persons indicated above, he will usually know where to turn for a given type of service. If he requires assistance in locating speech and hearing therapists or clinical psychologists, it is posible that colleges and universities in the area may be able to provide the names of available people known to them. Likewise, medical centers may serve the same purpose. Medical and psychiatric social workers are by virtue of their graduate training well qualified in family counseling; these professional people should not be confused with welfare workers who are primarily concerned with eligibility questions of persons seeking welfare aid. A Family Service Association of a city or county is generally able to provide expert family counseling or have available the names of qualified individuals who can provide the service. The services of a vocational rehabilitation counselor are more likely to be obtained at or through a rehabilitation center, either medical or vocational. At least such centers would be able to provide information as to where such service could be obtained. The vocational rehabilitation counselor is one trained in assisting physically and mentally handicapped individuals and assessing their skills and selecting suitable vocational opportunities. They should not be confused with vocational consultants who concern themselves primarily with normal individuals.

FAMILY COUNSELING

The physician may be capable of providing all the counseling necessary to the family. Much depends on the intelligence, resourcefulness and emotional stability of the parents. While such counseling may be adequate at one stage of the child's development, other resources may be indicated at a later date, depending on circumstances. In any case, whenever the emotional situation or family problems are beyond the counseling ability or available time of the physician, he may refer the family to one of several resources, depending on the nature of the problem and its magnitude. The psychiatrist, clinical psychologist, medical or psychiatric social worker, family welfare agency, public health visiting nurse and even a voluntary organization of parents interested in the problems of MBD are all possibilities. He may wish to refer the total responsibility for counseling to one of the professional resources and keep abreast of progress with periodic reports, or perhaps utilize any of these resources to supplement his own efforts at counseling.

New and different problems may arise as the child approaches the teen years or early adulthood. Relationships with the opposite sex, rejection of parental supervision, social behavior and vocational training needs are examples of problem areas differing from those of childhood. Still another problem relates to the dependent MBD adult who may have lived quite successfully under parental supervision for a number of years; the parents looking to old age may now have to seek means of providing domiciliary care and financial support for their offspring when they no longer exist. All these areas of concern may call for professional counseling beyond the childhood years. In addition to those already mentioned, the vocational counselor, the State Division of Vocational Rehabilitation and attorneys knowledgeable in wills and trust funds, a financial advisor or a public welfare agency are other resources that may be indicated. The need for these special services may not be extensive in terms of numbers to be served, but where they exist, solutions are essential.

RELIEF IN CHILD CARE

Baby sitting may appear to be a trite subject in a presentation of this nature, but obtaining an individual to care for the markedly hyperactive, perseverating child can present difficulties. The understanding baby sitter may be essential in the time of the mother's illness. At other times, it may provide periodic temporary relief of parental responsibility and the opportunity for recreation needed by parents to carry on the day-to-day challenge of dealing calmly and effectively with the MBD child. The significance of this problem, of course, depends on the degree of the child's behavior disorder. It may be mild and thus not require any unique solution. On the other hand, special resources may be necessary in the form of trained baby sitters.

"Trained" implies a mature person whose understanding of the child has been increased through parental explanation. Willing and able sitters for MBD children are not found easily. It is feasible for a parental organization to underwrite a program of training for selected, interested persons who would serve as baby sitters. Feasibility would depend upon the demands for service, availability of interested persons and fees offered. Such training programs might be offered periodically under the direction of an appropriate professional person. Whatever the solution, whether by trial-and-error method on the part of the individual family or by organized effort of parental groups, there is a significant need in some instances for capable baby sitters to provide periods of relief to the parents.

PRESCHOOL TRAINING AND EDUCATION

As in the case of all children, the nursery school or kindergarten provides a constructive environment for directed play activities and for social adaptation. Its activities often include reading readiness and general preparation for regular school routine.

In the case of the MBD child, the preschool program may serve an additional function. It provides an extended opportunity for objective day-to-day assessment of the child's defects and ways in which they might be minimized. Also, at the appropriate time, the nursery school or kindergarten is in a position to judge the child's readiness to accept the more formal routine of regular school classes or special education facilities. Parental conferences provide the opportunity for contributing to the parent's greater understanding of MBD and the need for special education techniques or programs that may be indicated. The nursery school or kindergarten may be the first to detect something different about the child and may provide a first indication to the parents that the child is in need of a physician's evaluation. Such conferences with parents will not always be successful in view of the great reluctance on the part of some to recognize their child as being different from the normal. Others are more accepting of the suggestion and will follow through with appropriate medical attention.

Thus, we can see that the preschool center can serve a twofold purpose. For the recognized MBD child, it provides a period of objective observation and may help to remedy some of the child's behavior; for the unrecognized brain-injured child, it may serve as a case-finding mechanism and alert the parents to the need for medical and related evaluation. The success of preschool training and educational facilities depends, of course, on the skills and understandings of the well-trained teachers.

It is sometimes difficult to locate a nursery or preschool program suitable for neurologically handicapped children. Although many nursery schools may be listed in the telephone directory, most of them are for normal children. Medical centers that sponsor special clinics for handicapped children are often aware of specialized schools. Information can also be obtained at times from Easter Seal Rehabilitation Centers for Children. More frequently the information can be obtained from parent organizations whose members are generally familiar with a wide range of nursery schools and special education facilities that serve various types of handicapped children.

SPECIAL EDUCATION

Special education, a specific program in our school systems for exceptional children including those with MBD, is a large topic with many ramifications. It is enough to say that a significant number of MBD children can benefit only in special education programs under the direction of properly trained teachers. It should be clear that children with perceptual impairments and more than ordinary difficulties with respect to reading and arithmetic cannot readily participate in the regular classes of our school systems. This is not to say that the MBD child is mentally retarded; in some cases, his IQ may exceed that of the normal child. His neurological impairments are such, however, that he is not able to readily master reading and calculations or symbolic thinking. Without special education, these children would have a dismal existence in many of the regular classes.

Generally speaking, such specialized school programs are possible only in the larger school systems. Classes are usually small; teachers require more than ordinary training, and the atmosphere and attitudes must be such that the children can progress at their own rate of maturation. In some instances, the special education program also provides prevocational training and opportunities which help the child to find ways of making the best use of his talents, particularly as he progresses through secondary schools. Some children, through special education, are able to overcome their particular defects and, at the appropriate time, can be transferred to the regular school classes. Indeed, some of these children may progress to high levels of education fully aware of their limitations but with certain abilities to compensate for them.

If the MBD child is to make the most of his abilities and avoid the frustrations of failure, he requires in many instances teachers adequately trained in ways of teaching around the defects. Providing such a service obviously is a community responsibility; the alternative is specialized private schooling, if it can be found and if the parents are financially able to meet the cost. Fortunately, many of our up-to-date public school systems recognize the need and provide the service. The unfortunate part is the lack of adequately trained teachers to meet the demand.

Some public school systems are so small, particularly in rural areas, that they are unable to sponsor a special education program for handicapped children. In this situation it may be necessary to seek a private school with a program of training and education, some covering preschool as well as elementary grade work. A number of such schools exist throughout the country. Inquiries may be directed to the state educational authorities which in most instances are required to license special education schools. Other inquiries may be directed to organized parent's groups, to medical centers conducting clinics for handicapped children and to local boards of education.

VOCATIONAL SERVICES

The probability of difficulty in vocational selection, job finding and job holding, will be significant for a sizeable portion of MBD children who reach adolescence or young adulthood with persistent problems in reading and arithmetic. Many of these children will constitute the "dropouts" from high schools. Their final adjustment to adult life will in large measure hinge upon their ability to earn a living. At this point, the vocational rehabilitation counselor provides invaluable, if not essential, service. The counselor's training provides him with a knowledge of psychological tests, of psychosocial phenomena, of occupational prerequisites and skills, of prevocational testing, of vocational training facilities and appropriate public assistance programs. With this background, he can provide tremendous assistance to the teenage or adult person with MBD in finding a meaningful place in a highly competitive labor market.

The vocational counselor cannot in all instances complete the necessary steps alone. After one or a number of interviews for assessment of the client's motivations, attitudes and general interest, he may refer him for prevocational testing to check on manual skills and the components of various types of occupations. A sheltered workshop may initially be indicated for the development of sound work habits, improvement of personal appearance, or for checking or improving interpersonal relationships with co-workers and supervisors. He may wish to refer the client to larger centers such as many of the Goodwill Industries for work evaluation and a wide variety of actual occupational activities.

Formal training in a specific occupation is indicated when the client manifests a specific interest and potential skills, combined with motivation. The counselor can assist in the selection of the training facilities and in obtaining financial aid from governmental resources to underwrite the training.

Finally, the counselor may provide help in job placement, either indirectly through employment agencies or through direct contact with industries. He may be instrumental in developing an understanding of the individual's disability on the part of management and thus help to create a better climate in which the MBD person can work.

The vocational counselor, with his background of psychology, should be in a good position to understand and appreciate MBD. It is possible, however, that he, like some physicians, social workers, or other professional people already mentioned, may have little appreciation or understanding for MBD as a diagnostic entity. The fact still remains that young adults with persistent behavior disorders or learning disabilities require the skills and professional help of the vocational counselor, regardless of what kind of diagnostic label is attached to the individual client.

As previously indicated, it may be difficult to locate a qualified rehabilitation counselor. If inquiries directed to rehabilitation centers are not successful, contact could be made with various colleges and universities where, in some instances, programs for the training of vocational rehabilitation counselors are well established. One example is the San Francisco State College in San Francisco.

RECREATION AND SOCIAL ACTIVITIES

The personality of the MBD child may hinder his ability to make or retain friends among the neighborhood children. Perceptual problems, mild impairment of coordination, inability to understand the rules of the game are all factors that could prevent his acceptance on the "ball team." Even the ordinary parlor games of childhood present difficulties for some MBD children. Just as such may require special education, they may also require special recreation and the opportunity to make friends.

Nursery schools and special education programs can fulfill these needs to some extent, but the after-school hours, weekends and summer months present difficulties to the friendless child. Summer camps and summer day programs designed for exceptional children may provide one outlet. Year-round recreation and social programs for exceptional children offered by such organizations as the YMCA are other possibilities. The Scouting programs for both boys and girls have from time to time manifested interest in providing special opportunities for handicapped children. The success of these and similar programs sponsored by organized groups as applied in any given situation depends on the circumstances of the individual child, the degree to which he fits into a program and the understanding and abilities of those directing it.

Here again, community organizations can provide the leadership. It may take some prodding on the part of organized parents groups. It also requires able leadership and necessary funds and equipment. Lacking interest on the part of community organizations, the parents themselves, through their own organization, may develop or sponsor an appropriate recreational and social activity, directed by volunteers or paid personnel. There are both parental groups and programs sponsored by community organizations that have been successful. Such programs fill a most important gap in providing social opportunities for children whose needs cannot otherwise be met.

A very useful Directory of Camps for the Handicapped has been published by the National Society for Crippled Children and Adults, 2023 West Ogden Avenue, Chicago, 60612. Here may be found resident camps and day camps listed by state and also according to types of disability groups served.

RELIGIOUS EDUCATION

The child, unable to adapt to the regular routines of school, will in all probability find difficulty in adapting to a regular religious education program. The problem is equal to the extent of the family's desire for the child's religious training. Either they must provide it themselves or seek the aid of a religious group in developing special services. In the case of mentally retarded children, individual churches, synagogues or a council of churches have attempted with some success to meet this need with volunteer help. Within the community, a single church might assume responsibility for serving children from all of the churches of similar faith. It is conceivable that an overall program for exceptional children, similar to special education in the school system, might meet the needs of the MBD child, as well as other exceptional children. Feasibility, in this respect, as might be anticipated, depends on the numbers and kinds of children involved.

Whatever may be best in the terms of service, religious organizations have a moral responsibility for at least considering the religious needs of the child with MBD who cannot benefit from the routine religious education program. Churches and synagogues are taking increasing interest and action in this respect. The church not only is capable of providing religious education but can also serve to meet the social and recreational needs of exceptional children. The local council of churches is the most likely source of information regarding religious programs for handicapped children.

GUARDIANSHIP AND LIFETIME CARE

On the basis of impressions discussed in the introduction to this section, it would appear that a certain proportion of MBD children require varying degrees of supervision, ranging from periodic counseling to complete custodial care throughout their entire lives. In the absence of any long-range follow-up studies of MBD children, one can only speculate as to the extent and nature of these needs.

Children who reach maturity and are able to adapt to society with only minor or no deficits, present no special problem. Even those with persistent learning difficulties may be able to retain certain routine jobs which are devoid of periods of stress and unusual demands. Marriage, child-rearing and other responsibilities may be associated with only minor difficulties. Others with more serious, persistent deficits may require a certain amount of supervision, at least until such time as their situation may stabilize. Undoubtedly, in a certain number of cases, the parents or, subsequent to them, close relatives may provide all the assistance that is necessary, as long as their services are available and accepted. Their supervision may at times require supplementary services from community resources, but the major contribution and responsibility rests with the family.

When the family resources are not adequate, those in the community may make the difference between a totally dependent individual and one capable of meeting the minimal criteria for self-support, or at least acceptable survival in the community. The resources required may be one or more of the following:

1. The vocational counselor whose services have already been discussed. They have special significance for those having difficulty with job placement and job holding.

2. The professional social worker can assist the individual who may have difficulties in certain social, marital or financial areas. And with a good knowledge of other community resources, he can direct the individual to specific sources of help. Success is contingent upon the social worker's awareness of the client's functional deficit and on the client's ability to profit from social service.

3. The pastoral counselor, specifically trained for the role of counselor, functions in a similar capacity to the social worker, but may be especially helpful for those individuals who are more religiously oriented.

4. Attorneys who are understanding in the problems of handicapped persons are essential to the family wishing to establish a trust fund for the support of the MBD adult who is incapable of financial management. The attorney, a well-chosen bank, or surviving relatives are equally important in serving as executors of such funds.

5. The terminal type of sheltered workshop may fill a definite need for those individuals unable to cope with a competitive labor market but who are otherwise capable of community living. Here, the intent is to permit the individual to engage in a productive occupation, consistent with his abilities and in a sheltered environment. Pay may be scaled to the individual's production. In addition to the useful occupation of time, the workshop also provides opportunity for socialization and, in some instances, recreation.

RESIDENTIAL CARE

Little is known regarding the need for one other resource: namely, residential care for those MBD children or adults who require supervised living arrangements but who lack financial resources, family or relatives. The probability is that many such individuals can be found in state hospitals; where hospital policy permits, some may already be residing in foster homes at the community level.

To what extent MBD is recognized as a diagnostic entity in state hospitals is not known. Further, data are lacking as to the number of MBD persons who may be living under supervision in the community in private homes or under auspices other than those of the state hospitals. It is conceivable that sufficient numbers may exist in certain areas to warrant establishing community residential facilities specifically oriented to the needs of the MBD individual who is in need of supervised living. A facility of this sort, under appropriate management, could make use of a number of community resources in meeting the needs of its residents, while at the same time providing shelter and general guidance, sociability and recreation.

Experience has shown, however, that this sort of a community residential center is not a panacea. A ten-year experience in Philadelphia with such a center for cerebral palsy children was established based on the expressed need of a number of families for such a facility. Despite the high quality of services, the center finally had to close its doors because demand for services did not match the expressed need. It was soon found that families regarded institutional living only as a last resort, when all other possibilities were exhausted. Any attempt to establish residential facilities for neurologically handicapped children or adults should be thoroughly explored and cautiously planned.

ATTITUDES

Thus far, this presentation has dealt primarily with professional people and services. What about the attitude of friends, neighbors and relatives? What about the attitude of the population at large who must bear the tax burden for many of the services which have been mentioned? Here is where the parent as an individual and as a member of a voluntary organization can and must exert his influence to create a community atmosphere of understanding and helpfulness.

As indicated earlier in this presentation, the family must begin with itself in developing a home environment and familial interrelationships that permit the MBD child to grow and develop most favorably. This calls for emotional as well as intellectual acceptance of the child's handicap. This assumes, of course, that such a handicap has been definitely established through competent medical and related studies. When the family has achieved the necessary adjustment and developed a constructive attitude toward the problems, it can then turn its attention to influencing relationships outside the home.

It can begin by explaining the nature of the child's handicap to neighbors and friends who are in frequent contact with the child. They in turn can help to influence and guide their children in dealing with the handicapped child in the course of neighborhood play and activities. The neighbors should be encouraged to discuss with the parents any untoward neighborhood incidents in which the child is involved. Such discussions, if kept in an objective vein, are helpful in guiding the parents' efforts in training the child. Such a relationship minimizes neighborhood problems and tensions. The greatest gain, however, consists of neighbors and friends who are accepting of the child and who can be helpful in creating a positive neighborhood environment in which the child can grow and learn.

The alternative is to permit the child to participate in community living as though he were normal. In some cases this may be feasible. But the child who is hyperactive, impulsive in his behavior and perhaps confused in his thinking is bound to get into difficulties with other children and even adults. He will soon become recognized as a "different" child and he runs the risk of nonacceptance. Failure to explain the child's condition may save embarrassment to the parents, but in the long run it is the child who will suffer through neighborhood rejection and social isolation.

When it comes to influencing the community as a whole, realistic parents well know the advantages of organized effort through formal types of associations. Educating the community is essential to the establishment of the resources enabling handicapped individuals to achieve their maximum socially and vocationally. I do not need to elaborate as to the groups in need of education — the legislative bodies, the school boards, service clubs, industrial organizations and social and recreational organizations. It is hardly necessary to say that no matter how capable the family is in managing its handicapped child, it cannot prepare the child for community living unless the community itself is understanding and prepared to accept him.

PART THREE
DIAGNOSTIC TESTING, REMEDIATION AND RESEARCH

Chapter 8

The Psychologist and Case Finding

SAM D. CLEMENTS

PERHAPS THE FIRST requirement of a comprehensive presentation concerning the psychologist and his role in case finding of children with learning disabilities (minimal brain dysfunction) would be to avoid a concept as abstract as "the" psychologist. It is self evident that among psychologists, there is as much variance as there is within any other professional group.

So much depends upon the *individual clinician* that one should want to know many things about the psychologist before determining the part he might play in case finding. For example:

1. Has he had specialty training in work with children? If so, was it attained in a professional preparation program which required training and experience with the full spectrum of atypical children, and in a wide variety of settings? Clinical child psychology is a specialty unto itself, and the individual psychologist, if he works with children, must have expertise above and beyond that obtained in a general graduate school program.

2. How well does he communicate with representatives from other disciplines who serve children, particularly educators, pediatricians, child psychiatrists? Does he appreciate the advantages and is he comfortable working within the framework of the "team approach" to diagnosis and treatment of exceptional children?

3. Does he appreciate and respect parents and their feelings, especially if they are caught on the "referral merry-go-round"? Is he able to indicate this to them? *Do listening and assessment precede judgment?*

4. Is he honest and realistic in his imparting of diagnostic information and in treatment recommendations? By honest, if he is not certain about some aspect of the child, is he willing to say, "I don't know," but then add, "I will make it my busines to find out"? By realistic, is he ready with several alternate therapeutic plans, or does he instead recommend a residential school for the child which costs $6,000 per year, when the total yearly income of the family is but $7,000?

5. Is he aware of, personally familiar, and in current contact with all available community and state resources for children? Is he "public health" minded and concerned for the general welfare of his fellowmen? Is this substantiated by his participation in community action programs which will expand and upgrade services to *all* children and families?

171

6. Does he keep abreast of the ever-changing aspects of his own profession? This is particularly essential with regard to refined diagnostic techniques and innovative therapeutic programs. Or, is he so tradition bound that he is unpliant in his thinking and unresponsive to the constant flow of new knowledge regarding children?

These are but some of the areas of appraisal of the individual psychologist, but are indispensable in the determination of the role he will play in case finding of children with learning disabilities.

*   *   *

The term *case finding*, in this instance, can be equated with individual diagnostic assessment of the child. Thus, with regard to children with learning disabilities, the contributions of the psychologist lie in two major areas: (1) the diagnostic process, and (2) treatment planning and contribution.

Perhaps the most prevalent case "finders" are parents and teachers, who suspect something wrong with a child when his learning efficiency and behavior are out of keeping with expectations and developmental sequence. During the preschool years, the family physician is a frequent case finder due to concern over a lag or deviation in the child's development, particularly in the areas of language and motor proficiency. The case finders would then seek to refer the child to the appropriate case "evaluators," for aid in diagnostic definitiveness and ameliorative programming.

Definitive diagnosis of minimal brain dysfunction (learning disabilities) should be approached by means of simultaneous assessment of the child's learning ability and style, behavior and physical status.

A major deterrent to congruence and advancement in clinical child work has been the failure to develop a *standardized* diagnostic procedure which would be used *routinely* by *all* facilities involved in the evaluation of the behavior and learning disorders of children.

This plight becomes more paradoxical when one considers that this failure to attain agreement and precision in the evaluation of children is due more to the attitudes and capriciousness of the individual child specialists than to a lack of general knowledge of causative factors or the availability of specific diagnostic tools and techniques.

In the general sense, children with learning disabilities, are a *social concern* and hence are the responsibility of all. Neither education, psychology, medicine, nor any other health-related profession can be designated their sole and proper patron. Certain problem areas and their alleviation are, of course, properly applicable to specific disciplines.

It would seem that a definitive diagnostic evaluation, too, should be a synthesis of the skills, techniques, and approaches of the various disciplines, each contributing parts to fashion a comprehensive wholeness.

The purposes of such a diagnostic evaluation are as follows:

1. To demonstrate the existence or absence of symptoms of learning disabilities (minimal brain dysfunction).
2. To search for causative factors, of past or present, which may be responsible for the condition.
3. To establish the child's unique profile of specific deficits and skills which relate to learning proficiency, style and acquisition.
4. To enable the clinicians to chart and institute the most logical program of educational and medical therapies.

To attain these objectives, a multidisciplinary diagnostic evaluation is requisite.

The guidelines for such a diagnostic evaluation were incorporated into the documental report of Task Force One of the National Project on Minimal Brain Dysfunction (Learning Disabilities) in Children.[1] The general format follows.

GUIDELINES FOR THE DIAGNOSTIC EVALUATION OF DEVIATING CHILDREN

Part A — Medical Evaluation

1. Histories:
   a. *Medical* — To include pre-, peri-, and postnatal information. Details of all childhood illnesses should be obtained, including age of child at time of illness, symptoms, severity, course and care (such as physician in attendance, hospitalization required, etc.)
   b. *Developmental* — To include details of motor, language, adaptive and personal-social development.
   c. *Family-Social* — To involve parents, child and others as indicated. The family-social history should include detailed information regarding family constellation, acculturation factors, specific interpersonal family dynamics, emotional stresses and traumata.

2. Physical examination:
   a. *General* — To evaluate general physical status and to search for systemic disease. The physical examination should be done as part of the current evaluation of the child, and not obtained at a previous time for some other purpose, e.g., routine preschool checkup or in conjunction with a previous illness. Many child study clinics require a report on the "physical status" of the child from the family physician or pediatrician as part of their referral policy. It is not uncommon, however, for the physician simply to fill out the clinic's requested form from his past records on the child without conducting a current examination.

    b. *Neurologic* — To evaluate neurologic function and to search for specific disorders of the nervous system. The developmental aspects of neurologic integration assume primary importance for this examination, especially with reference to integrated motor acts and skills as opposed to simple reflexes.

3. Special examinations:
    a. *Ophthalmologic* — To include visual acuity, fields and fundi examinations.
    b. *Otologic* — To include audiometric and otoscopic examinations.

4. Routine laboratory tests:
    a. *Serologic*
    b. *Urinalysis*
    c. *Hematologic*

5. Special laboratory tests (only when specifically indicated) :
    a. *Electroencephalographic* — To include wake, sleep and serial tracings.
    b. *Radiologic*
    c. *Pneumoencephalographic*
    d. *Angiographic*
    e. *Biochemical*
    f. *Genetic Assessment:* Chromosome Analysis

Part B — Behavioral Assessment

1. Academic history:

To involve child's teachers and principal, with their observations regarding school behavior as well as academic progress and achievement. The child's school records, including samples of schoolwork and test results, should be available to the diagnostic team.

2. Psychological evaluation:

The following areas represent the core of the psychological evaluation:
    a. Individual comprehensive assessment of intellectual functioning.
    b. Measures of complex perceptual functioning involving all sensory channels.
    c. Behavioral observations in a variety of settings.
    d. Additional indices of learning and behavior as indicated.

3. Language evaluation:

Involves detailed assessment of speech production and language behavior. To include audiometric screening; assessment of articulation, voice quality and rate; and thorough appraisal of the receptive, integrative and expressive aspects of language.

4. Educational evaluation:

An educational diagnostician should conduct detailed analyses of academic abilities, including achievement assessment for details of levels and methods of skill acquisition, e.g., in reading, computation, spelling and writing.

*   *   *

You will note that these areas of assessment are not detailed, and do not indicate to the clinician, in cookbook fashion, the exact manner in which they should be done. These guidelines were included in the report to point up the fact that *each* of these areas *should* be evaluated on *every* child. Otherwise, the child and his parents do not receive full benefit from present knowledge regarding diagnostic procedures for children. And, of more importance, gross errors in diagnosis, hence treatment, can result.

One shudders to consider the toll in personal tragedy and monetary outlay endured by parents as a result of incomplete, hence spurious evaluations of their children.

*   *   *

At this point, a review of the characteristics associated with minimal brain dysfunction (learning disabilities) seems appropriate, since these attributes can serve as *case finding "signs,"* and illustrate certain aspects of the individual case assessment:[2,3]

THE MAJOR SIGNS AND SYMPTOMS OF MINIMAL BRAIN DYSFUNCTION[2]

1. *Average or above intellectual capacity* as determined by comprehensive individual intellectual assessment by a qualified clinician.
2. *Specific learning disabilities.* The most commonly affected academic skills are reading, arithmetic and/or spelling. There are concomitant difficulties with abstract concepts such as time and space and in mastering tasks which are dependent upon fine perceptual discrimination and intact integrative processes within the various perceptual systems.
3. *Perceptual deficits* may occur in one or several of the sensory channels, i.e., visual, auditory, kinesthetic, tactile, etc. Printing, writing and drawing may be poor for age and measured intelligence. Figure-ground and/or whole-part discriminations and relationships may also be affected.
4. *Coordination deficits.* The child may appear clumsy or awkward. Motor coordination deficits may involve either *fine* muscle performance such as buttoning, tying, etc., or activities which require *gross* motor coordination such as walking, riding a bicycle, swimming, baseball and other such sports.

5. *Abnormal motor activity level:*

    a. *Hyperactivity* — Child appears to be in constant motion, flitting from one object or activity to another; or he may display extreme restlessness. Hyperactivity can also manifest as voluble, uninhibited speech, or in disorganized thought processes.

    b. *Hypoactivity* — Child described as slow and daydreamy, in that he moves, thinks and speaks at a markedly reduced rate. Often such slow-responding children will have an "aphasoid" quality in their expresive oral language.

6. *Emotional lability.* The child may be considered highstrung, overly sensitive, fluctuating. He may have quick changes of emotional response from high temper to easy manageability. He may be panicked by what would seem to others as a minimally stressful situation. Such mercurial behavioral shifting is most characteristic of the hyperactive child. On the other hand, the hypoactive youngster is most commonly sweet and even tempered, cooperative, diligent and displays a high tolerance for failure and frustration.

7. *Short attention span and/or distractibility.* The child is unable to concentrate on one activity for the length of time appropriate for his age and intelligence. He is drawn to irrelevant stimuli in his environment which interfere with academic and social learning situations. Some children show a tendency to become locked in a simple repetitious motor activity or preoccupation with one verbal topic. This latter characteristic is referred to as "perseveration."

8. *Impulsivity.* This characteristic is again most commonly associated with the hyperactive child. The youngster seems incapable of controlling or inhibiting his impulses to touch or handle objects, and sometimes persons, when in a new or overstimulating environment. He frequently speaks without checking himself. Such impulsivity easily leads the child into conflict with the demands for conformity as established by family, school and society. Some of the more involved children may commit striking antisocial acts, to the point of fire-setting, stealing, etc., with only a modicum of provocation. The immediacy of the act prevents the child from foreseeing the consequences of his behavior.

9. *Equivocal or "soft" neurological signs.* Among the most often noted among these youngsters are transient strabismus, poor hand-eye coordination, mixed laterality, confused laterality, speech impairment or a history of slow speech development or irregularity, developmental discrepancies and general clumsiness.

Note: This list of characteristics should not be used as a check-list for a nonclinical diagnosis of minimal brain dysfunction. It can, of course, be used as the starting point of an individualized educational program for specific children who show disabilities in learning. It is important to emphasize that a given child may not have symptoms in all or even many of these areas, since each child will have his own particular cluster of symptoms (for example, reading disability, hyperactivity and short attention span). The level of the child's innate intelligence and the nature of his underlying temperament as they interact with various environmental factors, will determine the form and excellence of his maneuvers to compensate for his deficits or deviations.

The following material concerning the psychological evaluation as part of a total diagnostic assessment is drawn, in part, from unpublished material developed at a special meeting sponsored by the Ciba Pharmaceutical Company, and held in Fort Lauderdale, Florida in May, 1966. Approximately twenty specialists from the United States and Canada, representing the fields of clinical child psychology, pediatrics, child psychiatry and neurology, met to consider and formulate a comprehensive diagnostic evaluation for the child with minimal brain dysfunction.

The psychologists were in astonishing agreement as to what should constitute the psychological evaluation. Moreover, it seemed advantageous to approach psychological assessment from at least two levels of completeness.

There was complete agreement among the psychologists that the *basic* or *minimal* evaluation should include *all* of the following measures. This survey was designated as the Level One Assessment. It is the writer's opinion that the Level One Assessment is essential for *any* child, regardless of reason for referral to a child study center.

Level One Assessment

1. The *complete* Wechsler Intelligence Scale for Children, consisting of 5 Verbal Subtests and 5 Performance Subtests. (There can be no short-cuts in the assessment of the intellectual functioning level of children.)
2. The Bender Visual-Motor Gestalt Test.
3. The Draw-A-Person Test (Goodenough-Harris).
4. The Gray Oral Reading Test (1965 Revision).
5. The Wide Range Achievement Test (1965 Revision).

Compiling the Level Two Assessment was a more difficult matter, since it was necessary to separate the ideal from the practical, and a routine clinical assessment from research evaluation. It was agreed, however, that each of the following measures should be obtained or the components mentioned should receive diagnostic attention:

Level Two Assessment

1. Detroit Test of Learning Aptitude.
2. Measures of visual perception.
3. Measures of auditory perception.
4. Measures of motor performance.
5. Measures of concept formation.
6. Appraisal of emotional lability.
7. Personal observations of the child in a variety of settings, in addition to observations and information from parents, teachers and others.
8. Illinois Test of Psycholinguistic Abilities.
9. Other measures as indicated for individual child.

For research purposes, the psychologists designed a master list of forty tests and measurements. Such an evaluation would require approximately three eight-hour days to administer, and this does not include the time necessary for scoring, evaluation and reporting the data obtained. Time alone and wear and tear on the child (and psychologist) would make such a procedure impractical in a diagnostic clinic. It is of scientific importance that clinical and research professionals are giving such serious thought to these matters, and that similar evaluations are being included in research designs. Present and future clinical and experimental research will enable us to distill the essential components of the psychological evaluation for children with learning disabilities.

A vital issue confronting us today can be incorporated into the following question: Is such an elaborate diagnostic procedure necessary in order to establish a diagnosis of learning disabilities and to enable the clinicians to initiate a useful therapeutic program for the child?

The answer, in my opinion, is a resounding No!

What then can be concluded? The Level One Assessment is absolutely necessary and represents the core of a psychological evaluation for children with learning disabilities. This, in addition to a complete educational evaluation should be sufficient for inaugurating an educational program based on the unique needs of the child.

*   *   *

The results of the diagnostic evaluation, simply stated, are for the major purpose of enabling the diagnostic team to make appropriate and logical decisions regarding habilitation of the child. These decisions are frequently limited by the services available in the community and/or the financial status of the family. If, for example, the child requires prescriptive teaching and this is available in an existing learning disabilities program in the public school system, then a decision regarding educational therapy is simplified. On the other hand, if the public school system is not meeting the needs of children with learning disabilities through special programming, then the team must consider alternate recommendations such as private tutoring, enrollment in a local private school, assignment to the educational therapist within the clinic facility, instructing the parents in certain techniques of home teaching and training, etc. When required services are not available in the local community, the clinic team may have to negotiate for enrollment of the child in a private out-of-state residential school which specializes in teaching disordered children.

Many of the needed services for the child and his family may be provided by the psychologist and/or other members of the clinic team. These would include parent counseling, child psychotherapy, medication management of the child, consultation with school personnel, etc.

The role of the individual psychologist will vary according to many factors including his particular experience, interests and talents; responsibility assignments in his work setting; the availability of ancillary service personnel; leadership abilities, etc.

REFERENCES

1. CLEMENTS, S.D.: *Minimal Brain Dysfunction in Children: Terminology and Identification.* Washington, U.S. Government Printing Office, 1966.
2. CLEMENTS, S.D.: *Some Aspects of the Characteristics, Management, and Education of the Child with Minimal Brain Dysfunction.* Little Rock, Arkansas Association for Children with Learning Disabilities, Inc., 1966.
3. EDGINGTON, R., and CLEMENTS, S.D.: *An Indexed Bibliography on the Educational Management of Children with Learning Disabilities.* Chicago, Argus Communications, 1967.

Chapter 9

Testing Children with Learning Disabilities

LESTER TARNOPOL

INTRODUCTION

THE PRESCRIPTIVE TEACHING approach for children with learning disabilities depends primarily upon two things: first, a differential diagnosis of the child's specific abilities and disabilities based upon an adequate psychological testing program, and second, that the results of these tests be provided to a specially trained teacher who can both teach in the areas of the child's strengths and strengthen his weaknesses.

The key persons in a prescriptive teaching program for educationally handicapped children appear to be the psychologist, the language therapist and the teacher. Current teaching practices suggest that in the group, the teacher should teach to the child's sensory strengths. In individual instruction, the teacher is advised to strengthen his areas of perceptual weakness. Such individualized teaching depends upon knowledge of the child's specific sensory strengths and deficits from testing.

There are several points of view currently in vogue with respect to testing. At one extreme, there are those who propose that testing is the key to proper teaching. Thus they are attempting to develop better, more specifically diagnostic tests of visual perception, motor functioning and auditory perception. As this is accomplished, they are also attempting to develop a highly individualized, specific teaching-prescription for each child based upon precise knowledge of his ability level in each different learning-related, sensory area. At the other extreme, there are those who propose that diagnostic testing may be unnecessary since, for example, all children are said to respond best to auditory methods of teaching reading regardless of diagnosis (based on a sound-symbol, phonics emphasis). And indeed, there is some preliminary evidence to this effect. Others believe that specific diagnosis in depth is unnecessary since a good teacher will arrive at her own diagnosis and prescription based upon experience. Finally, some advocate that it is more important to examine and correct the teaching methods to achieve best results.

We are fully cognizant of the fact that there is considerable controversy concerning both diagnosis and methods of teaching children with learning disabilities. Our present position remains eclectic since both of these areas

Note: Parts of this paper were published in the *Academic Therapy Quarterly*, III, 2 Winter, 1967-68.

have been only minimally researched and there appear to be a number of different approaches to teaching these children, each of which seems helpful for some children. At any rate, no method has proved to be completely effective so far, and no definitive research has been performed to assure us of the relative merits of the several methods now under study. Since the treatment of learning disabilities gives promise to become the largest single field within the scope of special education, it is vital that the research in this field be greatly expanded.

Since diagnosis and prescriptive teaching are being used in many programs, it is felt that the psychologists and teachers connected with programs for children with learning disabilities should be well acquainted with a complete test battery. At present, many psychological testing programs are inadequate. It might be helpful to look at some of the more complete testing programs which have been developed.

Attempts are being made to develop an adequate psychological testing program for children with learning disabilities. With this type of help, schools and clinics may be able to develop their own testing programs. At the Symposium on Learning Disabilities held in San Francisco in 1966, it was suggested that psychologists connected with programs for educationally handicapped children should become familiar with the following tests plus some alternate ones so that they may be able to give each recommended test battery. The first test battery is for identification or case finding purposes only. The second test battery is the assessment or diagnostic battery which is used to make a differential diagnosis. The diagnosis should specify the child's educational and perceptual abilities and specific learning disabilities. This is the important information which must be supplied to the teacher. Clements has suggested the following tentative test batteries in his chapter on case finding.[1] The batteries are repeated here for convenience.

TEST BATTERIES FOR CHILDREN WITH LEARNING DISABILITIES
Identification Test Battery

The Identification Test Battery should be used for case finding purposes only. It should be used to tell which children are educationally handicapped and need special help. It is *not* sufficient testing to make an assessment or differential diagnosis of the child's specific disabilities.

1. Wechsler Intelligence Scale for Children.
2. Bender Visual-Motor Gestalt Test.
3. Draw-A-Person Test, Goodenough-Harris.
4. Jastak Wide Range Achievement Test — 1965.
5. Gray Oral Reading Test — 1965.

Assessment Test Battery

The Assessment Test Battery is used to make the differential diagnosis of the child's abilities and specific disabilities. In cases where no specific test is given below, there are several tests available in the literature from which a selection may be made.

1. Detroit Test of Learning Aptitude.
2. Tests of Visual Perception.
3. Tests of Auditory Perception.
4. Motor Performance Tests.
5. Tests of Concept Formation.
6. Measures of Emotional Lability.
7. Illinois Test of Psycholinguistic Abilities.
8. Other measures as indicated.
9. Observations of Parents and Teachers.
10. Observations of Child Psychologist.

Identification Test Batteries are now in fairly general use and should not present too many difficulties to psychologists. In all cases, it is recommended that the testing program be headed by a competent psychologist, preferably at the Ph.D. level, who should both train and review the work of the testers. When first confronted with the Assessment Test Battery, some may demur. The major problems will be that some psychologists will not be familiar with all the tests, and some may not have enough time to give them all. Since they can learn the tests, given a competent chief psychologist, the only real problem is time. In order to have time, it will be necessary to allot funds to increase the number of psychologists in many school testing programs.

The complete assessment test battery probably will take the equivalent of a full day or even more for each child. It is also important to recognize that many children, especially the hyperactive, distractible variety, may not be testable for more than a few minutes at a time. Thus, a test such as the Wechsler Intelligence Scale for Children may take a week or more to complete with some children who may only be able to cooperate for one subscale at a time. On the other hand, this widely believed concept needs to be investigated further as there is evidence reported by Bateman that handicapped children, who were literally pushed through a full test battery, did not make materially different IQ scores than they had when very carefully tested to maintain cooperation and rapport.[2]

Another example of an interesting diagnostic test battery has been presented by Bannatyne of the Institute for Research on Exceptional Children at the University of Illinois.[3] His battery includes the following:

1. Wechsler Intelligence Scale for Children.
2. Illinois Test of Psycholinguistic Abilities.
3. Frostig Visual-Motor Perception Test.
4. Bender Visual-Motor Gestalt Test.
5. Lincoln-Oseretsky Motor Test.
6. Graham-Kendall Memory-for-Designs Test.
7. Examination by speech therapist.
8. Achievement Tests by teacher.

Bannatyne suggests that an important section of the report be written by the educational psychologist, the speech therapist and the teacher as a team. This section should include a tentative program of diagnostic remediation to train the deficit areas and reinforce through intact sensory areas.

Silver and Hagin have been studying the specific reading disability syndrome in children for fifteen years at New York University — Bellevue Medical Center.[4] Their research has contributed a great deal to both diagnosis and remediation in this field. The teaching plan which they have devised was based upon five learning modalities which they considered to be important from both diagnostic and pragmatic considerations. The teaching modalities included laterality, visual perception, auditory perception, tactile and kinesthetic procedures. They found that children both from disadvantaged and middle class backgrounds with specific reading disability tended to have similar perceptual and neurological deficits. As the result of follow-up studies of these children from about age ten to age twenty, they have decided that it is most important to concentrate their remedial efforts on stimulating the areas of perceptual deficit.

The test battery used by Silver and Hagin is reproduced below since it details the types of tests which are required in an assessment battery.

TESTS USED BY SILVER AND HAGIN

Neurological: Classical Examination Plus
  1. Right-Left Discrimination
  2. Handedness, eyedness, footedness
  3. Extension Test

Perceptual Integrative
  1. Visuo-motor
      a. Bender Visual-Motor Gestalt Test
      b. Visual Figure-Background: Marble-Board Test (Strauss and Werner)
      c. Reversible Figures
      d. Embedded Figures (Gottschaldt)

2. Auditory
   a. Auditory Discrimination
   b. Auditory Figure-Background
   c. Auditory Blending (Roswell-Chall)
   d. Matching Initial Consonants
   e. Matching Final Consonants
3. Tactile
   a. Face-Hand Test (M. Bender)
   b. Stereognosis (recognition of shapes by touch)
   c. Tactile Figure-Ground (Strauss and Werner)
4. Body Image
   a. Goodenough Drawing
   b. Finger Gnosis
5. Sequencing
   a. Objects
   b. Digits
   c. Words
   d. Sentences
   e. Days of the Week
   f. Months of the Year
   g. Clock Test (H. Head)
6. Educational
   a. Wide Range Achievement Test: Reading and Spelling Sections (Jastak)
   b. Appropriate level of Metropolitan Reading Test
   c. Writing Sample
7. Articulation Inventory

RESEARCH

Since about 1960, controlled empirical studies of children with learning disabilities have begun to appear in the journals. Previously, the work in this field tended to be primarily clinical-observational. Rigorous research is more difficult than clinical observation. However, no field of study can mature into a science without such research. Because of the critical nature of the learning problem in the lives of today's children it is essential that both clinical observation and research proceed at an accelerated pace. Some of the results of scientific research in the learning disabilities field will be cited to indicate some of the recent findings of value.

Wolf conducted an investigation of 198 measurement procedure variables in an attempt to find those significant to specific language disability (dyslexia).[5] He used thirty-two boys who were diagnosed as dyslexics with average or better intelligence but who had no apparent medical or emotional problems, and who were in the latter part of the third or fourth grades. They also were from the middle to above socioeconomic level. The control group consisted of twenty-three normal readers of the same average intelligence who also met the same criteria.

For this group, it was found that only one of eight types of reading errors measured was significant, indicating that only one type of reading error was common to these dyslexics. This proved to be the well-known word reversal error, such as *was* for *saw*. The experimental group were found to be significantly poorer than the control group in reading, spelling, handwriting and reproduction of the alphabet.

An important auditory perception test which is not sufficiently used in the diagnosis of children with learning disabilities is the Seashore Measures of Musical Talents.[6] This is one of the best special aptitude tests on the market. Because it is primarily a music aptitude test, it is not always recognized as a test of auditory perception. Wolf found that four of the six areas of auditory discrimination measured by the Seashore test differentiated the dyslexics from the normal readers. These were rhythm, time, tonal memory and auditory blending, all of which were significant at better than the 0.01 probability level. This finding further reinforces the concept that more intensive work needs to be done in auditory perceptual diagnostic testing and remediation with children with learning disabilities.

Tests For Brain Damage

Another area of research which has assumed importance, partly because it is controversial, and partly because prevention and remediation may in the long run depend upon specific knowledge, is determining if, when, and to what extent brain damage is involved in the condition. Reitan has been especially active in this research area and has attempted to develop a test battery for detecting brain damage.

Reitan has listed a battery of tests selected for routine use in the Neuropsychology Laboratory at the Indiana University Medical Center.[7] This battery of tests covers a wide range of psychological functions each of which contributes some validity to the whole. Halstead's Neuropsychological Test Battery[8] is used in conjunction with a number of supplementary tests. Halstead's battery consists of tests measuring a number of different sensory functions which are listed below.

1. *Category Test.* The subject attempts to find the common principle underlying each of seven groups of pictures.
2. *Critical Flicker Frequency and Critical Flicker Frequency Deviation.* The subject states the point at which a flickering light from a stroboscopic type of instrument appears to fuse into a steady light.

3. *Tactual Performance Test.* The subject is blindfolded and places blocks into spaces on a board. Then with the blindfold removed and the board out of sight he is asked to draw the board and blocks.

4. *Rhythm Test.* This is the subtest of the Seashore Tests of Musical Talent.

5. *Speech Sounds Perception Test.* The subject attempts to select the correct one of four printed alternatives for each item while listening to a recording of sixty spoken nonsense words which are variations on the *ee* sound.

6. *Finger Oscillation Test.* The subject's finger-tapping speed is measured.

7. *Time Sense Test (Visual and Memory Components).* The subject is required to press a key causing a clock hand to rotate ten times and then to stop it as close to the starting position as possible. After twenty trials, he repeats the test with the clock face turned away.

Additional Tests Used by Reitan

8. *Modification of Halstead-Wepman Aphasia Screening Test.*[9] This test involves naming common objects, spelling, reading, writing, calculating, enunciating, identifying numbers, letters and body parts, knowing right from left and understanding spoken language.

9. *Trail Making Test.* The subject is required to connect circles on a sheet of paper as quickly as possible.

10. *Sensory Imperception.* The subject is tested for ability to perceive tactile, auditory, and visual bilateral simultaneous stimuli in separate tests.

11. *Tactile Finger Recognition.* The subject is required to identify individual fingers after each is touched.

12. *Finger-Tip Number Writing Perception.* The subject is asked to tell which numbers have been written on his finger-tips without looking.

13. *Tactile Form Recognition.* The subject is asked to identify coins by touch alone.

Tests for Minimal Brain Dysfunction

It has been generally noted that children who exhibit the learning and behavioral problems associated with the concept of minimal brain dysfunction usually may be found to have no observable neurological deficits on a rountine neurological examination. However, many pediatric-neurologists have established a more extensive type of examination for these children where they look for certain indicators which they call "soft signs." Peters *et al.* have suggested that these procedures do not tend to involve classical reflexes.[10] Rather they look at the relative efficiency of integrated actions, sequences of movements, ability to change directions, etc., indicating less than adequate muscular control at each age level. It is further suggested that such muscular effort tends to cause minor irrelevant movements which may interfere with the main muscular effort and which may be observed. These are important indicators and should be noted, even if the child can correct them when they are pointed out to him. Peters *et al.* also have developed a Special Neurological Examination to detect minimal brain dysfunctions in children with learning disabilities.[10] In this test, each child receives almost one hundred separate ratings as well as possible subtotals and a total rating.

Dykman and Peters are also engaged in attempting to correlate a number of physiological tests with minimal brain dysfunction and learning disabilities. Their tests include conditioning, skin resistance, heart rate, respiration, muscle action potentials, level of physical activity and electroencephalograms plus the Special Neurological tests mentioned above. They state that their data suggests that children with minimal brain dysfunction "are less reactive in skin resistance and heart rate than normal controls. Tentatively, we have interpreted this data as indicating faulty coupling between cortex and brainstem arousal mechanisms important in attention and perception."[11]

Development of Kindergarten Tests

It is well known that early habilitation of children with learning disabilities is easier to accomplish than later rehabilitation. If possible, habilitation should start before first grade when the children normally start to learn to read. It is recommended that public schools screen all children in kindergarten and be prepared to start remedial work with those who need it. For kindergarten use, screening tests that the teachers can use are most important. Many California School Districts have started to test all kindergarten children using screening batteries which they have developed. Therefore, it would be most important and beneficial if an adequate, standardized, valid test battery were made available.

DeHirsch, Jansky and Langford are developing an important test battery to be used in kindergarten to screen children who will most likely have difficulty learning to read.[12] This battery of ten tests is now being validated. In a longitudinal study of three years duration they tested the efficacy of thirty-seven kindergarten tests in predicting reading failures at the second grade level. From these thirty-seven tests, ten were selected as most promising to constitute a predictive test battery. Their predictive index tests are as follows:

1. Pencil use: The child is observed using a pencil.
2. Bender Visual-Motor Gestalt Test.
3. Wepman Auditory Discrimination Test.
4. Number of Words Used in a Story: The number of words used by a child in telling "The Three Bears" is counted.
5. Categories: The child is asked to state class names for three groups of words: i.e., boys (Tom-Charley-Henry) .
6. Horst Reversals Test.
7. Gates Word-Matching Subtests.
8. Gates Word Recognition I.
9. Gates Word Recognition II.
10. Gates Word Reproduction Test.

The authors suggest that these tests will not only be predictive of reading failure but will also be useful for diagnostic purposes leading to prescriptive teaching.

PROBLEMS OF DEVELOPING PSYCHOLOGICAL TESTS

The development of a psychological test, no matter how simple, is a long, arduous, expensive task. It is not possible to produce a set of specific test items from one's knowledge of a subject such as motor proficiency, auditory perception, visual perception or even a simpler modality, which can surely constitute an adequate test. The selection of a really good set of items only results from years of use of the test and many revisions. For this reason, the oldest tests such as the intelligence tests are generally the best. Most of the tests used to detect specific sensory deficits related to learning are either new tests or are in process of development. Thus, they should logically be expected to contain many limitations. No psychological test is a perfect measuring instrument, in fact, most tests are rather gross instruments for measuring the quality they attempt to assess. Such tests are used primarily because they are the only ones available and because they can measure the quality better than chance or guessing. Although the many limitations of tests, including reliability, validity, norms, etc., are generally stressed in courses on testing, it seems that testers too often forget these aspects of tests as soon as they leave college. Somehow, tests tend to develop a magical quality off campus!

When tests are first made available to the market, they are generally labeled "Experimental Edition" and users are requested to make their findings available to the authors in order to help develop more extensive norm groups, reliability and validity data, to inform the authors about problems discovered when using the test and about new uses. If the test is in an area of great need, many psychologists ignore the fact that it is labeled "experimental" and rush to use it. This, in and of itself, is not bad. The important question is, How is the test used?

Unfortunately, the "experimental" test is sometimes used as a clinical instrument to determine children's deficiencies with only minor reservations concerning the reliability and validity of the observations made. When this is done, the resulting diagnosis may be improper. Even the Stanford-Binet Intelligence Test, which is generally considered to be a highly reliable, valid instrument is, at times, misused with the result that children of normal intelligence are placed in classes for the mentally retarded, especially in the cases of educationally deprived or handicapped children. It is probably best to use experimental editions of tests as part of a research program which both gives some clinical diagnostic information about the children and simultaneously produces further information about the degree of validity of the test as a measuring instrument. This is a way of determining the diagnostic validity of the test for your specific population of children. At any rate, all tests, no matter how well validated, are limited in the clinical diagnostic information which they can render by their coefficients of reliability and validity and by the nature of the populations which have been used to make up the tables of norms.

INTELLIGENCE TESTING

It will be observed that almost all of the recommended test batteries use the Wechsler Intelligence Scale for Children (WISC) rather than the older Stanford-Binet Intelligence Test. This is because the Verbal and Performance IQ scores plus the twelve subtest scores which the WISC provides have been found very useful for diagnostic purposes. However, the Wechsler tests cannot be used with children under four years of age which is the lower limit of the Wechsler Pre-School Intelligence Scale, so that two- and three-year-olds must still be tested with the Stanford-Binet.

Since intelligence tests were originally developed to determine whether or not a child could learn in a normal school environment, it is not surprising that they are good predictors of how well children might be expected to do in school. The Binet test was developed around the concept of intelligence as the abilities to reason, judge and to be self critical in order to correct one's errors. Wechsler defined intelligence for the purposes of his test as the overall ability to act purposefully, to reason and to deal effectively with the environment.

The present concept of the Intelligence Quotient (IQ) is that it changes for many people by significant amounts from age two on. Below age two, there are no reliable intelligence tests as yet. For a child less than two years of age, the mid-parent IQ may be the easiest obtainable indicator of the child's probable IQ at age six, the coefficient of correlation being about 0.50. It is believed that both genetic inheritance and environmental influences contribute to intelligence, but to what extent each contributes is not yet understood. Many studies have demonstrated that intelligence test scores can be raised significantly by an improved environment.

How can we determine the intelligence of a child with learning disabilities in order to place him in the most adequate educational environment? It is probably best to consider a child's intelligence test score as representing his minimal level of ability at the time tested. For purposes of establishing what he may be expected to do in a favorable prescriptive teaching environment, either the Performance or Verbal IQ may be used, whichever is higher, rather than the full IQ for these children. In cases where medication remarkably increases attention span, the increased test scores achieved while under the influence of medication should be considered indicative of the child's potential. In some cases, widely differing subtest scores will depress both the Performance and Verbal IQ ratings. In this case, the psychologist may wish to estimate the child's potential to learn based upon which abilities are intact and how adequate prescriptive teaching has proven to be in the areas of deficit. Finally, in many cases, the psychologist will observe strong evidence of good thinking ability which the test scores do not seem to reflect. This type of subjective clinical evidence should, of course, always be reported precisely as observed with conclusions related to the child's potential drawn.

It will be noted that, whereas in a normally developing child, the full scale IQ may generally be considered to be quite meaningful as a measure of his present intelligence level, with the educationally handicapped or educationally deprived child a good deal of clinical judgment enters the decision. This is because we are interested in determining the child's intelligence (ability to learn) for purposes of assigning him to a special placement which will attempt to help him overcome his deficits.

WISC Sub Tests

Bannatyne reported a study in which he tested three groupings of the WISC sub-scales.[13] He grouped the Comprehensive, Similarities and Vocabulary Subtests into a category which he termed Conceptualizing Ability; the Picture Completion, Block Design and Object Assembly Subtests into the category of Spatial Ability; and the Digit Span, Coding and either Picture Arrangement or Arithmetic Subtests into a category called Sequencing Ability.

In a study carried out in Lancashire, eighty-seven boys were tested who were between the ages of eight and eleven years and were poor readers but who were functioning well in the normal school system. It was found that the poor readers tended to score highest on the Spatial Ability Subtest group, lowest on the Sequencing Ability Subtests, and intermediate on the Conceptualizing Subtests. A control group of adequate readers was found to perform equally well, on the average, on all three WISC Subtest groups.

Bannatyne then used Penfield and Robert's WISC Subtest groupings to restudy the same population with most interesting results. These authors grouped the Information, Arithmetic and Digit Span Sub-scales into Left Brain Hemisphere Tests comprising Symbol Manipulation; and the Picture Arrangement, Block Design and Object Assembly Sub-scales into Right Brain Hemisphere Tests comprising Spatial Organization. For the control group of normal readers, 50 per cent did better on the Left Hemisphere Tests and 50 per cent did better on the right Hemisphere Tests, indicating no special hemispheric effect. For the poor readers, on the other hand, 82 per cent did better on the Right Hemisphere Tests than on the Left Hemisphere Tests. Bannatyne concluded that dyslexic boys functioning well in normal schools seem to be predominantly using their right hemispheres for learning, and mainly in terms of spatial concepts. No mention was made by Bannatyne of handedness, etc., which would give an indication of which hemisphere was dominant for motor activity as a basis for comparison.

Several studies have been performed on the effects of unilateral brain damage on cognitive functions. In general, these studies indicate that verbal deficits appear to be related to left hemisphere damage while nonverbal, visual-motor or spatial deficits seem to be related to right hemisphere damage. Although Bannatyne's subjects were not generally considered to be brain damaged, some may have been minimal neurological dysfunction cases, but all were operating in the normal school. The reading difficulties of his population were generally correlated with poor Symbol Manipulation and good Spatial Organization which in turn appeared to be related to inadequate left hemisphere function.

Other studies of children who have difficulty learning to read indicate that many have high Verbal and low Performance IQ scores on the WISC, others have the opposite relationship of scores and a few have about the same Verbal and Performance IQ scores. These findings coincide with the many different possible causes of learning disabilities which must be individually diagnosed for purposes of prescriptive teaching.

CRITERIA OF ACCEPTABILITY OF TESTS

The major areas of testing for sensory dysfunction related to learning disabilities are at present visual perception, auditory perception and motor function. Several tests have been mentioned in these areas. Most tests are fairly new and require considerable work to perfect them. A number of new tests are being developed which attempt to determine very specific deficits in each different sensory modality within the three major areas mentioned. These determinations may prove to be very valuable, or alternatively, we may be disappointed to discover that nothing important is added to diagnosis and remediation by these extra refinements.

In order to be acceptable, all of the tests must pass established rigorous criteria. For our purposes, even this is not enough. Beyond the seven criteria listed below, we will also wish to know that remedial procedures can be significantly improved by the diagnostic information supplied by each test.

In general, the minimal criteria which all tests must meet are that they must have the following:

1. Standardized administration procedures.
2. Objective standardized scoring procedures.
3. Acceptable reliability coefficients.*
4. Validity coefficients against acceptable criteria.†
5. Norms or standardization groups.
6. Tables of standard scores vs raw scores.
7. Information about how to interpret test scores.

Since a test of visual perception and visual-motor coordination has been recommended as part of any assessment test battery for educationally handicapped children, and many school districts and clinics are using the Marianne Frostig Developmental Test of Visual Perception,[14] it may be useful to review this test briefly as an example.

If a child is having difficulty in school, his teacher may observe evidence of a visual problem and ask that his eyes be examined. The eye examination will often test only the child's visual acuity or his gross ability to see. If the child has a neurological problem, he may generally be found to have adequate vision by this test. Since the child's problem tends to be a perceptual one and is not a matter of visual acuity, the usual eye test will fail to reveal this abnormality.

Visual perceptual abnormalities may be found by optometric and psychological tests of which the Frostig is an example. The child with minimal neurological dysfunction characteristically tends to have perceptual deficiencies.

The Frostig test has the advantages that it meets most of the criteria of acceptability, it may be given by a trained teacher or psychologist, it

---

*Simply defined, reliability is precision of measurement, or the extent to which test scores are reproducible on retesting. The coefficient of reliability is found by giving a test to the same group of subjects twice and correlating the two sets of test scores.

†Simply defined, validity is the extent to which a test measures what it is supposed to measure. The coefficient of validity is found by correlating the test scores with criterion ratings for a group of subjects.

may be given to individual pupils or groups, it tests five independent areas of visual perception, and *remedial exercises are available* so that the teacher can help each child improve in the areas of his specific visual perceptual and visual-motor weaknesses.

When assessing the Frostig test, it is important to keep in mind that tests for children are subject to many difficulties which are inherent in the problems of testing young children. Thus the problems of getting adequate reliability, validity and norms are common to most tests at this age level.

Since inadequate visual perception and motor coordination have both been demonstrated to be related to learning and behavioral problems in many children, some school districts have started to test all kindergarten children with some such test as the Frostig. It should be noted that these tests may be used on *all* children and are not specific to neurologically impaired children. After testing, training to improve visual-perception and motor coordination may be introduced before the children start to learn reading or concurrently. Experience with the Frostig test indicates that it should be administered and interpreted by either a psychologist or teacher *trained* in this test.

The test-retest reliability coefficient for the total test is quite adequate being greater than the accepted minimum of 0.80. However, no reliability studies are given for children below age five. It is assumed that below age five the reliability would be low since other tests have this problem. This means that the results of a single administration to a preschool child should *not* be considered definitive and final judgment about his visual-perception and eye-motor coordination impairment may not be made without further testing or other information. Similarly, the reliabilities of all subtests tend to be low and they vary with age so that one always has to refer to these reliability coefficients when making judgments. On the other hand, there seems to be little reason to disbelieve average or better scores on the subtests since adequate performance is undoubtedly less subject to error.

Failure to understand the meaning and use of the reliability data tends to make the tester's evaluation of the child's scores unreliable. For example, the coefficient of reliability of subtest #1 (eye-hand coordination) for kindergarten children is 0.33. This means that the true variance of the scores is 33 per cent and the *error variance* of the scores is 67 per cent. Thus the probable error in a given score is so great that it is *not* possible to make a reliable judgment of a kindergarten child's eye-motor coordination deficiencies on the basis of a single testing.

The most important single criterion of the usefulness of any test is its validity. Evidence has been presented to indicate that there is a relationship between Frostig Test scores and intellectual functioning, motor coordination, and classroom adjustment for children from kindergarten through the second grade. The teacher should note that these coefficients of validity, while adequate, indicate that there are other important variables affecting the children's ratings on reading ability and classroom adjustment. Frostig gives the validity correlation between the Frostig Developmental Test of Visual Perception and intellectual functioning as 0.50.[14]

Olson correlated the Frostig test with reading as follows:[15]

TABLE 9-I
FROSTIG TEST VS READING

	Coef. of Correlation
1. Frostig test vs Gates paragraph reading test	0.32
2. Frostig test vs. Gates word recognition test	0.42

From Olson, R.[15]

It will be noted that these correlations indicate that relationships exist between visual perception and eye-motor coordination as defined by the Frostig tests and such variables as adjustment and reading. These coefficients of validity are adequate but moderate and are about as high as most good tests are able to achieve. At the same time, it is important to note, as an example, that a correlation of 0.50 accounts for only 25 per cent of the common variance or overlap between the Frostig test and intellectual functioning. Thus 75 per cent of the Frostig test variance and of the criterion (intellectual functioning) variance is accounted for by other unstated variables. This indicates that visual perception and motor coordination are only two among many possible variables which affect reading and learning. This is suggested because many programs for educationally handicapped children stress training in visual perception and motor coordination and tend to neglect the very important area of auditory perception. A child who is unable to hear the differences among *b, d* and *p* will certainly have difficulty distinguishing them in written form.

Finally, although it is recognized that diagnostic testing and its relationship to remediation has not yet been fully explored and that there is controversy concerning the value of specific diagnoses, it is suggested that psychologists and teachers working with educationally handicapped children should learn a great deal about testing lest they be handicapped themselves.

REFERENCES

1. CLEMENTS, S.: The psychologist and case finding. *Symposium on Learning Disabilities.* 1966.
2. BATEMAN, B.: Personal Communication, 1967.
3. BANNATYNE, A.: Matching remedial methods with specific deficits. *1967 International Convocation on Children and Young Adults with Learning Disabilities.* 1967.

4. SILVER, A.A., and HAGIN, R.A.: Specific reading disability—an approach to diagnosis and treatment. *J Special Educ,* Winter 1967, vol. 1, No. 2.

5. WOLF, C.W.: An experimental investigation of specific language disability (dyslexia). *Bull Orton Soc, 17:*32, 1967.

6. SEASHORE, C.E.; LEWIS, D., and SAETVEIT, J.G.: *Seashore Measures of Musical Talents.* New York, Psychological Corp., 1960.

7. REITAN, R.M.: Psychological Assessment of Deficits Associated with Brain Lesions in Subjects with and without Subnormal Intelligence. Mimeographed, Bloomington, Indiana University Medical Center, 1966.

8. HALSTEAD, W.C.: *Brain and Intelligence.* Chicago, U. of Chicago, 1947.

9. HALSTEAD, W.C., and WEPMAN, J.M.: The Halstead-Wepman aphasia screening test. *J Speech Hearing Dis, 14:*9-15, 1949.

10. PETERS, J.E.; CLEMENTS, S.D.; DANFORD, B.H.; DYKMAN, R.A., and REESE, W.G.: A Special Neurological Examination for Children with Minimal Brain Dysfunctions. Mimeographed, Little Rock, University of Arkansas Medical Center, 1966.

11. DYKMAN, R.A., and PETERS, J.E.: Personal Communication, Dec., 1967.

12. DeHIRSCH, K.; JANSKY, J.J., and LANGFORD, W.S.: *Predicting Reading Failure.* New York, Harper, 1966.

13. BANNATYNE, A.: The Etiology of Dyslexia and Color Phonics System. Mimeographed, U. of Ill., 1966.

14. FROSTIG, M., and MASLOW, P., *et al.: Developmental Test of Visual Perception.* Palo Alto, Consulting Psychologists, 1966.

15. OLSON, R.: Relation of achievement test scores and specific reading abilities to the Frostig test of visual perception. *The Optometric Weekly,* July 14, 1966, p. 33.

Chapter 10

Auditory Processes in Children with Learning Disabilities

NAOMI KERSHMAN ZIGMOND

T HE BRAIN, SHIELDED from the world in its bony casing, has no direct contact with the external environment. It must receive information about the environment through data fed to it by sensory organs and must respond to the outer world through the effector organs of the neuromuscular system. Man's five senses, vision, hearing, olfaction, taction and gustation help him to establish a relationship between internal and external worlds. Most useful to him are his "distance senses" of hearing and vision through which he gets information about, and maintains contact with, the environment. Vision is basically a directional sense; it cannot function beyond the peripheral visual field. It is also a selective sense; it ceases to function in sleep, in the dark, and cannot travel through walls or around corners. By contrast, audition is nondirectional and nonselective. We can hear from all directions simultaneously, and we are always "tuned in." We can hear through walls, around corners, in light and darkness, and, although hearing "shifts gears" in sleep, it does not cease. We can learn to ignore large segments of the sound world during sleep, but are easily awakened by the faint crying of the baby.

Hearing is man's primary scanning sense. Moreover, it is the primary channel for language acquisition and interpersonal communication. Yet a survey of the broad field of perception soon discloses an abundance of material, both theoretical and empirical, on the topic of visual perception while the study of hearing lags far behind. In part, difficulty with instrumentation for production of controlled auditory stimuli has been a major drawback to research in auditory perception. From 1873 to the present, toys and noise-makers, clackers and bells, whistles, tuning forks and a myriad of other devices have been used to elicit responses in infants and children. These instruments have produced stimuli of varying and variable loudness and timbre differences which make it difficult and often impossible for experimenters to compare their results.

A second area of difficulty has been in determining a meaningful and reliable response. Such diversified responses as eyeblink, startle response, eye movements, heart rate, respiration rate, increase or decrease in general movement, conditioned sucking or conditioned foot withdrawal, and waking from sleep have been used to determine the presence of auditory sensitivity in infants and young children. Some of these same responses plus verbal responses, pointing responses, button pushing and EEG have been attempted with older children. These results have not been comparable because of differences in attentional and adaptational factors, and because a total lack of response to auditory stimulation cannot be considered as specific evidence that a child cannot hear.

Finally, because the deaf and severely hard-of-hearing child has been found to be extremely limited in his ability to communicate with others, in his personality development and in his educational achievement, researchers have tended to concentrate on techniques for the detection of auditory handicaps (see DiCarlo, Kendall and Goldstein, 1962; Reichstein and Rosenstein, 1964), and on the improvement of the communicative skills of such children, rather than on the development of auditory skills in general.

As a result, there are considerable clinical material on the evaluation of hearing in children and data on the sensory mechanism and the psychophysical properties of the ear (see Stevens and Davis, 1928; Wever, 1949) although little information is available on the development of auditory processes.

MATURATION OF AUDITORY PROCESSES

In the normal child, auditory capacities develop as part of the behavior of the maturing organism and become the foundation on which language is built. First the child learns to recognize and identify sounds, then to make fine discriminations between sounds in his environment. Finally he develops skill in auditory memory and the ability to reauditorize.

Recognition and Identification of Sounds

The normal infant passes through successive growth stages with respect to his sensitiveness to speech vibrations. Most of the data on the time and completeness of the stages of auditory perceptiveness come from the work of Gesell and Armatruda (1956), Cattell (1950), Griffiths (1954) and Darley and Winitz (1961). In general, the stages of response to sounds follow this pattern of maturation: The newborn infant responds to loud noises by crying or startling. By two weeks he assumes a listening attitude to the sound of the human voice. By four weeks he is quieted by sound, and activity is reduced by an approaching sound. By eight weeks he is no longer violently disturbed by loud noises but accepts them as part of his environment, and there is immobilization with attention to the human voice. By four months, there is a blink, smile or some response to the sound of bells, and deliberate head turning in search of sounds or voice. By the fifth to sixth month the normal infant can distinguish friendly from angry talking, demonstrates real interest in the human voice and correctly localizes a bell rung to either side of him.

By the eighth month there is deliberate imitation of sounds and responses to "no-no" and his name. By nine months there are associations of definitely articulated sounds with a particular object, person or action and the bare rudiments of language comprehension.

These stages represent development of the ability to listen as opposed to the innate ability of a child with an intact auditory mechanism to hear. A dysfunction in the brain can inhibit this auditory learning. The child with auditory agnosia hears, but does not interpret what he hears. He is unable to structure his auditory world, to sort out and associate sounds with particular objects or experiences. This child is severely disturbed in fundamental aspects of auditory perception, and is often mistakenly considered deaf or hard-of-hearing. In teaching a child with this generalized deficiency in auditory learning, the primary objective is to help him to utilize his auditory capacities. It is important to avoid treating this child as a deaf child and teaching him compensatory (visual or manual) methods for learning language. In the initial steps of training, the auditory environment is structured as much as possible and training begins by teaching the child an awareness of sound. Then he must be helped to develop consistent and appropriate responses to sounds. Eventually, when these basic skills have been developed, he will learn which sounds to ignore and which sounds require his attention; he will learn to listen.

Discrimination of Sounds

For the purposes of understanding and reproducing speech sounds, it is not enough that the child be able to listen to sounds; he must be able to hear differences between and among complex sounds which vary with respect to individual pitch, quality and intensity characteristics. It is only after listening skills have begun to develop that the child becomes aware of specialized sounds and differences between sounds. Children with auditory language disabilities, difficulties in comprehension of spoken language, often need special training in discrimination. They can distinguish gross but not fine differences. They might be able to differentiate between a knock on the door and the ring of the telephone, but not between a telephone and the door bell. They may confuse meanings of similar sounding words like *cup, cap,* or *cat,* not because of comprehension difficulties but as a result of poor auditory discriminations.

Templin (1957) has related the growth of speech-sound discrimination skills to the emergence of correct articulation patterns in normal children. Other speech pathologists have suggested that inadequate auditory discrimination may result in the development of defective articulation (see Van Riper, 1963; Berry and Eisenson, 1956). This hypothesis is strengthened by research such as that of Kronvall and Diehl (1954). They studied a group of elementary school children with severe functional articulation disorders and concluded that these children exhibit significantly more errors in speech-sound discrimination than a matched group of normally speaking children.

Auditory Memory and Reauditorization

It is not enough to say that auditory impressions must be identified and discriminated from each other; they must also be retained and available in memory storage. Every facet of the language process is dependent to some extent on memory, whether it be of a sound, or a sight, or the capacity to make a remembered noise in speaking, or a remembered movement in writing. Receptive language, which begins to develop in the normal child at about nine months, requires recognizing, discriminating, coding, classifying and storing symbols received by the brain. Many children with neurogenic learning disorders have no difficulty in comprehending single words but are limited in the *amount* of information they can remember at any one time; consequently they have difficulty taking a series of commands or comprehending complex verbal instructions. This difficulty is often referred to as a limited auditory memory span. Anderson (1953) defined "span" as the ability of an individual to retain and associate together for purposes of immediate reproduction, a series of impressions, auditory or visual. In any discussion of auditory processes, auditory memory span cannot be overlooked. Measurements of the maturation of auditory memory span are largely in the literature concerning the development of intelligence. Span tests were first introduced by Binet and have remained an integral part of the evaluation of mental ability. Terman and Merrill (1937) placed the ability to repeat two digits at two years, three digits at three years, four digits at four years. Memory for short sentences was placed at four and a half years. Digit span tests remain on the revised Stanford Binet Intelligence Tests (Terman and Merrill, 1962), and on the Wechsler intelligence tests at both the child (Wechsler, 1949) and adult (Wechsler, 1955) levels.

Putting information into storage is only one aspect of the memory process. In addition to this storing system, there must be a mechanism for retrieval and reproduction of the stored data. Many children with language disorders have no problem in understanding the spoken word, but are deficient in using it to express themselves. They perform well on nonverbal tasks such as drawing or putting puzzle parts together, and on verbal activities not demanding an oral response such as following a series of directions. These children understand and recognize words, have stored words, but they cannot retrieve them; they cannot remember them for spontaneous usage. These children have reauditorization difficulties. Children with reauditorization deficits, or dysnomia, experience great frustration in communicating. They resort to pantomime and gesture to indicate the needed words, or use a functional definition to describe the object whose name cannot be recalled. They try to relate happenings but often give up in desperation because they cannot remember how to say what they have in mind.

The reauditorization difficulties may affect not only the use of simple words or phrases in communicative acts but also the formulation and organization of words according to correct language structure. Children with formulation difficulties tend to omit words, distort the order of words, use incorrect verb tenses and make other grammatical errors long after such erorrs have been recognized and corrected by the normal child. Findings from the field of linguistics are helpful in understanding these syntax disorders (see Brown and Bellugi, 1964; Chomsky, 1967; Ervin, 1964; Lenneberg, 1964). While it appears that a child merely listens, learns, remembers and repeats sentences, the development of syntax is far more than simple repetition. Ability to formulate sentences is a complex skill requiring many integrities, including ability to understand, to remember word sequences, to manipulate symbols and to generate principles for sentence structure. A child cannot remember every sentence he hears, but he holds in mind certain structural patterns, makes abstractions about the relationships of words, and then generates sentences of his own. Even though syntax involves more than simple repetition, the role of memory in learning language cannot be overlooked.

AUDITORY PROCESSES IN WRITTEN LANGUAGE

Thus far our attention has been on the development of auditory language skills and on the disorders of comprehension and use of spoken words. But auditory language is not the only symbol system available to man. Upon this language is superimposed a visual conceptualization, reading. Although recently there has been increasing emphasis on the visual perceptual skills essential to reading (see Frostig and Horne, 1961; Kephart, 1960; Strauss and Lehtinen, 1947) and on intersensory functioning (see Birch, 1962; Myklebust, 1964), the specific role of auditory abilities has received little attention.

Initially, the process of learning to read entails superimposing the read symbol onto the auditory one. Only much later does one read "visually" or "silently" — and it appears that no one ever achieves complete success in reading by vision alone. We all regress and *sound out* words when they are difficult or unfamiliar (Myklebust and Johnson, 1962).

Auditory impressions of words consist not only of sound qualities but also of the temporal distribution of sounds in a pattern. Words are articulated as a sequence of sounds. However, the listener does not deal with each sound separately but rather with groups of sounds taken together (Ladefoged and Broadbent, 1960). The sequence of sounds in speech is presented so rapidly as to appear almost simultaneous; yet a child must be able to differentiate the sequence of sounds as well as the spatial pattern of letters in vision before he can begin to develop a phonetic system by which he can read strange or unfamiliar words (Monroe, 1932). For example, the Gates Diagnostic Reading Test (Gates, 1950) designed for children of 5 and one-half to six years of age, contains a picture test of rhyming words and several other subtests concerned with auditory aspects of word analysis and synthesis, including blending sounds into words or giving words that begin with a specific sound.

In addition to the auditory skills of analysis and synthesis, memory span and reauditorization are necessary for facility with word attack and comprehension (Monroe, 1932; Johnson and Myklebust, 1962). The maturation of auditory processes would seem to be essential for skillful reading and writing. The difficulties encountered by the deaf in learning to read by visual means alone attest to the importance of the auditory system in written language. Also, the study of children who have dyslexia has provided further evidence of the relationship between the auditory and the read word.

Dyslexia may be defined as a reading problem due to primary brain dysfunction. Clinically, children are diagnosed as dyslexic when they have a reading problem despite adequate intellectual capacities, sensory acuity, motor abilities, normal opportunities for learning in home and school and no primary emotional disturbances. Neurological dysfunction, often demonstrable through a neurological examination or EEG, is presumed.

Recently, an experiment was undertaken to evaluate auditory, visual and intersensory functioning in a group of dyslexic boys (Zigmond, 1966). These boys demonstrated at least average intelligence (IQ = 90) on both the verbal and nonverbal scales of the Wechsler Intelligence Scale for Children (Wechsler, 1949), adequate hearing and vision as determined by screening tests of acuity, no gross motor disturbances, no primary problems in emotional adjustment and normal opportunities for learning in school. Tests of oral and silent reading comprehension were administered individually, and a boy was considered to be dyslexic if he could not score within one year of the national norm for his mental age. On the average, the dyslexic group was 2.7 years retarded in reading.

A control group of twenty-five nondyslexic boys of equivalent age and intelligence was selected for comparison. Each control subject obtained a reading score at, above, or within one year below his mental age score; on the average, the reading scores of the control group were within 0.2 years of their mental age scores.

Fifteen tests were selected to appraise auditory, visual and intersensory abilities among the normal and dyslexic children. The battery was drawn from a variety of sources. The basic criterion for inclusion of a test was the assumption that it measured a function related to the acquisition of reading. To some extent, the auditory and visual measures were selected so that direct comparisons could be made between the two sensory systems. Although a completely parallel design was not accomplished, measures of discrimination and memory were included for both sensory modalities. The auditory and visual tests were designed to utilize a single modality for stimulus and response; in contrast, the intersensory tests required exchange of information from one sensory modality to another.

Auditory Measures

Six tests, five measures of auditory memory and one of auditory discrimination, were selected to evaluate auditory functioning. In each test, an auditory stimulus was presented which required a spoken (auditory-vocal) response.

Auditory Discrimination. The Rhythm subtest from the Seashore Test of Musical Talents (Seashore *et al.,* 1939) was selected as a measure of auditory discrimination. The subject heard two prerecorded rhythmic patterns tapped out in quick succession and he was required to tell the examiner whether they were the same or different. There were thirty pairs of patterns with five, six, or seven beats in each pattern.

Memory for Nonsense Words. Nonsense syllables are one of the most frequent devices for measuring auditory memory span. The value of the nonsense syllable lies in the fact that these sound combinations are easily discriminable yet are devoid of conventional meaning and associative imagery. Spencer (1958), in a study of auditory perception in preschool children, used a list of nonsense syllables made up of common English sound elements found in the vocabulary of children by the age of five. In Spencer's study, the syllables were given at the tempo of slow speech with a slight accent on the last syllable and some variations in the melodic line so that there was relatively close correspondence to the rhythm and melody of actual speech.

In this study, Spencer's list of nonsense syllables was revised and expanded so that the results of this test would be comparable to auditory span tests using digits and words. Twelve series were given, ranging from two to six syllables, presented at the conventional rate of one-per-second. Subjects were required to repeat each set of syllables; there were no penalties for distortions of articulation consistent with the child's general speech habits.

Memory for Digits. Tests of digit span have found prominence in mental test batteries since Jacobs (1887); in each test, however, the selection of digit combinations seems arbitrary. The sequence used in the present investigation were adapted from the Wechsler Memory Scale, Digits Forward subtest (Wechsler, 1945). Twelve series were administered, ranging from three to eight digits per series.

Memory for Words. This test was taken from the Detroit Tests of Learning Aptitude, Auditory Attention Span for Unrelated Words subtest (Baker and Leland, 1959). The test was constructed to be equivalent to tests of auditory memory span for digits, using nouns rather than numbers. It consists of fourteen word series, ranging from two to eight words. Words were presented at the conventional rate of one-per-second.

Memory for Sentences. A second subtest from the Detroit Tests of Learning Aptitude, Auditory Attention Span for Related Syllables (Baker and Leland, 1959) introduces the effect of connected language and syntax to the study of immediate auditory memory. The child is asked to repeat the complete sentence given by the examiner. There were forty-three sentences in the test, increasing both in length and structure, as well as in complexity of content. The test was discontinued when a subject made more than two errors in the repetition of three consecutive sentences.

Memory for Rhythmic Sequences. A test of nonverbal auditory memory was devised by Stambak (1951) for use with children with reading and speech problems. It measures ability to reproduce nonverbal, temporally well organized auditory impressions. The subject listens to a rhythmic sequence, a series of irregularly spaced taps, and taps out the pattern just heard. He retains a temporal sequence and translates it into an equivalent auditory-motor response. Twenty-one rhythmic sequences, varying in length from three to eight taps were administered.

Visual Measures

Four tests were selected as measures of visual functioning: visual discrimination, visual-motor memory, visual associative skill and visual analytic and synthetic reasoning. In all instances, a visual stimulus was presented which required a visual-motor response.

Visual Discrimination. Subtest V from the Chicago Nonverbal Examination (Brown, 1940) was incorporated into the battery as a measure of visual discrimination. The subject is required to match the stimulus design with one of four similar designs. In addition to discrimination, it was considered a test of visual scanning and memory since the subject can complete more designs in less time if he retains the stimulus design while looking for the correct match.

Memory for Designs. The Revised Visual Retention Test (Benton, 1955) was used to assess visual memory. Ten cards upon which one or more figures had been drawn were shown for ten seconds each after which the subject was asked to reproduce them.

Coding. A digit symbol test, Subtest I from the Chicago Nonverbal Examination (Brown, 1940), was chosen as a test of visual associative learning. Although the digits and symbols remain in view, the subject can achieve a higher score if he learns the associated units, thus being able to complete the items more quickly without reference to the sample illustrations. This type of associative learning was interpreted as a symbolic process and evaluated accordingly.

Block Design. The Kohs Block Design Test (Kohs, 1923) is reputed to be a reliable nonverbal measure of analytic reasoning. It consists of seventeen designs with a wide range of difficulty. The child was presented with the appropriate number of cubes and was required to construct the design within a time limit. The designs, printed on the center of a card, were one-quarter the size of the actual designs constructed with the cubes. The time limits for each design were about one minute longer than the time within which the correct response reasonably could be expected.

Intersensory Measures

Five tests were used to evaluate intersensory functioning. In two, Oral Directions and A-V Equivalents, an auditory stimulus was presented which required a visual-motor response. In the remaining three tests, Memory for Visual Digits, Memory for Pictures and Syllabication, a visual stimulus was presented which required a spoken (auditory-vocal) response.

Oral Directions. In the test of Oral Directions, a subtest of the Detroit Tests of Learning Aptitude (Baker and Leland, 1959), the child was confronted with a page of printed letters, pictures and forms. The examiner gave directions and the child carried them out by making appropriate markings on the page within a required time limit. This test consisted of seventeen items increasing in complexity and in length of the directions given.

A-V Equivalents. The test of nonverbal Auditory-Visual Equivalents was adapted from the test by Birch and Belmont (1964). The original test was designed to explore the development of intermodal equivalences in normal children and to analyse disturbances in intersensory integration in neurologically damaged persons. The test demands matching of a visual dot pattern with a corresponding patterning of a rhythmic auditory stimulus. The relationship explored is, therefore, between a temporally structured set of auditory stimuli and a spatially distributed set of visual stimuli. Since over 40 per cent of the normal boys in the Birch study received perfect or near-perfect scores on his test, the present investigator felt it necessary to increase the number of items from ten to fifteen. The visual stimuli from which each response was to be chosen were printed on individual 8 x 11 inch cards.

Memory for Visual Digits. The digit series for this test were taken from the Wechsler Memory Scale, Digits Reversed subtest (Wechsler, 1945). The test was expanded, however, to include a total of fourteen items, ranging from two to eight digits per series. Each digit was printed on a white card, and the cards were presented successively, at the rate of one per second. After each series of digits had been shown, the child was required to tell what numbers he had seen. In order to recall the entire series, the visual image or memory of each card had to be retained. This serial presentation of the digits served to make this intersensory memory test comparable to the auditory memory tests (Blair, 1955).

Memory for Pictures. Immediate recall of pictures was incorporated into the early Simon-Binet scales, but the form of presentation was simultaneous; thirteen pictures were displayed at the same time for thirty seconds to be recalled in no particular order. Squire (1912), Baldwin and Stecher (1942) and Eysenck and Hallstead (1945) also used memory for pictures with simultaneous presentation and no particular order required on recall.

The present test was adapted from the Detroit Tests of Learning Aptitude, subtest Visual Attention Span for Objects (Baker and Leland, 1959) for presentation by the serial method. Fourteen series of pictures ranging from two to eight were presented to each subject and, following each presentation, the subjects were required to name as many of the pictures as they could remember.

Syllabication. The Syllabication test, a subtest of the Gates-McKillop Reading Diagnostic Test (Gates and McKillop, 1962), simulated the auditory-visual integration required in oral reading. The subject is required to read and pronounce aloud twenty nonsense syllables. These nonsense words are made up of syllables which are most frequently encountered in elementary school word lists. The test measures the ability to break up and to auditorize a new, complex group of visual symbols and then to combine them. It is necessary for the child to pronounce each nonsense word in an analytic way as no content cues are given.

A summary of the test battery is given in Table 10-I.

Results

Auditory Measures

All six of the auditory tests showed the dyslexic subjects to be inferior to the controls. The means, standard deviations and Student's *t* values are presented in Table 10-II. It is evident that the dyslexic group was deficient in both discrimination and memory aspects of auditory functioning.

TABLE 10-I
SUMMARY OF MEASURES OF AUDITORY, VISUAL AND INTERSENSORY ABILITIES

Test Title	Source	Score
	AUDITORY MEASURES	
Auditory Discrimination	Seashore Tests for Musical Talents: Rhythm, Seashore, 1939	Raw score
Span for Nonsense Words	Memory for nonsense syllables, Spencer, 1958	Span score
Span for Digits	Wechsler Memory Scale: Digits Forward, Wechsler, 1945	Span score
Span for Words	Detroit Tests of Learning Aptitude: Auditory Attention Span for Unrelated Words, Baker and Leland, 1959	Span score
Memory for Sentences	Detroit Tests of Learning Aptitude: Auditory Attention Span for Related Syllables, Baker and Leland, 1959	Raw score
Memory for Rhythms	Reproduction de structures rhymiques, Stamback, 1960	Raw score
	VISUAL MEASURES	
Visual Discrimination	Chicago Nonverbal Examination: Test V, Brown, 1940	Raw score
Memory for Designs	Revised Visual Retention Test, Benton, 1955	Raw score
Coding	Chicago Nonverbal Examination: Test I, Brown, 1940	Raw score
Block Designs	Kohs Block Design Test, Kohs, 1923	Raw score
	INTERSENSORY MEASURES	
Oral Directions	Detroit Tests of Learning Aptitude: Oral Directions, Baker and Leland, 1959	Raw score
A-V Equivalents	Test of Auditory-Visual Equivalences, Birch and Belmont, 1964	Raw score
Span for Visual Digits	Wechsler Memory Scale: Digits Reversed, Wechsler, 1945	Span score
Span for Pictures	Detroit Tests of Learning Aptitude: Visual Attention Span for Objects, Baker and Leland, 1959	Span score
Syllabication	Gates-McKillop Reading Diagnostic Test: Syllabication, Gates and McKillop, 1962	Raw score

Visual Measures

Three of the four tests of visual functioning produced *non*-significant *t* values: Block Design, Visual Discrimination, and Memory for Designs. Only on the Coding test did significant differences appear ($p = .01$), the reading disability children being inferior. These data are summarized in Table 10-III.

The three nondiscriminating visual tests required that the subject match his response with the stimulus, either in the presence of the stimulus or from memory. The Visual Discrimination test required matching of the stimulus with one of four possible choices. In the Block Design test, the subject had to construct a pattern which matched the stimulus, while in the Memory for Designs test, he had to draw a figure to match the stimulus. In each case, the task was to match or reproduce the stimulus. In contrast, the Coding test required the child to learn associations between symbols in order to perform rapidly. It was at this level, in learning to relate one symbol to another, that the dyslexics were inferior. This suggests that, while the latter had no difficulty seeing (perceiving) and reproducing visual patterns, they were unable to learn to associate visual symbols in a manner equivalent to the normal child.

TABLE 10-II
MEANS, STANDARD DEVIATIONS AND STUDENT'S *t* VALUES
FOR AUDITORY MEASURES

		Dyslexics N=25	Controls N=25	t	p
Span-Digits	Mean	5.0	6.2	4.67	.001
	S.D.	.8	1.0		
Span-Words	Mean	4.1	4.8	3.88	.001
	S.D.	.6	.7		
Memory-Sentences	Mean	64.1	76.2	3.74	.001
	S.D.	10.4	11.9		
Memory-Rhythms	Mean	11.3	14.0	3.11	.01
	S.D.	3.2	2.9		
Auditory Discrim	Mean	21.3	24.6	3.02	.01
	S.D.	4.1	3.8		
Span-Nonsense Wds	Mean	4.4	4.8	2.28	.05
	S.D.	.7	.5		

TABLE 10-III
MEANS, STANDARD DEVIATIONS AND STUDENT'S *t* VALUES
FOR VISUAL MEASURES

		Dyslexics N=25	Controls N=25	t	p
Coding	Mean	47.4	56.4	2.91	.01
	S.D.	11.1	10.4		
Block Design	Mean	52.5	60.7	1.14	NS
	S.D.	22.1	27.3		
Visual Discrim	Mean	5.5	6.1	1.09	NS
	S.D.	1.6	2.0		
Memory-Designs	Mean	8.6	8.8	0.64	NS
	S.D.	1.1	1.0		

Intersensory Measures

The means, standard deviations and *t* values for the intersensory functions are given in Table 10-IV. On all seven tests the dyslexics were inferior to the normal readers. These findings are consistent with those of Birch and Belmont (1964, 1965), Katz and Deutsch (1963), Walter and Doan (1962), Williams (1965) and Muehl and Kremenak (1966). These authors have suggested that individuals with reading difficulties are disabled because they have nervous systems in which the development of equivalences between sensory systems is impaired.

When the results of the fifteen tests are reviewed, it is evident that on the eleven measures in which there was at least one auditory component, the dyslexics were inferior. However, only one of the four visual measures discriminated the groups. These results suggest that the deficiencies in dyslexic children of this age may be specifically related to an *auditory involvement* rather than specifically to intersensory difficulties or to visual perceptual problems.

TABLE 10-IV
MEANS, STANDARD DEVIATIONS AND STUDENT'S *t* VALUES
FOR INTERSENSORY MEASURES

		Dyslexics N=25	Controls N=25	t	p
Auditory Stimulus-Visual Response					
Oral Directions	Mean	9.1	12.4	2.92	.01
	S.D.	3.4	4.4		
A-V Equivalents	Mean	10.4	12.2	2.77	.01
	S.D.	2.4	2.2		
Visual Stimulus-Auditory Response					
Syllabication	Mean	9.9	16.9	6.25	.001
	S.D.	5.0	2.3		
Span-Visual Digits	Mean	4.8	5.8	3.74	.001
	S.D.	1.0	1.0		
Span-Pictures	Mean	3.6	4.1	2.21	.05
	S.D.	.7	.6		

Johnson and Myklebust (1967) indicate that many dyslexic children show deficits in auditory perception, memory and integration which makes it difficult for them to acquire skills of phonic analysis. These children may respond best to a "whole word" approach in the initial stages of reading instruction, but will require intensive training in auditory functioning before structural and phonic skills can be developed. However, Johnson and Myklebust suggest that the auditory dyslexic represents one segment of the dyslexic population and that there are considerable numbers of children with neurogenic reading disabilities who develop normal auditory processes. In the above study, the dyslexics were defined only on the basis of the discrepancy between their reading abilities and their mental abilities in the absence of intellectual, sensory, emotional and educational deficits. They were not selected as auditory dyslexics. The findings indicate that auditory problems underlie this neurogenic reading disorder.

There are findings in the literature consistent with this interpretation. Sandstedt (1964) measured auditory and visual memory span in an unselected group of forty-five retarded readers age 8-0 to 13-0 years, selecting tests from the WISC and the Detroit Tests of Learning Aptitude. She learned that pupils scored higher in total visual memory span then in total auditory memory span. Behrens (1963) also demonstrated that school children diagnosed as having neurogenic learning disabilities have more difficulty with learning when stimuli are auditory as opposed to visual. Behrens suggested further that the major difficulty encountered by children with learning problems is less a deficiency in auditory memory *per se* than an inability to sequentialize and maintain the structure of an auditory perception. It may be postulated that neurologically impaired children demonstrate a specific diasbility in the ordering and structuring aspects of auditory memory. These children cannot impose order on, or maintain order in, a given auditory stimulation. This disorder, most evident on tests of immediate memory, is not simply an impairment of auditory memory span; rather it may be a qualitative difference in the ability to structure the auditory stimuli as compared with normal children (see Kershman, 1962).

TABLE 10-V
MEASURES OF GROSS MEMORY AND MEMORY SPAN IN
DYSLEXIC AND CONTROL CHILDREN

Measure	Modality		Dyslexics N=25	Controls N=25	t	p
Gross-Digits	A	Mean	55.7	60.8	5.02	.001
		S.D.	3.6	3.4		
Span-Digits	A	Mean	5.0	6.2	4.67	.001
		S.D.	.8	1.0		
Span-Words	A	Mean	4.1	4.8	3.88	.001
		S.D.	.6	.7		
Span-Visual Digits	VA	Mean	4.8	5.8	3.74	.001
		S.D.	1.0	1.0		
Gross-Words	A	Mean	43.4	48.3	3.67	.001
		S.D.	4.7	4.5		
Gross-Nonsense Words	A	Mean	26.5	30.3	3.30	.01
		S.D.	4.0	4.0		
Gross-Pictures	VA	Mean	41.4	45.2	2.31	.05
		S.D.	5.8	5.6		
Span-Nonsense Words	A	Mean	4.4	4.8	2.28	.05
		S.D.	.7	.5		
Span-Pictures	VA	Mean	3.6	4.1	2.21	.05
		S.D.	.7	.6		
Gross-Visual Digits	VA	Mean	46.0	48.3	1.96	NS
		S.D.	4.0	4.0		

ORGANIZATION OF AUDITORY PERCEPTION

To test this hypothesis, a second analysis of the auditory memory data from the previous experiment was undertaken (Zigmond, 1966). Two scores were derived for each memory test: (1) the traditional span score, and (2) a measure of gross memory function derived from summing the number of items correctly reproduced (regardless of sequence) in each trial. Means, standard deviations, and *t* values for dyslexics and controls are given in Table 10-V. From these results, it is evident that the dyslexics were inferior in memory with and without consideration of sequence; performance requiring sequential reproduction was no better at differentiating the dyslexics from the normals than were measures of gross memory.

Harris (1963) utilized a different technique to assess the organization of auditory stimulation in children with reading difficulties. He presented words binaurally, except that he used a low-pass filter in one ear and a high-pass filter in the other. Each ear, therefore, received a different part of the word-sound spectrum. One ear received only certain low frequency elements and the other received only certain high frequencies. The words could not be distinguished when either ear heard its frequency element alone, but, when both ears were used and a binaural fusion effect occurred, subjects could obtain a high speech discrimination score. If the information coming to the two ears did not fuse, if the binaural fusion process failed, the results would be significantly poorer speech discrimination scores. The results of Harris' tests were equivocal. In a pilot study involving twenty-five subjects, with a history of brain damage and twenty-five apparently "normal" subjects he obtained statistically significant differences between the groups. A second study was undertaken involving ninety-six subjects, aged seven through eleven years. The group was divided into two sets of forty-eight subjects, matched for age, sex and intelligence. The reading disability group included pupils with a Betts reading index of 0.80 or lower (Betts, 1957). In this study, Harris obtained no statistically significant relationship between auditory integration and levels of reading ability.

While the Zigmond (1966) and Harris (1963) studies show negative results, the clinical symptoms of confusion in serial order and jumbled verbal output which seem to characterize the child with psychoneurological learning disabilities persist. It is possible that the techniques of auditory memory testing or auditory fusion are not sensitive enough measures of auditory integration.

There is yet another way of analyzing subjective organization in the auditory perceptual process, using simultaneous binaural presentation of material. A foremost pioneer in this area has been the British psychologist, D. E. Broadbent. The work began as experimental research in the field of aviation on selective listening. Broadbent asked the question, "What would be the effect of applying different auditory stimulation simultaneously to the two ears, thus putting the input from the right ear in competition, so to speak, with that from the left?" In his experimental paradigm (Broadbent, 1956), the subject wore earphones to which were delivered two series of three digits simultaneously to both ears at half-second intervals. The right ear received 3-5-7, for example, while the left ear received 8-2-9; the 3 and 8 were delivered simultaneously and so on with the two following pairs 5 and 2, 7 and 9. The subject was asked to report all the digits he heard, in any order. In 157 out of 160 trials, normal subjects spontaneously reported the whole series from one ear (3-5-7) before reporting from the other ear. The perceptual process had imposed a temporal order on the material received. It had changed the order of the sensory events from three pairs of simultaneous events to two series of three single events. According to Broadbent (1957), sounds must pass through the perceptual mechanism successively rather than simultaneously, and information presented to one channel must be stored momentarily while the other channel is being attended to.

This reorganization of information from simultaneous to successive occurs in everyday experiences. When we are concentrating on a task, and someone approaches and speaks to us, our immediate reaction is to say, "What?" But the stranger does not have to repeat what he said for us to respond to his statement. The time during which we say "what" serves to delay the response and allow the information received simultaneously to be dealt with successively. The statement appears to be temporarily and momentarily stored until attention can be shifted to it.

A variation of the Broadbent technique of dichotic listening affords an opportunity to investigate the way in which the two hemispheres of the brain may work together in perception and learning. In this case, the presentation of the stimuli is slowed down, so that the time interval between presentation of stimuli is increased from one-half second to two seconds. A frequent procedure in reporting numbers presented at this rate is to report them in pairs in the order of their arrival at the ears, although no constraint is given as to the direction within each pair (Bryden, 1962; Witelson, 1962). Using the numbers from the previous example, the order of report for this two-second presentation might be 3-8, 2-5, 7-9. Bryden has conceptualized this order of report as the *temporal order* as opposed to the *ear order* reported when digits are presented at one-half-second intervals. According to Bryden, the *temporal order* involves an "active reorganization of the traces by rehearsal, transforming the material from the two channels into a single sequence." By contrast, he considers the *ear order* as keeping the two series separable, a relatively simple task involving rote repetition of numbers. The fact that the *temporal order* is not seen until a two-second interval is presented between the pairs of digits suggests that this time interval is critical to the ability to integrate dichotic stimulation. The restructuring and reorganizing of the stimuli takes time and breaks down if the system is bombarded with these simultaneous bits of information too rapidly. Witelson (1962), working with a small sample of children with learning problems, demonstrated that these children tended to respond with *ear order* rather than *temporal order* even at the slower, two-second interval, presentation. Her data indicate that these children require more time to restructure the auditory input and that organization of auditory stimuli does not proceed in these children at the same rate or in the same manner as for normal children of the same age, sex and intellectual capacities.

CONCLUSIONS

The child with learning disabilities presents us with a challenge. He appears so normal, yet he demonstrates subtle and complicated problems. He has not been able to learn, yet he has the potential for learning and *can* learn. With appropriate educational management he can and will become a productive and effective member of society. The single most important factor in planning for a child with learning disabilities is an intensive diagnostic study. This child learns differently from the normal child, and it is only when we understand the specific problems he encounters that we can initiate adequate remedial procedures to give him the help he so desperately needs. Without a comprehensive evaluation of his areas of strength and weakness, the educational program may be ineffective.

The diagnostic study should include measures of sensory acuity, intelligence, academic achievement, language abilities, motor function and emotional and social maturity. The very basic role of audition to language and learning processes seems to warrant complete investigation in children of this aspect of their functioning. A partial list of tests which might be useful in assessing auditory processes is given in the Appendix. Measures of discrimination, memory, analysis and synthesis, reauditorization and auditory sequentialization should be included in the diagnostic evaluation. There is also a need for thorough investigation of the structuring and organizational aspects of the auditory perceptual process. How the individual receives, organizes and makes use of the conglomerate of auditory stimulation in his environment will directly influence the level of language and learning that he can attain. Tests analyzing the ability of these children to perceive sequential events and to reproduce temporal orders may help to explain precisely and more specifically the deficit in auditory functioning which is impeding the learning process.

REFERENCES

1. ANDERSON, V.A.: *Improving the Child's Speech.* New York, Oxford U.P., 1953.
2. BAKER, H.J., and LELAND, B.: *Detroit Tests of Learning Aptitude.* Indianapolis, Bobbs, 1959.
3. BALDWIN, B.T., and STECHER, L.I.: *The Psychology of the Preschool Child.* New York, Appleton, 1924.
4. BEHRENS, T.R.: A Study of Psychological and Electroencephalographic Changes in Children with Learning Disorders. Unpublished Doctoral Dissertation, Northwestern University, 1963.

5. BENTON, A.L.: *The Revised Visual Retention Test: Clinical and Experimental Applications.* New York, Psychological Corp., 1955.

6. BERRY, M.F., and EISENSON, J.: *Principles and Practices of Therapy.* New York, Appleton, 1956.

7. BETTS, E.A.: *Foundations of Reading Instruction.* New York, Am. Bk. Pub. Co., 1957.

8. BIRCH, H.G.: Dyslexia and the maturation of visual function. In Money, H.J. (Ed.): *Reading Disability: Progress and Research Needs in Dyslexia.* Baltimore, Johns Hopkins, 1962.

9. BIRCH, H. G.: Perceptual analysis and sensory integration in brain-damaged persons. *J Genet Psychol, 105:*173, 1964.

10. BIRCH, H.G., and BELMONT, L.: Auditory-visual integration in normal and retarded readers. *Amer J Orthopsychiat, 34:*852, 1964.

11. BIRCH, H.G., and BELMONT, L.: Auditory-visual integrations, intelligence, and reading ability in school children. *Percept Motor Skills, 20:*295, 1965.

12. BLAIR, F.X.: A Study of the Visual Memory of Deaf and Hearing Children. Unpublished Doctoral Dissertation, Northwestern University, 1955.

13. BROADBENT, D.E.: Successive responses to simultaneous stimuli. *Quart J Exp Psychol, 8:*145, 1956.

14. BROADBENT, D.E.: Immediate memory and simultaneous stimuli. *Quart J Exp Psychol, 9:*1, 1957.

15. BROWN, A.W.: *The Chicago Nonverbal Examination.* New York, Psychological Corp., 1940.

16. BROWN, R., and BELLUGI, U.: Three processes in the child's acquisition of syntax. In Lenneberg, E. (Ed.): *New Direction in the Study of Language.* Cambridge, M.I.T., 1964.

17. BRYDEN, M.P.: Order of report in dichotic listening. *Canad J Psychol, 16:*291, 1962.

18. CATTELL, P.: *Measurement of Intelligence of Infants and Young Children.* New York, Psychological Corp., 1950.

19. CHOMSKY, N.: *Syntactic Structures.* The Hague, Mouton, 1957.

20. DARLEY, F.L., and WINITZ, H.: Age of first word: review of research. *J Speech Hearing Dis, 26:*272, 1961.

21. DiCARLO, L.M.; KENDALL, D.C., and GOLDSTEIN, R.: Diagnostic procedures for auditory disorders in children. *Folia Phoniat, 14:*206, 1962.

22. ERVIN, S.: Imitation and structural change in children's language. In Lenneber, E. (Ed.): *New Direction in the Study of Language.* Cambridge, M.I.T., 1964.

23. EYSENCK, H.J., and HALSTEAD, H.: The memory function: I. A factorial study of fifteen clinical tests. *Amer J Psychiat, 102:*174, 1945.

24. FROSTIG, M., and HORNE, P.: *The Frostig Program for the Development of Visual Perception.* Chicago, Follett, 1964.

25. GATES, A.I.: *The Improvement of Reading.* 3rd ed., New York, Macmillan, 1950.

26. GATES, A.I., and McKILLOP, A.: *The Gates-McKillop Reading Diagnostic Tests.* New York, Columbia University Teachers College, 1962.

27. GESELL, A.L., and ARMATRUDA, C.S.: *Developmental Diagnosis.* New York, Hoeber, 1956.

28. GRIFFITHS, R.: *The Abilities of Babies: A Study in Mental Measurement.* London, U. of London, 1954.

29. HARRIS, R.: Central auditory functions in children. *Percept Motor Skills, 16:*207, 1963.

30. JACOBS, J.: Experiments on "prehension." *Mind, 12:*75, 1887.

31. JOHNSON, D.J., and MYKLEBUST, H.R.: *Learning Disabilities: Educational Principles and Practices.* New York, Grune, 1967.

32. KATZ, P., and DEUTSCH, M.: Relation of auditory-visual shifting to reading achievement. *Percept Motor Skills, 17:*327, 1963.

33. KEPHART, N.C.: *The Slow Learner in the Classroom.* Columbus, Merrill, C.E., 1960.

34. KERSHMAN, N.: Auditory perception in children with learning problems. Unpublished research, McGill University, 1962.

35. KOHS, S.C.: *Kohs Block-Design Test.* Chicago, C.H. Stoelting, 1923.

36. KRONVALL, E.L., and DIEHL, C.F.: The relationship of auditory discrimination to articulatory defects in children with no known organic impairment. *Speech Hearing Dis, 19:*335, 1954.

37. LADEFOGED, P., and BROADBENT, D.E.: Perception of sequence of auditory events. *Quart J Exp Psychol, 12:*162, 1960.

38. LENNEBERG, E. (Ed.) : *New Direction in the Study of Language.* Cambridge, M.I.T., 1964.

39. MONROE, M.: *Children Who Cannot Read.* Chicago, U. of Chicago, 1932.

40. MUEHL, S., and KREMENAK, S.: Ability to match information within and between auditory and visual sense modalities and subsequent reading achievement. *J Educ Psychol, 57:*230, 1966.

41. MYKLEBUST, H.R.: Learning disorders: Psychoneurological disturbances in childhood. *Rehab Lit, 25:*354, 1964.

42. MYKLEBUST, H.R., and JOHNSON, D.: Dyslexia in children. *Exceptional Child, 29:* 14, 1962.

43. REICHSTEIN, J., and ROSENSTEIN, J.: Differential diagnosis of auditory defects: A review of the literature. *Exceptional Child, 31:*73, 1964.

44. SANDSTEDT, B.: Relationship between memory span and intelligence of severely retarded readers. *Reading Teacher, 17:*246, 1964.

45. SEASHORE, C.E.; LEWIS, D., and SAETVEIT, J.: *Seashore Test of Musical Talents,* Camden, N.J., Educational Department, Radio Corporation of America, 1939.

46. SPENCER, E.: An Investigation of the Maturation of Various Factors of Auditory Perception in Pre-school Children. Unpublished Doctoral Dissertation, Northwestern University, 1958.

47. SQUIRE, C.R.: Graded mental tests. *J Educ Psychol, 3:*363, 1912.

48. STAMBAK, M.: Le problème du rythme de developpement de l'infant, et dans les dyslexics d'evolution. *Enfance,* 480, 1951.

49. STEVENS, S.S., and DAVIS, H.: *Hearing: Its Psychology and Physiology.* New York, Wiley, 1938.

50. STRAUSS, A.A., and LEHTINEN, L.E.: *Psychopathology and Education of the Brain-Injured Child.* New York, Grune, 1947.

51. TEMPLIN, M.C.: *Certain Language Skills in Children: Their Development and Interrelationships.* Minneapolis, U. of Minn., 1957.

52. TERMAN, L.M., and MERRILL, M.A.: *Measuring Intelligence.* New York, Houghton, 1937.

53. TERMAN, L.M., and MERRILL, M.A.: *Stanford Binet Intelligence Scale.* Boston, Houghton, 1962.

54. VAN RIPER, C.: *Speech Correction: Principles and Methods.* 4th ed., Englewood Cliffs, Prentice-Hall, 1963.

55. WALTER, R.H., and DOAN, H.: Perceptual and cognitive functioning in retarded readers. *J Consult Psychol, 26:*355, 1962.

56. WECHSLER, D.: *Wechsler Memory Scale.* New York, Psychological Corp., 1945.

57. Wechsler, D.: *Wechsler Intelligence Scale for Children*. New York, Psychological Corp., 1949.

58. Wechsler, D.: *Wechsler Adult Intelligence Scale*. New York, Psychological Corp., 1955.

59. Wever, E.G.: *Theory of Hearing*. New York, Wiley, 1949.

60. Williams, J.: Auditory-visual Equivalence of Stimuli Among Normal and Retarded Readers. Unpublished Master's Thesis, University of Iowa, 1965.

61. Witelson, S.: Perception of Auditory Stimuli in Children with Learning Problems. Unpublished Master's Thesis, McGill University, 1962.

62. Zigmond, N.: Intrasensory and Intersensory Processes in Normal and Dyslexic Children. Unpublished Doctoral Dissertation, Northwestern University, 1966.

APPENDIX

Measures of Auditory Functioning

Discrimination

Wepman, J.: *Auditory Discrimination Test*. Chicago, Language Research Associates, 1958.

Seashore, C.E., Lewis, D., and Saetviet, J.: *Seashore Test of Musical Talents*. Camden, N.J., Educational Department, Radio Corporation of America, 1939.

Memory

Wechsler, D.: *Wechsler Intelligence Scale for Children*. New York, The Psychological Corporation, 1949.
Verbal Scale—Digit Span

Baker, H.J., and Leland, B.: *Detroit Tests of Learning Aptitude*. Indianapolis, Indiana, Bobbs-Merrill Co., Inc., 1959.
Auditory Attention Span for Unrelated Words
Auditory Attention Span for Related Syllables

McCarthy, J.J., and Kirk, S.: *Illinois Test of Psycholinguistic Abilities*. Urbana, Illinois, Institute for Research on Exceptional Children, 1961.
Auditory-Vocal Sequencing Test

McCarthy, J.J., and Olson, J.L.: *Validity Studies on the Illinois Test of Psycholinguistic Abilities*, University of Wisconsin, 1964.
Appendix I—Random Word Test
Appendix M—Sentence Memory Test

Stambak, M.: Trois épreuves de rythme. In Rene Zazzo (Ed.): *Manuel pour l'Examen Psychologique de l'Enfant*. Neuchatel, Suisse, Delachaux & Niestle, 1960.

Analysis

Gates, A.I.: *The Improvement of Reading*. New York, The Macmillan Co., 1950.
Rhyming Test
Matching Test

Gates, A.I., and McKillop, A.: *The Gates-McKillop Reading Diagnostic Tests*. New York, Bureau of Publications, Columbia University Teachers College, 1962.
Initial Letters
Final Letters

Synthesis

Roswell, F.G., and Chall, J.S.: *Roswell-Chall Auditory Blending Test*. New York, Essay Press, 1963.

McCarthy, J.J., and Olson, J.L.: *Validity Studies on the Illinois Test of Psycholinguistic Abilities.* University of Wisconsin, 1964.
Appendix K—The Auditory Closure Test

Reauditorization

McCarthy, J.J., and Kirk, S.: *Illinois Test of Psycholinguistic Abilities.* Urbana, Illinois, Institute for Research on Exceptional Children, 1961.
Auditory-Vocal Automatic Test
Auditory-Vocal Association Test
Vocal Encoding Test
Baker, H.J., and Leland, B.: *Detroit Tests of Learning Aptitude.* Indianapolis, Indiana, Bobbs-Merrill Co., Inc., 1959.
Verbal Opposites
Free Association
Hejna, R.F.: *Developmental Articulation Test.* Madison, Wis., College Printing and Typing Co., 1955.
Templin, M.C., and Darley, F.L.: *The Templin-Darley Tests of Articulation.* Iowa City, Iowa, Bureau of Educational Research and Services, Extension Division, State University of Iowa, 1961.

Auditory Organization

Broadbent, D.E.: *Perception and Communication.* New York, Pergamon Press, 1958.
Dichotic listening
Matzker, J., and Ruckles, J.: A new hearing test for the diagnosis of brain stem lesions. *Ger. Med. Monthly, 3:*258, 1958.
Auditory fusion

Chapter 11

Visual Perception and Early Education

MARIANNE FROSTIG *and* PHYLLIS MASLOW

T HIS PAPER DISCUSSES the visual perceptual training of children with learning difficulties. Training of any individual ability, such as visual perception, has to be considered in relation to the total educational program of the child. The paper, therefore, will be concerned with broad aspects of the education of children with learning difficulties, although it will emphasize the remediation of visual perceptual defects.

First I want to explain what I mean by the term "learning difficulties," because the teacher's ability to help children progress smoothly and at a maximum rate in school may depend upon an understanding of this concept. I propose defining a learning difficulty as *the outward manifestation of a lag or lags in development.*

To diagnose and remedy a lag in development, the teacher has to be familiar with the basic teachings of developmental psychology. Meticulous observation of the behavior of young children has led to the conclusion that certain functions are learned in a definite sequence and at more or less predictable age levels. The *exact* time at which these developmental abilities emerge varies somewhat, partly because individuals tend to vary in their rates of development, and partly because the particular culture has an effect, but the sequence in which the abilities unfold is independent of culture. They occur in the same order in the Eskimo child as in the Sudanese or the American child.

A disturbance or a lag in any developmental function impairs the adjustment of any individual to his environment. In the case of a child, it nearly always impairs his ability to learn at the same tempo as the rest of the children in his class. If the teacher is to help the child to make maximum progress, she must be aware of any developmental lags, and she must be able to take into account in her teaching.

I use the plural in regard to lags, because as a rule a developmental defect in one area will influence other psychological functions. We rarely find a visual perceptual defect, or an emotional maladjustment, or a speech disorder, by itself. Usually each deficit will affect other areas of behavior and therefore the total adjustment. It is because developmental lags are so frequently multiple that I cannot discuss perceptual dysfunctions without considering other aspects of the child's development also.

The first functions which develop in the infant are the so-called sensory-motor functions. These develop maximally during the first eighteen or twenty-four months of life. During the sensory-motor phase, the child becomes aware of the world around him through *simultaneous* application of all sense modalities and of movement. A baby does not learn to recognize his mother by sight alone, but by touch also. As he plays with his blanket with his hands, he is likely to suck and kick it as well. A baby playing with toys will typically touch, throw and lick them, hide and retrieve them, push, pull and shake them, simultaneously listening to the sounds as he bangs them around, and at the same time watching what happens to the objects as he handles and moves them. He thus becomes cognizant of the outer world, and learns to achieve some mastery over it.

The baby also learns in this way to gain a certain mastery over himself. He learns how to change his position, move in space, and use parts of his body independently of the others. He finds out how to move his hands and manipulate objects, how to move his head in order to look in different directions, and how to move his feet and hold his body in order to walk. In learning to move himself, and in coming to grips with the world about him, he also learns to recognize himself as a being separate from the outer world.

In summary, he learns to move himself; he learns to move objects; he becomes aware of the world around him; and he becomes aware of himself. He learns these fundamental skills, as I have stated, during the first eighteen or twenty-four months of life, which constitute the phase of maximum sensory-motor development.

The teacher may ask, "Why should we be interested in this period? After all, we work with much older children." The reason is that we still find lags in school-age children which can be referred to this early phase of development. We even find children who cannot differentiate between themselves and the environment; these are the severely disturbed children who are known as autistic. There are other children who have difficulties in locomotion; they may be able to walk, but not to skip or to gallop or to walk upstairs without putting both feet on each tread. There are children who have difficulties in handling objects and do not learn to build well with blocks, or lace shoes, or cut out a picture. In short, many school children with learning difficulties are handicapped because they lag in abilities normally gained in the first eighteen or twenty-four months of life.

The second developmental phase begins during the second year of life and lasts until about three to four years of age. This is the period of maximum speech development, when the child learns to understand language and to express ideas through speech. Defective language development is often seen in children of school age also. Teachers are well acquainted with children who cannot talk well in sentences, who have articulation defects, or who have difficulty in understanding what the teacher says to them.

The third group of abilities which develop in the preschool child are the perceptual abilities. Their maximum development occurs roughly between three and one-half or four and six and one-half to seven years of age. Piaget refers to perception as the *intuitive* aspect of intelligence.[1] What he means is that the young child now recognizes objects and the world around him directly, intuitively, without deliberation, and without the simultaneous use of motor functions, such as touching and turning, pulling or biting. Piaget also speaks of this developmental phase as the *representational* phase, referring to the inner "pictures" which the child forms of the world around him — "engrams" if you wish — which permit him to recognize and understand immediately what he encounters in his daily environment.

Jerome Bruner uses a different term. He speaks of the *iconic* mode of cognition.[2] "Iconic" has the same meaning as representational and refers to the same functions. The world is understood by looking and by listening. The main avenues for recognition are the distance receptors, vision and hearing. In recognizing the things around him, the child relies on memories of previous experiences — he does not need to repeat previous explorations by detailed inspection.

Although the maximum development of perceptual ability occurs between about three and one-half and seven and one-half years of age, Bower and Fantz and others have shown that infants are able to recognize three-dimensional shapes almost from birth on.[3,4] But Bower's experiments show that the infant does not develop recognition of shapes in two-dimensional space, a much more difficult perceptual task. Perceptual difficulties frequently involve lack of perception of forms, or of direction, or of relationships in two-dimensional space. Visual perceptual disabilities usually affect reading and writing because these are activities which are done on a plane surface.

The next developmental phase, that of higher cognitive functioning, begins when the child is about six and one-half to seven and one-half years of age. The exact time of onset depends on the culture, on the child's intelligence level, and on his previous experiences. During this phase the child develops the ability to figure things out, to ponder and weigh them in his thoughts, to classify, to draw conclusions and to check on hypotheses. Because these higher cognitive functions are still bound to the child's perception to a certain degree — he observes, and then thinks about what he has observed — Piaget calls this the phase of "concrete operations." Purely abstract thinking, which Piaget terms "'formal operations," occurs later, in the prepubertal period, after eleven or twelve years of age.

There are two other groups of developmental functions to which I have not yet referred. These are emotions and social behavior. These differ from the other functions in that they do not show a single peak of maximum development, but rather a series of transformations throughout the total life span. I refer those of you who are interested in these developmental aspects to the work of Erik Erikson, especially his book *Childhood and Society*.[5]

I have stated before that difficulties in learning can be conceptualized as being caused by lags in developmental abilities. Therefore all psychological functions should be explored so that we can find any existing deficit and can plan the best remedial program. The most effective remedial program is probably one which is based on a detailed evaluation consisting of comprehensive testing, interviews and observations. The school psychologist and the trained teacher can translate the results of such an evaluation into a program specifically designed to help the child develop those basic psychological functions which are found to be deficient.

I want to emphasize that I am referring to remedial programs, not to preventive programs. Formal ability testing is not necessary for the school child who can progress well and does not exhibit specific difficulties. But for the child with learning difficulties, a careful choice of testing instruments is important. There are two quite widely used tests which were specifically designed to serve as a partial basis for remedial programs. Samuel Kirk and his associates at the University of Illinois were aware of the need for an instrument with which to evaluate specific language disturbances and they developed the Illinois Test of Psycholinguistic Abilities.[6]

The staff at the Center for Educational Therapy for Children in Los Angeles were moved by a similar concern, and constructed the Frostig Developmental Test of Visual Perception.[7] How this test was constructed and a report on some of the first validity and reliability studies will be found in the technical manual for the Frostig Developmental Test of Visual Perception.

These two tests, the ITPA and the Frostig, have become an integral part of the evaluation of children with learning difficulties in many institutions in the United States and elsewhere. Their prime virtue, I think, is that they were designed to serve as a basis for remedial programs and not to classify children, as is the purpose of most intelligence tests. The concept of a remedial test is a very important one, because tests which are to serve the purpose of remediation are constructed in a very different way from those constructed for the purpose of classification. The test which serves remediation is designed to isolate as many abilities as possible and to evaluate them; intercorrelations between the subtests will therefore be low. General intelligence tests, to the contrary, arrive at a global measure of functioning, and intercorrelation of subtests should be higher.

In addition to the ITPA and the Frostig test, we invariably use two other tests for children of the appropriate age level referred to our Center because of learning difficulties. These are the Wepman Test of Auditory Discrimination (a test which also serves remedial purposes) and the Wechsler Intelligence Scale for Children.[8,9] With children below six and one-half or seven years of age, however, the WISC is replaced by the Wechsler Pre-School and Primary Scale of Intelligence (WPPSI) or the Binet.[10,11]

The total test battery used at the Center always includes other measures also. The choice of these measures depends on the needs of the particular child. Observation and interviews are also included in the assessment of the child's abilities; these are particularly important for evaluating his emotional and social adjustment. The entire evaluation program — testing, interviewing and observing — is designed to assess each child's specific strengths and weaknesses in the six developmental areas which have been mentioned: sensory-motor functions, language, perception, thought processes and social and emotional development.

Figure 11-1 shows the test results of two children in the four tests that I have mentioned — the Frostig, the Wepman, the Wechsler and the Illinois Test for Psycholinguistic Abilities. Both children have similar IQ's; one of 85 and the other of 87. But here the similarity ends. Where the graph for one child is high, it is low for the other. One of the children (Harna) shows low scores in visual perception, low performance IQ, and low ability in the visual-motor association and visual-motor sequencing subtests of the Illinois Test of Psycholinguistic Abilities. In the other child (Holda), visual perceptual abilities in general seem to be adequate, but verbal IQ, the score of the Wepman Auditory Discrimination test, and grammar and verbal expression as measured by the Illinois Test for Psycholinguistic Abilities, are low. We see that in the abilities in which one child is deficient, the other is adequate, and vice versa. One child has visual perceptual disabilities, the other auditory ones. One child has verbal facility, the other visual-motor ability.

This wide diversity in test result patterns is typical of children with learning difficulties, and it proves that no single reading method or physical education program or perceptual program, *or any other educational measure,* can be the same for all children and still achieve optimum results for all of them. Some children need training in auditory discrimination, others need concentration on the amelioration of their visual perceptual deficits. Some children need help with expressive language, others with the memory for visual sequences, and so on. The implication of these findings is that individualizing of instruction is necessary for children with learning disabilities.

This fact poses a severe problem for the classroom teacher. How can she individualize while conducting a class? One way to do this is to group children in the classroom in such a way that their need for individual instruction is reduced. There will be several children in each classroom who show similar difficulties. These children can have some of their remedial work together in the areas of their deficits — in visual perception or auditory perception, and so on. When the teacher does not have test results to guide her in grouping, she must rely on her own observations. Her best measure of each child's abilities will result from comparison of the child's level of performance with the rest of the group.

Whatever techniques the classroom teacher uses, however, she will always be handicapped if she has to teach academic skills and content subjects at the same time as she provides the necessary remediation. It is therefore important that at the kindergarten or early first grade level, each child's program should provide the necessary training in all the psychological functions which should be acquired prior to intensive academic work.

Cross-sectional studies show that at least 15 to 25 per cent of children in the beginning school grades suffer from perceptual disabilities, language difficulties and sensory-motor dysfunctions, or a combination of these disabilities. Training in sensory-motor functions, language and visual and auditory perception should therefore be part and parcel of all kindergarten programs. At the same time it should be remembered that all of those children who have difficulties in learning, however varied their difficulties, share the common characteristic that they work under considerable stress in public school. To a lesser degree, the first weeks in school are stressful for all children. The beginning school program must therefore help them to cope with the new intellectual and social demands which public school entrance entails and prepare them for later academic work.

I would like to give an example which indicates the importance of such measures. The achievement test scores of fourth and fifth grade school children in a big underprivileged district of a metropolis in the United States are uniformly two years below those of the national average. But one school in this district is an exception. Year after year, the children of this school test at the national average grade achievement level. A physician working for health services for school children went to the principal of this school and asked her if she had an explanation for this relatively high achievement. The principal said, "We use the first half year of the first grade for a readiness program. During this time we devote our attention to perceptual and language functions. The program also helps the children to become acquainted with classroom procedures."

Language training, training in sensory-motor functions and training in visual perception are of equal importance, but it is not necessary to set up three separate and different readiness programs. The Frostig Program for the Development of Visual Perception attempts to provide the child with a global readiness training including most of these skills, although the emphasis is on visual perception. This program will be used as an example of material based on an integrated readiness concept.

As the Program was constructed to help provide training and amelioration of the difficulties assessed by the Frostig test, I would like to give you a short history of this test and of its theoretical orientation before discussing the Program itself. The test was founded on the observation of visual perception deficits in children who had known brain damage as the result of an epidemic of encephalitis in Europe some years after the first World War. It was apparent that the visual perceptual deficits of the children were not uniform. The variety of symptoms in this area has also been noted by such workers as Cruickshank, Wedell and Thurstone.[12,13,14,15] The inference could therefore be made that there are in fact several visual perceptual abilities.

At the Frostig Center our observations led us to conclude that children could be disturbed in any or all of the following abilities: perception of form or size independent of distance, background, pattern and so on (form constancy and size constancy); perception of the direction in which an object is turned (perception of position in space); perception of the relationship of one point in space to another (perception of spatial relationships), and the ability to direct the attention to a particular part of the visual field (figure-ground perception). I do not maintain that these abilities comprise the total of what we call visual perception. In fact, perception of color, of depth and of other parameters are perceptual functions which may be defective also. But these four abilities — figure-ground perception, constancy, perception of position in space and perception of spatial relationships — seem to have special importance for school learning, and they are therefore evaluated by four of the subtests of the Frostig test. An additional subtest is included for eye-hand coordination, partly because a measure of the child's ability to control his hand movement is needed to be able to judge his ability to outline on subsequent test items, and partly because eye-hand coordination is important for many activities in kindergarten and the early school grades, including writing and drawing.

The final version of the test was administered to more than 2000 children for standardization, and it was given to many more in the course of refining the test items.

The next step was to devise a visual perceptual program to train the abilities evaluated by the test. This program has now been published in two forms. The first is a series of worksheets for each visual perceptual area, which is called the Frostig Developmental Program for Visual Perception.[16] The worksheets are accompanied by a single Teacher's Guide, containing theory, suggestions for use and the instructions to be given to the children. The other form consists of three workbooks called *Beginning, Intermediate* and *Advanced Pictures and Patterns,* respectively, each of which has its own Teacher's Guide.[17,18,19] The *Pictures and Patterns* workbooks have almost identical exercises to those in the Developmental Program of Visual Perception, but each workbook is used with a different level of perceptual proficiency. Each workbook contains exercises at the appropriate level for all five visual perceptual areas. *Beginning Pictures and Patterns* is appropriate for roughly the nursery school-kindergarten level, *Intermediate Pictures and Patterns* for the kindergarten-first grade level and *Advanced Pictures and Patterns* for the first-second grade level. Both editions may be used for either preventive (readiness) programs or for remedial programs, although *Pictures and Patterns* is designed primarily for preventive purposes at younger age levels.

The worksheets and workbooks are concerned with perception in two-dimensional space. The training of perception in regard to a plane surface is very important because it is required in all paper and pencil work. Obviously a child who cannot recognize and reproduce written symbols or letters or numbers is indeed very handicapped in school. But training with worksheets is only a part of the Frostig Program.

The Teacher's Guides explain how two-dimensional work should be preceded and accompanied by sensory-motor training, by activities with three-dimensional materials in every perceptual area, by training in body awareness and by many other activities. We usually suggest that there should be at least two weeks of work with these materials and exercises preceding the use of the worksheets in kindergarten, and there may be many months of introductory work when the Program is introduced in nursery school. As a rule, the *Beginning Pictures and Patterns* workbooks should not be given to the child before he is about four and one-half years old. But visual perceptual training with the worksheets should not be postponed until the child has mastered the manipulative materials. Training in both kinds of activities can proceed simultaneously after a short preparatory period.

Visual perception, I repeat, does not occur isolated from other human abilities. The Teacher's Guides therefore explain how training in visual perception can be integrated with training in sensory-motor and language functions and later with the training of higher cognitive (thought) processes.[20] For example, training in receptive language is provided as the teacher explains each worksheet or workbook exercise and gives instruction for its use. The child must follow the verbal directions. Training in expressive language is provided when the child is encouraged to discuss or elaborate upon the pictures or stories illustrated by the worksheets.

The exercises were deliberately planned to be as pleasing and interesting to children as possible. The program will be much more helpful if it is fun.

The integration of various abilities is essential. In training visual perception, other sense modalities and motor activities should be considered also. So far as visual perception and especially spatial ability is concerned, perception will be enhanced if stimuli are presented simultaneously to other sense channels. For example, if a child moves or touches an object while he looks at it, the kinesthetic and tactile experiences will reinforce his perception. Language facilitates perception as well. If the child is told the name of an object while looking at it, he will be helped to form and remember the concept. It is helpful if the teacher explains what the child sees on the worksheet, and requires him to repeat what she says, or to point to the figures or attributes mentioned. For example, the teacher may say: "Here is a big square and here is a little square. They have the same shape but a different size; one is big, one is little. Point to the big one. Good. Point to the little one. In what way are the big one and the little one the same? —— Yes, they are both squares. They are of the same —— (shape)."

For a detailed description of the perceptual program I refer you to the Teacher's Guides. Examples of worksheets and directions to them are appended.

Up to now, my discussion of the rationale of the training and the characteristics of the program has given little idea of either its purpose or efficacy. The most frequent question asked concerns the correlation of visual perception and reading.

In nearly all studies published to date, the correlation of visual perception and reading has been shown to be medium high for beginning readers. However, the correlation between visual perceptual ability and reading probably depends on the methods used with each child, and the manner in which these methods relate to his specific pattern of abilities and disabilities. I am quite certain that the greater stress on phonics, the introduction of a linguistic approach, the use of the initial teaching alphabet (i/t/a), and the use of tape recorders and other new teaching methods, will not only help children with reading difficulties but will also prevent many reading difficulties altogether. Thus the correlation between visual perception and beginning reading should become somewhat lower. In any case, the medium high correlation between reading and visual skills usually disappears about the third grade level.[21]

Observation of our elementary and junior high school students at this Center indicates that a much more significant correlation is that between visual perceptual disabilities and the general, more pervasive and global learning difficulties. As a rule, only those children are referred to our

Center who have such severe difficulties in learning that they neither progress in public school nor can be helped by the usual tutoring methods. Children who are thought to be able to profit from regular tutoring are sent elsewhere. Roughly three-fourths of the children accepted by the Center have difficulties in visual perception as shown by the Frostig Test. About three-fourths of the children also have difficulties in visual sequencing — that means the ability to reproduce a visually perceived sequence, as required in spelling a word, for example. In one example, sixty-nine children out of eighty-nine had visual perceptual difficulties. It is this high correlation of visual perceptual deficits with persistent learning difficulties which leads us to recommend early introduction of visual perceptual training.

A visual perceptual training program is used with nearly all of the children at the Center, even for children above nine and one-half or ten years of age, if they show evidence of deficiencies in visual perception. For children above nine and one-half or ten years of age, materials are used which have not yet been published. We found that not only did the vast majority of the children improve in visual perception, but that there was overall improvement. These findings were based on retesting the children periodically with the Frostig, the Wepman, the ITPA, the WISC, or another intelligence test; by achievement testing; the incidence of readmission to public school, and finally, by follow-up after the child's return to public school through reports from both teachers and parents. The results indicate that all children who show a visual perceptual defect should have perceptual training whether or not they are able to read. In fact, it should be emphasized again that I firmly believe that visual perceptual training should be part and parcel of any readiness program in nursery school, in kindergarten or in beginning grade school.

This point can be illustrated by an experiment carried out at the elementary school of the University of California at Los Angeles under the direction of Miss Edith Appleton, Kindergarten Supervisor.[22] A group of children ranging in age from four years and ten months to six years and one month were exposed to a program in which a great variety of materials and activities were made available. A large number of student teachers aided the head teacher, thus permitting much individual attention. In this classroom, no child was made to feel that reading was of any greater value than the other activities offered. About six months later it was found that all of the children with a perceptual quotient above 90 except one had learned to read, but that the children with a perceptual quotient of below 90 did not learn to read. An intensive readiness program to train the abilities basic to reading was then provided for all of the children, and they were all exposed to reading. This time all of the children were soon reading, with the single exception of the child with the most severe disturbances in visual perception.

The above mentioned study indicates that children with visual perceptual difficulties may be able to learn to read if there is a certain amount of pressure to learn to read, but that they will avoid reading if they can do so without being stigmatized or punished. In public school, however, withdrawal from reading is impossible. Children must try to read even if they have considerable visual perceptual disturbances, in spite of the added stress and the anxiety which often results.

One of our own research studies demonstrated a high correlation between visual perceptual abilities and classroom adjustment at beginning public school entrance. The Frostig Developmental Test of Visual Perception was given in the spring semester of 1962 to all children in kindergarten, first and second grades of Hermosa Beach School District. There were 374 kindergarten children, 277 children were in first grade, and 285 children in second grade. The children were also rated independently by their teachers on a five-point scale for classroom adjustment. Classroom adjustment was defined as the child's ability to function acceptably in the school situation — to hang up his coat, to pass out crayons, to refrain from shoving his neighbor, to listen quietly and follow directions when required, to work in a group, to share the teacher's attention, to profit from instruction and so on.

When the classroom adjustment scale ratings were compared with the total scores, or perceptual quotients, on the Frostig Test, it was found that the chi-square correlation between scores in the lowest quartile on the Frostig Test and low ratings for classroom adjustment were significant beyond the .001 level for children in kindergarten and first grade, but were no longer significant at the second grade level.

Our findings in this study therefore support the hypothesis that a disturbance or lag in the main developmental task at a given age level is likely to be reflected in all areas of behavior. As we have stated, development of perceptual skills is the main task up to about seven or seven and one-half years of age; after that, at about the middle of the second grade, the child becomes more independent of immediate perceptions.

It is probably not only the pressure to read that causes poor behavior in children with visual perceptual disturbances. As I have mentioned, such children have difficulty with other academic subjects as well as with a variety of activities, such as cutting, coloring, writing and so on. Their failures are therefore multiple and must lead to feelings of inadequacy, to anxiety, to unhappiness and to tension due to fear of further failure; in other words, to emotional disturbances.

A clinical example can illustrate this point. Scott, a somewhat clumsy boy, nine and one-half years old, had visual perceptual difficulties which led to learning difficulties in public school and poor adjustment at home. Tutoring did not help him, and he was finally enrolled for full time school in our Center in the fall of 1966. During his evaluation he was given a story completion test. His answers showed a normal, generally happy, clever boy, who related well with other children, who liked his parents, and had no irrational fears — except that to the question, "Why might father be angry at the table?" he gave eight different reasons, adding, "This is how it is with me." The eight reasons were all on these lines: "The boy stepped on his father's new shoes; he did not notice them . . . The boy spilled milk over his suit . . . The boy could not find the salt shaker on the table . . . The boy let food fall from his fork, he did not put the whole fork in, just part of it," and so on. All of these answers reflected his worry about his own clumsiness and the fear of being punished for it.

But Scott was found to have good coordination. His clumsiness derived from his difficulties in figure-ground perception and perception of spatial relationships. He usually excused himself after a mishap by saying, "But I did not see it." He showed worry, not only about his performance at home, but also in relation to the school situation, for he found that he would not be able to learn what the other children could learn. Scott's case provides a typical example of how children with visual perceptual difficulties feel about themselves.

It is hoped that early visual perceptual training will prevent many learning difficulties, and therefore much suffering of children and of those who work with them.

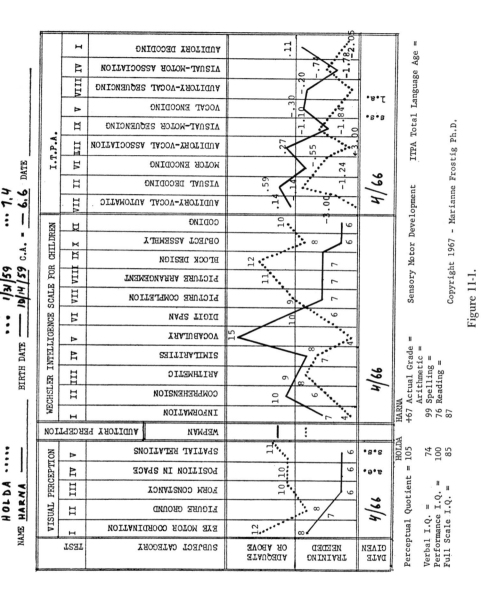

Figure 11-1.

Some examples of exercises for visual perceptual and visual-motor training are given in Figures 11-2 through 11-7.

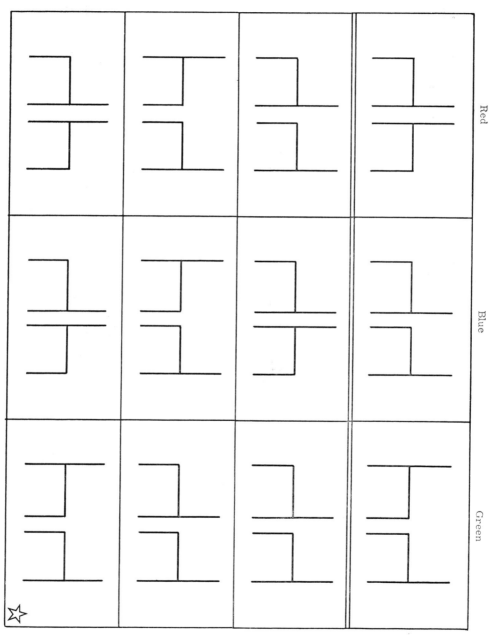

FROSTIG VISUAL PERCEPTION PROGRAM
© 1964 by Follett Publishing Company • Chicago

Figure 11-2. Spatial Relationships: Similarities and differences (SR-11).

"Let's look at the drawing at the top left corner of the page. It shows two chairs facing in different directions. Put a red mark on that drawing. Now look at all the other drawings on the page. In some of them, the chairs are exactly like the chairs in the drawing you just marked. Do you see the drawings that are just the same? Put a red mark on each of them, too. Good."

"Look at the middle picture at the top of the page. Put a blue mark on that one. Do you see how the chairs are facing the same way? See how many drawings you can find just like that one, and put a blue mark on each of them." Give similar instructions for the third stimulus figure.

For children with perceptual difficulties, demonstrate with two schoolroom chairs before they do the exercise.

Discuss where people may look while sitting on the chairs: at each other, away from each other, as in some trains where they sit back to back.

Figure 11-3. Figure-ground: Intersecting lines (FG-12).

"Here is a picture of three cars that are going different places. Put a red mark on the car at the top of the page. The family in that car wants to make a trip to the hot dog stand. (*Indicate*) Draw along the road from the car to the hot dog stand with your red crayon. Try to do it without taking your crayon from the page."

"Now put a green mark on the car below the top one. The family in that car wants to go to the pond with a boat on it. Can you trace their road with your green crayon so that the people can see where they are going?"

"Put a brown mark on the car at the bottom left of the page. The family in that car wants to visit the city. (*Indicate*) Can you trace their road with your brown crayon?"

For integration with memory training, language skills and concept formation, have the children tell stories about what the people in the cars might have seen while traveling. Ask what a factory is and have the children discuss it.

For integration with development in auditory discrimination, the child may be asked to find names which begin with the same letters as the colors of the cars or to give the first letter of the places where the cars go: *Hot Dog Stand, Factory Building, Lake, Sailboat*, etc.

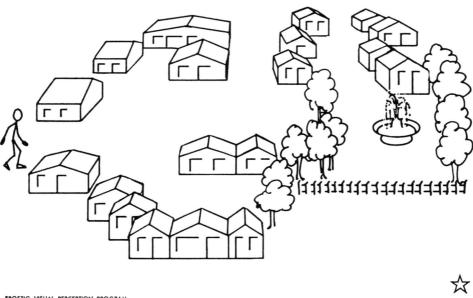

Figure 11-4. Spatial Relationships: Shortest path to a goal. (SR-21) .

"Look at the picture at the top of the page. The little girl at the left wants to play with the little girl at the right. Draw a line showing how she walks along the street between the rows of houses to the other little girl. Make the line so that it does not touch the roofs of the houses."

"Now look at the bottom picture. It's a hot day, and the boy at the left wants to get a drink at the fountain. (*Indicate*) Draw a line showing how he walks between and around the houses to reach the fountain. Be careful not to let him lose the path. He cannot go over the trees or the houses or outside the fence."

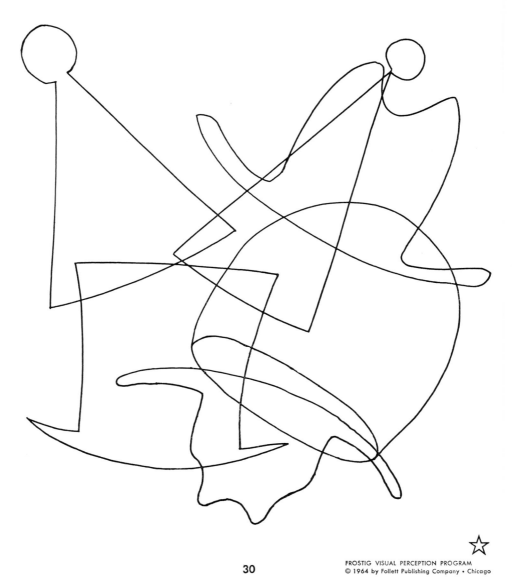

FROSTIG VISUAL PERCEPTION PROGRAM
© 1964 by Follett Publishing Company • Chicago

Figure 11-5. Figure-ground: Intersecting figures (FG-19).

Intersecting figures are usually a little harder to distinguish than intersecting lines. Children are used to seeing pieces of rope or string crossing, but not hats, for instance.

"Oh, Oh! Someone dumped all the party hats out in a pile. Let's outline them in different colors so that we can see how many we have. First take a red crayon and outline one of the hats. Try to do it without taking your crayon off the paper. Good. Take a green crayon and outline another hat." Continue, telling the children to use a different color crayon for each hat. "Now how many hats do we have? Right. We may have six people at our party."

Check so that the children do not make mistakes. Give help whenever necessary. Follow up by making party hats with the children, and let them play that they are having a party. Discuss first what children do at a party and what it would be fun to do.

37

Figure 11-6. Figure-ground: Hidden figures (FG-21).

What is that? Discuss what it is in the picture that makes the clown look funny (mask, clothes, ruff, very large feet).

In the box at the top of the page is a shape. (*Indicate*) Outline the shape first. Now look at the clown again. If you look hard, you can see shapes just like the one in the box. Outline all the shapes you can find that are just like the one in the box."

If a child has difficulty in perceiving or outlining the shapes, have him cut out a shape like that in the box, use it to cover the similar shapes in the picture, and draw around it.

PC: **Exercise 45**

Figure 11-7. Perceptual Constancy: Size constancy (PC-45).

"On the left side of this page you can see three tents. Inside each tent is a boy. The boy in the big tent wants to visit the other big tent. He is going to walk there on his hands. Can you draw a path for him from one big tent to the other? Make just one line."

Give appropriate instructions for connecting the two small and the two medium size tents.

Discuss scouting, outdoor equipment, etc.

REFERENCES

1. PIAGET, J.: *The Origins of Intelligence in Children.* New York, Int. Univs., 1952.
2. BRUNER, J.: *Toward a Theory of Instruction.* Cambridge, Harvard, 1966.
3. BOWER, T.G.R.: The visual world of infants. *Sci Amer, 215* (6) :80-92, 1966.
4. FANTZ, R.: Pattern discrimination and selective attention as determinants of perceptual development from birth. In Kidd, Aline, and Rivoire, Jeanne (Eds.) : *Development in Children.* New York, Int. Univs., 1966.
5. ERIKSON, E.: *Childhood and Society.* New York, Norton, 1950.
6. KIRK, S., and McCARTHY, J.: *Illinois Test of Psycholinguistic Abilities.* Urbana, U. of Ill., 1961.
7. FROSTIG, M.; LEFEVER, D., and WHITTLESEY, J.: *The Marianne Frostig Developmental Test of Visual Perception.* Palo Alto, Consulting Psychologists, 1964.
8. WEPMAN, J.: *Wepman Test of Auditory Discrimination.* Chicago, Language Research Associates, 1958.
9. WECHSLER, D.: *Wechsler Intelligence Scale for Children.* New York, Psychological Corp., 1949.
10. WECHSLER, D.: *Wechsler Pre-School and Primary Scale of Intelligence.* New York, Psychological Corp., 1963.
11. TERMAN, L., and MERRILL, M.: *Stanford-Binet Intelligence Scale.* Manual for Third Revision, Form L-M. Boston, Houghton, 1960.
12. CRUICKSHANK, W.M.; BICE, M.V., and WALLEN, N.E.: *Perception and Cerebral Palsy.* Syracuse, Syracuse, 1957.
13. WEDELL, K.: The visual perception of cerebral palsied children. *J Child Psychol Psychiat, 1*:215-227, 1960.
14. WEDELL, K.: Variations in perceptual ability among types of cerebral palsy. *Cereb Palsy Bull, 11*:149-157, 1960.
15. THURSTONE, L.L.: A factorial study of perception. *Psychometric Monographs,* No. 4., Chicago, U. of Chicago, 1944.
16. FROSTIG, M., and HORNE, D.: *The Frostig Program for the Development of Visual Perception.* Pictures by Bee Mandell. Chicago, Follett, 1964.
17. FROSTIG, M.; MILLER, A., and HORNE, D.: *Teacher's Guide to Beginning Pictures and Patterns.* Chicago, Follett, 1966.
18. FROSTIG, M., and HORNE, D.: *Teacher's Guide to Intermediate Pictures and Patterns.* Chicago, Follett, 1967.
19. FROSTIG, M., and HORNE, D.: *Teacher's Guide to Advanced Pictures and Patterns.* Chicago, Follett, 1967.
20. Examples of how training in visual perceptual abilities may be integrated with the teaching of beginning reading, writing, spelling, and arithmetic skills are given in the *Teacher's Guide to Advanced Pictures and Patterns.*
21. BRYAN, Q.: Relative importance of intelligence and visual perception in predicting reading achievement. *Calif J Educ Res, 15*:44-48, 1964.
22. MASLOW, P.; FROSTIG, M.; LEFEVER, D.W., and WHITTLESEY, J.R.B.: The Marianne Frostig developmental test of visual perception, 1963 standardization. *Percept Motor Skills, 19*:463-499, 1964, Monograph Supplement, 2-V19.

Chapter 12

The Dyslexias — A Psycho-educational and Physiological Approach

VIOLET E. SPRAINGS

T HREE SIGNIFICANT FACTS emerge regarding the phenomena of the dys- lexias: (1) with our present state of knowledge, there are more unanswered than answered questions; (2) medical specialists, psychologists, speech and language clinicians and educators use the term with varying degrees of pre- ciseness and often with different connotations; (3) these phenomena have more frequently been described in the singular than in the plural.

The recognition of dyslexia as a clinically observable phenomenon dates back to 1896 when James Kerr, an English school physician, and W. Pringle Morgan[19] described reading problems or word blindness in children who were intellectually normal.

One of the early great contributions to the field was by J. Hinshelwood, an ophthalmologist, whose monograph, *Congenital Word Blindness* was published in London in 1917.[15] This contribution was significant because it not only described the symptomatology, but also stressed the importance of differentiating difficulties in reading due to congenital word blindness from defects of reading due to other causes. He further suggested that congenital aplasia (absence) of the angular gyrus (folded convolution in the inferior parietal lobule) of the dominant hemisphere might be the cause of develop- mental dyslexia, and also noted no perceptual defect which would account for failure to learn to read. In the United States, Samuel T. Orton, a Neuropathologist, was a leading contributor to knowledge in this field. From 1925 to the time of his accidental death in 1948, he devoted himself to research and teaching of children with specific language disabilities. In 1928 he presented his famous paper and used the term "strephosymbolia" (twisted symbols).[25] On the basis of his investigations conducted over a period of years, he concluded that in dyslexia there was no generalized de- fect in form perception, but that the perceptual disability was specific to letters and words.[24] There was no supporting evidence for this view.

There have been others who have made significant contributions to knowledge in this area: Myklebust,[20] Drew,[5] Ettlinger and Jackson,[7] Critchley,[3] Fildes,[9] Gallagher,[10] Money,[17,18] etc.

Note: An abbreviated version of this paper appeared in ICAA's *Word Blind Bulletin*, Vol. 1 Nos. 6 and 7, Winter 1966, London, England.

An attempt has been made to arrive at a definition of dyslexia which would be meaningful from both a psychological and an educational point of view. Many have defined dyslexia as the condition of being unable to read adequately because of brain disorder, or because of minimal neurological deficits. In working with dyslexics, both from a diagnostic and teaching point of view, psychologists, speech and language clinicians and educators lack the tools, technical skill and knowledge to diagnose cerebral dysfunction. Hence, for them such a definition is not entirely a realistic one. Perhaps even for the skilled physician, this definition may not always be adequate since some of these children, after having been rigorously examined neurologically, are said to appear normal.

For purposes of this discussion, dyslexia is defined as a symbolic language disorder, with a somewhat characteristic syndrome, where there is poor ability to learn to interpret and retain the symbols needed for reading in the absence of major mental ability defect or perceptual aberration, and where the child has been exposed to an organized attempt to teach him to read over a minimum period of one year.

To diagnose a child as dyslexic from this definition, presupposes that certain diagnostic criteria have been met:

1. A child is at least seven years of age or is at the end of first grade before an attempt is made to classify him as dyslexic. One, however, looks forward to the day when diagnostic procedures will be so refined as to permit definitive diagnosis of the pre-dyslexic by at least kindergarten and preferably at the preschool level.

2. There has been a thorough assessment of the child's intellectual functioning to determine as accurately as possible his present level of functioning and to predict with some degree of accuracy his potential.

3. Perceptual functioning at all levels has been explored; so that the possibility of a perceptual disability precluding reading can be eliminated.

In our discussion of testing, several factors should be considered. Tests have been standardized on children of whom only a small number have had reading and language problems; so normative data are but relatively applicable to the dyslexic. This means that the dyslexic is probably capable of functioning a little better than indicated by the quantitative test data. Dyslexia is a type of language disorder, hence the dyslexic may appear to be functioning lower than he actually is on verbally oriented tests. Not infrequently, in addition to the reading disorder, this group also presents some generalized language deficits, which are dysphasic-like in character. They often lack age-level skills in communicating, evidence a poverty of well-oriented ideas, lack fluency in speech, evidence a slowness in response time, and need several starts to answer questions adequately even when they know the correct answer. The latter is often suggestive of formulation as well as naming problems. It is interesting to observe that in the older dyslexic, the dysphasic-like language disorder might go unnoticed in his conversational speech but becomes exceedingly apparent when he is placed in situations where he must structure his verablization in such a manner as to answer specific questions or describe specific events or material. An instrument like the Wechsler Intelligence Scale for Children, where the verbal and performance components are separated and yield two separate Intelligence Quotients, will be more revealing regarding the intellectual functioning of this child than the Stanford Binet with its very large verbal component.

The number of studies related to reading probably exceeds those in any other content area. *In a review of some one hundred studies postulating causes for reading disability, few even remotely suggested dyslexia or or- ganicity as being a cause for children failing to learn to read.* Of those suggesting this possibility, none suggested the possibility that this is a dis- ability better thought of in the plural than in the singular.

Research seems to suggest at least three distinguishable types of dyslexia, and possibly a fourth:

1. Visual dyslexia in which the child is unable to learn and retain the appearance of letters.
2. Auditory dyslexia in which the child is unable to learn and retain the sound of letters.
3. Visuo-auditory dyslexia in which both of the above defined states exist.
4. Possibly a familial dyslexia having some of the aforementioned char- acteristics and some unique characteristics. An attempt is being made to decide whether this is indeed another and separate type of dyslexia.

The type of dyslexia seems closely related to prognosis, with a visual or auditory type having a better prognosis than a visuo-auditory type. If a child has a visual type of dyslexia, one may often use auditory approaches very effectively and vice versa. However, if there is disablement in both the auditory and visual spheres, effective approaches to learning are much more limited.

It is further felt that type should dictate the nature of the program of remediation. Dyslexia is a disability which seems rather resistant to the usual remedial reading techniques. Hence, it is felt that remedial programs should be prescribed on an individual basis at the outset, and this means that the problems involved in the individual's audio-visual-verbal processing system must be delineated prior to program formulation.

In order to dileneate the problems that might be involved in dyslexia, the question arises as to what should be included in the psycho-educational evaluation so that remedial educational programs can be formulated, remembering that *Diagnosis precedes program planning*. The following will comprise a brief listing of the constituents:

DIAGNOSTIC TESTS

Perceptual Testing — Visual, Auditory and Manual

Perception has often been viewed as a single process to be studied in children, rather than as a sequential and developmental process. Most standardized tests designed to assess perception do so only at the lowest levels, namely, those of discrimination. The higher levels, analysis and synthesis, virtually are ignored. In this assessment of the dyslexic child, an experimental battery of visual and auditory perceptual tests is used.

The Spraings' *Visual Perceptual Analysis Battery* includes the following tests*:

Test 1: Differentiation of Likenesses and Differences Among Simple, Uncluttered Geometric Forms

At this level, the task of the child is to differentiate likenesses and differences among simple, uncluttered geometric forms. The choices include figures like the stimulus figure, but smaller; those like the stimulus figure, but larger; like the stimulus figures but with some distortion as well as figures like the stimulus figure, but oriented differently. In repeated testing of children with perceptual disorders, it has been consistently noted by this writer that orientation problems occur with considerably more frequency than reversal problems. (See Fig. 12-1.)

Test 2: Differentiation of Likenesses and Differences Among More Complicated Patterns of Geometric Forms

At this level, the task of the individual is to differentiate likenesses and differences among somewhat more complicated patterns of geometric forms. Here the forms have some relationship to each other and require more astute scrutiny. (See Fig. 12-2.)

Test 3: Differentiation of Likenesses and Differences Among Complicated Patterns of Geometric Forms

Differentiation at this level is among complicated patterns of geometric forms and requires quite astute scrutiny. Nonsymbolic sequential per-

---

*All tests are scored in terms of four variables: (1) Raw Score; (2) Time; (3) Per cent Correct; (4) Attention. There is also a system for qualitative appraisal of frequency of types of errors.

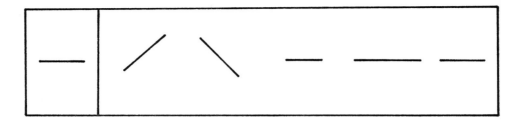

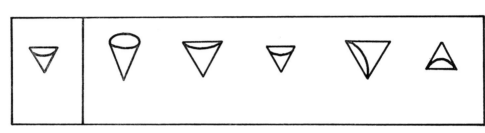

Figure 12-1. Differentiation of Likenesses and Differences Among Simple, Uncluttered Geometric Forms. Match the form on the left with each form on the right to find all matching forms.

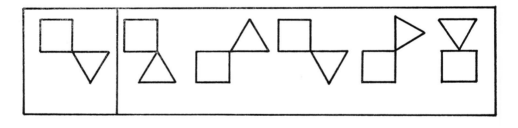

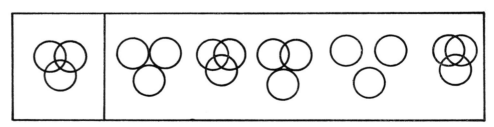

Figure 12-2. Differentiation of Likenesses and Differences Among More Complicated Patterns of Geometric Forms. Match the form on the left with each form on the right to find all matching forms.

ceptual skills are introduced for the first time. The previous levels involved more static and non symbolic perception. (See Fig. 12-3.)

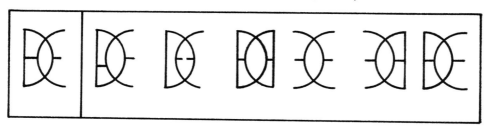

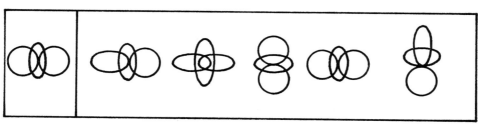

Figure 12-3. Differentiation of Likenesses and Differences Among Complicated Patterns of Geometric Forms. Match the form on the left with each form on the right to find all matching forms.

Test 4: Differentiation of Likenesses and Differences Among Simple and Uncluttered Pictured Items

At this level, meaning is introduced for the first time. Where it is possible to consider meaningfully that which is being perceived, the individual will do so. This increases the time required to perceive the items. (See Fig. 12-4.)

Test 5: Differentiation of Likenesses and Differences Among Complicated and More Cluttered Pictured Items

At this level, differentiation is to be made among complicated pictured material. (See Fig. 12-5.)

Test 6: Differentiation of Likenesses and Differences in Symbolic-type Material Such as Letters and Numbers

Although letters and numbers are not involved at this level, symbolic-like material is utilized so that the individual must make many of the same kinds of discernments that are utilized in correctly perceiving symbolic material. (See Fig.12-6.)

Figure 12-4. Differentiation of Likenesses and Differences Among Simple and Uncluttered Pictured Items. Match the item on the left with each item on the right to find all matching items.

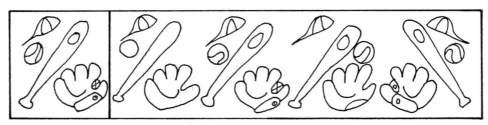

Figure 12-5. Differentiation of Likenesses and Differences Among Complicated and More Cluttered Pictured Items. Match the item at the left with each item on the right to find all matching items.

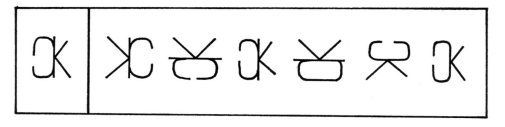

Figure 12-6. Differentiation of Likenesses and Differences in Symbolic-type Material Such as Letters and Numbers. Match the item on the left with each item on the right to find all matching items.

Test 7: Differentiation of Likenesses and Differences Among Nonsense Words

At this level, sequential and symbolic visual perceptual skills are required and the differentiations must be made among nonsense words. (See Fig. 12-7.)

caemu:	caewn	caemn	ceamu	clelozmre
tijles:	tjiles	seljit	tijles	caemu
clelozmer:	cleplzmer	clelozmer	cellozmer	tlijes

Figure 12-7. Differentiation of Likenesses and Differences Among Nonsense Words. The child matches the nonsense word on the left with each word on the right to find all matching words.

Test 8: Test for Visual Discrimination of Words

For the first time, visual memory is introduced. The level of difficulty of the words is such that reading is not a factor, but instead emphasis is on perceiving, perceiving in the proper sequence and retaining the general gestalt. Some examples from this test are in Figure 12-8.

black: bark   crack   sack   black   clock
berth: bestir   berry   beryl   beret   berth   bereft   bequest
regulation: regular   registration   negotiation   recognition   regulation   radiation

Figure 12-8. Test for Visual Discrimination of Words. The child matches the word on the left, after a brief exposure to it on a separate card, with the proper word on the right.

Test 9: Perceptual Synthesis Test

Reading involves not only the ability to make discriminations among letters, syllables and words, perceiving these in sequence, but also to make these discriminations while synthesizing and analyzing. At this level, one assesses the individual's ability to synthesize perceptually. (See Fig. 12-9.)

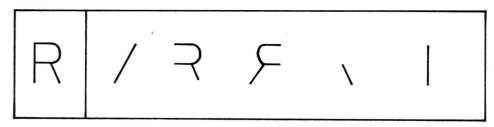

Figure 12-9. Perceptual Synthesis Test. Select the two parts on the right which should be synthesized to form the letter on the left.

Test 10: Perceptual Analysis Test

At this level,* one is able to evaluate the child's ability to analyze perceptually and to discern the accuracy and speed with which he is able to engage in this process. (See Fig. 12-10.)

---

*Although the test material is organized according to levels, more than a hierarchy of perceptual levels, there may be in some cases more differences in kind rather than levels.

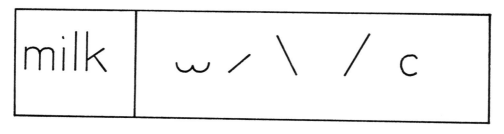

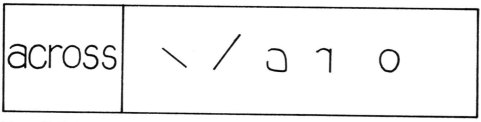

Figure 12-10. Perceptual Analysis Test. Select the part on the right which is part of the word on the left.

Subsequent to an administration of the above battery, each subject is administered a perceptual speed test. Sometimes this is an area requiring a separate specifically designed remedial emphasis. While these visual skills are essential in the reading process, the individual must also and simultaneously relate these skills to a system of sounds.

Tests of Auditory Perception

The Spraings' *Auditory Perceptual Battery* includes the following tests:

Test 1: Nonsocial — Nonverbal Auditory Tests

    Part I   Tone Discrimination
    Part II   Tonal Pattern Discrimination

Test 2: Social Nonverbal Auditory Tests

    Part I   Auditory Matching Test
    Part II   Auditory-Visual Matching Test

Test 3: Test of Auditory Discrimination Among Words

Test 4: Auditory Temporal Integration Test

    Part I   Sound Blending Test
    Part II   Auditory-Visual Test

Test 5: Hearing Sounds in Words Test
Part I   Initial Test
Part II   Endings Test
Part III   Blending Test

Manual perceptual skills are assessed and a gnosic age computed on each child. Gnosic disorders have been identified in the cerebral palsied child with some frequency. It has been pointed out that some children cannot tell what position in space the various parts of their limbs occupy; some cannot tell whether their joints are flexed or extended. When their eyes are shut, they cannot recognize objects put into their hands.

There is now some evidence that children with minimal cerebral dysfunction who are experiencing difficulties in writing, and for whom visual-motor coordination is an aberrant function, also have difficulties in manual perception which make writing even more askew and difficult. When a gnosic age is computed for these children, often it is found to be significantly less than their mental age.

Intelligence Tests
1. Wechsler Intelligence Scale for Children.
2. Other types of intelligence measures, verbal and nonverbal, to assess the child's ability to "act purposefully, to think rationally, to deal effectively with his environment."
3. Additional testing to bring data to bear on intellectual ability, intelligent behavior and the intellectual processes: recognition, retention, divergent thinking, convergent thinking, decision-making and social behavior.

Visual Motor Assessment
1. Body image testing.
2. Testing that yields data indicating status of visual-motor coordination skills if at a prewriting level, or status of these skills if at a writing level. It is to be remembered that in the hierarchy of language development, the expressive skill of writing is acquired *subsequent* to reading.

Right-Left Orientation
1. Verbal versus nonverbal assessment. For the child who might have some difficulty either in expressive or receptive language, a nonverbal assessment of right-left orientation is apt to be more revealing with respect to an accurate status of these skills.

2. Sequencing Abilities. These involve the child's ability to understand nonverbal and sequentially presented material including the ability to synthesize these data into meaningful and well organized wholes.

Learning Ability Assessment

There always needs to be an assessment of *how* a child learns which is quite apart from *what* he has learned and the approach should include both visual and auditory assessment. In experimenting with dyslexics, it appears that one of the most crucial and aberrant areas in some is learning ability, and that prognosis in some cases can be predicted with considerable accuracy on the basis of the learning ability data.

Conceptualization Assessment

1. Nonverbal
2. Verbal

Memory Assessment

1. Visual
   a. Static — recall of material, the gestalt of which can be perceived at a single viewing. For example: a simple geometric form.
   b. Sequential — recall of material that must be perceived in a proper sequence. For example: a trigram, a word, a sentence.
2. Auditory
   a. Static
   b. Sequential

Language Assessment

1. Inner
2. Receptive
3. Expressive

Cross Modality and Integrative Assessment

1. Visual to verbal
2. Auditory to verbal
3. Visual to auditory
4. Auditory to visual, etc.

Academic Achievement Assessment

1. Reading — word recognition, paragraph reading
2. Arithmetic — fundamentals, concepts, problem solving (oral and written)

Behavior Assessment

1. Subjective Data
   a. Rorschach
   b. Thematic Apperception Test
   c. Parent Interview Data
2. Objective Data
   a. Spraings' Behavior Rating Scale
   b. Parent Interview Data

DYSLEXIA SYNDROME

As one views retrospectively the data from a number of dyslexics, a syndrome can usually be discerned. All dyslexics, however, will not have all the symptoms, but the following can be seen to generally characterize the group:

1. Reading ability is definitely not commensurate with mental age and with the opportunities offered him to learn to read.
2. Poor ability to relate letter and letter sound, so spelling often appears bizarre in that the child's spelling often bears little or no relationship to the stimulus word.
3. Visual hyperactivity, especially in older subjects.
4. Topographical disturbances evidenced in map reading, directional orientation, etc.
5. Right-left discrimination problems.
6. Dischronometrical disturbances — a basic disturbance in time as an aspect of a symbolic language disorder.
7. Emotional problems especially in children of third grade and above, usually due to frustration sustained because of low achievement.
8. Visual and/or auditory memory problems.
9. Rare in girls. Perhaps four or five times as many boys than girls affected.
10. Sequencing difficulties.
11. Visual-motor coordination problems that often begin at the level of body image disturbance and are not infrequently also accompanied by gnosic disorders.
12. Spontaneous and creative writing poor. *Note:* In the developmental hierarchy of language development, reading precedes writing.
13. Often bizarre maturational patterns — much further advanced in one area and quite slow in others.
14. Ofttimes general language deficits — dysphasic in character.
15. Audio-visual and/or visual-auditory integration impaired as well as other integrational aberrations.

16. Conceptualization deficits.
17. Poor time concepts.
18. Achievement in arithmetic higher than in language arts area.
19. Learning ability problems.
20. Learning Quotient considerably less than Intelligence Quotient.

In the remediation programming for the dyslexic, it is vital to define the type for this will ultimately dictate the kind of corrective procedures which should be utilized.

The auditory dyslexic will be poor in his acquisition and use of phonetic skills, have difficulty blending sounds into words, have difficulty remembering auditory sequences, often show limited ability to use word attack skills, often evidence more speech and language disabilities, auditorization problems, auditory sequencing disturbances, etc. When beginning to teach the auditory dyslexic to read, one will need to utilize whole word approaches, techniques that employ matching words that can be represented concretely with pictures, for example.

On the other hand, the visual dyslexic will show visual sequencing problems, perceptual speed difficulties, poor visual feedback, visual memory disabilities, higher level visual discrimination problems, etc. When beginning to teach the visual dyslexic to read, one will need to use analytic approaches. For example, teach letter sounds before letter names, recognition before recall, blending skills that begin with short vowels, integration skills — making transitions from visual to verbal and visual to auditory.

RESEARCH RESULTS

A two-year study was made of forty-five dyslexic children who were brought to the Diagnostic School for testing. The results of this retrospective study by Crowther* and Spraings are listed below.

Forty-five children with dyslexia were evaluated over a two-year period. These children were selected from a minimally neurologically handicapped population of children, three to twenty-one years of age, evaluated in a Medical-Educational Diagnostic Center. The diagnosis of dyslexia was made by a team of specialists in medicine, language and education. Forty were male and five female. Their ages ranged from six years seven months to nineteen years five months. It is of interest to note that twenty-four of the children evaluated presented between the ages of nine and eleven years. Of this number, the greatest number, i.e., ten patients, presented at the

*Douglas Crowther, M.D., Assistant Professor, Pediatric Neurology, University of California Medical Center and Consulting Pediatric Neurologist, Diagnostic School for Neurologically Handicapped Children, Northern California.

age of nine years. This seems to indicate that despite a significant reading problem, over 50 per cent of the patients are apt to spend four to six years in school before being referred for evaluation.

The neurological evaluation of these children included a careful history and physical examination, together with electroencephalographic studies in certain patients.

1. Family History

   Fifty-eight per cent of the patients showed a family history in which there was a learning problem either in siblings or parents. The family histories have not been adequately analyzed yet to ascertain the type of learning problems present in the families. A cursory view seems to indicate a predominance of problems in the area of language arts: reading, spelling and handwriting.

2. Pregnancy History

   Fifty-seven per cent presented with an abnormal history of pregnancy in the mother prior to their birth.

3. Neonatal History

   Thirty-one per cent showed significant problems during the birth and/or neonatal period.

4. Motor Development

   Motor development was said to be normal in 71 per cent of the patients. In 29 per cent it was delayed.

5. Speech Development

   Speech development was normal in 40 per cent of the patients. Sixty per cent of the children evidenced abnormal speech development with the largest number of these showing a moderate to mild defect. Only one had a severe defect.

6. Handedness

   Seventy-three per cent of the patients were right handed and 27 per cent left handed. Forty-four per cent showed mixed hand-eye dominance. In view of the complexity of assessing dominance in relation to eye, hand and foot, the complete breakdown on the specific defects in the mixed dominance group has not yet been completed.

7. Seizure History

   Only 7 per cent of the group suffered with convulsive seizures either before or at the time of the examination.

8. Electroencephalographic Data

   Tracings were taken on thirty-three (73%) of the forty-five patients. Of this number, fifteen (46%) were normal, four (12%) "borderline" normal and fourteen (42%) abnormal. Of the fourteen abnormal electroencephalographic tracings, eleven showed a diffuse dysrhythmia, while three showed focal abnormalities. Further analyses will need to be made on these EEG findings.

9. Psychological Data

    a. The Wechsler Intelligence Scale for Children was administered to the children. The Verbal Scale IQ ranged from 66-106, Performance Scale IQ from 76-124, and the Full Scale from 75-109.

    b. The discrepancy between the Verbal and Performance Scale ranged from 0-33 points.

    c. Fourteen per cent had a higher Verbal than Performance Scale IQ. Eighty-four percent had a higher Performance Scale IQ. One per cent evidenced no discrepancy between the Verbal and Performance Scale IQ, and for 1 per cent of the cases, only a Verbal or Performance Scale was administered. An analysis of these data seems to indicate that initially the potential of the dyslexics is better measured by Performance than Verbal Tests. More than 50 per cent of the group evidenced a generalized language deficit that often appeared nonspecific in type, but sometimes appeared aphasic-like in type.

    d. The Bender Gestalt and other tests used to assess the visuo-motor and visual perceptual functions indicated visual-motor coordination deficits in more than 90 per cent of the cases, but visual perceptual disorders in less than 25 per cent.

    e. The Peabody Picture Vocabulary scores ranged from 70-108.

    f. Thirty-three per cent of the children had complications involving other kinds of symbolic language disorders: dyscalculia, aphasia, aphasic-like disturbances and dysgraphia.

    g. On the Raven's Progressive Matrices Test, 51 per cent scored in the below average to defective range.

    h. Fourteen per cent evidenced disturbances in body image.

    i. Forty-one per cent evidenced disturbances in auditory memory. Forty per cent evidenced disturbances in visual memory.

10. Reading Achievement.

Twenty-five per cent were nonreaders for practical purposes. Only one child was reading at the third grade level.

From the above preliminary data, it is seen that there are a large number of factors to analyze in this retrospective study. However, it is hoped that because of inaccuracies that every retrospective study leads to, more pertinent information will be forthcoming with the prospective study which is in progress.

REFERENCES

1. BENDER, L.: Problems in conceptualization and communication in children with developmental alexia. In Hoch, P.H., and Zubin, J. (Eds.) : *Psychopathology of Communication*. New York, Grune, 1958.

2. CRITCHLEY, M.: Inborn reading disorders of central origin. *Trans Ophthal Soc UK, 81*:459-480, 1961.

3. CRITCHLEY, M.: *Developmental Dyslexia*, London, Heinemann, 1964.

4. DE HIRSCH, K.; JANSKY, J.J., and LANGFORD, W.S.: The Prediction of Reading, Spelling and Writing Disabilities in Children: A Preliminary Study. Final technical report to the Health Research Council of the City of New York, 1965.

5. DREW, A. L.: A neurological approach of familial congenital word blindness. *Brain, 79*:440-460, 1956.

6. EISENBERG, L.: Office evaluation of specific reading disability, *Pediatrics, 23*:997-1003, 1959.

7. ETTLINGER, G., and JACKSON, C.: Organic factors in developmental dyslexia. *Proc Roy Soc Med, 48*:998-1000, 1955.

8. FABIAN, A.A.: Clinical and experimental studies of school children who are retarded in reading. *Quart J Child Behav, 3*:15-37, 1951.

9. FILDES, L.G.: A psychological inquiry into the nature of the condition known as congenital word blindness. *Brain, 44*:286-307, 1921.

10. GALLAGHER, J.: Specific language disability: dyslexia. *Bull Orton Soc, 10*:5-10, 1960.

11. GATES, A.I.: *The Psychology of Reading and Spelling with Special Reference to Disability*. Teachers College Contributions to Education #129, New York Bureau of Publications, Teachers College, Columbia University, 1922.

12. GILLINGHAM, A., and STILLMAN, B.: *Remedial Training for Children with Specific Disability in Reading, Spelling and Penmanship*. 6th ed., Cambridge, Educators Publishing Service, 1960.

13. GOODY, W., and REINHOLD, J.: Congenital diplexia and asymmetry of cerebral functions. *Brain, 84*:231-242, 1961.

14. HERMAN, I.: *Reading Disability*. Springfield, Thomas, 1959.

15. HINSHELWOOD, J.: *Congenital Word Blindness*. London, H.K. Lewis, 1917.

16. INGRAM, T.: Pediatric aspects of specific developmental dysphasia, dyslexia and dysgraphia. *Cereb Palsy Bull, 2*:254-277, 1960.

17. MONEY, J. (Ed.) : *Reading Disability — Progress and Research Needs in Dyslexia*. Baltimore, John Hopkins, 1962.

18. MONEY, J. (Ed.) : *The Disabled Reader: Education of the Dyslexic Child*. Baltimore, John Hopkins, 1966.

19. MORGAN, W.P.: Word blindness. *Brit Med J, 2*:1378, 1896.

20. MYKLEBUST, H., and JOHNSON, D.: Dyslexia in children. *Exceptional Child, 29*:14-25, 1962.

21. MYKLEBUST, H.: Learning disorders: psychoneurological disturbances in childhood. *Rehab Lit, 25*:354-360, 1964.

22. MYKLEBUST, H.R.: *The Psychology of Deafness*. 2nd ed., New York, Grune, 1965.

23. MYKLEBUST, H.: *A Picture Story Test*. New York, Grune, 1965.

24. ORTON, S.T.: *Reading, Writing and Speech Problems in Children*. New York, Norton, 1937.

25. ORTON, S.T.: Specific reading disability — strephosymbolia. *JAMA, 90*:1095-1099, April 1928.

26. REBINOVITCH, R.; DREW, A.; DE JONG, R.; INGRAM, W., and WITHEY, L.: A research approach to reading retardation. *Res Publ Ass Res Nerv Ment Dis, 34*:365-396, 1954.

27. ROBINSON, H.: The study of disabilities in reading. *Elementary Sch J, 38*:1-14, 1937.

28. SCHILDER, P.: Congenital alexia and its relation to optic perception. *J Genet Psychol, 65*:67-88, 1944.

29. SILVER, A.A., and HAGIN, R.: Specific reading disability: delineation of the syndrome and relationship to cerebral dominance. *Compr Psychiat, 1*:126-134, 1960.

30. SPRAINGS, V. (Ed.): *The Educationally Handicapped: The Spectrum of Learning Disabilities.* (Syllabus) Education Extension, Berkeley, U. of Calif., 1966.

31. THOMPSON, L.: Specific reading disability — strephosymbolia I: diagnosis. *Bull Orton Soc, 6*:3-9, 1956.

The Illinois Test of Psycholinguistic Abilities: Implications for Diagnosis and Remediation

STANFORD H. LAMB

PERHAPS NO SINGLE TEST in recent years has generated as much research and discussion in the area of learning disabilities as the Illinois Test of Psycholinguistic Abilities (ITPA). Researchers, clinicians and teachers within almost every area of learning disabilities have paid attention to the work with this instrument. Their interest was generated because this test has opened a way of bridging the gap between diagnosing and remediating language disabilities which have been found in almost all children with learning handicaps.

Language is composed of numerous tasks involving several modes of reception and expression including the more complicated tasks of integration, storage and retrieval. Previous language tests for children have sampled too few or only single psycholinguistic abilities. Thus, it has been difficult to perceive relationships among several different language skills and to observe how one may influence the other from a diagnostic standpoint and as the result of a remediation program. The utilization of test profiles such as the ITPA's, which illustrate several language skills, has become increasingly valuable in making more adequate diagnoses of learning disabilities, and in observing gains from remediation procedures. However, it should be stressed that the ITPA was only intended to open the door to the understanding of language disabilities. The test was designed as an *initial* diagnostic tool in the assessment of specific language disabilities. Furthermore, if the tester maintains the attitude that the ITPA, in its initial form is only experimental, he will be more conscious of the assets and limitations of its uses.

The purpose of the ITPA is to aid; (1) in precise diagnosis of special areas of psycholinguistic strengths and weaknesses, and (2) in planning an individual remedial program to ameliorate the disabilities. The test evolved out of our increasing knowledge of the complexities of language, the essential abilities for comprehending and conveying information. The use of a theoretical behavioral model has become a significant tool in the description and illustration of language abilities and such a model was used by McCarthy and Kirk in the development of the ITPA.[38]

DEVELOPMENT OF ITPA

From the theoretical framework of a behavioral model, nine subtests were developed. The first six were at the Representational Level (the ability to mediate activities dealing with the meaning of linguistic symbols), and were divided into three psycholinguistic processes. Two were decoding processes (the ability to obtain meaning from incoming linguistic symbols — receptive language ability). Two were association processes (the ability to meaningfully manipulate linguistic symbols internally — inner language abilities). And two were encoding processes (the ability to express oneself meaningfully with linguistic symbols — expressive language ability). The remaining three subtests were at the Automatic-Sequential Level (the ability to mediate activities involving nonmeaningful uses of symbols), which are termed "whole level" tests, meaning that no separation of processes was made (McCarthy and Kirk).[39]

Subtest Descriptions

The order that follows corresponds to the order of the subtests as they appear on the profile grid on the record form and will be followed throughout this discussion, although this is not the order of administration.

Subtest 1

Auditory Decoding assesses the subject's ability to comprehend the spoken word. It is a "controlled vocabulary" subtest requiring that the subject respond to a question with a simple Yes or No answer. The material was compiled from early word lists of the Peabody Picture Vocabulary Test (PPVT) and the syntax of all questions was kept constant, e.g., "Do airplanes fly?" "Do cars cry?" "Do daughters marry?" "Do chateaux chastise?"

Subtest 2

Visual Decoding measures the subject's ability to understand pictures and written words. The subject is initially shown a stimulus picture and following its removal is asked to find from four comparison pictures the one most nearly like the stimulus picture on a meaningful basis, not a physical basis. For example, the stimulus picture may be a square table, while among the comparison pictures is a round table. The authors state that the selection should be based on those items that are "perceptually similar." Selection by matching is eliminated as the stimulus picture and the comparison pictures are not exposed simultaneously. However, because of this, memory is a contributing factor in selection.

Subtest 3

Auditory-Vocal Association tests the subject's ability "to relate spoken words in a meaningful way." This subtest utilizes a sentence completion form of opposite analogies, e.g., "I sit on a chair; I sleep on a ——." "A cube is square; a sphere is ——." To have the major emphasis of the task on the association process, the requirements for decoding and encoding were constructed at two years below the level of the analogy. However, it was found that auditory decoding has a "regular and substantial degree of relationship" with auditory-vocal association.[39] As discussed in the section on Validity, this subtest is highly correlated with mental age.

Subtest 4

Visual-Motor Association evaluates the subject's ability to relate visual symbols or stimuli on a meaningful basis by selecting from a group of four pictures the one which "goes with" the stimulus picture. The relationships are of two types, the first being transitional "sock goes with shoe" and the second substitional "boys and girls are people." Little relationship was found between this subtest and visual decoding and motor encoding.[39]

Subtest 5

Vocal Encoding measures the individual's ability to describe verbally simple objects in a number of unique and meaningful ways, e.g., "Tell me all about it," while being shown a marble, ball, chalk, etc. This test is mainly quantitative. Articulation proficiency or language structure are not considered in the scoring. The relative familiarity of the objects reduces the potential problem of lack of recognition (decoding). Because the test is open-ended, allowing for innumerable responses, acceptable and unacceptable responses are listed to aid in the objectivity of the scoring.

Subtest 6

Motor Encoding assesses the child's ability to express ideas through gestures appropriate for the manipulation of objects which are held or viewed in pictures, e.g., "Show me what you should do with this," while holding a hammer or viewing a picture of a musical instrument. In selecting the stimuli for the test, decoding was reduced as an influence in performance by having children select, by use ("the one you pound with"), the appropriate stimulus from a group of pictures before supplying the motion. In this way, it was assured that children could identify the pictures even though they might be unable to supply the appropriate gestures.

Subtest 7

Auditory-Vocal Automatic tests the subject's ability to use appropriate grammatical forms. Because of the highly redundant nature and incidental verbal learning of our language we learn to predict, without conscious effort, future linguistic events by what preceded them. This subtest utilizes a sentence completion form to be completed with a common inflected word, e.g., "Here is a bed. Here are two ——." The evidence to indicate that this task was at the nonmeaningful level was found by Berko when she observed that children could supply the correct inflections (changes in word forms) to nonsense syllables.[10] However, the authors (McCarthy and Kirk) decided to use meaningful, familiar objects because they found a tendency for children to give meaning to the inflected responses of nonsense syllables, e.g., "Here is a wug." *Here are two rugs.*[39] Like subtest 5, articulation proficiency is ruled out of the subject's performance. Although pictures are used to aid the younger children, after the task has been learned the test can be performed without the visual stimuli.

Subtest 8

Auditory-Vocal Sequencing measures the person's ability to repeat correctly a sequence of digits. This test of immediate auditory recall differs in several respects from the standard digit span test in that: the examiner presents the digits at two per second; he lowers his voice at the end of the sequence; digits may be said more than once within a sequence; and a sequence is given a second time if failed on the initial trial. Nonsense words were originally designated to be used, but it was found that articulation errors common to younger children would call for excessive use of subjective judgments on the part of the examiner.

Subtest 9

Visual-Motor Sequencing evaluates the child's ability to reproduce a sequence of visual stimuli, either pictures or geometric designs. Like subtest 8, this measures immediate rote memory, gives two trials if needed, and utilizes two of the same stimuli within a sequence. Unlike subtest 8, this task requires the child to select and to code before sequencing the data. An example of a coded sequence would be "o-d-z-3-z-" which is used in the Manual for a circle, diamond, trapezoid, triangle and trapezoid sequence.

A point of interest for future research was pointed out by the authors (McCarthy and Kirk) when they found that both sequencing tests showed no tendency to "level out" at the older age levels, thus suggesting that these tests could be extended beyond the maximum age level of nine years and prove valuable in assessing older children.[39]

The authors stated that after many unsuccessful attempts to construct a suitable test of visual-motor automatic for all age levels, they abandoned the effort.

STANDARDIZATION AND STATISTICAL CHARACTERISTICS

The normative data were obtained on 700 children from Decatur, Illinois between the ages of 2-6 and 9-10 out of a total 1,100 who were tested. All children, an equal number of boys and girls, were tested with the Stanford-Binet Intelligence Test, Form L (1937 revision). In an attempt to assure "a relatively homogeneous reference group" only those with IQs between 80 an 120 were used. No children of the negroid race or children attending parochial schools were used. The socioeconomic status of the group was controlled in order to assure that the sample reflected a cross section found in other parts of the United States. No attempt was made to control nationality and the children were largely from urban districts. Testing was performed within two months of each child's birthday by sixteen trained examiners.

The data from both sexes were combined at each age level because it was found that, in general, there was "no marked sex bias." However, certain subtests tended to favor boys (Visual Decoding and Vocal Encoding) and others favored girls (Visual-Motor Sequencing, Visual-Motor Association and Auditory Decoding). When comparing age differences, the authors found that total ITPA raw score means increased regularly with age except between 7-6 and 8-0 and between 9-0 and 9-6. Consequently for the normative data, these age levels were combined resulting in twelve age groupings instead of the original fourteen.

Reliability

Two forms of reliability were studied: (1) internal consistency, and (2) stability.[39] Internal consistency measurements evaluate the homogeneity of the items within a subtest; these overall coefficients of correlation for the subtests ranged from 0.89 to 0.95. However, these coefficients for specific age levels of subtests were as low as 0.50 and 0.51 for subtest 2 at the 7-6 and 8-0 levels, and subtest 3 at the 6-6 age level respectively.

Stability was measured by a test-retest method on a restricted group of sixty-nine children from the 6-0 to 6-6 age groups with a minimum three-month interval between tests. This method measures how consistently the test will predict future performance if administered on repeated occasions. Product-moment coefficients of correlation ranged from 0.18 (Visual-Motor Sequencing) to 0.86 (Auditory-Vocal Sequencing), with the coefficient for the ITPA total score 0.70 for this restricted age range. Full age range estimates (2-6 to 9-0) were computed with coefficients of stability ranging from 0.73 for both encoding subtests to 0.96 for the Auditory-Vocal Association subtest; the ITPA total score correlated 0.97. As a group, the auditory-vocal subtests showed the highest test-retest coefficients, especially subtests 3 and 8. The encoding subtests showed the lowest full age range stability coefficients.

Another method of estimating reliability employed was the split-half method, where the test was split into odd and even halves. Overall coefficients, for all ages combined, ranged from 0.90 for Motor Encoding to 0.96 for Auditory-Vocal Association and Auditory Decoding, with the ITPA total score correlated at 0.99.

Weener, Barritt and Semmel in their critical evaluation of the ITPA reported a study analyzed by them on the test-retest stability of preschool children in Ypsilanti, Michigan.[58] Their results from two groups of children with pre and post-test intervals of twelve and twenty-one months respectively, were similar to those of McCarthy and Kirk. As a result of their study and an analysis of the data presented by McCarthy and Kirk, Weener, Barritt and Semmel conclude that the ITPA subtest reliabilities are "too low for adequate prediction and diagnosis from individual profiles."[39,58] However, according to Bateman, of seemingly greater importance than statistical reliability may be the increasing data supporting the tests' clinical reliability.[4,7] The test is said to be able to detect reliably, characteristic profiles that aid in the diagnosis and remediation of children with learning disabilities. Furthermore, emphasis should be placed on the fact that this edition of the test is experimental and that a revised edition may be available soon.*

Validity

Several studies have been completed that shed light on the validity of the ITPA.[4] Validity determines to what extent a test measures what it purports to measure. The work of McCarthy and Olson seems to deal most directly with the problem.[40] In their study, eighty-six subjects from Middleton, Wisconsin, between the ages of 7-0 and 8-6, were matched with the equivalent age group in the standardization sample with respect to social class, sex, mental age, birth order, nationality, race, handicaps, school settings and urban-rural factors. Five types of validity were examined; (1) concurrent, (2) predictive, (3) content, (4) construct, (5) diagnostic. Types 1, 2 and 5 will be discussed in this paper; for a discussion of the other types of validity studies, see McCarthy and Olson.[40]

Concurrent and predictive validity were determined by administering criterion tests at approximately the same time as the ITPA (concurrent) and then readministering them about three months later (predictive). Criterion tests were selected on the basis of similar qualitative nature to the ITPA.

---

*The revised edition of the ITPA is essentially the same as the 1961 edition with some revisions in content, higher reliability for the subtests, greater ease in administration and scoring and an extended age range, up to 11-6. Three tests have been added to the battery — a visual closure test, a sound blending test and an auditory closure test. The basic battery will consist of ten subtests which include the visual closure test. The auditory closure and sound blending subtests are primarily supplementary tests to be given when a diagnosis of reading disability is made.[33]

Existing language tests and the linguistic portions (reading, spelling) of achievement tests were used. The question to be answered was, how well does the ITPA battery as a whole, correlate with similar but not identical language tests and will the correlation hold up over time. A summary of the results can be seen in Table 13-I. The concurrent validity coefficients between the ITPA and criterion tests ranged from 0.13 (sentence complexity) to 0.50 (Stanford Achievement Test—Paragraph Reading section) with all coefficients significant at the 0.01 level, except for the mean length of response and the sentence complexity criterion tests. For predictive validity, again all coefficients were significant at the 0.01 level except for the same two criterion tests as stated above. The coefficients ranged from -0.04 (sentence complexity) to 0.46 (Durrell-Sullivan Word Meaning section).

TABLE 13-I
SUMMARY OF THE VALIDITY CHARACTERISTICS OF THE ITPA AND
ITS INDIVIDUAL SUBTESTS
(McCarthy *And* Olson, 1964)

| *ITPA* | *Types of Validity* | | | |
	Concurrent & Predictive	*Content*	*Construct*	*Diagnostic*
Whole Test	Yes[a]	Omissions Noted	e,f	Moderate to Significant
Visual Decoding	Yes	c,d	Yes	g
Auditory Decoding	Qualified[b]	c,d	Yes	g
Visual-Motor Ass'n.	Yes	c,d	Yes	g
Auditory-Vocal Ass'n.	Qualified[b]	c,d	Yes	g
Motor Encoding	Doubtful	c,d	Yes	g
Vocal Encoding	Questionable	c,d	Yes	g
Visual-Motor Seq.	Qualified[b]	c	Qualified[b]	g
Auditory-Vocal Seq.	Yes	c	Yes	g
Auditory-Vocal Auto.	Doubtful	c	No	g

[a]Criterion Tests and Retests included the reading and spelling section of the Stanford Achievement Battery, the reading section of the Durrell-Sullivan Capacity Test, the Raven's Progressive Matrices, the Goodenough Draw-A-Man Test, the Peabody Picture Vocabulary Test, and the mean-length-of-response and "sentence complexity" scores derived from a sample of the subject's speech.
[b]A qualified Yes.
[c]Standard Error ranges recommended. Subtests internally consistent but fairly heterogenous with respect to one another.
[d]Basically "single ability" in character.
[e]Inversely related to social class, number of sibs, and position among sibs; positively related to mental age; zero relation to sex of subject.
[f]Stability coefficients vary from .70 to .95.
[g]Classification, by type of child, can be made reasonably well by "experts" on linguistically handicapped children; the test is not sufficiently sensitive to confirm teachers' ranking of ITPA subtests for linguistically "normal" children.

Estimates were made for each of the ITPA subtests. Two procedures were followed. Initially, a preselected criterion test was compared to the subtests and then each subtest was correlated with every other possible criterion test to find the optimum correlation. The postselected criterion tests tended to show more accurately what each subtest was measuring, whereas the preselected data reflected the best estimate by the authors. To illustrate the differences, the preselected criterion test for subtest 1 (Auditory Decoding) was the Peabody Picture Vocabulary Test (PPVT). The PPVT versus Auditory Decoding gave a negligible correlation coefficient of 0.09. The postselected criterion test, the Similarities subtest of the Wechsler Intelligence Scale for Children (WISC), correlated 0.31 with Auditory Decoding. Subtest 6 (Motor Encoding) versus the preselected criterion test, Draw-A-Man, correlated 0.08. On the other hand, the postselected test, the Vocabulary Test of the Stanford-Binet Intelligence Test, correlated 0.40 with Motor Encoding.

As a result of these comparisons the following summary statements were made by McCarthy and Olson.[40]

1. *Auditory Decoding.* Nonsignificant correlations with the PPVT and Binet Vocabulary Test and a significant correlation with the WISC Similarities Test and Stanford Achievement Test, Paragraph Reading section, suggests that this test assesses the "ability to comprehend and/or remember related word sequences" and is not a test of a simple function.

2. *Visual Decoding.* A significant correlation with the same test for pre- and postselection, Durrell-Sullivan Paragraph Meaning Section, and with the PPVT and the Raven's Progressive Matrices strengthens the view that the test measures comprehension of visual stimuli.

3. *Auditory-Vocal Association.* In addition to the significant correlation with the preselected criterion test (Similarities Test of the WISC), this subtest corelated well with two-thirds of the criterion tests, especially with the Spelling section of the Stanford Achievement Test. The subtest apparently assesses general intellectual and linguistic abilites with the latter factor being larger than thought originally.

4. *Visual-Motor Association.* The character of this test was supported by both pre and postselected criterion tests (Raven's and Draw-A-Man) as indicated by significant correlations of similar magnitudes.

5. *Vocal Encoding.* It seemed logical to the investigators that this subtest would correlate well with the Vocabulary Test of the Binet as a preselected test, which it did not (0.03). They were further perplexed by the fact that the postselection test with which Vocal Encoding correlated was the Knox Cube Test (0.27). However, in making comparisons between this subtest and the preselected test using the original standardization group, the concurrent validity of the subtest was supported. Due to these differences, however, this subtest remains questionable in measuring what it purports to measure.

6. *Motor Encoding.* The lack of an appropriate criterion test and the low reliability of this subtest were stated as possible reasons for the fact that a very low correlation (0.08) was found for the preselected test, Draw-A-Man. An unexpected high correlation was found with the Vocabulary Test of the Binet (0.40). These results relegated this subtest to the doubtful category.

7. *Auditory-Vocal Automatic.* The most logical preselected criterion test, Sentence Complexity score, was found to have a low correlation (0.14) with this subtest, while the Word Reading section of the Stanford Achievement Test was found to be the strongest postselected test (0.53). These results, and others, suggest that this subtest measures some sort of general linguistic factor "which is somewhat less 'grammatical' (in a purely mechanical sense) and far more meaningful than previously thought." Because of these factors, this subtest has doubtful validity.

8. *Auditory-Vocal Sequencing.* The preselected criterion test, the Random Word Test, was specifically designed by the investigators (McCarthy and Olson) to ascertain if the same ability could be measured whether using digits or words.[40] Such was the case as the correlation was high (0.65) for both pre and postselection comparisons.

9. *Visual-Motor Sequencing.* The low correlation with the preselected criterion test, the Knox Cube Test (0.15) and the significant correlation with the Stanford Achievement section on Paragraph Reading (0.32) and other auditory-vocal ability criterion tests, suggests a transfer ability from visually perceived elements to auditory memory elements. This factor seems to confirm the clinical observation of the investigators "that subjects often name the stimuli of this subtest aloud as if to assist their visual memory."

The final phase of McCarthy and Olson's validity studies examined the "diagnostic validity" of the test.[40] This was accomplished by asking four "experts" to classify ten profiles each of six different diagnostic categories, (normal, trainable mentally retarded, educable mentally retarded, cerebral palsied, deaf and articulation defectives). All experts correctly classified the profiles beyond the chance level. However, classifications were never perfect. The most characteristic profile was from the deaf group and the least from the articulation defective group. (See Figs. 13-1, -2, -3). It must be emphasized that this study employed total profile analysis.

McCarthy and Olson conclude their discussion with the following:[40]

"1. Our data suggest that the Encoding subtests and especially, the Auditory-Vocal Automatic subtest, may deviate from the definition in the Examiners Manual. It is particularly critical that, when a diagnosis or a prescription for remediation is based on the results of these subtests, ad hoc tests and clinical observation be used to confirm performance on them. Of the three, the Vocal Encoding subtest appears to be the most valid.

"2. In the diagnosis of children with linguistic defects, particularly dyslexia, it is recommended that auxiliary tests accompany the use of the ITPA. A good interim array is suggested by Kass."[29]

The reader is referred to Weener, Barritt and Semmel for a critical view of the aforementioned validity studies, and to McCarthy for a cursory overview of his and Olson's work.[58,41]

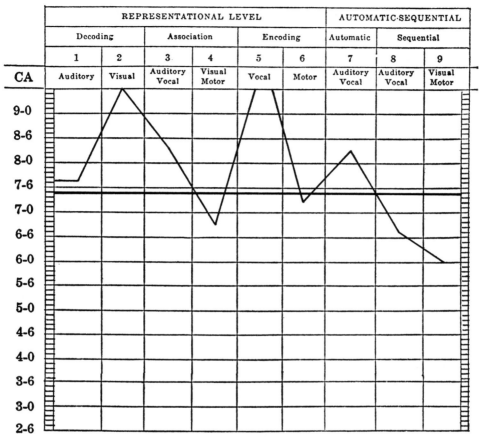

Figure 13-1. Profile from diagnostic validity study. Normal Profile. From McCarthy and Olson, 1964.

TEST ADMINISTRATION AND SCORING

Many factors contribute to the usefulness of a diagnostic instrument; proper standardization and statistical characteristics to name only two. However, these factors and others that must be considered in constructing the test are no more important than the factors of who uses the test and how it is used. With respect to who should give the test, it is felt that anyone who knows what the test is measuring and how the results can be applied to a remediation program should be using it. All psycholinguistic tests are *tools* to be used for purposes of aiding in making appraisals of language disorders. They are there to be used by those individuals who see and understand the value of their results. However, it is incumbent upon the person using the instrument to know thoroughly, not only the test, but also the procedures for administration and scoring of individual tests. In addition, the tester

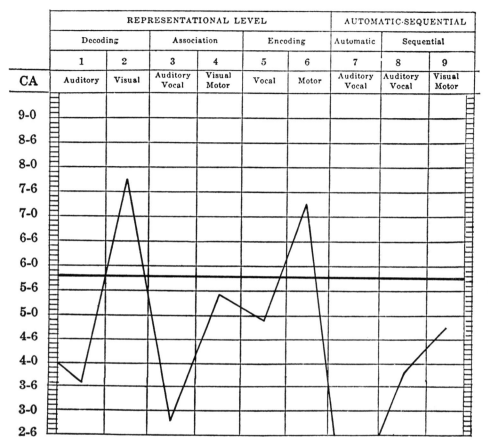

Figure 13-2. Profile from diagnostic validity study. Deaf Profile. From McCarthy and Olson, 1964.

must keep in mind that the test is no substitute for accurate observations of the child's language behavior and should be used primarily for supplementary or initial diagnostic procedures. To know thoroughly the administration and scoring of the ITPA, the reader is referred to the Examiners Manual. Below are some comments which are intended to amplify and/or clarify the instructions that are found within the Manual. In addition, there are some suggestions for changing the instructions or procedures which have developed out of clinical experience.

As in the case with all standardized tests, strict adherence to the procedures is essential if one is to apply the results to the normative data. However, this does not prevent the examiner from changing the procedures to obtain information that will be useful to him in his appraisal, as long as the changes are noted and the results viewed in that light.

One of the most important procedures in the administration of the ITPA is the task of teaching the child the behavior to be tested. The examiner needs to know whether the child understands the task before administering the test. Consequently, the demonstration items must be used before beginning each subtest. Revisions, repetitions, use of other items and so on, may be utilized to teach each task that will be tested. If the child is unable to successfully perform on the demonstration items, it is fairly clear that he will be unable to perform on the actual test items. A common criticism of beginning or inexperienced examiners is that they do not use the demonstration items enough before proceeding to the test items. All subtests except Auditory-Vocal Association and Auditory-Vocal Sequential have specific demonstration items. In the two subtests without demonstration items, the test items or substitute items may be used. If test items are used, they are never scored in computing the raw score.

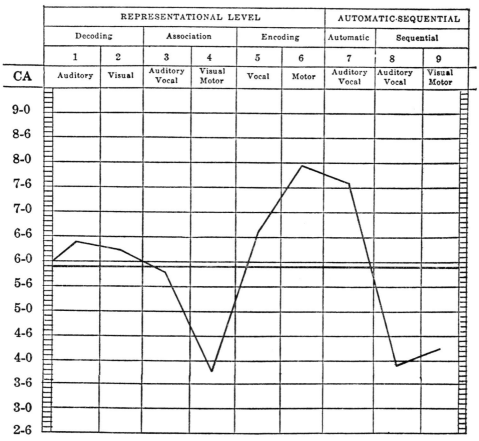

Figure 13-3. Profile from diagnostic validity study. Articulation Disorder Profile. From McCarthy and Olson, 1964.

The use of a basal level and ceiling in the ITPA, in seven of the nine subtests, allows for a substantial saving in test administration time. If the subject passes the basal level, the examiner can give credit for the beginning items that were not administered. When the ceiling is met, by the child failing a certain number of items, the test is discontinued at that point under the assumption that the child would continue to fail the remaining items which increase in difficulty. Basals and ceilings vary among tests and must be memorized. The two subtests without these measures are the encoding tests. In general, the authors recommend obtaining the ceiling before the basal. However, the reader is cautioned to review carefully the rules for each subtest, especially for subtests 1 and 4 in this regard. It is assumed that even though no basal is established, such as three consecutive correct, the subtest is scored by totaling the number correct. However, this is based on the assumption that the subtest was learned by the subject by use of the demonstration items. To effectively use the basal level and ceiling, it is necessary that the examiner score each item as he goes. This has been found to be a major shortcoming of the inexperienced administrator.

The order of subtest administration is seen on the front of the Record Form (see Fig. 13-2) . The authors stress that this order should not be altered without a valid reason. It would seem that one such valid reason would be when the examiner does not know the child's mental age. All subtests, except the encoding tests, use the concept of a basal level. To be able to use this convenience, by starting at more difficult subtest items instead of the first item, the examiner must know the child's mental age, e.g., "if S's mental age is less than 7-0, begin with item 1; if over 8-0, begin with item 5." In some cases when the ITPA is used as the initial test instrument, the mental age of the child may not be known. In that case it is suggested that subtest 3, Auditory-Vocal Association, be administered first because of its high correlation (.93-.97) with mental age. Bateman has stated that clinically she has found it to agree very closely, within three points, with the Binet IQ.[5] However, more recently she has stated that it frequently underestimates the Binet MA on the order of 5-10 per cent.[7]

Perhaps another reason for altering the order of administration is when the subject has severe visual or auditory impairment. The auditory-vocal channel subtests can be used with the severely visually impaired and the visual-motor channel subtests with the deaf.[2,46]

One repetition of the spoken material for all subtests, except for Auditory-Vocal Sequencing, is allowed if requested by the subject. In addition, the subject is given credit for all self-corrections. Concerning this procedure, it may be clinically useful to keep a total of all self-corrections made by the subject, a procedure followed in the scoring of the Language Modalities

Test for Aphasia (Wepman and Jones), in order to evaluate the subject's monitoring capabilities.[59] Under no circumstances are responses other than those demanded by the task scored as correct.

Subtest 6, Motor Encoding

This subtest has no basal or ceiling, therefore all items are given to every subject. In the administration of this subtest, if the subject has not responded, it i shelpful to name the objects, e.g., "show me what you should do with this drill." It may be helpful to pretend to lift the object from the book and hand it to him. Through the use of the demonstration items, encourage large motor movements. In addition to the regular demonstration item, the first picture item, a pencil-sharpener, must be used as a demonstration item if it is failed. Furthermore, if it appears that in performing the response correctly the child has difficulty shifting from the objects to the pictures by attempting to perform the response on the book, use the item as a demonstration item as if he has failed. This will allow the examiner the opportunity to show the subject how the responses can be given by hand movements off the book.[7] The examiner must keep in mind that this subtest is not measuring decoding and therefore more flexibility is allowed in getting the message to the subject. In some cases you may not want to use the pictures at all and just give auditory instructions. In using the pictures, because two appear on one page, it is helpful in some cases to cover the picture not being used when exposing the other.

Subtest 3, Auditory-Vocal Association

Because there is no demonstration item, either item 1 or 6 may be used if necessary for that purpose, and when this is done, no credit is allowed for that item. It is suggested that the examiner should use as many cues as possible through vocal inflection to convey the notion of opposites. Bateman recommends starting with item 8, "soup is hot; ice cream is ——," instead of item 6, which has been found to be too difficult, for those subjects with a MA (mental age) below six years.[7]

Subtest 9, Visual-Motor Sequencing

Perhaps the most confusing aspect of this subtest is the way the chips are placed in the tray. If the examiner does not read the manual carefully, he may not recognize that the order given in the record form is the reverse of the order that should be seen and reproduced by the subject. For example, in item 4, the examiner views the order as s-s-3, whereas the subject must view it and reproduce it from left to right as 3-s-s. When placing the chips in the tray, work from right to left with respect to the order in the record form. Timing must not begin until after advising the subject to look carefully at the sequences. The chips are always dumped toward the examiner so that nothing is between the subject and the tray and the chips must be mixed quickly after dumping so that there is no interference with the subject's memory.

Subtest 5, Vocal Encoding

This subtest is one of the most difficult to give because of a more complicated scoring system. Bateman has stated that two major concerns in giving this subtest are: (1) that the examiner must use the demonstration item to the hilt; and (2) the examiner must know the scoring criteria so that he knows when to question and when not to.[7] With respect to the first concern, direct and leading questions should be used to teach the child the variety of responses that he can use. Concerning the second item, it should be kept in mind that whenever a response is elicited with a question, the response receives only one point regardless of whether it was a two or more point response. If the examiner is unaware of what responses are correct, he may question a two point response that was given initially and therefore inadvertently penalize the subject by the fact that he can now gain no more than one point for his follow-up response. Only misinformed and ambiguous responses must be questioned. If the examiner fails in this he again is penalizing the subject. Because of the difficulties in administering this subtest, it along with the Auditory-Decoding subtest, compose the "inexperienced tester profile," which is characterized by a high Auditory-Decoding and low Vocal Encoding pattern.[7]

Subtest 4, Visual-Motor Association

A procedural chart for determining basal and ceiling items is provided to eliminate "complex explanations of procedure." It would seem that a simpler explanation would be to state that for subjects with MA below 6-0, a score of two out of four is needed to go on to the picture items. If the subject misses more than two in the first four, the test is stopped. All other procedures are similar to those for the other subtests. It is permissible, as in the case of Motor Encoding, to name "any picture or object" for the subject before he responds. However, unlike its use for Motor Encoding, this writer believes that this procedure should be used sparingly and noted on the record form. This form of stimulation could significantly contaminate the results of this association subtest as it seems to add factors which do not appear to be within the intent of the subtest.

Bateman found few children who had difficulty with the first few picture items and was not pleased with using the objects, consequently, she seldom starts with or ever uses the objects.[5]

Subtest 1, Auditory Decoding

The procedural chart used for this subtest, similar to subtest 4, is the most involved of all the subtests. To simplify the explanation, two statements should be kept in mind. (1) For children with MA below 6-0, if they cannot pass more than two of the first four items, stop testing. (2) For the older children, if they cannot pass more than four items of the first eight administered (5-12), administer items 1-4 and then stop testing. When children pass more than the minimum, continue testing in the usual manner. Because personalized items (1-4), e.g., "Do you run?" and nonpersonalized items (5-36), e.g., "Do babies eat?" are used, demonstration items "must always" precede the administration of each set of questions.

In Bateman's clinical experience, she has found that the first four personalized items are more difficult than the first few nonpersonalized items.[5] Consequently, she may begin with item 5, and go until the ceiling is reached, four wrong in eight. At that point she stops testing; she completely eliminates items 1-4, believing that their administration will not yield additional useful information about the child's language abilities. Some examiners have asked if guessing by the child would contaminate the results on this subtest and others. Bateman stated that this factor was built into the norms for the Visual Decoding, Visual-Motor Association and Auditory Decoding subtests when they were standardized by requiring that the child give an answer to each item.[7] You cannot accept a "don't know" response for these subtests.

Some individuals have asked the question about giving the ITPA to children older than provided by the norms. If there is an indication that this test could provide some useful information about a severe language disability it seems that there should be little question as to whether the test should be administered. If deficits show up for older children, that seems more important than whether his chronological age or mental age is above the norms. The potential value of using the test with older mentally retarded children was discussed by Bateman and Wetherell.[8]

TEST SCORES AND USE OF NORMS

Normative data were prepared for both language age and standard score. These latter norms are based on a theoretical, "normalized" distribution of scores. The authors recommend the following: " (1) that the language age norms be used for comparing the results of the ITPA with other instruments whose scores are expressed in terms of age; (2) that standard score norms be used for comparing tests within the battery with each other, and (3) that raw scores be used for comparing test and retest results for the same S."[38]

Although it is valuable from a remedial standpoint to compare the subject's overall language age to his mental age, the ITPA's greatest value is estimating strengths and weaknesses of specific psycholinguistic abilities. To accomplish this, it is essential that the examiner know whether the differences that exist between the scores on the various subtests are reliable differences and not simply a reflection of test unreliability. To this end McCarthy and Kirk suggest the use of a range of scores by adding and subtracting the standard error of measurement from the standard score.[38] This procedure is illustrated best by the following quotation:

"A child of 4-0, for example, who receives a raw score of 15 and a standard score of +1.69 on the Visual Decoding test has a 'true score' that lies in the range of +1.69 ±.32 or from +1.37 to +2.01. If this S could be given an infinity of equivalent forms of the Visual Decoding test, simultaneously, two out of three times his score would be between +1.37 and +2.01."

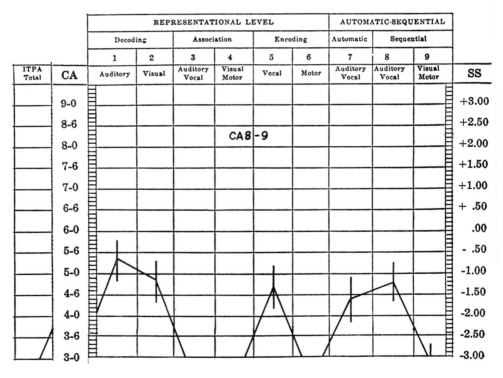

Figure 13-4. A comparison of tests on the ITPA battery. Subtest scores for one subject. From McCarthy and Kirk, 1961.

If the range of standard scores for one subtest overlaps with the ranges of other subtests, no reliable differences exist between subtests. On the other hand, if no overlap exists then the differences are reliable or significant and therefore separate strengths from weaknesses. Figure 13-4 illustrates this procedure. These are the subtest scores for one subject. It can be seen that there are no significant differences between subtests 1, 2, 5, 7 and 8; however, these subtests are significantly above tests 3, 4, 6 and 9, indicating fairly clearly weaknesses in Visual-Motor and Auditory-Vocal Association, Motor Encoding and Visual-Motor Sequencing. Although less precise, as a general rule differences of less than 1.00 standard score between subtests are not considered significant, and for language age scores, a significant difference between scores occurs only if the difference is greater than two years.

In addition to diagnosing specific areas of deficit, the norms can be used to measure the effectiveness of a remediation program over a prescribed period of time. By test-retest comparisons of raw scores, using the standard error ranges, differences can be evaluated in the same manner as described above for subtest standard scores. In general, however, test-retest differences of less than four points for a subtest and less than ten points for the total raw score should not be considered significant.

Recently, Bateman, after discussing the disadvantages of using the aforementioned norms, suggested the use of a mean language age score as the "reference line" for denoting "discrepant abilities."[6] In a pilot study comparing judges selections with selection by total discrepancy scores, the scores were computed by summing the differences between subtest language ages and the mean language age. After converting them to years, a total discrepancy score of nine years was arbitrarily selected as the "minimum criterion for 'psycholinguistic disability.'" The judges were asked to select from tests of twenty-four mentally retarded children those ten whom they felt had "psycholinguistic disability or disabilities." Twelve out of the twenty-four cases were selected by the discrepancy score as having a disability. All ten choices for two judges and nine of the third judge were the same as those selected by the mean language age method. Therefore, it was suggested that following the establishment of criteria separating assets from deficits, this method could be used as an objective way to facilitate the grouping of profiles with respect to deficit combinations. However, for total profile analysis it was found during further study that it was necessary to subtract the mean language age from the total discrepancy score. From this information definite disabilities were seen only if differences were greater than four years.

Other methods for interpreting profiles have been suggested, such as using "Profile Quotients" and "Coded Deviation Profile" analysis.[7]

CLINICAL INTERPRETATION OF ITPA PROFILES

It is beyond the scope of this paper to go into great detail relative to the following diagnostic profiles. The reader is directed to the references and to Bateman's work for an in depth analysis.[4,7]

Mental Retardation

The most typical characteristic of the mentally retarded, with IQs below 75, are as follows: (1) a deficit in the automatic-sequential level, Tests 7, 8 and 9; (2) a generally lower auditory-vocal channel than visual-motor channel; and (3) a deficit in the association process, especially auditory-vocal. Above an IQ of 75, the profiles tend to show less of a flattening characteristic with more variability (See Fig. 13-5) .[8,43,44]

Mongoloid children show an even greater disability at the automatic-sequential level, especially Auditory-Vocal Automatic, with a significant

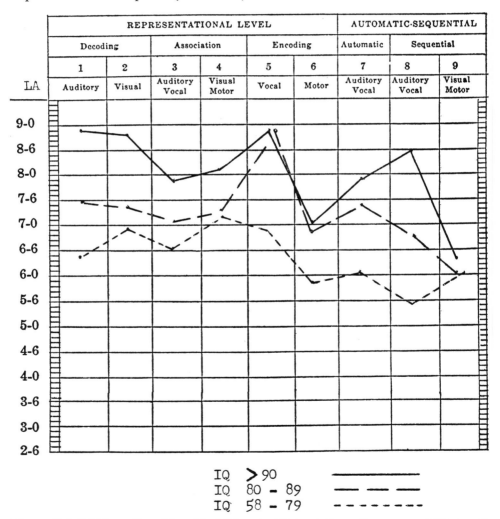

Figure 13.5. ITPA profiles of low IQ children by IQ level. From Bateman and Wetherell, 1965. Reprinted by permission from *Mental Retardation*, 1965, April 3, Vol. 3, p. 10.

peak in Motor Encoding (Test 6) as seen in Figure 13-6 (Jeanne McCarthy, Bilovsky and Share) .[41,11]

Cultural Deprivation

These children are seen to have their main strengths in the visual-motor channel with two consistently typical characteristics in the auditory-vocal channel. They, as a rule, do their poorest on Auditory-Vocal Automatic and the best, often even above the visual-motor subtests, on Auditory-Vocal Sequencing. This latter characteristic, as seen in Figure 13-7, is most pronounced with Negro children, and has been confirmed using both experi-

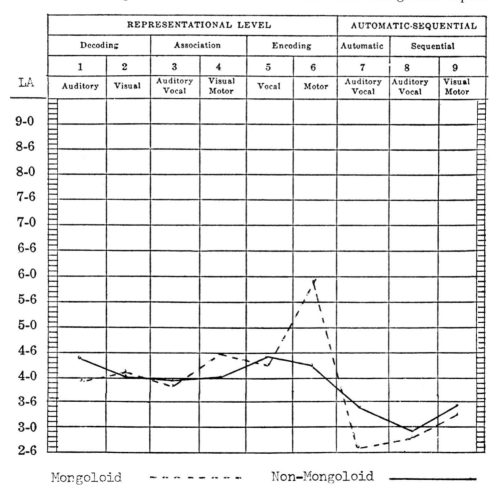

Figure 13-6. ITPA profiles of thirty mongoloid and thirty nonmongoloid children. From Jean McCarthy, 1965, as illustrated in Bateman and Wetherell, 1965. Reprinted by permission from *Mental Retardation*, 1965, April 3, Vol. 3, p. 10.

enced examiners (Weaver, Bateman) and inexperienced examiners (Lamb and Tarnopol) .[57,7,34]

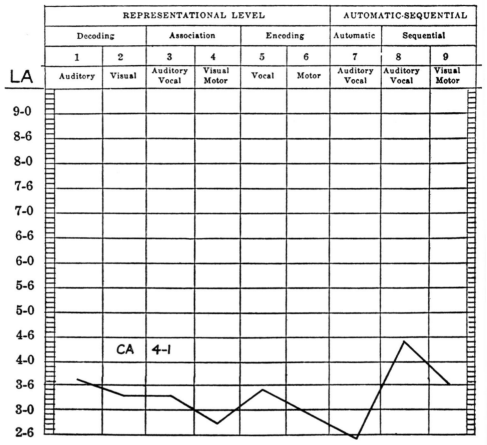

Figure 13-7. ITPA profile of twenty-six culturally deprived preschool Negro children. From Lamb and Tarnopol, 1967.

Gifted

The gifted children in contrast to retarded children show their strengths in the auditory-vocal channels over the visual-motor, and in the association processes in contrast to decoding and encoding. They also may show peaks in the Auditory-Vocal Association and Vocal Encoding subtests (Mueller, Bateman) .[44,7]

Aphasic Children

In a study by Olson (Olson, Sievers *et al.*) which successfully compared and contrasted the performance of receptive and expressive aphasics, (organic language symbolization disorders) with that of deaf children, it was found that the profiles of the receptive aphasics (RA) were predictable beyond chance, while the profiles for the expressive aphasics (EA) were too unstable to be predictable.[46,52] Olson suggested that this latter characteristic could be accounted for by the observation that this "group" did not appear to be "psycholinguistically speaking, a homogeneous clinical entity." In Figure 13-8, the language ages were plotted from the mean scores as given by Olson (Sievers *et al.*).[52] The results of a statistical analysis of raw scores indicated the RA group to be superior on only Motor Encoding, while the EA group was superior on Auditory Decoding, Auditory-Vocal Association, Auditory-Vocal Automatic and Auditory-Vocal Sequential. Consequently,

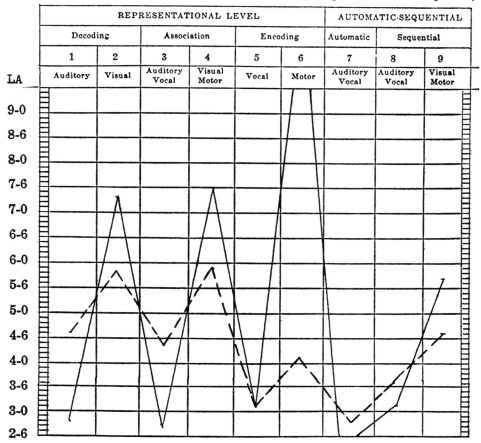

Figure 13-8. ITPA profiles of twenty-seven receptive and fourteen expressive aphasic children. From Olson, in Siever *et al.*, 1963.

Key:
Receptive ——————— (CA 7 — 7)
Expressive – – – – – – (CA 7 — 7)

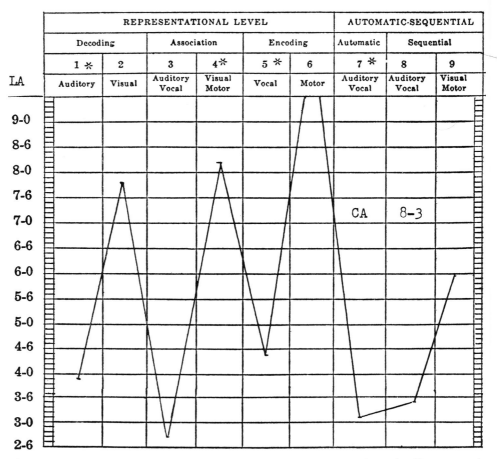

Figure 13-9. ITPA profiles of twenty-five deaf children. From Olson, in Sievers *et al.,* 1963. (*) Adjusted mean scores significantly different from those obtained by receptive aphasics.

the major contrasting characteristics seem to be the ability to use the "auditory mode of language input and the motor or gesture mode of output." However, due to the poor predictability of the EA profile, few if any comparisons can be made between Olson's results and profiles of other EA individuals. Bateman offered a valuable suggestion for using the test with aphasic youngsters by recommending it be administered in two ways: one by the standardized procedures and the other by using any available clinical means to assess the child's performance on each specific task, and then compare the two.[5] This will aid the examiner in finding out how the child functions in two clearly different situations, which will in turn be useful in planning a remediation program.

Stark reported results from twenty-two "aphasic children" on the three visual subtests of the ITPA, and indicated that no characteristic pattern emerged.[55] However, he stated that the greatest deficit was observed in the sequential subtest. This differs from Olson's (Sievers *et al.*) results which showed the association subtest to be the lowest.[52] The decoding subtest was the least impaired for both studies.

Deaf

As stated above, Olson (Olson, Sievers *et al.*) also studied deaf youngsters.[47,52] The characteristic profile of this group which is the most predictable of the three (0.93), is seen in Figure 13-9. Although there are similarities betwen this group and the RA group, Olson found statistically significant differences favoring the deaf group in Visual-Motor Association, Auditory Decoding, Vocal Encoding and Auditory-Vocal Automatic. Reichstein used the ITPA as a tool to differentiate an RA group from a hard of hearing (HOH) group and reported similar findings to Olson's.[51] However, Reichstein found his HOH group to be superior on all auditory-vocal subtests, Visual Decoding and Visual-Motor Association. These differences in results may be due to differences in age between subjects as suggested by Reichstein or perhaps due to the differences in the quantity and quality of the disorder in the HOH and deaf samples, not to mention the possible differences in the RA groups.

Cerebral Palsy

In a study of athetoid (characterized by excessive involuntary, purposeless muscular activity) and spastic (characterized by excessive muscular tension and an exaggerated stretch reflex) cerebral palsied (CP) children by Myers, a factor analysis isolated a "Representation Level Factor" and an "Automatic-Sequential Level Factor."[45] It was reported that spastics were superior in the automatic-sequential level factor and athetoids in the representational level factor. For a review of the results of a previous study on a group of CP children using the Differential Language Facilities Test (DLFT) which was the ITPA's predecessor, see Sievers *et al.*, and McCarthy.[52,36]

Reading Disabilities and Visually Handicapped

Several studies have been completed in this area. In general, they find that reading disabilities are associated with deficits in the Automatic-Sequential Level subtests. Kass found this to be particularly true when supplemental tests are also used in conjunction with the subtests of the ITPA.[29,30] Figure 13-10 gives the supplemental tests and how her subjects performed.

Representational Level	Automatic-Sequential Level
** 1. Auditory Decoding	+ 7. Auditory-Vocal Automatic
* 2. Visual Decoding	** 8. Auditory-Vocal Sequential
++ 3. Auditory-Vocal Association	++ 9. Visual-Motor Sequential
** 4. Visual-Motor Association	+ a. Visual Automatic
** 5. Vocal Encoding	++ b. Sound Blending (Monroe)
** 6. Motor Encoding	++ c. Mazes (WISC)
	++ d. Memory-for-Designs (Graham-Kendall)
	++ e. Perceptual Speed (PMA)

*=Strength   **=No deficit   +=Marginal deficit   ++=Deficit

Figure 13-10. Clinical model of reading processes indicating areas of strength, no deficit, marginal deficit and deficit of twenty-one dyslexic children. From Kass, 1966.

It can be seen that deficits occurred in all but one area — at the Automatic-Sequential Level, and the Auditory-Vocal Association subtest at the Representational Level. Both Ragland and Bateman reported similar findings with the latter study indicating positive and significant correlations between reading achievement and Automatic-Sequential Level subtests.[50,2,52] Figure 13-11 shows the group profile for Bateman's study. A comparison made between Bateman's and Kass' results shows similarities in performance on the Visual-Motor Sequential subtests but apparently opposite results for the Visual Decoding subtest. Kass indicates this latter subtest as a strength in her group, while it appears to be more of a deficit in Bateman's group. This difference could be accounted for by the fact that Bateman included children with peripheral visual impairments while Kass excluded peripheral sensory deficits. See Bateman for a discussion of the above.[7]

Articulation Disorders

Ferrier found that his subjects were significantly below the normative sample in all areas except Visual Decoding.[19,20] The greatest differences were noted in all the Automatic-Sequential Level subtests and Vocal Encoding and Auditory-Vocal Association. (See Fig. 13-12). These findings were substantiated for the most part by Foster although there is some criticism of the way in which the data was handled.[21,4] Bateman has brought up an interesting point in stating that if articulatory disorders are the only communicative deficit, then as a group they should not differ significantly from the normative group, especially since this disorder is controlled to some degree in the test administration procedures.[4,5] The results of the aforementioned studies seem to suggest that there are other deficits accompanying the disorders in articulation.

REPRESENTATIONAL LEVEL						AUTOMATIC-SEQUENTIAL			
Decoding		Association		Encoding		Automatic	Sequential		
1	2	3	4	5	6	7	8	9	
Auditory	Visual	Auditory Vocal	Visual Motor	Vocal	Motor	Auditory Vocal	Auditory Vocal	Visual Motor	SS

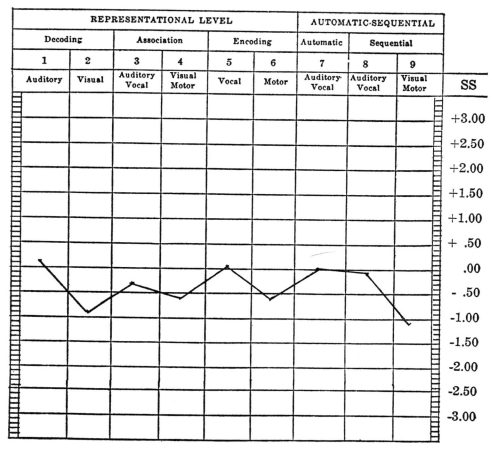

Figure 13-11. ITPA profile of ninety-three partially seeing children. From Bateman, in Sievers *et al.*, 1963.

Minimal Brain Damage

Strong (as reported in McCarthy and Olson) found that the Auditory Decoding and Visual-Motor Sequencing subtests correctly classified children with "minimal brain damage" beyond chance, when compared to a matched group of normals.[40] However, Strong stated that the most valid measure resulted from using a multiple cutoff technique combining the scores of the Auditory Decoding and Auditory-Vocal Automatic subtests which correctly clasified 80 per cent or more of both groups.

Children with "Strauss-Syndrome," characterized by hyperactivity, perseveration, poor motor coordination and perceptual disturbances, have one of the most characteristic profiles that remain regardless of age or IQ. The so-called "two-six profile" is characterized by significant dips in Visual-

Decoding and Motor-Encoding as seen in Figure 13-13. (Bateman and Wetherell, Bateman) .[8,7]

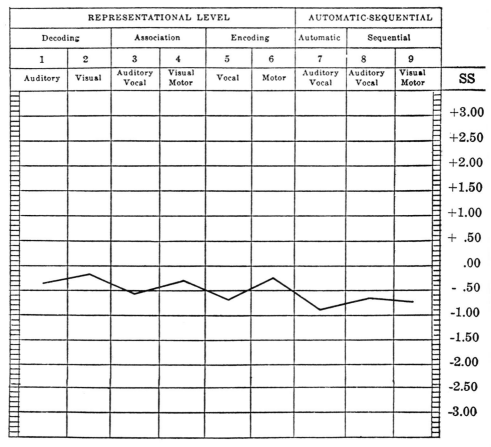

REPRESENTATIONAL LEVEL						AUTOMATIC-SEQUENTIAL			
Decoding		Association		Encoding		Automatic	Sequential		
1	2	3	4	5	6	7	8	9	
Auditory	Visual	Auditory Vocal	Visual Motor	Vocal	Motor	Auditory Vocal	Auditory Vocal	Visual Motor	SS

+3.00
+2.50
+2.00
+1.50
+1.00
+ .50
.00
- .50
-1.00
-1.50
-2.00
-2.50
-3.00

Figure 13-12. ITPA profiles of total sample of forty children with functional articulation
disorders. From Ferrier, 1966.

Emotionally Disturbed

Bateman has stated that this group has not been thoroughly studied.[5]
However, her feeling was that the term *emotionally disturbed* was too general and consequently would not constitute a homogeneous group. The
differences that might be found would tend to counterbalance one another
causing the group profile to appear flat. On the other hand, she did state that
inhibition may be indicated by a depressed encoding channel which suggests
a reluctance on the child's part to express himself, and a peak in Auditory-
Vocal Automatic (grammar) may indicate overdemanding "pushy" parents.
Although inconclusive by themselves, one or both of these characteristics

could aid in an adequate diagnosis when used in conjunction with other test findings.

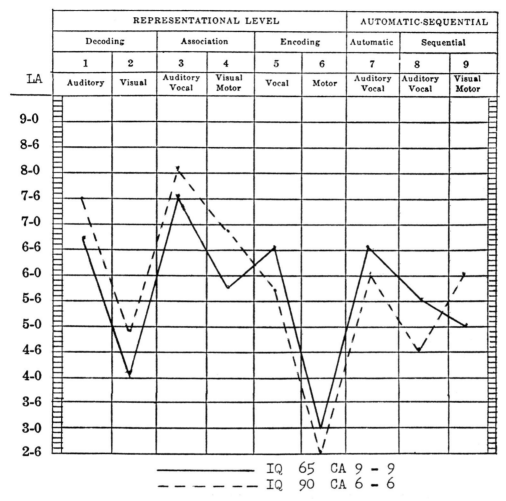

Figure 13-13. ITPA profiles of two "Strauss-syndrome" children. From Bateman and Wetherell, 1965. Reprinted by permission from *Mental Retardation*, 1965, April, Vol. 3, p. 12.

IMPLICATIONS FOR REMEDIATION

In the past it has not been particularly difficult to identify children with overall language impairments. However, it has been difficult to objectively estimate the quantitative and qualitative dimensions of their impairments. The major contribution of the ITPA has been its ability to identify both of these characteristics so that the clinician and/or teacher can not only identify specific areas of deficit, but also the extent and relationship of the deficits to areas exhibiting strengths. As a result of this quality of the test, some individuals have assumed that if the clinician could train the individuals to improve specifically their ability to repeat digits or properly sequence the geometric designs or know that chateaux do not chastise, this would remediate the child's language impairment. The point is that the ITPA is not a remediation program and was never intended to be. Furthermore, the test was not designed to be even a model for a "new" remediation program. The psycholinguistic abilities of the ITPA are not new. Consequently, the methods, in general, of remediating deficiencies in them are not new. If a child has a decoding problem which could be identified by other tests or by observation of a trained and sensitive clinician, the therapy program is directed toward the amelioration of that problem by the methods known best to the clinician. Many methods are and have been available for use with decoding deficits.[3] The ITPA is simply another effective way of evaluating this and other psycholinguistic disabilities. As stated earlier, if the diagnostician knows specifically what he is to be testing, he will evaluate the ability with several diagnostic tests and likewise if the clinician and/or teacher knows specifically what the deficit is, he will use those procedures appropriate for the remediation of the problem.

Numerous studies have been reported in which the remediation programs were developed specifically for deficit in ITPA profiles and/or in which the ITPA was used as the criterion test for determining success of a specific therapeutic approach. The reader is referred to the following sources for a review of some of these studies: Bereiter and Engelmann,[9] Blessing,[13] Blue,[15] Bradley, Maurer and Hundziak,[16] Gray and Klaus,[23] Gray et al.,[24] Hart,[25] Hermann,[27] Johnson, Capobianco and Miller,[28] Olson, Hahn and Hermann,[48] Painter,[49] Smith,[53,54] Stark,[55] Stearns, Hodges and Spicker,[56] and Wiseman.[60]

Strength Versus Weakness

The question of whether to work with the strength or the weakness has long been debated by therapists and teachers. With the capability of the ITPA to identify areas of strengths and weaknesses in certain language abilities, the question remains perplexing as illustrated by the comments from some writers (Bradley, Maurer and Hundziak, Stark, Kirk and Bateman, Bateman) .[16,55,32,7]

Bateman, in her paper in this text, has reported a study that was designed to shed some light on the question of strength versus weakness. A large group of kindergarten children were tested and placed into first grade classes as a result of their ITPA profiles. There was one class of "visual learners" who received a visual approach to reading; one class of "visual learners" who received an auditory approach to reading; one class of "auditory learners" who received a visual approach and a second class of "auditory learners" who received an auditory approach to reading. In addition, there were four control groups. The conclusion of the study was that it did not make any difference about strengths or weaknesses as far as a reading program was concerned; the "auditory learners" performed better regardless of the teaching method and the auditory approach was superior regardless of the child's style of learning. These findings tend to be corroborated by Bliesmer and Yarborough's study which found that ten beginning reading programs, those which emphasized a "synthetic" approach — teaching certain letter-sound relationships or word elements before beginning to read (a predominately auditory approach) — tended to be "significantly more productive in terms of specific reading achievement in grade one" than the "analytic" approach — going directly from readiness procedures to the teaching of whole words (a predominately visual approach) .[14]

The ultimate decision seems to depend on the goals that are being set for the individual. These goals, in turn, depend on the basic potential for learning within the individual. If the teacher is working with a trainable mentally retarded child or a so-called minimally brain damaged child, the potential for learning and therefore the goals will be vastly different. With the former, because the potential is low the emphasis may be toward the strengths whereas with the latter individual because the potential is greater the strengths may be controlled to compel him to develop his weaknesses. Furthermore, it might depend on what task is to be taught, for example, strengths may be utilized in learning academic skills with weaknesses being stressed in a separate remediation program. Many factors, of course, must be considered and certainly the most important one seems to be that of each individual child's own unique qualities which must be viewed separately from those of every other exceptional child.

REFERENCES

1. AUSEBEL, D.P.: The use of advance organizers in the learning and retention of meaningful verbal material. *J Educ Psychol, 51*:267-272, 1960.
2. BATEMAN, BARBARA D.: Reading and psycholinguistic processes of partially seeing children. *CEC Res Monogr*, 1963, Series A, No. 5.
3. BATEMAN, BARBARA D.: Learning disabilities — yesterday, today, and tomorrow. *Exceptional Child, 31*:167-177, 1964.
4. BATEMAN, BARBARA D.: *The Illinois Test of Psycholinguistic Abilities in Current Research.* Urbana, U. of Ill., 1965.
5. BATEMAN, BARBARA D.: The Illinois Test of Psycholinguistic Abilities. A short course given at the CSHA Convention, San Francisco, Apr. 1967a.

6. BATEMAN, BARBARA D.: A reference line for use with the ITPA. *J Sch Psychol, 5:* 128-135, 1967b.

7. BATEMAN, BARBARA D.: *Interpretation of the 1961 Illinois Test of Psycholinguistic Abilities.* Seattle, Special Child, 1968.

8. BATEMAN, BARBARA D., and WETHERELL, JANIS: Psycholinguistic aspects of mental retardation. *Ment Retard, 3:*8-13, April 1965.

9. BEREITER, C., and ENGELMANN, S.: *Teaching Disadvantaged Children in the Pre-school.* Englewood Cliffs, Prentice-Hall, 1966.

10. BERKO, JEAN: The child's learning of english morphology. *Word, 14:*150-177, 1958.

11. BILOVSKY, D., and SHARE, J.: The ITPA and Downs Syndrome: an exploratory study. *Amer J Ment Defic, 70:*78-82, 1965.

12. BIRCH, G.H., and LEFFORD, A.: Intersensory development in children. *Monogr Soc Res Child Develop,* 1963, vol. 28.

13. BLESSING, K.R.: An Investigation of a Psycholinguistic Deficit in Educable Mentally Retarded Children: Detection, Remediation and Related Variables. Unpublished Doctoral Dissertation, University of Wisconsin, 1964.

14. BLIESMER, E., and YARBOROUGH, B.A.: Comparison of ten different beginning reading programs in first grade. *Phi Delta Kappan,* June, 1965, pp. 500-504.

15. BLUE, C.M.: The effectiveness of a group language program with trainable mental retardates. Unpublished report, Appalachian State Teachers College, 1963.

16. BRADLEY, B.; MAURER, R., and HUNDZIAK, M.: A study of the effectiveness of milieu therapy and language training for the mentally retarded. *Exceptional Child, 33:* 143-150, 1966.

17. DELACATO, C. H.: *The Diagnosis and Treatment of Speech and Reading Problems.* Springfield, Thomas, 1963.

18. FERNALD, G.: *Remedial Techniques in Basic School Subjects.* New York, McGraw, 1939.

19. FERRIER, E.E.: An Investigation of Psycholinguistic Factors Associated with Functional Defects of Articulation. Unpublished Doctoral Dissertation, University of Illinois, 1963.

20. FERRIER, E.E.: An investigation of the ITPA performance of children with functional defects of articulation. *Exceptional Child, 32:*625-629, 1966.

21. FOSTER, SUZANNE: Language Skills for Children with Persistent Articulatory Disorders. Unpublished Doctoral Dissertation, Texas Women's University, 1963.

22. FROSTIG, MARIANNE, and HORNE, D.: *The Frostig Program for the Development of Visual Perception.* Chicago, Follett, 1964.

23. GRAY, S., and KLAUS, R.: An experimental preschool program for culturally deprived children. *Child Develop, 36:*887-898, 1965.

24. GRAY, S.; KLAUS, R.; MILLER, J., and FORRESTER, B.: *Before First Grade.* New York, Teachers College, Columbia, 1966.

25. HART, N.W.H.: The differential diagnosis of the psycholinguistic abilities of the cerebral palsied child and effective remedial procedures. *Special Schools Bulletin, No. 2,* Brisbane, Australia, 1963.

26. HEGGE, T.G.; KIRK, S.A., and KIRK, WINIFRED: *Remedial reading drills.* Ann Arbor, Wahr, 1940.

27. HERMANN, ANITA: An Experimental Approach to the Educability of Psycholinguistic Functions in Children. Unpublished Master's Thesis, University of Illinois, 1962.

28. JOHNSON, G.; CAPOBIANCO, R., and MILLER, D.: Speech and language development of a group of mentally deficient children enrolled in training programs. *Exceptional Child, 27:*72-77, 1960.

29. KASS, CORRINE E.: Some Psychological Correlates of Severe Reading Disability. Unpublished doctoral Dissertation, University of Illinois, 1962.

30. KASS, CORRINE E.: Psycholinguistic disabilities of children with reading problems. *Exceptional Child, 32*:533-539, 1966.

31. KEPHART, N.: *The Slow Learner in the Classroom.* Columbus, Merrill, 1960.

32. KIRK, S.A., and BATEMAN, BARBARA: Diagnosis and remediation of learning disabilities. *Exceptional Child, 29*:73-78, 1962.

33. KIRK, S.: Personal Communication, April 1968.

34. LAMB, S., and TARNOPOL, L.: A pilot study of psycholinguistic abilities of culturally deprived Negro preschool children. An unpublished study carried out at the Booker T. Washington Community Center, San Francisco, 1967.

35. LOWELL, E.L., and STONER, M.: *Play It By Ear.* Los Angeles, John Tracy Clinic, 1960.

36. McCARTHY, JAMES: A test for the identification of defects in language usage among young cerebral palsied children. *Cereb Palsy Rev, 21:* (1) , 1960.

37. McCARTHY, JAMES: Notes on the validity of the ITPA. *Ment Retard, 3*:25-26, 1965.

38. McCARTHY, J.J., and KIRK, S.A.: *Illinois Test of Psycholinguistic Abilities, Examiners Manual.* Urbana, U. of Ill., 1961.

39. McCARTHY, J.J., and KIRK, S.A.: *The Construction, Standardization and Statistical Characteristics of the Illinois Test of Psycholinguistic Abilities.* Urbana, U. of Ill., 1963.

40. McCARTHY, J.J., and OLSON, J.L.: *Validity Studies on the Illinois Test of Psycholinguistic Abilities.* Urbana, U. of Ill., 1964.

41. McCARTHY, JEANNE McRAE: Patterns of Psycholinguistic Development of Mongoloid and Nonmogoloid Severely Retarded Children. Unpublished Doctoral Dissertation, University of Illinois, 1965.

42. McGINNIS, M.A.: *Aphasic Children: Identification and Education by the Association Method.* Washington, D.C., Alexander Graham Bell Association for the Deaf, 1963.

43. MUELLER, M.W.: Comparison of psycholinguistic patterns of gifted and retarded children. Unpublished report, George Peabody College, 1963.

44. MUELLER, M.W., and WEAVER, S.J.: Psycholinguistic abilities of institutionalized and non-institutionalized trainable mental retardates. Unpublished study, George Peabody College, 1963.

45. MYERS, P.: A study of language disabilities in cerebral palsied children. *J Speech Hearing Dis, 8*:129-136, 1965.

46. OLSON, J.L.: A Comparison of Receptive Aphasic, Expressive Aphasic, and Deaf Children on the Illinois Test of Psycholinguistic Abilities. Unpublished Doctoral Dissertation, University of Illinois, 1960.

47. OLSON, J.L.: Deaf and sensory aphasic Children. *Exceptional Child, 27*:422-424, 1961.

48. OLSON, J.; HAHN, H., and HERMANN, A.: Psycholinguistic curriculum. *Ment. Retard, 3*:14-19, 1965.

49. PAINTER, GENEVIEVE B.: The Effect of a rhythmic and Sensory-motor Activity Program on Perceptual-Motor-Spatial Abilities of Kindergarten Children. Unpublished Master's Thesis, University of Illinois, 1964.

50. RAGLAND, G.G.: The Performance of Educable Mentally Handicapped Students of Differing Reading Ability on the ITPA. Unpublished Doctoral Dissertation, University of Virginia, 1964.

51. REICHSTEIN, JEROME: Auditory Threshold Consistency: A Basic Characteristic for Differential Diagnosis of Children with Communication Disorders. Unpublished Doctoral Dissertation, Teacher's College, Columbia University, 1963.

52. Sievers, Dorothy J.; McCarthy, J.J.; Olson, J.L.; Bateman, Barbara D., and Kass, Corrine E.: *Selected Studies on the Illinois Test of Psycholinguistic Abilities.* Urbana, U. of Ill., 1963.

53. Smith, J.O.: Effects of a group language development program upon the psycholinguistic abilities of educable mental retardates. *Special Education Res. Monogr., No. 1,* George Peabody College, 1962a.

54. Smith, J.O.: Group language development for educable mental retardates. *Exceptional Child, 29:*95-101, 1962b.

55. Stark, Joel: Performance of aphasic children on the ITPA. *Exceptional Child, 33:* 153-158, 1966.

56. Stearns, K.; Hodges, W., and Spicker, R.: Interim report: a diagnostically based language curriculum for psychosocially deprived preschool children. Paper read at the Amer. Educ. Res. Assn., Chicago, Feb. 1966.

57. Weaver, S.J.: Psycholinguistic abilities of culturally deprived children. In Early Training Project, Murfreesboro, Tenn., Tennessee City Schools and George Peabody College, 1962.

58. Weener, P.; Barritt, L., and Semmel, M.: A critical evaluation of the Illinois Test of Psycholinguistic Abilities. *Exceptional Child., 34:*373-384, 1967.

59. Wepman, J., and Jones, L.: *The Language Modalities Test for Aphasia.* Chicago, U. of Chicago, Ind. Rel. Ctr., 1961.

60. Wiseman, D.: A classroom procedure for identifying and remediating language problems. *Ment Retard, 3:*20-24, 1965.

Chapter 14

Reading: A Controversial View Research and Rationale

Barbara Bateman

READING, A NONMEANINGFUL PROCESS

T HE CONCEPT THAT THE activity popularly and commonly known as reading can and should be viewed as a nonmeaningful process is by no means a new one, nor is it one that should be considered grossly heretical. In the teacher's manual accompanying Lippincott's *Basic Reading* series (Mc-Cracken & Walcutt, 1963) this position is clearly and forcefully stated:

"The written words are in fact artificial symbols of the spoken words, which are sounds. So reading must be the process of turning these printed symbols into sounds. The moment we say this, however, someone is sure to ask (and probably in a tone of the greatest anxiety), 'But what about meaning? Do you propose to define reading as mere word-calling, without regard for meaning?' Yes, we do."

Jastak, and Bloomfield and Barnhart have also clearly and emphatically pointed to the distinction between (1) reading as a process of converting letters to sounds and (2) the ultimate goal of this process, which is to obtain meaning from the resultant sounds.[1,2] Teachers sometimes refer to these as "word calling" and "comprehending." It appears unfortunate that the former, which is herein called reading, is sometimes viewed as a "necessary evil." In our eagerness to help children reach the eventual goal of obtaining meaning or comprehending what they have read, we perhaps have sometimes neglected the all-important prior stage of mastering the mechanical, rote process of letter-to-sound conversion. One might well ask why another statement of this position is necessary when it has been stated earlier and so well by others. It has been observed that many, if not most, elementary teachers and reading specialists are reluctant to consider seriously the possibility that initial reading instruction could or should neglect to emphasize meaning. Cases have been encountered where teachers who are using materials such as the Lippincott series, espousing this point of view, have denied ever hearing of such a position!

Others assert, after an initial presentation of the concept of reading as

Note: The material for this chapter is reproduced from *Curriculum Bulletin* No. 278 with permission of the School of Education, University of Oregon, Eugene, Oregon. Portions of this material were presented at the International Reading Association Convention, Seattle, Washington, May, 1967, and are reproduced with permission from the International Reading Association.

289

a nonmeaningful process, that all it means is that word recognition is also important but they prefer to define reading as more inclusive. While it would be easy to pretend the issue vanishes by being labelled a matter of "semantics," the fact is that how one views the basic nature of the reading process should have a determining role in how reading is taught. It is because of these important implications for reading instruction that it seemed time to look once again at the differences between the process of reading and the purpose of reading.

Two lines of evidence — clinical and research — will be advanced in support of the position that reading should be viewed as a rote, automatic, conditioned nonmeaningful process which precedes (and thus is separable from) comprehension.

Logical and Clinical Approach

Clinical work with children who have difficulty in reading leads to the observation that very, very few of them have difficulty in comprehending symbols such as the spoken word "dog." But they almost all share a pro-nounced difficulty in converting the letters *d-o-g* into the spoken sounds "dog." One way to view this distinction would be to think in terms of two stages.

Stage One is the process of reading. It differs only in quantity, not quality, from what the rat does when he learns to jump to the circle, but not to the triangle (differential responses to visual stimuli). Stage Two is that of comprehending or attaching meaning to the symbols which have been identified in the previous step. This second stage should indeed be taught to children and taught very directly and explicitly, but it is the con-tention of this paper that in the early stages of so-called reading instruction, the child has quite enough to do in Stage One and his task ought not to be unduly complicated by simultaneously requiring Stage Two. The process of learning to drive a car (this same illustration was used by McCracken and Walcutt) is perhaps analogous.[3] It is certainly true that we learn to drive to eventually be able to transport persons and goods from one place to an-other, just as we learn to read for the eventual purpose of obtaining mean-ing. But, we would consider it somewhat ill-advised to combine teaching a novice to drive with a task such as driving a dignitary to the airport during rush-hour traffic when the time schedule is tight. We recognize that the me-chanics of driving must be practiced *without* the pressure of any immediate purpose beyond mastering the mechaniscs. It is also true in both driving and reading that after the mechanical (Stage One) part has been mastered it seems to disappear. As adults we are seldom aware of the actual process of converting printed symbols to sound equivalents as we read, just as we fre-quently shift gears, brake and accelerate without consciously attending to those behaviors. This is one of many instances in which introspective knowledge of how we as normal adults perform a given task does not necessarily provide helpful guides in teaching that task to young children who have not yet become proficient in it.

In order to check the accuracy of the contention that children who have trouble in reading are in need of instruction in Stage One, not Stage Two, it would be very simple for classroom teachers to administer two forms of a test like the Gates Reading Tests (e.g., Advanced Primary Paragraph Reading) in two different ways and compare the scores. If the teacher were to read the paragraphs aloud to the class ("Draw a line under the little cat.") and have them do the required comprehension of the spoken word (symbol) and make the appropriate marks on the test, Stage Two would be measured.

If a comparable form of the test were then administered in routine fashion, the child would be required to perform both Stages One and Two. The difference between the two scores would thus constitute a measure of the need for instruction in Stage One.

Earlier it was indicated that Stage Two, attaching meaning to symbols, should be taught directly. However, obtaining meaning from printed letters is only one kind of comprehension and we are advocating that it not be taught until after the child is comfortable with the process of converting printed letters to sounds. However, the world is full of many symbols and signals which children need to learn to comprehend. We would suggest that teaching the meanings of facial expressions, moss on a tree, and traffic flow (e.g., in terms of what it means or tells us about the time of day, the direction of the downtown area, the socioeconomic class of the area, etc.), are all legitimate educational pursuits and that they do not differ from the teaching of the meanings of words which have been previously read. In short, we are urging that reading be taught as a rote, conditioned, mechanical process of converting letters to sounds and that the comprehension of many symbols (including sounds combined into words) be taught as a separate process. It is a highly significant, but widely overlooked fact that reading disability is usually defined as a discrepancy between proficiencies in comprehending symbols (mental age, loosely translated) and in converting visual symbols to sounds and then obtaining meaning from them (reading as traditionally measured, including both Stages One and Two.) Thus, by definition, reading disabilities occur in Stage One! If a child is strong in Stage One (word-calling) but poor in Stage Two (comprehension), as does occasionally happen, we say he has a problem in "comprehending what he reads," acknowledging in spite of ourselves that we really do equate word-calling with reading, as well we should.

An important qualification to this discussion is that a very substantial percentage of children, perhaps three-fourths of them, seem to acquire the skills of reading and comprehending almost by "osmosis." The method of instruction seems to matter very little compared to the fact of exposure. While in theory we would argue that reading should be taught to all children as the nonmeaningful process it really is, in practice it would probably matter only to those few children who actually need systematic reading instruction because they do not learn by "osmosis."

Research Approach

The distinction we have made between Stage One and Stage Two as symbol conversion or identification versus symbol recognition or comprehension, appears to parallel that made in the psycholinguistic model of Illinois Test of Psycholinguistic Abilities (ITPA). In this test two levels of language are assessed — the representational or meaningful and the automatic-sequential or rote, nonmeaningful. The ITPA has generated recent research which is quite relevant to the concept of reading as a nonmeaningful process. Two of the earliest studies utilizing the ITPA (Kass, Bateman) found that reading achievement correlated positively with the nonmeaningful language subtests, and not with the meaningful ones.[4,5] In fact, Kass found a negative relationship between reading achievement and the ability to comprehend meaningful visual stimuli. Ragland also reported that retarded readers performed better than non-retarded readers on the comprehension of meaningful visual stimuli.[6] Additional data, to be presented, also indicate that good readers and poor readers are differentiated psycholinguistically by their performances in the use of language at a nonmeaningful level. These four studies just mentioned included mentally retarded, partially seeing, dyslexic and normal subjects.

Evidence which bears on the validity of the assertion that reading can and should be taught as a symbol-sound conversion process can also be adduced from new research on methodology in reading instruction. But it is first necessary to point out that "Stage One" instruction, in our terminology, is most closely approximated in today's practice by intensive phonics programs in which the initial instructional emphasis is on symbol-sound conversion with comparatively little attention to meaning per se. These systems have been described as synthetic — "in which the child is taught certain letter-sound relationships or word elements (Stage One) before beginning to read (Stage One plus Stage Two)" (Bliesmer and Yarborough).[7]

The other widely used approach embodies an initial emphasis on meaning and learning whole words prior to the introduction of specific letter-sound relationships. It is often called the analytic approach or the look-say method. In our terminology, it requires the child to perform Stage Two first and then later introduces him to Stage One.

Bliesmer and Yarborough compared ten different beginning reading programs in first grade — five of these were synthetic (phonics) and five were analytic (whole word and meaning). Reading achievement was measured by five subtests of the Stanford Achievement Test: Word Reading, Paragraph Meaning, Vocabulary, Spelling, and Word Study Skills. When the means of the two programs were compared on these five measures, ninety-two differences were significantly in favor of the phonics programs and none significantly favored the analytic programs (125 total comparisons). With specific regard to comprehension skills, twenty of twenty-five comparisons significantly favored the phonics program and none significantly favored the analytic programs. This study was well controlled (e.g., programs were randomly assigned to teachers, in-service training was provided by consultants from the program publishers, covariance procedures were applied to adjust mean criterion scores, etc.) and the authors' conclusion that ". . . reading programs which give attention to sound-symbol relationships prior to teaching of words . . . tend to be significantly more productive . . . than do analytic reading programs which involve the more conventional approach of going directly from readiness procedures to the reading of whole words" is well founded.

In an excellent review of available rigorous (carefully defined by the authors) comparisons of reading achievement of groups which had early intensive phonics with groups that had not, Gurren and Hughes found that the evidence "clearly favors intensive teaching of all the main sound-symbol relationships from the start of formal reading instruction" and that "such teaching benefits comprehension as well as vocabulary and spelling."[8] Of the twenty-two rigorous comparisons of "conventional" and "phonetic" reading programs, nineteen were favorable to "phonetics," three to neither group, and one to "conventional." Sub-analyses revealed that sixteen comparisons favored the "phonetics" in specific regard to comprehension, while none favored the "conventional."

In summary, it is this observer's opinion that logical analyses of the reading process, clinical experience and research data all point unmistakably toward the currently unpopular notion that reading can and should be taught as the formation of a series of rote, nonmeaningful, conditioned bonds between visual stimuli (letters) and vocal responses (sounds). This nonmeaningful process is, of course, carried on for the eventual purpose of obtaining meaning from the symbols, but this fact ought not remain an obstacle to teaching the process of reading.

If one were to test the merit of this position (and one certain merit, however small, is that it is testable) he would perhaps carry the position to its extreme and employ a program in which (1) the symbol-sound relationship were always constant, e.g., i/t/a, and (2) *all* "meaningful words" were excluded until after the child had thoroughly mastered the conditioned associations using only individual sounds and nonsense combinations. Teachers often ask how long it would take for the child to master the forty-four sound-symbol bonds in i/t/a, especially if all meaningful words were excluded. Research would of course be required to answer this with certainty, but if the best application of known principles of learning were systematically employed, a couple of months would appear to be a reasonable guess.

Another objection frequently raised to this type of proposal is that the children might not be "motivated" to learn forty-four rote associations. This, too, would have to be tested, but it would seem that careful application of reward and precise structuring to insure task success could eliminate such anticipated difficulties.

The nature of the process of learning the forty-four sound-symbol associations advocated here should be no different from that of learning forty-four children's names, or forty-four baseball players' batting averages, or forty-four models of automobiles. In all cases an arbitrary label is assigned, and if one forgets that label, there is no way to meaningfully deduce it. It is in just this sense we urge that the process of converting letters to sounds, which we have called reading, should be viewed as a rote, nonmeaningful process.

EFFICACY OF AN AUDITORY AND A VISUAL METHOD OF FIRST-GRADE READING INSTRUCTION WITH AUDITORY AND VISUAL LEARNERS

Most educators probably agree with the proposition that reading instruction ideally should be geared to individual children's learning style. However, most attempts to do this kind of matching of method and child have actually centered on flexibility in planning for varying rates of learning and for interests rather than for styles of learning. Within regular classrooms, the basic method of teaching, i.e., of presenting the process of reading, has not been individualized. In contrast, some remedial teachers do, however, use radically different methods — e.g., kinesthetic, visual, phonics — with different children.

In a recent study of reading disabilities in children, de Hirsch, Jansky and Langford compared relative strength in visual and auditory perceptual areas.[9] All of the children rated as superior visual-perceptual subjects (N=3) in kindergarten achieved high scores on reading tests at the end of second grade, but of the superior auditory-perceptual children (N=7) only those who had received intensive phonic training were able to read satisfactorily. The authors concluded, therefore, that teaching methods should to a large extent be determined by modality strength and weakness. Conversely,

Harris failed to find any significant association between the specific teaching method used and the presumed aptitude for that method.[10] In addition to visual and auditory methods and aptitudes, he also explored kinesthetic patterns.

The basic purpose of this study was to explore the efficacy of an auditory approach to first-grade reading compared to a visual approach, both when children were homogeneously grouped by preferred learning modality (auditory or visual) and when they were not so grouped.

Subjects and Procedure

This study was initiated by the Highland Park, Illinois, School system* as part of its program to evaluate and continually improve first-grade reading instruction.

In the spring of the year, eight kindergarten classes were given the Detroit Group Intelligence Scale and the Metropolitan Reading Readiness Test. In addition, the Illinois Test of Psycholinguistic Abilities (ITPA) was administered to the children in four of the classes.

On the basis of these test results the children were assigned to their first-grade classes. The four classes which were not administered the ITPA were designated as nonplacement classes. Two of these nonplacement classes received auditory method reading instruction and the other two received visual method instruction. These nonplacement children were assigned to their first-grade classrooms in the usual manner utilized by the school system — an informal "sorting process" in which an effort is made to have all classes heterogeneous and similar to each other on chronological age (CA) and IQ and to control boy/girl ratio within each class. The classes were not known to differ from each other in any respect other than method of reading instruction employed by the teacher. There were no significant differences among the four classes on IQ, mental age (MA), or total reading readiness.

Each child in the other four classes — the placement classes — was labelled an "auditory" or a "visual" subject on the basis of his performance on the two ITPA subtests of memory which measure automatic-sequential language abilities and have been found to correlate with reading. The total group of placement children (N=87) was stronger in auditory memory

*The excellent cooperation and assistance of the entire Highland Park school system including the members of the school board, the administration, the kindergarten and first-grade teachers, the guidance department, and especially Mr. Allen Trevor, Principal of Sherwood School, and Miss Sue Hunt, Director of Guidance Services, is gratefully acknowledged. Thanks are also due to the staff of the University of Illinois' Institute for Research on Exceptional Children who provided guidance, time, and personnel for all individual testing. And special thanks go to Sr. Joane Marie, O.S.F., Ph.D., Cardinal Stritch College, for her assistance in the preparation of this paper and to Miss Janice Wetherell, University of Illinois, for the statistical analyses.

(auditory-vocal sequential, subtest #8), where the mean language age was 80.75 months, than in visual memory (visual-motor sequential, subtest #9), where the mean language age was 71.30 months. The "typical" child in this group thus scored nine months higher on auditory memory than on visual memory. The difference was used as the base line in the determination of whether a child was labelled "auditory" or "visual." If his auditory memory score exceeded his visual memory score by more than nine months, he was designated an auditory subject and if it exceeded the visual by less than nine months he was a visual subject. There were some borderline cases which were labelled on the basis of the total profile (comprised of four additional auditory tests and three additional visual tests).

Many of the children in the auditory group showed only a very slight preference for the auditory modality, and the same was naturally true in the visual group. But all the strong preference children were clearly in their appropriate group. The inclusion of "borderline" subjects has the effect of minimizing obtained differences.

Table 14-I shows the constitution of all eight classes.

TABLE 14-I
EIGHT CLASSES

Tests given in Kdgtn.	Placement Classes	Subjects	Method	N	IQ*
Group IQ	1 (AsAm)	Aud.	Aud.	24	126.0
Reading Readiness	2 (VsAm)	Vis.	Aud.	24	124.7
	3 (AsVm)	Aud.	Vis.	20	124.8
ITPA	4 (VsVm)	Vis.	Vis.	19	126.2
			Total	87	
	Nonplacement Classes				
Group IQ	5 (A-Vs, Am1)	Aud. & Vis.	Aud.	25	124.3
Reading Readiness	6 (A-Vs, Am2)	Aud. & Vis.	Aud.	23	127.0
	7 (A-Vs, Vm1)	Aud. & Vis.	Vis.	25	121.6
	8 (A-Vs, Vm2)	Aud. & Vis.	Vis.	22	125.6
			Total	95	

*denotes mean value

Profile 1 shows the mean ITPA scores of the two Placement Classes of auditory subjects (N=44) and the two Placement Classes of visual subjects (N=43). The greatest differences occur in auditory memory and visual memory since these subtests were the bases on which the children were divided. However, the auditory subjects' mean score was slightly higher on all five auditory subtests and the visual subjects' score was higher on the four visual subtests.

The auditory method classes utilized the Lippincott beginning program and the visual method classes used the Scott, Foresman series. None of the teachers of the placement groups was told whether his class was composed of auditory or of visual subjects (the two auditory-method placement teachers guessed correctly which group they had within the first few weeks of school, but this was not confirmed for them). All eight first-grade teachers in the study attended in-service orientation sessions in which the use of only those supplementary reading materials and techniques consistent with the basic approach used in that classroom (auditory or visual) was emphasized and discussed.

Only one instance of "contamination" was discovered in which a teacher of a nonplacement visual method class employed some supplementary auditory materials.

At the end of first grade the Gates Primary Word Recognition and Paragraph Reading tests were administered to all eight classes. Each pupil's

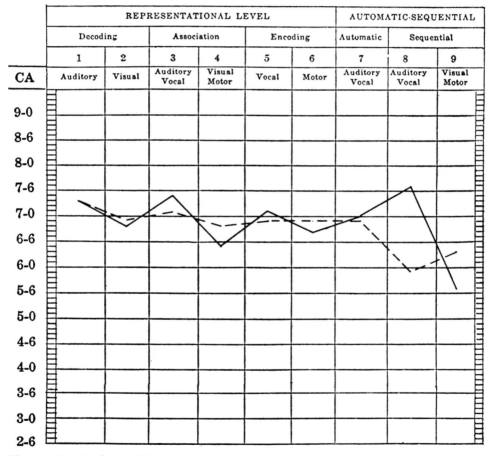

Figure 14-1. Profile 1. ITPA Performance of Auditory (N=44) and Visual (N=43) Subjects.

— — — — Visual

———————— Auditory

scores on these two tests were averaged to obtain his reading grade. A spelling test (author-constructed) consisting of twelve words and six nonsense words was also administered to all subjects.

Results: Nonplacement Classes

The results obtained are presented in three sections: (1) A comparison of the auditory and visual methods in the nonplacement classes; (2) a comparison of the auditory and visual methods with auditory and visual subjects; (3) a comparison of good and poor readers from the placement classes. Summary data for the nonplacement classes are presented in Table 14-II.

The 2-point IQ difference between the combined auditory method classes (N=48) and visual method classes (N=47) was not significant. The auditory method was significantly superior (t = 2.17, p<.05) to the visual method. The mean reading achievement of the children in the auditory classes was three and one-third months higher than the visual classes.

TABLE 14-II
NONPLACEMENT CLASSES (N=95)
READING AND SPELLING ACHIEVEMENT

	N	Class Subjects - Method	IQ*	Average Rdg. Grade X*	SD	Spelling X* No. Right
	25	A-V, A_{M1}	124.3	3.34	1.14	7.04
	23	A-V, A_{M2}	127.0	3.27	.57	6.57
Total	48	Auditory Method	125.6	3.31	.91	6.81
	25	A-V, V_{M1}	121.6	2.95	.51	2.88
	22	A-V, V_{M2}	125.6	3.00	.53	2.65
Total	47	Visual Method	123.5	2.98	.52	2.77

*denotes mean value

The same clear superiority of the auditory method over the visual is seen in the spelling scores as presented in Table 14-III.

TABLE 14-III
NONPLACEMENT CLASSES
SPELLING ACHIEVEMENT

Spelling Score	Auditory Method Classes	Visual Method Classes
0-5 words right	14 (29%)	39 (83%)
6+ words right	34 (71%)	8 (17%)
N	48	47

The above data reveal that when children were heterogeneously grouped without regard to preferred learning modality, the auditory method of instruction produced results significantly superior to those of the visual method in both reading and spelling.

Results: Placement Classes

Analysis of variance (two-way fixed effects model) of reading achievement revealed that for the four placement classes the auditory method was significantly superior to the visual method ($F = 16.28$, 1 df, $p<.01$) and that the auditory subjects were significantly superior to the visual subjects ($F = 9.28$, 1 df, $p<.01$). Method accounted for 14 per cent of the variance and subjects for 7 per cent. There was no interaction between subject and method ($F = 1.62$, NS). Table 14-IV summarizes reading and spelling achievement of the four placement classes.

TABLE 14-IV
PLACEMENT CLASSES
READING AND SPELLING ACHIEVEMENT

N	Placement Classes Subject - Method		IQ*	Average Rdg. Grade X*	SD	Spelling X* No. Right
24	A	A	126.0	3.62	.37	11.29
24	V	A	124.7	3.43	.38	7.92
20	A	V	124.8	3.34	.59	7.85
19	V	V	126.2	2.90	.51	1.79

*denotes mean value

The superiority of the A_sA_M group and the poorer performance of the V_sV_M group in reading are apparent.

Analysis of variance of spelling scores revealed the auditory subjects were superior to the visual subjects ($F = 49.4$, 1 df, $p<.01$) and the auditory method was superior to the visual method ($F = 42.7$, 1 df, $p<.01$). Method accounted for 24 per cent of the variance and subjects for 28 per cent. Again, there was no interaction between subject and method ($F = 2.0$, 1 df, NS).

Good Readers Versus Poor Readers

The children in the placement classes who scored at the 3.9 grade level or above were designated "good" readers and those who scored below 2.9 grade level were "poor" readers. These highly arbitrary cutoffs were dictated by the necessity of choosing points which would yield groups of a size suitable for study.

Of the sixteen good readers, fourteen had received the auditory method and only two the visual method. Of the eighteen poor readers, sixteen were visual subjects, twelve of whom had received the visual method.

The clear superiority of the auditory method over the visual and the less marked superiority of the auditory subjects (as found in the analysis of variance) are both apparent in Table 14-V.

TABLE 14-V
CLASS PLACEMENT OF GOOD AND POOR READERS

	N	AsAm	AsVm	VsAm	VsVm	As	Vs	Am	Vm
Good	16	10	2	4	0	12	4	14	2
Poor	18	1	4	1	12	5	13	2	16

The mean IQ for the good readers was 129.6 compared to 120.2 for the poor readers. Table 14-VI shows the IQ breakdown by preferred modality.

TABLE 14-VI
IQ OF GOOD AND POOR READERS

	N	As	Vs	T
Good	16	127.8	135.0	129.6
Poor	18	111.4	123.6	120.2

The visual subjects who were good readers were substantially above the average IQ for the total group, while the auditory subjects who were poor readers were appreciably below the group mean in intelligence. These data again confirm the earlier observation that *children who prefer the visual modality are handicapped, relative to those who prefer the auditory modality, in reading.* An interesting possibility is suggested — did the few visual subjects who became "good" readers by the end of first-grade also become more auditorially oriented?

When the ITPA profiles of the sixteen good readers and eighteen poor readers were plotted (see Profile 2) it was apparent that the psycholinguistic patterns were different in shape as well as in level. The level difference was to be expected since the IQs and MAs of the good readers were higher than those of the poor readers. The good readers were predominantly auditory subjects (12 of -6) so their highly auditory profile is not unexpected. However, the poor readers were predominantly visual subjects (13 of 18) but their profile is not predominantly visual. Profile 1, presented earlier, shows that the mean difference between the total group of auditory subjects and the total group of visual subjects on auditory-vocal automatic is less than one month. Yet on Profile 2 it is fifteen months. Also, Profile 1 shows only a two-month superiority of the auditory subjects in vocal encoding, while the good readers (Profile 2) are fifteen months higher than the poor readers. This suggests that, given good auditory memory, other auditory-vocal skills (incidental verbal learning and vocal expression) may play a more important role in reading than previous ITPA studies have indicated.

The poor readers' ITPA profile differs from their "parent" visual group in that they show a peak in motor encoding and are below the total visual group in visual memory. The low visual memory might be related to the presence of the five auditory subjects in the poor reader group. But this assumption poses a difficulty in accounting for the strong showing of the poor readers in motor encoding, which is a visual-motor test. The high motor encoding score of the poor readers does suggest that some very active (hyperactive), "acting-out" children may have difficulty adjusting to the auditory-vocal world of reading.

The unexpected finding that the A_SA_M group produced ten good readers and only one poor reader, while the V_SV_M group had twelve poor and no good readers, has precluded the kind of intergroup comparisons of good

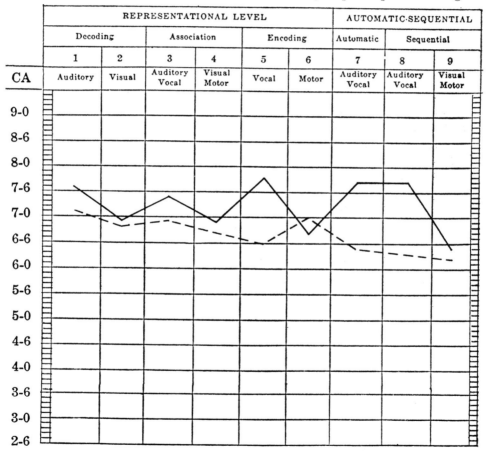

Figure 14-2. Profile 2. ITPA Performance of Good (N=16) and Poor (N=18) Readers.
Good IQ* 129.6
Poor IQ* 120.2
— — — — Poor Readers
————— Good Readers
*Mean Value

and poor readers that would have been most meaningful, in regard to psycholinguistic abilities.

There was no overlap whatever between the distribution of spelling scores of the good readers ($X^* = 12.3$ words correct) and the poor readers ($X^* = 2.2$ words correct).

Summary and Discussion

The major findings of this study may be stated: the auditory method of reading instruction was superior to the visual method for both reading and spelling; the auditory-modality-preferred subjects were superior in both reading and spelling to the visual-modality-preferred subjects; and there was no interaction between subjects' preferred modality and the method of instruction used.

Within the fields of remedial and corrective reading one of the recurring issues centers on whether instruction should be geared to the child's pattern of cognitive strengths or to his weaknesses. It was hoped that this study might provide evidence on this point as two groups (A_SA_M and V_SV_M) were taught to their strengths and two groups (A_SV_M and V_SA_M) to their weaknesses. However, one of the strength groups was significantly superior (A_SM_M) to all other groups and the other (V_SV_M) was significantly inferior. The weakness groups (A_SV_M and V_SA_M) were intermediate in results produced and were highly similar to the nonplacement classes. One way to talk about these results is to say that it is not enough to ask, "Should we teach to the child's strengths or his weaknesses?" but that we must specify about which child we are asking. The data from this study suggest the answer would then be to teach to his strengths if he is an auditory learner or to his weakness if he is a visual learner. However, a simpler way of stating this is to say that the auditory method is superior, regardless of the child's own pattern of learning.

It is, of course, possible that this may be true for a homogeneous, above-average group such as this, and still not be true for the extreme cases found in a reading disability population.

The close correspondence found between reading and spelling achievement was striking and possibly supportive of the observation that both reading and spelling are basically processes of making sound-symbol associations.

The findings of this study support those of Harris who found no interaction between subject and method and those of Bliesmer and Yarborough who compared the effectiveness of ten beginning first-grade programs of reading, including Lippincott and Scott, Foresman and found the Lippincott program was significantly superior to the Scott, Foresman on every measure of reading employed (Stanford Achievement Tests subtests of

---

*denotes mean value

Word Reading, Paragraph Meaning, Vocabulary, Spelling, and Word Study Skills) .[10,7] The 484 children included in this study were from middle and lower socioeconomic levels, in contrast to the higher level of the present investigation. Bliesmer and Yarborough use the description "synthetic approach, in which sound-symbol relationships (letter sounds) are taught before words are taught" to designate what the present study called "auditory method" and they use "analytic approach of going from sight words to sounds" to describe what this study called "visual method." In the Bliesmer-Yarborough study the four "auditory methods" (including Lippincott) were all significantly superior to the three "visual methods" (including Scott, Foresman) .

The evidence appears to be mounting that reading is basically a sound-symbol association process and should perhaps be taught to all children as such. The assumption has often been made by many (including the writer) that some kind of matching procedure in which instruction is differentially geared to individual children, replete with their individual differences, must be better than an arbitrary application of one method to all children. However, it is just possible that our lack of knowledge of adequate or best methods of teaching a given set of behaviors such as reading has made this assumption too easy.

Limitations of the Present Study and Suggestions for Further Research

One of the major limitations of this study is that the sample was drawn entirely from a high socioeconomic level. The general ability and achievement level was unusually high (e.g., only one child in the entire sample had a group IQ of below 100) and it is somewhat ironic to describe a first-grader who reads at a 2.9 grade level as a "poor" reader! However, it should not be overlooked that the major findings of this study in regard to the superiority of the auditory method have also been obtained on low and middle socioeconomic level children (Bliesmer and Yarborough) .[7]

The second major limitation appeared only when the results were available — namely, the auditory method produced only two poor readers while the visual method produced only two good readers, thus making many planned analyses impossible.

This study yielded many data which remain unanalyzed, and also suggests further data gathering. Examples of possible analyses include the following: (1) correlational studies including both predictive and content validity studies employing the subtests of the ITPA, the Detroit Group Intelligence Scale and the Metropolitan Reading Readiness Tests; (2) redefinition of good and poor readers to allow comparisons of those two groups within each modality preference; (3) ITPA retest of good and poor readers to check for any changes in preferred modality, as a function of method of instruction employed.

REFERENCES

1. Jastak, J.: *Wide Range Achievement Test and Manual.* New York, Psychological Corp., 1946.
2. Bloomfield, L., and Barnhart, C.L.: *Let's Read: A Linguistic Approach.* Detroit, Wayne, 1961.
3. McCracken, G., and Walcutt, C.C.: *Basic Reading: Teacher's Edition.* Philadelphia, Lippincott, 1963.
4. Kass, C.E.: Some Psychological Correlates of Severe Reading Disability. Unpublished Doctoral Dissertation, University of Illinois, 1962.
5. Bateman, B.D.: Reading and psycholinguistic processes of partially seeing children. *CEC Res Monogr,* 1963, Series A, No. 5.
6. Ragland, G.G.: The Performance of Educable Mentally Handicapped Students of Differing Reading Ability on the ITPA. Unpublished Doctoral Dissertation, University of Virginia, 1964.
7. Bliesmer, E.P., and Yarborough, B.H.: A comparison of ten different beginning reading programs in first grade. *Phi Delta Kappan,* 1965, pp. 500-504.
8. Gurren, L., and Hughes, A.: Intensive phonics vs. gradual phonics in beginning reading: a review. *J Educ Res, 58* (8) :339-346, 1965.
9. de Hirsch, K.; Jansky, J.J., and Langford, W.S.: *Predicting Reading Failure: A Preliminary Study.* New York, Harper, 1966.
10. Harris, A.J.: Individualizing First-Grade Reading According to Specific Learning Aptitudes. Office of Research and Evaluation, Division of Teacher Education, City University of New York, April 1965, Mimeographed, 12 pp.

Chapter 15

Delinquency and Learning Disabilities

LESTER TARNOPOL

INTRODUCTION

It IS WELL KNOWN THAT there is a high correlation between delinquency and school failure. Among minority, lower socioeconomic delinquents the school drop-out rate is perhaps higher than in the general population of delinquents. Generally, Negro and Latin ghetto children tend to be below average in reading level, grades completed in school, intelligence test scores and employability skills when compared with middle-class children. Also, these minority poor tend to be above average in proportion of high school dropouts, and in delinquency rate.

Studies of the Negro poor especially, show substantially below average reading levels, high school-dropout rates and high arrest and delinquency rates in cities where such studies have been made. These relationships have led many researchers to suggest a characteristic sequence starting with failure to learn in school followed by dropping out and delinquency. In some instances, the primary cause of this sequence has been suggested to be a genetically low intelligence level. In others, the causes have been stated as being primarily environmental. The environmental causes have usually been stated as stemming from an educational handicap related to an experience-impoverished preschool environment followed by overcrowded schools, and teachers who are unprepared to teach children who do not come to class equipped with a middle-class background of experience and language.

These genetic and environmental hypotheses are well known. What is not so well known is that in many instances, northern school superintendents and school testing administrators have insisted that the low reading scores achieved by these ghetto children are due to their low IQ scores and therefore very little could be done about it. Since these school administrators were either unable or unwilling to attempt to correct this situation, they excused their own failures by placing the blame on the genetic and/or

Note: This study was undertaken as peripheral research related to a larger delinquency control project; namely, the Youth Leadership Training Project: Utilizing Indigenous Youth Leaders in Poverty Areas for Constructive Community Change. Dr. Mario D'Angeli, Director; Dr. Lester Tarnopol, Research Director; Hezekiah Singleton, Training Director; J. Scott Breed, Ronald Cowan, Research Associates; Sheldon Berkowitz, Research Assistant; James Jacobs, Alice Moses, Ralph Schneider, Research Technicians. Grant #66210, Office of Juvenile Delinquency and Youth Development, U. S. Department of Health, Education and Welfare.

family backgrounds of the children. They considered the low IQ scores to be irreversible, at least so far as the schools were concerned. In cases where superintendents have refused to release the children's reading scores to public scrutiny, they tended to say that it would put the teachers in the lower socioeconomic neighborhood schools at a disadvantage. They claimed that the teachers were already doing the best they could and so it would not help the children but would create dissension in the community.

The environmentalists have postulated that low IQ scores can be raised sufficiently, on the average, to overcome the disparity between the poor and the middle-class children by various means. Some suggestions which are being tried include a number of different types of preschool programs, school integration, educational parks and the More Effective Schools Program initiated in New York. So far, none of these programs of intervention has been in effect long enough to establish its relative merit. Perhaps more important, in too few instances have school districts attempted to test the value of their interventions in a rigorously scientific manner. Until this is done, it will not be possible to sort out the useful from the useless programs and valuable time and tax money will continue to be wasted.

None of these intervention programs which are aimed at raising the reading and educational levels of the educationally disadvantaged lower socioeconomic children seem to have considered that a significant segment of this population might need individual psychological and educational diagnosis followed by prescriptive teaching in order to learn. There is evidence that between 5 and 10 per cent of the total population of children have learning disabilities related to minimal brain dysfunction in the presence of the complete range of intelligence quotients. This type of dysfunction creates a number of different types of learning disabilities. Children with minimal brain dysfunction may exhibit difficulties in visual perception, auditory perception, motor coordination, balance, tactile perception and kinesthetic perception, singly or in any combination. A small number may have a genetic reading disability in the absence of any clearly distinguishable sensory dysfunction. Children with these learning disabilities seem to require differential diagnosis of their specific learning problems followed by prescriptive teaching starting as early as possible, preferably before starting to learn to read, if they are to be helped to learn.

HYPOTHESIS OF MINIMAL BRAIN DYSFUNCTION

It is hypothesized that *the delinquent school dropout population from minority ghettos should contain a greater percentage, than the total population, of children with minimal brain dysfunction in the presence of an adequate IQ, i.e., above the retarded range.* This would tend to account in part, both for the school dropout and delinquency rates. The following sequence has been hypothesized. Minimal brain dysfunction leads to learning disabilities in many cases which gives rise to very low reading levels and poor school performance leading to frustration and school phobia, followed by early school dropout and a high probability of delinquency.

The term "Minimal brain dysfunction" (MBD) is used to designate the medical entity related to the education term "learning disabilities" because that was the medical term selected by the Terminology and Identification phase of the National Project.[1]

Evidence for Hypothesis of Minimal Brain Dysfunction

It has been observed by a number of psychologists and physicians that both the distribution of intelligence quotients and reading levels do *not* form a normal curve for the total population of school children. Instead, these distributions appear to be bimodal with a small hump at the lower end of intelligence. According to Critchley,[2] a small hump was first described below IQ 45 by Jaederholm which has since been verified by several others.* This hump suggests the possibility of a pathological process which is thought to be developmental dyslexia, a primary constitutional reading disability. From the point of view of the education of these children, the most significant consideration is that when this condition is diagnosed early, habilitation is very often possible, especially for those with at least low-normal intelligence.

Although the hump in the distribution of intelligence quotients was observed below 45 IQ, it is suggested that a careful study of a sufficiently large population should reveal a shift of the total curve to the lower IQ range due to the intrusion of the MBD population. The Terman and Merrill 1937 standardization of the Stanford-Binet Intelligence Test on 2904 children shows the hump below about 45 IQ, while the distribution of IQs for Negro children by Tanser in Kent County, Ontario, Canada, shows a hump below 70 IQ based on a sample of 103.[3] Although Tanser's curve approximates what one might expect based on the hypothesis of minimal brain dysfunction, the small sample of 103 could create a spurious bimodal effect. Also, since the standard intelligence tests are devised in such a manner that the distribution of intelligence quotients versus the number of children comes out normal, it would be necessary to make a very careful study of the distribution to determine the true nature of the bimodal curve.† At any rate, the bimodal distribution seems to indicate that there

---

*See Chapter 4, Richard Masland, "Children with Minimal Brain Dysfunction — A National Problem."

†It is not known what the distribution of intelligence actually is since the normal distribution is an artifact of the intelligence tests now in use.

is a sub-population which is different from the normal population. Moreover, there is reason to believe that this is the population with minimal
brain dysfunction.

Another indication which casts suspicion that the school drop-out delinquent population may contain a high percentage of persons with minimal
brain dysfunction comes from electroencephalographic studies. The electroencephalograph may be used as an adjunct to neurological and psychological diagnoses. However, it is not considered to be very reliable as a
diagnostic insrument by many neurologists. On the other hand, some
neurologists claim that they can read electroencephalograms (EEG's) well
enough to detect or predict children with learning disabilities in 85 per
cent of the cases. At any rate, various studies have reported up to 70 per
cent of juvenile delinquents with abnormal EEG's as compared with 15
to 27 per cent abnormal EEGs in the total population. This type of evidence supports the need for further investigation of the delinquent population to determine the incidence of minimal brain dysfunction.

A certain fraction of the children with minimal brain dysfunction will
undoubtedly have suffered brain damage. Any population which has been
subject to more than average perinatal brain insult should also evidence
above average minimal brain dysfunction. Since the poor tend to suffer
dietary deficiencies and to have less adequate medical care than the total
population, they should constitute a high risk group. The poor Negro population certainly is in this category. Both infant mortality and premature
birth rates may be considered to be indicators of the health of a population
and of the relative amount of minimal brain damage to be expected in the
population.

According to Albee, former director of the Task Force on Manpower of
the Joint Commission on Mental Illness and Health, about one-fifth of the
indigent mothers who deliver babies in tax-supported hospitals have complications in pregnancy and birth for which special services are required,
but which they seldom receive.[4] Moreover, the prematurity rate in low-
income families tends to be from two to three times that of the middle class.
Among urban indigent Negro mothers, the retardation rate for their children is ten times the white rate. These Negro mothers often have received
no prenatal care or dietary instruction and tend to come to the hospital for
the first time when they are about to deliver. Albee suggests that a most
important area for American medicine and financial support is adequate
and proper medical care for the poor which would tend to prevent a great
many cases of retardation.

A review of vital statistics for the United States of America discloses that
in 1965 the infant mortality (deaths of infants to one year) rate was 24.7

per 1,000 live births.[5] It has been reported that these figures place the United States fifteenth among the world's nations with respect to infant mortality. In 1964, white infant deaths were 21.5 per 1,000 live births while the nonwhite rate was 40.3. The lowest nonwhite infant death rate was 10.9 in New Hampshire while the highest rate, excluding Alaska, was 54.4 in Mississippi. The nonwhite infant mortality rate in California, where this study was done, was 28.1 compared with 21.2 for whites.

A further breakdown of California infant death rates is given for 1964 in Table 15-I.* This table shows that the Negro infant death rate of 34 was one and one-half times as great as the white rate and accounts for most of the total nonwhite rate of 28. This data leads one to suspect that the Negro population should evidence a higher rate of both brain damage and minimal brain dysfunction from perinatal trauma than the white or other nonwhite populations of California.

TABLE 15-I
INFANT DEATH RATE, CALIFORNIA 1964

	Infant Deaths per 1,000
Negro	34
Total nonwhite	28
White	21
Chinese	19
Other nonwhite	12

Courtesy: State Department of Public Health, California

As early as 1861, the possible consequences when the asphyxiated or apoplectic infant was saved were stated by Dr. Little. *"The proportion of entire recoveries from the effects of asphyxia neonatorum is smaller than has hitherto been supposed.†* . . . The muscles of speech are commonly involved, varying in degree. . . . The intellectual functions are sometimes quite unaffected, but in the majority of cases the intellect suffers . . . from the slightest impairment . . . to entire imbecility . . . the individual may acquire a fair knowledge of music, the memory is good . . . a fair capacity for arithmetic and languages may be displayed, but there commonly exists a great want of application, a slowness of intellect similar to a slowness of volition. In other cases, where intellectual powers are good, a preternatural impulsive nervous condition of mind exists, combined with an agitated, eager, anxious mode of performing acts of volition."[6] Although Dr. Little was describing cerebral palsy to a skeptical audience of physicians, it is

---

*Figures supplied by the California State Department of Public Health. These figures were rounded off to the nearest whole number.

†Emphasis not in original.

noted that in the selected quotation he was also describing minimal brain dysfunction. The effect of anoxia at birth in depressing the intelligence of children is well illustrated in the graphs of Figure 4-4.†

Further evidence which indicates that the Negro population should sustain a higher rate of minimal brain dysfunction than other groups in California (and in the nation) comes from the statistics on premature births. Table 15-II indicates that the premature (under $5\frac{1}{2}$ pounds) birth rate for Negroes in California is twice that for whites. The effect of premature births on infants may not be proportional to the percentages given in the table since Negro women tend to have smaller babies than white women and the mortality rate for premature infants of the same weight is said to be relatively higher for whites than Negroes. At any rate, de Hirsch's studies of premature infants at school age indicates that they constitute a very high risk group with respect to learning disabilities.[7] This study included a group of fifty-three premature children weighing from about three to five pounds at birth and fifty-three matching children over five and one-half pounds at birth weight as a control group. It was found that in both the first and second grades the maturely born children were significantly ahead of the prematurely born children in reading and writing.

TABLE 15-II
PREMATURE BIRTHS, CALIFORNIA 1964

Negro	13%
Other nonwhite	7.3%
White	6.7%

From U.S. Bureau of the Census, Washington, D.C.

Other studies cited by de Hirsch supported her findings. For example, Wortis and Freedman found that for children in a lower socioeconomic deprived environment, premature children had a lower average IQ than term children.[8] They also found that prematurely born children are more susceptible to both neurological dysfunctions and the deleterious effects of impoverishment than term children. It has also been found by other researchers that there is a high incidence of learning disabilities and academic failure among premature children who have an adequate IQ. The study of correlates of low birth weight by Wiener *et al.* cited by Masland, also indicates a direct relationship between low birth weight and neurological damage to children. (See Figure 4-6 in Doctor Masland's chapter.) Finally, the learning difficulties of these children in the presence of disturbances in visual perception, visual-motor integration, auditory perception, etc., are

†See Chapter 4, Richard Masland, "Children With Minimal Brain Dysfunction — A National Problem."

indicative of minimal brain dysfunction. Thus, there is good reason to expect to find an above normal incidence of minimal brain dysfunction and learning disabilities in the lower socioeconomic Negro population related to the high incidence of premature births.

Critchley also cites as evidence that studies of juvenile delinquency in both New York and France found that at least 75 per cent of the young offenders were termed illiterate.[2] However, he did not define illiteracy as used in these studies. He went on to state that society should give serious attention to the relationship between dyslexia and delinquency, especially the observed tendency of many dyslexic teenagers to become delinquent. Critchley reassuringly states that the secondary neurotic reactions of children with learning disabilities tend to be generally benign, and they seem to yield readily to treatment once the basic learning problems have been adequately treated.

Medical Examinations of School Dropouts

Another source of possible neurological impairment in the impoverished Negro population might be untreated chronic medical conditions and dietary deficiencies which could result in certain medical and dental problems. About 70 per cent of the youths who participated in our study either were or had previously been in a Neighborhood Youth Corps Program. This program was to provide work experience for jobless school dropouts from poverty areas. The results of medical examinations of 165 of these enrollees were published by Eisner *et al.* (Table 15-III).[9] Their age range was from fifteen to twenty-two years with 80 per cent male, mostly Negro and some Latins. It will be observed from this table that physician No. 1 found that 62.5 per cent of his forty examinees required no care whereas No. 2 found only 32.8 per cent of his 125 in this category. This difference in findings may be attributed to the fact that physician No. 1 was given about five to ten minutes per person for a medical history and physical examination whereas physician No. 2 took about thirty to forty-five minutes per individual and included a urinalysis and serologic test for syphilis. Medical

TABLE 15-III
CARE REQUIRED BY 165 ENROLLEES IN NEIGHBORHOOD YOUTH CORPS,
BY EXAMINING PHYSICIAN

Condition	Physician No. 1		Physician No. 2		Total	
	Number	%	Number	%	Number	%
No care required	25	62.5	41	32.8	66	40.0
Dental care required	11	27.5	20	16.0	31	18.8
Medical care required	4	10.0	38	30.4	42	25.5
Both dental and medical care required	0	0	26	20.8	26	15.7
Total	40	100%	125	100%	165	100%

histories proved to be difficult to obtain from the enrollees so that most defects were found by examination. In some cases, the enrollees could not
recall ever having previously seen a dentist or physician. The data indicate
that this population requires a complete physical and dental examination
rather than the ten-minute variety. With the longer examination, only
about one-third of the population was found to be relatively free of defects
requiring attention. It should also be noted that the longer examination was
by no means complete. The implication of this evidence for our hypothesis
that this population should contain an above average amount of minimal
brain dysfunction derives from the existence of an above average incidence
of unattended medical problems.

Delinquency and Organicity

Denhoff studied a group of 109 youths aged fourteen to nineteen years
with adjustment problems.[10] The group was composed of school dropouts
and delinquents. One-third had been referred as delinquents and the remainder as school adjustment problems. Of this total group, 53 per cent
were found to have problems of cerebral dysfunction. Unfortunately, the
percentage of organics among the thirty-five delinquents was not specified.
We are able to get an indication of both the nature and predictive validity
of the examinations used from other data in this same paper. Denhoff also
studied a group of 240 physically and intellectually normal first graders.
He screened these children using examination items of the type in general
use for the diagnosis of cerebral palsy and other related problems. It was
found that thirty-nine, or 15 per cent of the group, exhibited subnormal
speech development, language development, fine motor skills and gross
motor skills. Of these thirty-nine children, twenty-nine or 11 per cent of the
total sample failed first grade. *All of those who were not promoted came
from the group of predicted failures.* Denhoff concluded that cerebral dysfunction was the basic cause of these school failures.

Denhoff's finding of 11 per cent of inadequate learners with minimal
brain dysfunction is in substantial agreement with a number of other
estimates which range around 10 per cent. Since all of the predictions of
failure in the first grade were based on motor and language development
deficits, indicating organicity, the question arises as to why these problems
did not show up in all of the fourteen- to nineteen-year-old school dropouts
and delinquents where only 53 per cent exhibited organicity. A partial
answer to this question may be that by age fourteen some of the cases of
substandard motor and language development will have been rectified
since some may have been maturational. However, once these immature
children have experienced failure, many may continue to fail as they develop self-images as failures (with concomitant fear of exposing themselves to

ridicule by trying to learn) with increasing hostility towards everything connected with school. Thus, by their teens, they may no longer evidence cerebral dysfunction, but may instead display a deep-seated school phobia and neurotic syndrome. Also, in some cases, the severe emotional overlay in teenagers, developed as the result of school failure may obscure the underlying minimal neurological dysfunction. Finally, a certain number of teenagers may have developed a poor adjustment to school for other reasons even though their basic intelligence was adequate and they appeared to have no demonstrable neurological dysfunction.

DELINQUENCY IN SAN FRANCISCO

In Moncrief's study of delinquency in San Francisco, juvenile delinquents were defined as youth from five through eighteen years of age who were apprehended for committing an act contrary to law, were suspected of committing an unlawful act, or behaved in a manner considered by the police to indicate a delinquent tendency.[11]

Perhaps one of the more important findings of Moncrief's study was the fact that of the youth who made up the 5,038 juvenile court cases, only 56.2 per cent were living with both parents compared with 83.7 per cent for the total population in 1960. Among the Negro subgroup, only 46.9 per cent were living with both parents (including adoptive parents and step parents), while in the white subgroup 60.4 per cent were living with both parents. Among the Chinese and Japanese, 77.2 per cent and 80.0 per cent respectively were living with both parents. Undoubtedly, the factor of broken homes and one parent families is a most important determinant of education and delinquency status for many children. Children from one parent families constitute high risks for brain damage for a number of reasons including the following: They are often born to mothers who are under twenty years of age and who may have babies approximately annually, or to mothers past forty, both of which have been established as high risk groups. These mothers also lack the support of a family head, so that they tend to be indigent and may suffer from various forms of malnutrition during pregnancy. They tend to be delivered at home or in county facilities without adequate perinatal care. And their infants tend to receive poor nutrition and few medical services. When these factors are compounded by poverty and slum living, the combination is a powerful deterrant to good education, and fosters delinquency.

Changes in Delinquency Rates 1960-1964

There is no doubt that delinquency among minorities is becoming an increasing problem. Between 1960 and 1964, in San Francisco, the white delinquency rate increase was negligible, from 65 to 66 per 1,000 population of male youth. On the other hand, a marked increase occurred for the nonwhite male delinquent population from 79 to 110 per 1,000 youth. The nonwhite population was predominantly Negro but included Chinese, Japanese, Filipino, American Indians and Oceanians.

The subcommittee on Research and Statistics of the United Community Fund of San Francisco concluded from these statistics that ". . . there has been a sharp increase in delinquent Negro boys in San Francisco from 1960 to 1964. These increases are especially disturbing in view of the operation of anti-delinquency programs for this group and especially of the Youth Opportunities Center and the multitude of other programs designed to improve the economic status of Negro youth."[11]

Based upon the hypothesis of this study, a significant proportion of the educational handicap of the ghetto population is considered to be related to minimal brain dysfunction. Moreover, the resulting learning disabilities are considered to give rise to poor reading ability and early school dropout. These youth also tend to lack job skills relevant to the jobs available today. And finally, these deficiencies in youth who live in a society of abundance tend to create extralegal means of obtaining a share of these materials. Delinquency is thus postulated as being related to minimal brain dysfunction underlying the frustrations of nonachievement in school and inability to obtain money through gainful employment, for a great many youth.

Although the Subcommittee has suggested the need for compensatory and special education, in the form of the programs being developed with federal funds, they were typically unaware of the existence of the minimal brain dysfunction syndrome and its ramifications. It is contended that adequate education for this population will necessarily take into consideration the special needs of children with learning disabilities. Perhaps equally as important, when learning disabilities classes are established, the children in these special classes will begin to learn and the teachers of "normal" children will have fewer discipline problems and more time to teach. Finally, and perhaps most important, through the study of exceptional children we are learning how to teach *all* children better. Therefore, when the regular classroom teachers learn the methods of teaching reading, writing and arithmetic being devised for children with learning disabilities, there is good reason to expect the performance of "normal" children to improve measurably.

POPULATION OF THIS STUDY

In the current study, 102 male youths, ages sixteen to twenty-three were included.* The subjects were primarily nonwhite, delinquent school drop-

---

*The data from this research are still being broken down and interpreted. Only a preliminary report can be given at this time.

outs: 67 per cent Negro, 14 per cent oriental, 13 per cent Latin and 11 per cent other nonwhites (Table 15-IV). The subjects were composed of nineteen trainees and eighty-three controls who were in two groups comprising thirty-two aides and fifty-one rank and file.

TABLE 15-IV
102 MALE YOUTHS, AGES 16 TO 23

Negro	62%
Oriental	14%
Latin	13%
Other nonwhite	11%
Total	100%

The nineteen trainees, ages eighteen to twenty-two, were youth who had been selected to be trained as subprofessional, social service aides. They were to act as pro-social influences in their neighborhoods to help induce constructive community change and to influence younger boys to pro-social behavior. They had been selected from delinquent youth who had demonstrated some gang leadership. Less than half of them had given up their delinquency and were really interested in training which would lead to jobs and pro-social careers. The majority still maintained delinquent connections and were not yet ready to exchange the "hustle" for a "respectable" career.

The thirty-two aides were working-leadmen on a Neighborhood Youth Corps project.† These were youth between sixteen and twenty-one years of age who had dropped out of school and were generally unemployable. They were employed by the federally funded Neighborhood Youth Corps to develop basic job skills and to be placed on regular jobs whenever possible. The aids were selected as working bosses from among those who showed some leadership. The fifty-one rank and file controls were composed of young men from the Neighborhood Youth Corps plus some youths who were induced by their friends to come to the project to be tested (for which they were all paid) as part of the control group. A large control group was necessary because of the attrition expected on retesting and in order to attempt to get a pre- and post-test control group which might match the trainees on desired characteristics. For purposes of this study the control characteristics of the groups are not necessary so that the two control groups will be lumped together as a unit of eighty-three, and all three groups will act as a unit of one hundred-and-two when possible. This study will investigate the characteristics of these subjects as an indication of what one might expect to find in the delinquent, minority, ghetto population.

---

†A Youth For Service project.

Educational and Reading Levels

Educational level data were available on ninety-four subjects, 92 per cent of whom did not complete high school and about half of whom completed the tenth grade, Table 15-V. The mean grade level attained by the trainees was 10.7 and by the controls was 10.3.

TABLE 15-V
HIGHEST GRADE COMPLETED

Grade	Trainees %	Controls %	Total Group %
8	—	1	1
9	16	15	15
10	16	35	31
11	53	43	45
12	16	7	8
Total Number	19	75	94

On the Gates test of Reading for General Significance, 28 per cent of the total group would be considered functionally illiterate by a fourth grade reading level criterion, Table 15-VI.[12] This is almost three times the illiteracy rate in the total United States population which is estimated at about 10 per cent. On the Gates Reading to Understand Directions subtest, 45 per cent were below the fourth grade level.[12] This gives an indication of why it is difficult for them in school, on the job and when taking tests. Testing these subjects proved to be a most difficult task for this and many other reasons, including the factors of school-phobic fear of testing and little motivation other than to hustle a few dollars. Both the reading level tests and the grades completed in school indicate that the trainees were somewhat superior to the controls. Two factors often related to minimal brain dysfunction are prevalent in this population, namely, low reading ability and difficulty following directions. One of the important diagnostic signs in many cases is difficulty following directions.

INTELLIGENCE QUOTIENTS AND DELINQUENCY

It is well known that the nonwhite ghetto populations tend to do better on performance tests of mental ability than on verbal tests. For our subjects, the average Wechsler Performance IQ was 90 and the average Wechsler Verbal IQ was 87. This difference is spuriously low because in many cases the verbal IQ was the greater. Lower Verbal IQs have generally been ascribed to the factor of English being a second language for the children. In some homes a foreign language is spoken and in the lower class Negro environment a form of English is spoken which is only understood by themselves. These children enter school with specific language deficiencies which make it difficult for them to understand the middle class language of the teacher and which is considered to be a major handicap preventing them from learning at a rate commensurate with their intelligence.

TABLE 15-VI
GATES READING TESTS

READING FOR GENERAL SIGNIFICANCE

Grade Level	Trainees %	Controls %	Total %
1-4	38	24	28
4-6	13	38	30
6-8	19	24	23
8 up	31	14	19
Total Number	16	37	53

READING TO UNDERSTAND DIRECTIONS

Grade Level	Trainees %	Controls %	Total %
1-4	44	46	45
4-6	13	22	19
6-8	0	14	10
8 up	44	19	26
Total Number	16	37	53

On the other hand, large discrepancies between verbal and performance IQ scores are also characteristic of learning disabilities related to minimal brain dysfunction so that one cannot be certain of the etiology in cases where the Performance IQ is significantly greater than the Verbal IQ. However, in those cases where the Verbal IQ is significantly greater than the Performance IQ, the probability of a basic learning disability existing should certainly be considered. Of eighty-four subjects tested with the Wechsler Adult Intelligence Scale, twenty-three had Performance IQ scores 10 or more points above their Verbal IQ scores and seven such discrepancies occurred in the opposite direction.

It has often been stated that it is not really essential to have as high a Verbal IQ if the Performance IQ is at least normal. The concept being that for most practical purposes an adequate Performance IQ will suffice. It was, of course, recognized that for educational purposes the Verbal IQ was most meaningful. Our data seem to indicate that the Verbal IQ may have more practical importance than has been ascribed to it for the minority, poor population.

Data comparing Wechsler Verbal IQ scores and Performance IQ scores with the number of adult arrests and convictions for the trainees is presented in Table 15-VII. Adult arrests and convictions of the trainees are seen to be negatively correlated with intelligence, that is, the higher the intelligence score the fewer arrests and convictions.* The correlations also

---

*A negative correlation means that the two variables are inversely related, i.e., as one increases the other decreases.

indicate that the Verbal IQ is more important than the Performance IQ in relation to arrests and convictions.

TABLE 15-VII
VERBAL IQ AND PERFORMANCE IQ OF TRAINEES

	N	Verbal IQ		Performance IQ
		r	p	r
Adult Arrests	18	−0.44	0.06	−0.14
Adult Convictions	12	−0.60	0.05	−0.40
Sociometric Leader	17	0.54	0.05	0.31
Trainee Rating	15	0.64	0.01	0.02
Employability Rating	19	0.56	0.02	0.23

N = number of subjects
p = probability level
r = coefficient of correlation

The importance of verbal intelligence is further attested to by the Sociometric Leader ratings of the trainees, Table 15-VII. When the trainees rated each other on leadership, the sociometric ratings were more highly correlated with Verbal IQ than with Performance IQ. This is significant because one might expect performance factors to be more important to the trainees than verbal intelligence. Finally, ratings of the trainees by staff members on general competence (Trainee Rating) and employability after training proved to be correlated with verbal intelligence rather than performance abilities. These correlations attest to the importance of education directed at improving the verbal abilities of this population.

Consideration of the larger population under study provides further evidence of the same type with respect to intelligence, Table 15-VIII. Once again arrests are negatively correlated with intelligence factors. The correlations are low but significant. They are lower than the correlations for the smaller trainee group, probably in part due to the difficulty of getting reliable data from the control population. Once again adult arrests are shown to be inversely related to verbal ability for this population. However, the number of undetectable crimes committed is seen to be directly related to intelligence level. The data indicate that the *more intelligent delinquents*

TABLE 15-VIII
INTELLIGENCE QUOTIENTS VS ARRESTS

	N	Verbal IQ		Performance IQ		Full IQ	
		r	p	r	p	r	p
Juvenile Arrests	74	−0.27	0.05	−0.24	0.05	−0.28	0.02
Adult Arrests	70	−0.30	0.01	−0.17	−	−0.26	0.05
Family Arrests	75	−0.26	0.05	−0.28	0.05	−0.30	0.01
Undetected Crimes	76	0.27	0.05	0.32	0.01	0.32	0.01

N = number of subjects
p = probability level
r = coefficient of correlation

commit more crimes and are less often arrested than their less intelligent peers.

The relationships between reading ability and intelligence test scores for the trainees are depicted in Table 15-IX. Reading for Significance is related more to verbal than performance abilities. Reading to Understand Directions is also more related to verbal intelligence. The ability to follow directions is essential to both education and employment. Since difficulty in following directions is often part of the minimal neurological dysfunction syndrome, it may well be that the low Verbal IQ scores are, in part, the result of this syndrome.

TABLE 15-IX
VERBAL IQ AND PERFORMANCE IQ

	N	*Verbal IQ* r	*Verbal IQ* p	*Performance IQ* r	*Performance IQ* p
Verbal IQ	84	1.0		0.66	0.001
Full Scale IQ	84	0.93	0.001	0.88	0.001
Gates Reading for Significance	50	0.65	0.001	0.41	0.01
Gates Reading Follow Directions	50	0.48	0.001	0.26	0.06

N = number of subjects
p = probability level
r = coefficient of correlation

BENDER VISUAL-MOTOR GESTALT TEST

In the original plan of this study the Wechsler Adult Intelligence Scale and the Bender Visual-Motor Gestalt test were introduced to determine whether or not any significant degree of perceptual dysfunction would be detected in this population. Only after serious Bender abnormalities were detected were other tests introduced to ascertain the nature of the dysfunction in greater detail.

The Bender Visual-Motor Gestalt test is composed of nine geometrical figures which are presented to the subjects one at a time to be copied, Figure 15-1.[13] It is presumed that the ability to copy these designs is a measure of visual motor functioning. The results derived from 85 subjects tested are given in Table 15-X.* Only one third of the subjects were found to have normal Benders, whereas, 29 per cent were borderline and 38 per cent were abnormal.

The finding that only one-third of the delinquent, school dropout population tested had normal Benders compared with 85 per cent in the total population indicated that a significant degree of visual-motor dysfunction appears to exist in the delinquent, school dropout population under study.

*The Bender tests were scored by Miss Violet Spraings, Director, Psychological and Educational Services, Diagnostic School for Neurologically Handicapped Children, Northern California. The Pascal-Suttell scoring method was used.

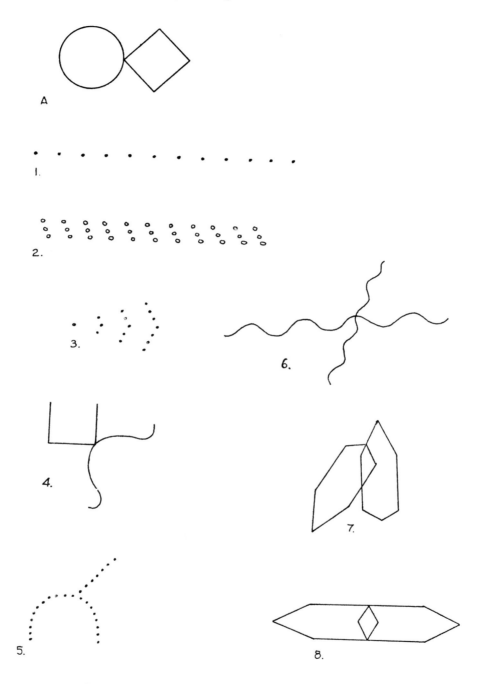

Figure 15-1. Designs of the Bender Visual-Motor Gestalt Test.

TABLE 15-X
BENDER VISUAL-MOTOR GESTALT TEST

Range	T-score	Trainees	Controls	Total	%Total
Normal	40-59	11	17	28	33
Borderline	60-69	5	20	25	29
Abnormal	70 up	3	29	32	38
	Totals	19	66	85	100

Therefore, *the hypothesis that a significant degree of minimal brain dysfunction should be found in this population is given further confirmation.*

In order to determine if the visual-motor problem was primarily one of visual perception, motor coordination or visual-motor integration, the Thrustone and Jeffrey Closure Flexibility Test (concealed figures),[14] and the Oseretsky Test of Motor Proficiency were given.[15] In the Closure Flexibility test, the subjects were to find geometrical figures concealed in designs as a test of visual perception. In the Oseretsky Motor test, the subjects performed a series of complex motor coordination and balance problems to test their motor functioning.

Correlations for the subjects between the Bender test and the Closure Flexibility and Oseretsky tests are given in Table 15-XI. The high correlation (—0.80 significant at better than the 0.01 probability level) between the Bender and Oseretsky tests indicates that the basic problem is either one of visual-motor integration or motor coordination. The lower correlation (—0.26) between the Bender and Closure Flexibility tests indicates that some visual perceptual dysfunction exists but to a much lesser extent than the motor problem.* The negative correlations indicate that as the Benders improve, visual perception and motor coordination and balance also improve. This is because the higher Bender scores indicate greater visual-motor abnormality, whereas higher Closure Flexibility and Oseretsky scores indicate better functioning.†

TABLE 15-XI
BENDER VS OSERETSKY MOTOR AND CLOSURE FLEXIBILITY

		Bender-Gestalt	
	N	r	p
Oseretsky Motor	15*	—0.80	0.01
Closure Flexibility	44	—0.26	—

N = number of subjects
r = coefficient of correlation
p = probability level
*Data available for trainees only.

*These findings are in agreement with those of Spraings on a nondelinquent dyslexic group ages six to nineteen, see The Dyslexias, Chapter 12.

†Because of the lack of norms for our population, it was not possible to draw conclusions about the degree of impairment on the Closure Flexibility and Oseretsky Test of Motor Proficiency for this population.

The Bender Visual-Motor Gestalt test is an important screening test for neurological dysfunction and for predicting learning disabilities in children. De Hirsch found that of the thirty-seven tests given in kindergarten to predict which children would have reading difficulties in the second grade, the Bender proved to be the second best predictor.[7] Since 38 per cent of the delinquent, school dropouts had abnormal Benders and another 29 per cent were borderline, it could have been predicted that this population would have a high rate of both minimal neurological dysfunction and learning disabilities. This could partly account for the fact that the usual "head start" and other special programs for the education of the minority ghetto children have tended to fail thus far. The evidence seems to indicate most cogently the need for early diagnosis and prescriptive teaching for this population.

DRAW-A-MAP TEST

It has been observed that people with neurological dysfunction or with brain damage often have difficulty with spatial orientation. Thus tests involving map reading and drawing have been used as indicators. As an added test, a number of our subjects were asked to draw from memory freehand maps of the San Francisco Bay area, indicating the Pacific Ocean, the San Francisco Bay, the bridges and the major local cities. The results were most interesting and enlightening. Although interpretation of the map tests and the other tests of our population is not complete a few examples will serve to indicate the nature of our findings.

A map of the Bay area is presented in Figure 15-2 for purposes of comparison with the subjects' maps. Figures 15-3 and 15-4 show the Bender drawings and map produced by subject C. J., age nineteen. Comparing these Bender designs with the originals in Figure 15-1, it is obvious that the copies are very poor and design 5 is rotated. Comparison of C. J.'s map with the correct map indicates considerable confusion about where the ocean and the Golden Gate Bridge are located. Also, the general configuration of the area is askew.

The drawings made by A. B., age twenty-two, are shown in Figures 15-5 and 15-6. The Benders are all cramped along one edge of the paper and the reproductions of the designs are quite poor. Correspondingly the map of the Bay area also indicates distortions and spacial disorientation. The total configuration lacks any concept of the true area. The Golden Gate Bridge and the Bay Bridge are shown as parallel whereas they are actually at about right angles to each other. The communities outside of San Francisco are bunched together in the same area, as though any city outside San Francisco was thought of as being "over there in the same direction."

Finally, a map drawn by T. C. is reproduced to show some features which recurred in several cases. All of the communities were placed in a straight line, improperly related. The relationship of the bay to the cities and the ocean was askew. And both bridges were depicted as heading out into the Pacific Ocean toward China. The spatial confusions exhibited by many of the maps when taken together with the Benders and other test scores indicate the probability of a high incidence of visual-perceptual-motor dysfunction in the subject population.

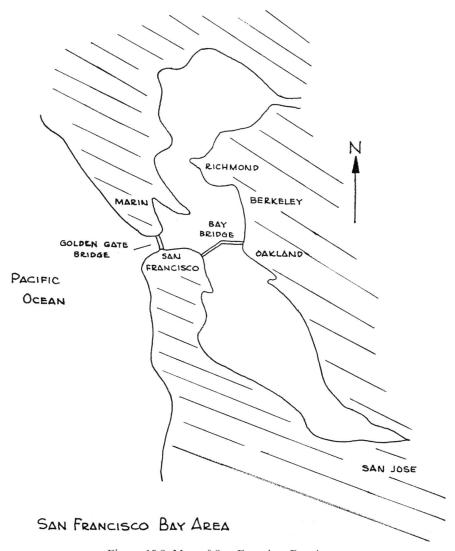

Figure 15-2. Map of San Francisco Bay Area.

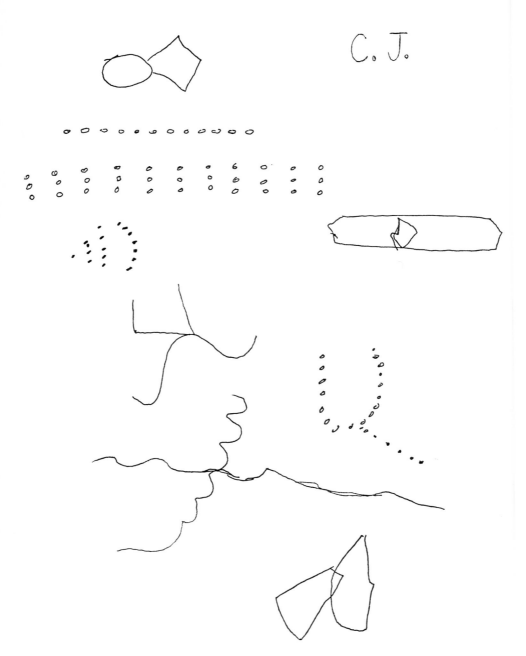

Figure 15-3. Subject C. J., age nineteen years. Copied Bender designs. Poor visual-motor coordination is apparent.

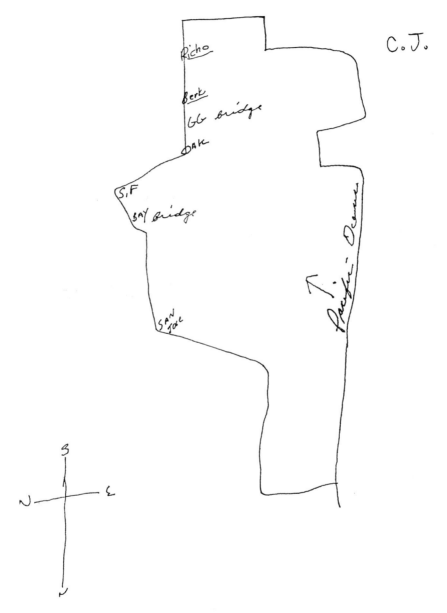

Figure 15-4. Subject C. J., age nineteen years. Map of Bay area from memory indicates distortion of spacial relations.

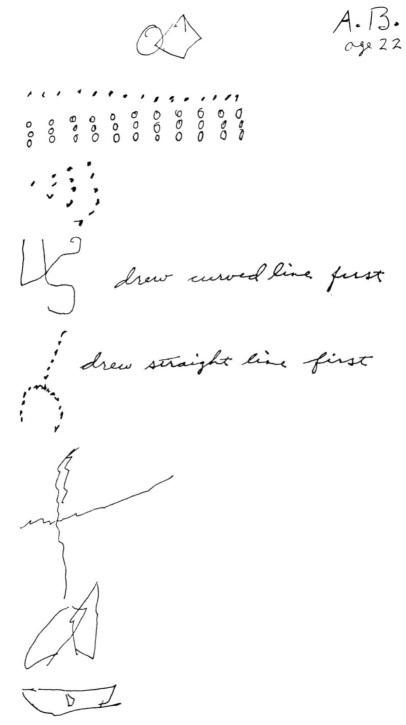

Figure 15-5. Subject A. B., age twenty-two years. Copied Bender designs. Considerable distortion present.

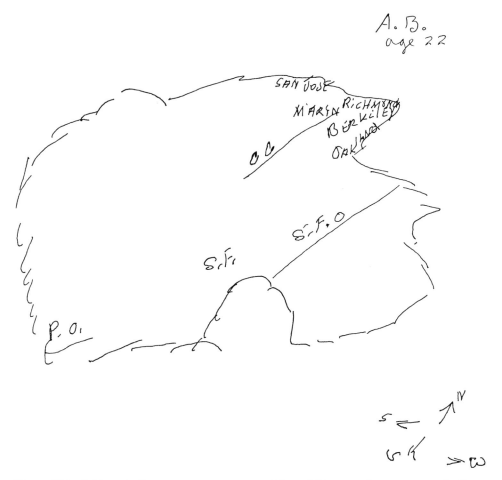

Figure 15-6. Subject A. B., age twenty-two years. Map of Bay area from memory indicates distortion of spacial relations.

HEMISPHERIC DOMINANCE

Bannatyne tested Lancashire boys, ages eight to eleven years, who were poor readers but who were functioning in the regular classroom, against a group of controls who were normal readers.[16] Using the Wechsler Intelligence Scale for Children, he separated their subtests into left hemisphere tests consisting of the Information, Arithmetic and Digit Span sub-scales; and right hemisphere tests comprising the Picture Arrangement, Block Design and Object Assembly sub-scales. It was found that the poor readers performed significantly better on the right hemisphere tests than on the left hemisphere tests as shown in Table 15-XII. Bannatyne concluded that poor readers tend to use their right hemispheres for learning more than

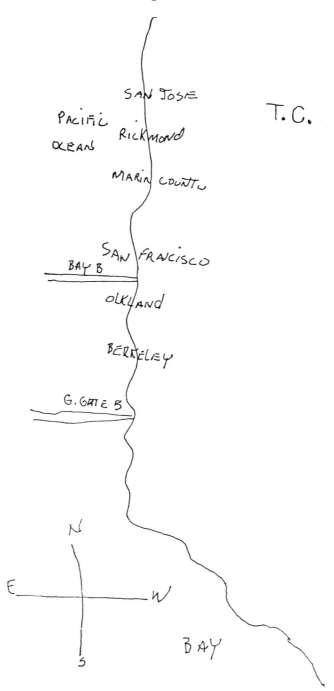

Figure 15-7. Subject T. C., age nineteen years. Map of Bay area. Typical of several showing Bay Bridge and Golden Gate Bridge heading out to sea, Bay and Pacific Ocean confused, and cities in a straight line and random order.

their left. For comparison purposes, the mean left hemisphere sub-scale scores were compared with the right hemisphere scores for eighty-four of the delinquents of our study. It was similarly found that the right hemisphere test scores were significantly higher than the left hemisphere scores. It may be surmised that delinquent poor readers also tend to have right hemisphere dominance. Others have also found dominance peculiarities among poor readers and have associated it with minimal brain dysfunction.

TABLE 15-XII
RIGHT HEMISPHERE VS LEFT HEMISPHERE TESTS
LANCASHIRE BOYS

87 Poor Readers vs 87 Normal Readers, ages 8 - 11

Poor Readers	Normal Readers
82% RH better than LH	50% RH better than LH
18% LH better than RH	50% LH better than RH

84 SAN FRANCISCO DELINQUENTS

	Mean	Std. Dev.	p
RH tests	8.31	2.41	0.001
LH tests	7.45	2.41	

Right hemisphere tests are Wechsler Information, Arithmetic and Digit Span. Left hemisphere tests are Wechsler Picture Arrangement, Block Design and Object Assembly.
p = probability level

SUMMARY

A preliminary examination was conducted of the evidence from testing nineteen trainees and eighty-three control subjects, ages sixteen to twenty-three years, who were primarily from minority ghettos. Almost all had dropped out of school and had engaged in varying degrees of delinquency. A substantial amount of untreated medical and dental problems were found in this population. On the Wechsler Adult Intelligence Scale, 39 per cent had significantly different Verbal and Performance IQ scores. The mean grade at which they dropped out of school was 10.5. Fifty-eight per cent were reading below the sixth grade level, and 64 per cent were below the sixth grade level on the Gates Reading to Understand Directions test. On the Bender Visual-Motor Gestalt test, only one-third were in the normal range. Comparisons of the Bender tests and the Draw-A-Map test proved that the subjects with poor Benders tended to be deficient in the spacial relations of local geography. Comparison of the Bender tests with the Oseretsky Test of Motor Proficiency indicated that most of their visual-motor problems were related to visual-motor integration and motor coordination. Comparison of the Bender test with the Closure Flexibility test showed that only a small proportion of the visual-motor problem was related to disturbances of visual perception. Finally, the right hemisphere Wechsler Subtest scores were found to be significantly higher than the left hemisphere scores.

All of the test deficiencies noted are known to be parts of the minimal brain dysfunction syndrome which is related to learning disabilities. This cumulative evidence, therefore, all tends to confirm the hypothesis that a significant degree of minimal brain dysfunction exists in the minority, delinquent, school dropout population. This evidence partially explains why the special programs to help educate this population have tended to lack success. A successful program of educational habilitation for the minority poor appears to require diagnostic testing and prescriptive teaching starting in preschool.

REFERENCES

1. CLEMENTS, S.D.: *Minimal Brain Dysfunction in Children.* NINDB Monograph No. 3. Washington, D.C., U.S. Government Printing Office, 1966.
2. CRITCHLEY, M.: *Developmental Dyslexia.* London, William Heinemann, 1964, p. 10.
3. HILGARD, E.R.: *Introduction to Psychology.* New York, Harcourt, 1967, pp. 425, 459.
4. ALBEE, G.W.: Needed a revolution in caring for the retarded. *Trans-Action*, 1967.
5. *Statistical Abstract of the United States.* Washington, D.C., Bureau of the Census, U.S. Department of Commerce, 1967.
6. PETERS, J.E.; CLEMENTS, S.D.; DANFORD, B.H.; DYKMAN, R.A., and REESE, W.G.: A Special Neurological Examination for Children with Minimal Brain Dysfunctions. Mimeographed, Little Rock, University of Arkansas Medical Center, 1967. (Cited in)
7. DE HIRSCH, K.; JANSKY, J.J., and LANGFORD, W.S.: *Predicting Reading Failure.* New York, Harper, 1966.
8. WORTIS, H., and FREEDMAN, A.M.: The contribution of social environment to the development of premature children. *Amer J Orthopsychiat, 35:*57-68, 1965.
9. EISNER, V.; GOODLETT, C.B., and MAYNARD, B.D.: Health of enrolees in neighborhood youth corps. *Pediatrics, 38:*1, 40, 1966.
10. DENHOFF, E.: Bridges to burn and build. *Develop Med Child Neurol, 7:*3-8, 1965.
11. MONCRIEF, F.M.: Juvenile Delinquency, San Francisco 1964 and 1960. Mimeographed, United Community Fund of San Francisco, 1965.
12. GATES, A.I.: *Gates Basic Reading Tests.* Bureau of Publications, Teachers College, Columbia University, April 1961.
13. PASCAL, G.R., and SUTTEL, B.J.: *The Bender Gestalt Test.* New York, Grune, 1951.
14. THURSTONE, T.G., and JEFFREY, T.E.: *Closure Flexibility (Concealed Figures) Test.* Chicago, Industrial Relations Center, U. of Chicago, 1956.
15. DOLL, E.A.: *The Oseretsky Test of Motor Proficiency.* Minneapolis, Educational Test Bureau, 1946.
16. BANNATYNE, A.: The Etiology of Dyslexia and the Color Phonics System. Mimeographed, U. of Ill., 1966.

PART FOUR
PROGRAM ADMINISTRATION AND TEACHER ROLES

Chapter 16

Case Finding and Treatment: The Teacher

SISTER EILEEN MARIE CRONIN

THE DILEMMA

I AM WELL AWARE of the dilemma in which classroom teachers often find themselves in dealing with the child who has special learning problems. I sympathize with them. They need some special technique to meet the needs of the child who suddenly runs around the classroom, or who looks out the window, or with whom they cannot establish a relationship or for the child who cannot read.

I should like to stress the basic assumption on which all teachers must operate regardless of problem manifestation. It is assumed that there is a sequential development of skills which all children, regardless of manifested behavior aberration, must achieve in order to become adequate learners. Currently, the special child is looked upon in education with respect, and success in teaching him is well rewarded with a sense of achievement. Nevertheless, further commitment to research and improved teaching techniques is expected and hoped for to reduce the recognized state of ignorance that continues to exist. Efforts presently shown by the disciplines of medicine, psychology and education to close the gap between clinical practice and classroom competency indicate hopefully better understanding and a more effective approach to the learning needs of the special child.

The special programs presently provided demonstrate more clearly the importance of recognizing the differences in the level of developmental skills *within* the child. The concept of individual differences *among* children has been familiar to educators for at least the past four decades. Programs established early in this country served to mark broad general categories for the blind, deaf, mentally retarded and the emotionally disturbed. Children with problems of undetermined origin were unfortunately often labeled as subnormal. In recent times a more definitive approach to the individual difficulties of children with average intelligence or better, but handicapped in school achievement, is being sought.

Teachers are often at a loss to define the difficulty of children who exhibit developmental gaps or lags in learning and/or behavior. The child easily discouraged, unpredictable in behavior and in school achievement, those with short attention span, or set off easily, or who cannot accept criticism pose a challenge to the classroom teacher, puzzling and difficult to solve. The gulf between neurology and the theories of human behavior is seemingly yet too wide to determine clear-cut guidelines as to etiology. This is not to say, of course, the etiology is unimportant nor that appropriate medical treatment is not a part of the total remedial program, but that the "shadow-boxing" with vague terminology and classification presently describing these children can only be confusing to the classroom teacher. Whether the label is one of brain-injured, cerebrally impaired, perceptually handicapped, neurologically handicapped, organic hyperactivity, or specific language disability, the afflicted child has, and is, a problem. For the teacher he presents a problem disruptive of classroom procedure and defying all effort at solution. No one knows the true extent of this problem. Careful guesses would place it at 5 per cent of the total elementary school population. The weight of evidence would suggest that while it is possible to have brain injury accompanied by developmental problems, it is also possible to have developmental deficits unaccompanied by brain injury. Critchley, an English neurologist and reputable authority in the field of dyslexia, cautions that most neurologists are reluctant to visualize in a severe learning problem any focal brain lesion.[1] To do so would risk ignoring the important factor of maturation in relation to chronological age, cortical development, and the processes of learning. He reminds us that with carefully controlled learning steps a child can overcome many of his problems. What is needed most of all are cooperative and centralized efforts including collaboration of neurologist, pediatrician, psychologist, and other experts. Only with the combined help of all experts can we hope to sort out some of the confusion that still exists in classification and terminology of the child with "hidden" learning handicaps.

SEQUENTIAL SKILLS

Because success in school for all children is predicated on the development of sequential skills, the teacher is sensitive to the behavioral controls appropriate to each of these skills. A failure to achieve in the skills necessary for learning is more manifest in reading than in any other school subject. But it is never a reading problem *per se*. It is a general learning problem owing to some underlying cause. Scant comfort is obtained from categorizing children "different" who cannot read or write or spell because of a tendency to reverse the form and sequence of the letters of the alphabet, or who cannot sit still long enough to attend a given task and who exhibit some degree of emotional disorder. Hence, teachers from primary grades through high school are more concerned with reading progress than with any other phase of the school program. This complex and complicated skill is based on the necessary prerequisites of factors that are largely physiological, emotional and mental, as well as maturational.

A child must have a healthy development and an enriching environment in order to have reached the stage of reading readiness. Specific language skills necessary to the acquisition of reading do not begin when the child enters school for the first time. Readiness consists of mastery of those simpler skills that permit one to reach higher skills. We expect a child of normal intelligence and balanced personality to be in command of an adequate sound vocabulary; we expect him to understand that symbols, auditory or visual, convey meaning; we expect that he can hold and guide a pencil and that his hand can copy what his eye or memory sees.

The development of language skills requires normal auditory memory and discrimination of sounds and words with the acquisition of a still wider vocabulary; it requires intact visual acuity and memory for the perception of forms and symbol constancy, of figure-ground and spatial relationships; it takes a well-developed muscle sense for coordinated fine motor movements as well as tactile and kinesthetic functions. A description of the various stages which contribute to reading skills shows that the reading process is dependent on sensory perception and language function. Similarly, the writing process lies between the language function and simple motor skills.

As every teacher knows only too well a relatively large number of children reach school age, or even high school, without adequately developed audio-visuo-motor skills. These children hear and/or say *pin* for *pen;* they write *b* for *d,* or read *saw* for *was;* they copy *69* for *96* or may be unable to draw a picture or write a word describing objects otherwise quite familiar. These are only a few examples of typical errors made by problem learners. They vary almost indefinitely from individual to individual.

While language is a distinct and important developmental task for learning to read, there are other aspects of the neurosensory syndrome evident in a child with specific learning disability. These phases are not sharply delineated but overlap and may be relatively discrete or found in combination with one another. A puzzling phenomenon to the teacher is the number of children who exhibit hyperactivity, a short attention span with laterality problems of crossed dominance, left-handedness, or ambidexterity. As is often revealed in parent conferences, a number of hereditary signs of similar difficulties are found in other members of the family. Early speech impediments are often predictive of future reading problems.

RASKOB SURVEY

A recent survey was made at the Raskob Institute of some three hundred children from first grade through high school.[2] These children, of average intelligence or better, mostly boys, were under remediation for problems of reading, writing, and/or spelling. Three-fourths of those tested demonstrated a problem of visual-perceptual and motor coordination. This complex problem showed a pattern of confusion in directionality, sequence, spatial orientation, figure-ground relationships, poor visual memory, reversals, or transpositions. Of the total group, one-third exhibited tension in impulse control by aimless walking about, shifting position frequently while sitting, throwing things about, running to the window, investigating contents of drawers and shelves, playing in a distracted manner with pencils, erasers and the like. That a good per cent of problem readers present a picture of hyperactivity and distractibility suggests forcefully the severity of the problem for the teacher in the classroom as well as for the parents at home.

The fact that one-third of the group investigated had relatives with abnormal laterality, poor motor coordination, reading problems, speech deficits, auditory problems, hyperactivity and/or visual-perceptual inadequacies would appear to support the hypothesis of genetic or familial trend in connection with the language disability syndrome. It was revealing to discover that many of the children had delayed speech development, in some instances for as long as two to three years.

READING PROCESS

As experts in the field of learning point out, the reading process is based on perception and the formation of numerous associations; therefore, it requires normal and mature neurosensory functions. It was suspected in the eighteenth century that learning and memory had a neural basis. At the turn of the century, William James theorized that neural connections occur when a stimulus is presented visually and auditorily at the same time. In learning to read and write, a conditioning of response takes place. To a child the sound of the spoken word is a familiar stimulus, the visual symbol of a printed word is a new stimulus. Through repeated associations of two stimuli, the child learns gradually to attach the same meaning to the sounds as well as to the symbol. He becomes conditioned to respond to visual stimuli as formerly to the spoken word. What facilitates the formation of association is the simultaneous presentation of two or more stimuli involving more than one of the senses.

With the multiplicity of physical and psychological processes entering into the reading process, it is no wonder that children can, and do, experience a breakdown in development. The surprising thing is that so many children do learn to read well and efficiently.

Reading problems cannot be approached in the same manner for all children. Many difficulties inherent in the process of learning to read are common to all children but for some are greatly accentuated and longer in duration. That a child cannot read at the expected time, under conventional methods, indicates the requirement of special techniques to meet particular strengths and weaknesses. Methods and techniques must obviously be adapted to the inadequacies associated in perception, language, memory and the higher thought processes. Instruction should begin at the point of the basic disturbed function, at the level of reading competency and according to the age of the disabled reader. The saying, "Meet the child where he is," is based on the premise that in cases of learning disabilities the exact level of function must be determined before remediation can profitably take place.

A major part of the teacher's armament includes knowledge of principles of learning. Although normal children can apparently learn in spite of occasional violation of these principles, children with learning disabilities cannot. Even in older children deficits in abilities basic to sensory-motor, perception, and language functions must be remediated before progress in cognitive thinking can take place. However, in regard to older problem readers, Dr. Marianne Frostig makes a good point when she advises that: "clinical experience suggests that beginning reading can often be introduced before the initial reading readiness training is completed. This is especially significant for the treatment of older children for whom time saved is of the greatest importance within the limits set by a slow step-by-step progress designed to insure continued success and to overcome the characteristic sense of hopelessness."[3]

No one of the multitude of remedial methods available will answer all the difficulties of the problem reader. In many instances special techniques of teaching and/or psychological assistance must be exercised on a one-to-one or small group basis to reinforce the individual's learning strengths and to remediate his weaknesses. Substantial assistance for teachers in meeting the special needs of deficient developmental abilities appears in the works of Myklebust, Kirk, Frostig, Kephart, Levi, Piaget, Bruner and de Hirsch — to mention but a few.

SOUND-SYMBOL APPROACH

The phonic method is basic to most remedial programs. In the normal process of learning to read children can be expected to recognize a number of words by the whole word method (configuration) before being introduced to the sound-symbol technique of building a sight vocabulary. But the child who is headed for reading problems cannot approach word recognition by visual recognition patterns alone. He needs a definite sound-symbol structure within which to operate in building a sight word vocabulary. A remarkable feature of the problem reader is the disturbance of the sound-structure of the written or printed symbol. Children with severe reading problems appear universally to operate on minimal clues in confusing not only the direction of letters such as *b* or *d, p* or *q,* but also the order of letters within words. The problem may be one of specifically visuo-spatial time sequence or the association of symbol to auditory stimulus. A stable association must function between auditory and visual stimuli for learning. Without a fusion of both, reading becomes haphazard. A child may even comprehend general ideas, for example, when reading silently but when required to read orally, he may skip the sound sequence in the association chain and refer directly to the meaning. Hence, he may read *money* for *dime, toy* for *ball, city* for *town,* and *large* for *huge.* Useful exercises in following directions for auditory-motor reinforcement besides describing a picture for visual-vocal association, and sometimes finding a specific object in a picture for auditory-visual association may be suggested.

An alphabetic-phonetic orientation from left to right, emphasizing proper sequence and clear visual-auditory perception with kinesthetic reinforcement of letter images is essential to remedial teaching. In the case of inadequate auditory discrimination, a visual and/or kinesthetic approach may be used while auditory perception is developed simultaneously. The use of the auditory-visual-kinesthetic technique as especially helpful in the acquisition of reading, writing and spelling is not unique. Reputable reading therapists, notably Fernald and Gillingham, have used this method effectively. The Raskob Institute makes use of such a method with a basic letter box and film strips. Several weeks of study at the Wordblind Institute in Copenhagen, Denmark, reinforced my own technique for structured exercises with reference to the Edith Norrie Letter Box. The Raskob Letter Box also emphasizes Montessori's principle that the child is never permitted to fail before he has succeeded.[4] The reinforcement of the concept of an alphabetic-phonetic technique *before* writing is basic to the Raskob Letter Box.

The use of the Letter Box is thoroughly explained before the pupil proceeds to use it. A disciplined order of procedure is important to the pupil who has never mastered the ability to concentrate nor formed orderly habits of work. The pupil confused in orientation and sequential order of letters within words (reading and spelling) cannot trust his visual memory. He must progress step-by-step in associating the auditory with the visual image of the symbol before kinesthetically reinforcing it in writing. With the letters or their combinations, the pupil manipulates on the table in *vertical* position (side of box) letters, sounds, or words dictated by the teacher or therapist. Pupils must never be permitted to manipulate a given exercise *during* dictation. It is important for the development of *auditory memory* that the pupil wait until the teacher or therapist has completed dictating an exercise before he puts it on the table. Errors are self-corrected as much as possible. Only after correcting his errors is the child permitted to transfer an exercise into writing. As the pupil establishes an auditory-visual-kinesthetic rountine, he begins to develop slowly but steadily independent, thoughtful, and correct study habits.

"Begin where the child is," we say. It is not necessary to begin always with the first exercise in the accompanying manual, but rather at the level of difficulty indicated by previous testing in areas of reading weaknesses. The ingenuity of the teacher is constantly challenged in providing more and similar tasks as the daily order of exercises continue as follows:

1. Pupil listens (auditory memory training) .
2. Pupil manipulates letter, word into vertical position on table to right of box (left-handed child positions letters, words to left of box) .
3. Exercise checked by pupil for errors.
4. Pupil manipulates exercise into horizontal position in front of box.
5. Exercise is covered and entered from memory into copy book or tablet (visual memory training) .
6. Final check for verification of both printed or written exercise (children print or write exercise) .
7. Each exercise of letter, sound, or word is replaced in box before next dictation.

PROBLEM WORDS

As a supplement to the Letter Box, the Institute makes use of its own film strips *Problem Words.*[5] The most troublesome disorder for the problem reader is that of building a stable basic sight vocabulary. The black marks on the page must become orderly, stable symbols of speech in the *how* to read before reaching a hoped-for stage of proficiency in the interpretation of all manner of printed material. The problem reader cannot identify words as wholes in global fashion nor remember them. Critchley calls it the normal "flash" of word recognition. Also, though to a lesser degree, the problem reader cannot synthesize a word out of its component letter-units. Problem readers frequently miscall such words as *horse* for *house* or *home, went* for *want, pretty* for *party* and the like. Erors made in the recognition of a sizable number of basic words have been narrowed down in thirty-six film strips to cover six different categories in the *Problem Words* films:

1. Words with one letter variable.
2. Words with two or more letters variable.
3. Words with single consonants.
4. Words with letter sequences easily confused.
5. Words with additonal letters.
6. Words confused by minimal clues.

It should be mentioned that the use of the tape recorder is an excellent way to coordinate the temporal sequence of hearing with the spatial sequence of seeing. The child audits his own recording, following along line for line with his eye the material read into the tape.

COGNITION

Important as words are to recognition skills, they are meaningful only to the relationship of ideas. Words and ideas in meaningful association establish the basis for reading. Comprehension is aided by imagery and by the memory of experiences which the reader brings to the printed page. A child's ability to learn depends chiefly upon his capacity to remember. A child who cannot picture in his mind previous experiences or who lacks concepts for the words and phrases he reads has difficulty understanding written material. Not only trainable by repetition, memory as a mental function can be materially aided by practice with images — by recalling the details and complex patterns found in them. Puzzles which are useful to perceptual training of figure-ground dimensions can also be utilized for memory training to recall, for example, what a horse looks like.

For more adequate discussion of cognitive development, the work of Aurelia Levi and Jerome Bruner are recommended.

I have only tried to point out briefly the teacher's concerns for the developmental skills and behavior manifestations of the child with learning problems whether brain-injured or not. Reading is used as an example of a learning skill since it is the single most important cause of school failure for all children today. The reading problems of the special child are particularly troublesome. He needs not only help in development of conventional reading skills but must have assistance in remediating retarded basic abilities. Further, I am fully aware of the necessity for a healthy emotional status in learning and the place of drug therapy in the case of the hyperactive child. Clinical experience leads us to believe that the needs of children with learning problems, provided all aspects of the problem be investigated, can with special teaching help be successfully met and with time, patience and intelligence, his handicaps may be overcome in many cases.

REFERENCES

1. CRITCHLEY, M.: *Developmental Dyslaxia*. Springfield, Thomas, 1964.
2. KLASEN, E.: Unpublished Research Project, Raskob Learning Institute, Oakland, California, 1967.
3. FROSTIG, M.: *Educating Children with Learning Disabilities: Selected Readings*. New York, Appleton, 1967.
4. CRONIN, E.M.: *Raskob Letter Box and Teacher's Manual*. College of the Holy Names Campus Book Store, Oakland, California.
5. CRONIN, E.M.: Filmstrips, LTS, Incorporated, Sunland, California.

Chapter 17

Administration of a Program

*Some Administrative Aspects of a Program
For Educationally Handicapped Children*

Leonard R. Levine

HISTORICAL BACKGROUND

As early as 1952 a committee of the California State Legislature became interested in programs for children with serious learning and behavior problems. A few years prior to 1960 a small number of California school districts had been exploring the feasibility of meeting the needs of children with severe learning disabilities. Some programs concentrated on helping the emotionally disturbed while others directed their efforts toward the neurologically handicapped child. The writings of Strauss and Lehtinen,[1] Howe,[2] Cruickshank *et al.*,[3] Haring and Phillips[4] and Mahler[5] all undoubtedly had an influence on and in some instances describe these very programs.

In the early 1960's an attempt was made to get legislative sanction for these programs. These early efforts to convince the legislators of the necessity for financial support by the State failed. Failure was probably due to the inability of the two major supporting groups to reach prior agreement and present a single proposal. One group wanted the emphasis to be on helping the emotionally disturbed. The other group concentrated on the organic, or neurological impairment approach.

Apparently taking heed of the advice of legislators to "get together" a single bill was drawn up which represented both groups. Assemblyman Jerome Waldie (now United States Congressman) carried the legislation through to its final passage in 1963.*

Legal aspects of this legislation can best be described by quoting from the California Education Code and its implementation document the California Administrative Code, Title 5.

The California Education Code, Section 6750 states that educationally handicapped minors are, "minors other than physically handicapped . . . or mentally retarded minors . . . who, by reason of marked learning or behavioral problems or a combination thereof cannot receive the reasonable benefit of ordinary education and facility."

Title 5, Section 221a of the California Administrative Code describes this in greater detail: "An educationally handicapped minor eligible for

---

*For details, see Tarnopol, Parent and Professional Relations, Chapter 3.

admission to a program is a minor described in Education Code 6750 whose learning problems are associated with a behavioral disorder or a neurological handicap or a combination thereof and who exhibits a significant discrepancy between ability and achievement."

From the words of the legislation it can be concluded that many of the children with learning problems make up the category designated as educationally handicapped (EH). They may be aggressive or withdrawn, coordinated or clumsy, perceptually involved or not. All are school failures.

The admission of children into this program is based on an individual evaluation and upon the recommendation of an Admissions and Discharge Committee which includes a teacher, school nurse or social worker, school psychologist or other pupil personnel worker, principal or supervisor and licensed physician.

The legislation also established instructional groupings for EH children. These may take one of three forms: Special Day Classes, Learning Disability Groups and Home and Hospital Instruction.

A Special Day Class is a self-contained unit with the pupils being taught for at least a minimum school day of 240 minutes. The maximum number of pupils allowed to be enrolled is eleven unless the age span is greater than three years which then reduces the size to nine. At the high school level the maximum enrollment is twelve except where the age span is greater than three years and then it is ten students.

The Learning Disability Group is arranged in a time block concept for individual or small group instruction. While it serves pupils at all grade levels it more nearly fits into the junior-senior high school day which is predicated on departmentalized instructional periods of time. In other words, the students are scheduled in the Learning Disability Group for one to five periods each day. When the student can also be programmed into a regular class period he is so scheduled. The group size is limited to eight for any single period, or six if the age span is over three years. If a Learning Disability Group is at the senior high school level the size is increased to ten each period, or eight if the age span is over three years.

For those children who cannot be maintained in a public school, Home and Hospital Instruction is available. This permits a program to be established in hospitals or residential institutions as well as in the home.

There are other legal elements of importance. The establishing of classes and groups for educationally handicapped children is on a permissive rather than mandatory basis. That is, local districts are not required to create such programs. If they do, only two per cent of the district's enrollment can be placed in the classes and groups and still be reimbursed by the State.

Financial aspects of the California EH program have been subjected to various changes. When the program first started the reimbursement of $565 per unit of average daily attendance (ADA) * was established for Special Day Classes. Learning Disability Groups were supported at the rate of $910 per unit of ADA. Added to these amounts was a $20 per ADA grant to defray consultation services which private psychological, psychiatric, medical, educational and guidance experts would render to the local districts.

It was soon determined that the reimbursement aspect needed further study and while this was being undertaken the amount was raised to $910 per unit of ADA for all EH programs.

In 1967 the studies indicated need for increasing the basic reimbursements. Legislation was changed which reimbursed Special Day Classes at the rate of $1140 per unit of ADA or $13,680 per class, $1880 per unit of ADA for Learning Disability Groups, and for Home and Hospital Instruction $1590 per unit of ADA. The special consultation fee was reduced to $10 per unit of ADA.

OPERATIONAL STRUCTURE

The success of any program for handicapped children is contingent on many factors. Some of these concern community interest, school district philosophy, financial resources, physical facilities, availability of trained personnel, administrative acceptance and support and teacher cooperation.

Before any program may begin a clearly defined need must exist plus an urge to do something positive to satisfy this need. Parent groups have often given the impetus to the beginning of many special education programs. They have pointed out the need. They have sought help for their children through any available source. They have contacted their local schools, their legislative representatives, professional groups and even the press. Their efforts have been just the start of a long process which may or may not lead to an acceptable program.

The realization of most special education programs depends on monetary considerations. Because these special classes are expensive when compared to regular ones local school districts find it difficult to support them financially without help from other sources such as the State.

Even when this financial hurdle has been overcome there still remains other problems to solve. An individual school district's philosophy must be such as to generate a desire to embark on special education programs. There is not as much resistance to providing education for children who by appearance show the need but when it comes to hidden handicaps, persuasion is a more difficult matter. Educationally handicapped children usually

---

*A unit of ADA is approximately equivalent to a child attending school for one year computed on a daily basis.

do not have noticeable disabilities when observed in a nonacademic setting. It is when they must compete in a classroom that their failures stand out. If local school districts can be convinced of the importance of establishing classes for these children then the programs have good chance for survival.

Physical Facilities

Physical facilities are an important consideration for EH classes. Since the goal of the program is to *reintegrate these children back into regular classes as soon as feasible* it follows that the special class's location should be in a regular rather than a special school. Even location within the school should be given careful thought. Since these children already feel different an effort should be made to reduce this feeling by assigning the class to a regular room in the main part of the building housing similar grade levels. Too many times special classes are relegated to the "boondocks," that is, the last room in the most remote wing of the school. This tends to increase the children's feelings of being different and may encourage other children to call them mentally retarded.

Some arrangements should be made to have the classroom environment accommodate small booths or "offices" for those students who are easily distracted. These offices should be moveable if possible. While affixing the sides permanently to the wall to form a **U** appears to be the easiest arrangement, it has disadvantages. When the teacher wants to do group work and place the children in that kind of configuration the rigid offices may be found to take up too much floor space and reduce the flexibility that most teachers find necessary for group activities. There is also the child who works better in the open than in a restricted area. Keeping him in a small semi-enclosed space may do more harm than good.

Lighting needs should be studied carefully in any school room setting and particularly in an EH class. The walls of the offices produce shadows not found in regular classes and the subdued colors tend to keep the light dim.

Areas in the room should be set aside for designated learning activities. For example, a "listening center" near electrical outlets can be used for recorded activities, while a "science corner" can be established in another part of the room and a space set aside as the "reading table." This also allows the teacher to routinize the learning and avoid unnecessary contacts between certain students who tend to have outbursts of temper.

A "time out room" *within* the classroom will be found helpful to the teacher and administrator alike. Some children having little or no self-control have a tendency to disturb other children and upset the atmosphere necessary for learning. When they lose control and are made to lie down on the cot in the "time out room" until they feel they can rejoin the group, it is beneficial to all. The teacher will have more time to instruct the class. The principal does not have to contend with the student in the administrative office area or prematurely rush him home.

An effort should be made to reduce distraction as much as possible. The color scheme of the room should be on the subdued side. Pastel greens and browns are better than excitable reds and oranges. If windows are at eye level, frosting them cuts off visual distractions with a minimum of light reduction.

Noise within the room can be reduced by use of carpeting over three-fourths of the floor. The indoor-outdoor variety affords good acoustical qualities at reasonable cost. Arts and crafts and other activities requiring a smooth hard floor surface can take advantage of the remaining uncarpeted area.

It is also helpful if the classroom has water facilities. This cuts down on the distraction caused by leaving the room to get drinks and bringing water in for the various art projects.

If arrangements can be made from the inception of the program to establish Learning Disability Groups in each elementary school then this concept should be seriously considered. Some authorities feel it is more effective for certain EH students to be assigned to a regular class initially and scheduled into the disability group for a designated number of periods. When they have overcome their learning problems they can be reassigned full time to their regular class. This avoids the problem of having to convince the teacher to take the child because he was assigned to her class originally even though he spent most of his time in the special program. Care should be taken, however, to return the student to an accepting teacher. If there is danger of a personality clash, or if the original assignment was untenable and developed into an irreparably harmful environment, then arrangements should be made to reassign the child to another teacher.

Equipment and Materials

Classrooms used for educationally handicapped programs should be as self-sufficient as is financially possible. This rationale is based on the individualized nature of the instruction, the almost minute-by-minute scheduling of students' work, and the teacher time needed to prepare the assignments. If equipment and materials have to be shared with many other teachers in the building the efficiency of the program is reduced.

The following teaching aids are necessary to a well balanced program: tape recorder, record player, recording device such as a Language Master[6] or Audio Flashcard System,[7] all with earphone attachments. A 35mm film strip projector is useful, particularly when a tachistoscopic device is attached to it. Single concept 8mm motion picture film loops have recently been produced for science and art instruction. A projector with a small daylight screen allows the student to view these films continuously with a minimum of disturbance to others since no room darkening is necessary. A full-length mirror is helpful in teaching right and left concepts and giving the student better body imagery. Many EH children cannot write legibly. A typewriter helps them get their thoughts on paper. The keys can be covered with different colored adhesive-backed circles and student's fingernails can be marked with corresponding colors to teach the keyboard. Walking boards and balance beams are excellent devices for improvement of large muscle coordination. Cots or foam rubber pads are necessary for the young children to lie on during the rest periods.

Another important piece of equipment is the telephone. With close parent contact necessary, a phone in the EH classroom avoids tying up the school phone and also permits a degree of privacy not usually available in most school offices.

Instructional materials are as varied as teachers' imaginations make them. Clear acetate sheets can be used indefinitely with water color ink pens for tracing writing lessons and solving arithmetic exercises. Mathematic concepts can be taught through the use of colored blocks such as found in the Katherine Stern[8] materials. Peabody Language Kits[9] are excellent for language development. They contain large clear pictures and clever hand puppets. One kit even has an intercommunication system capable of transmitting voices from one side of the classroom to the other. Dolch[10] materials and Botel[11] spellers are reported to bring good results in the teaching of writing and spelling. Young children with perceptual problems have also been helped through the use of Frostig[12] materials.

Reading is usually the most difficult academic area for EH children. Because most of them have weaknesses in several modalities a multisensory approach is often necessary to help them gain academic skills. In reading, an individualized program is almost mandatory. This will produce better results if it is correlated with the learning process required of reading rather than the content; that is, emphasis should be on methods and techniques which fit auditory, visual, kinesthetic modes of individual students.

Before most young children can undertake the learning necessary to read from a book an extensive amount of readiness is needed. Kirk[13] has developed a list of factors necessary for reading readiness. These are the following:

1. A mental age of six or more.
2. Adequate language development.
3. Memory for sentences and ideas.

4. Visual memory and visual discrimination.
5. Auditory memory and discrimination.
6. Correct enunciation and pronunciation.
7. Motor ability.
8. Visual maturity.
9. Maturity.

It is to be noted that most of the above factors are not present in the repertoire of skills of EH children. Thus, training in most of these has to be entered into before formal reading can take place.

Grace Fernald's work,[14] although emphasizing writing, contains many excellent reading readiness lessons. Gillingham[15] covers basic skill used in writing, spelling and reading. Her development of the phonetic approach is a technique that many EH teachers might find very useful with students.

Many kinds of readers have been found helpful after reading skills building has begun if they are adapted to fit the learning process, methods, and techniques selected by the teacher. Some of these are *Sullivan Programmed Readers,*[16] *Readers Digest,*[17] *Chandler Series,*[18] *SRA Reading Laboratories,*[19] *Behavioral Laboratory Series*[20] and *Teen-Age Tales.*[21]

Games, particularly those based on number concepts or requiring letter-word recognition are beneficial with children who have learning problems. Some of these are dominoes, scrabble, bingo and various flash card games.

Personnel

When one deals with a program as complex as that for EH children, things and ideas usually can be managed reasonably well. It is with people that the most difficult problems arise. This difficulty is not necessarily in the sense of negative qualities but is linked to personality attributes related to working with other professionals and children with learning disabilities. Thus it is the selection of personnel that is most crucial in establishing a high success potential for the program.

Teaching Staff

Those who have the primary responsibility for the on-going learning situation are the teacher and aide. These people must work together as a team if maximum benefit is to be derived from having two adults in the classroom simultaneously. Their successful relationship is dependent on the meshing of two personalities into a teaching unit where there exists both similar and complementary skills in each.

Teacher. The teacher is the key person around whom this program revolves. Moreover, the criteria for selection of this important person are most difficult to establish.

The basic requirements should be a standard teaching credential and several years of successful experience in a regular classroom. A few EH teachers have had a credential entitling them to instruct mentally retarded children. While a few of these teachers have been successful others have failed. It is felt that the latter group needed a baseline of teaching normal children before venturing into the intricacies of the unique EH class. In addition to the several years of successful regular class teaching experience the teacher should be a creative person and have the motivation to learn how to teach EH children. Further criteria should include demonstrated ability to teach small groups as well as individuals while providing for the remainder of students with meaningful work assignments. It would be well to pause here and reflect on the philosophy of the program.

Establishing the goals of the program before selection permits the matching of the candidate's personality against these goals. The goal of a program for EH children is to develop sufficient learning skills and strengthen self-concept to the extent that these children will return to the regular class and succeed. This will be accomplished best by having a structured environment, adequate and appropriate equipment and supplies, supportive services and administration. Thus the teacher should be comfortable working in a highly organized setting where each minute of the day is planned for every student. The teacher should be able to use equipment and supplies not necessarily found in the regular classroom. Being able to take advantage of the assistance of a classroom aide might be required. Working with a school psychologist in a manner that goes beyond just implementing psychometric data should be part of the criteria. The teacher should be able to work closely with the school principal and other administrators in carrying out the program within the framework of school and district policies. Added to the above which develop an image, or a model are the factors of maturity, patience, flexibility, sensitiveness, firmness, energy, friendliness and good health. One other consideration that should not be overlooked is that the candidate's motivation in seeking to teach these children should not be based on a desire to act out or solve problems of a personal nature.

Teacher Aide. Some programs operate without a teacher aide. Because of the individualized nature of instruction within the class, the use of an assistant makes this effort much more effective. The aide is responsible not only for clerical duties such as attendance accounting, preparing and distributing instructional material but also becomes the second teacher in the room. In some districts the aides are accredited teachers, while in most they are not. Where they are accredited, their work serves as a training ground for later assignment to an EH class of their own. This helps insure a steady supply of *trained EH teachers,* but it is more expensive than using non-accredited persons. The same qualities that are sought in an EH teacher candidate are looked for in an aide, i.e., maturity, patience, etc. However, another attribute is necessary — that of following the teacher's directions and yet having the ability to go ahead without depending on the teacher for constant guidance. This narrow balance of subordination with intelligent initiative is one of the most difficult tight ropes to walk. Initially, the aide's lot can be a trying one because the children may be sensitive to the status structure and try to play her off against the teacher. She has to be perceptive to these machinations and not allow herself to be put in an untenable situation which results in taking a position against that of the teacher.

Auxiliary Services

Auxiliary services comprise those persons assigned to the school as an adjunct to the teaching situation. These people are the school psychologist, nurse, curriculum consultant, social worker and other specialists such as the speech and language therapist. Because of the high degree of distractibility evidenced by EH children, care should be taken not to have too many services in the room at the same time or on the same day. This requires good communication and scheduling procedures.

School Psychologist. As mentioned above the law sets forth that the written identification of a child as educationally handicapped is the responsibility of three people, among whom is a psychologist, either with a designated school credential or certified as having clinical training with children. He is almost always a member of the Admissions and Discharge Committee. Usually the regular class teacher calls to the psychologist's attention a particular child who is having learning or behavior problems. This individual referral might develop into classroom observation and subsequent testing and evaluation of the child. The psychologist's report along with those of an educator and a medical doctor form the basic agenda items which are acted on by the Admissions and Discharge Committee. In some districts the collecting of this information is the responsibility of the psychologist while in others an administrator has the task. Since psychological services are such an integral part of the EH program it follows that the psychologist should also have the responsibility of handling the entire case. This results in strengthening continuity rather than a fragmentation which tends to weaken the contributions of others. In other words, when the psychologist is involved from the beginning observation, through psychometric evaluation, to liaison between the family, school, outside-the-school agencies, other professionals, and finally to presentation before the Admissions and Discharge Committee the whole case seems to be better integrated.

After the student has been placed in the class the psychologist still has a responsibility to work with the teacher assisting her in helping to solve the psychodynamics of the problems the child manifests in this unique environment. One of the best ways a psychologist can be effective is to consult with the teacher and aide on a regular basis in problem solving sessions which focus on rather specific problems of child management. It is also beneficial if the school principal can be present during these meetings.

It will be found that the psychologist will need to devote much more time in providing services to the EH program than any other person in special education. Thus his caseload should be adjusted to make allowance for this additional demand on his time. One way to alleviate the problem is to relieve the psychologist from all assignments except those pertaining to EH students.

Involvement with parents whose children have been admitted to the EH class is another important part of the psychologist's role. This can take the form of individual parent conferences called for a specific reason or group meetings to discuss matters of a more general nature.

Nurse. Many EH students have health problems. The nurse's involvement with the program can be a very beneficial one. She can make parent or family doctor contacts on matters concerning vision and hearing tests, general cleanliness and medication. A number of these children need to take medication to reduce hyperactivity, increase attention span and lessen anxiety. Consistency of dosage is usually necessary in order to derive benefit therefrom. With some frequency parents forget to give their children the prescribed amount of medication or neglect it altogether. This usually shows up in the child's behavior at school. Because of her training the nurse usually can handle these situations effectively.

Curriculum Consultant. It seems that the teacher's most frequent request is for some material or technique that she can use with her educationally handicapped students. The person who can give her the greatest help in this area is the curriculum consultant. The background and knowledge of this specialist can be very beneficial in matching materials and techniques with the needs of both teacher and student. It takes someone who is highly creative and keeps abreast of the rapidly increasing array of books, texts, devices, equipment, games and new teaching methods, to give the teacher assistance in this important facet of the program. A school district may have such a qualified person on its own staff or it may have to look to the outside and make arrangements on a contractual basis.

School Social Worker. School social workers are numerous in some districts in California while in others they are quite scarce or even nonexistent. The social worker can perform a valuable function in districts having an EH program. She can counsel the family in the initial stages of identification and can continue to work with them after placement is made. Some families having EH children are quite disorganized and the social worker can attempt to re-establish a degree of stability. If she has special skill in group work she can put this to use by working with the children in the class or their families.

Speech and Language Therapist. Language and articulation problems are very often found among EH children. The services of a speech and language therapist can be of great help to the EH teacher. The therapist, if the numbers warrant, can conduct group sessions or he can take the children out of the room and work with them on an individual basis. The EH teacher can reinforce the work of the therapist by incorporating language development in her daily assignments with the individual students. The speech and language therapist can make a most important contribution in testing children for problems of auditory perception — which most children with learning disabilities display. He is also the key person to develop a program for remediation of language and articulation problems.

Administrative Services

School Principal. Schools are similar to naval vessels with respect to morale. Just as the captain creates factors leading to a "happy ship" or a "taut" one the principal sets the tone and administrates the school in an easy-going manner or "by the book."

Educationally handicapped classes flourish best in an environment of encouragement, acceptance, flexibility and openness. The principal who will try to learn the basic elements of the EH program by reading pertinent material, attending lectures and talking to others experienced in the same program will probably establish a setting conducive to greatest growth. He should participate in as many class activities as possible, including EH staff conferences, Admissions and Discharge meetings and parent conferences and meetings.

After an EH class is assigned to a school and the students placed in it, the principal has the major responsibility to see that the class is successful. He will be the person on whom the teacher will depend for support in matters concerning student placement and reassignment, discipline, and parent contacts. It will be his responsibility to evaluate the teacher and aide and ultimately the program. For this he will need to make himself as knowledgeable as possible about the many facets of providing for the unique needs of educationally handicapped children.

Director of Special Education. This person is responsible for all special education programs at the district level. These may include the educable mentally retarded, gifted, educationally handicapped, blind, deaf, etc. Since the program for the educationally handicapped is the most recent one and the largest, more time will be spent by the director in its administration than the others. Any new program as unique as this requires special care and nurturing.

The most difficult task for the director is the selection of adequately trained personnel. The teacher and aide cannot be marginal people. They must have the ability to move quickly into a new field and be successful in the shortest possible time.

But how does he know who will be successful? There is no sure way to guarantee the selection of competent personnel. However, there are methods which tend to result in better choices. The candidate's records should be carefully checked and previous employers contacted by phone. Often accurate information is more easily obtained by personal contact than by written communication. There should be several interviews if possible. Even though the director uses all of his skills to pick the best people he can make the task more effective if he receives assistance from others such as the Director of Personnel, principal of the school to which the class is assigned, and psychologist who will be dealing with the students and teacher.

Another responsibility of the director is the providing of adequate supplies, equipment and consultation for the program. He should see that the purchase of necessary items is budgeted for and expedited to the classroom. A tape recorder does not do the teacher or pupil any good if it is still an item on a requisition form in someone's desk. Consultants should be contacted early enough to be able to make commitments of time convenient to the teachers and other personnel.

The director should also make it his duty to visit all the EH classes personally. In this way he sees for himself the program at its operational level and also indicates to the personnel he is interested in them.

In order to perform all of these duties effectively, *the director should carefully study the technical journals in these fields and attend technical conferences to insure that he keeps abreast of the latest developments.* Research is proceeding at such a rapid rate that it is easy to become mired in outdated, useless approaches to administering a program for handicapped children.

Finally, the director should make himself personally available to parents by attending meetings called for their benefit. This channel of communication is necessary both as a public relations measure and as a sounding board for feelings and concerns.

Parent Meetings

While there is a danger in generalizing, this may be risked in order to state that EH children seem to do better in class when their parents are cooperative with the school. Some parents cooperate from the very beginning. With others, cooperation is not easy to develop. Parent conferences with the teacher establish some understanding of the dynamics of the day-by-day class work. However, many parents have concerns which they are not comfortable discussing at such conferences. It takes a meeting with other parents present, some of whom are willing to talk about their feelings and concerns, to induce the reluctant ones to join in as contributing members.

The initial meetings are more effective if they are informational, that is, a description of the program, its needs and goals. At later meetings a discussion of specifics about child behavior and management can be undertaken successfully. When most of the parents are more comfortable about the fact that their child is in a special class and will enter into a discussion during the meeting, getting to the feeling level may help develop better understanding. Naturally, those who conduct the meeting should be skillful in group process and thus guide the parents effectively to help achieve their goals.

REFERENCES

1. STRAUSS, A.A., and LEHTINEN, LAURA E.: *Psychopathology and Education of the Brain-Injured Child.* New York, Grune, 1947, vol. 1.
2. HOWE, JOHN: *An Exploratory Study of Children with Neurological Handicaps in School Districts of Los Angeles County.* Los Angeles, Los Angeles County Superintendent of Schools, 1963.
3. CRUICKSHANK, W.M., and others: *A Teaching Method for Brain-Injured and Hyperactive Children.* Syracuse, Syracuse, 1961.
4. HARING, N., and PHILLIPS, E.: *Educating Emotionally Disturbed Children.* New York, McGraw, 1962.
5. MAHLER, DONALD: *Instructional Planning for Educationally Handicapped Children.* Orinda, California, Orinda School District, 1964.
6. Bell & Howell Company, 7100 McCormick Road, Chicago, Ill.
7. Electronic Futures, Inc., 57 Dodge Avenue, North Haven, Conn.
8. *Structural Arithmetic Kits 1 & 2,* Palo Alto, Houghton.
9. American Guidance Company, Publisher's Building, Circle Pines, Minnesota.
10. Garrard Publishing Company, 2 Overhill Road, Scarsdale, N.Y.
11. Follett Publishing Company, 1010 West Washington Blvd., Chicago, Illinois 60607.
12. *Program for the Development of Visual Perception,* Chicago, Follett.
13. KIRK, SAMUEL A.: *Teaching Reading to Slow-Learning Children.* Boston, Houghton, 1940.
14. FERNALD, GRACE: *Remedial Techniques in Basic School Subjects.* New York, McGraw, 1943.
15. GILLINGHAM, ANNA: *Remedial Training for Children With Specific Disabilities in Reading, Spelling, and Penmanship.* New York, 1956.
16. McGraw-Hill Book Company, Webster Division, 1871 Redwood Highway, Novato, California.
17. *Readers Digest New Reading Skill Builder Series,* Educational Division, Reader's Digest Services, Inc. Pleasantville, N.Y.

18. Chandler Publishing Company, 124 Spear Street, San Francisco, California.
19. Science Research Associates, Inc., Rt. 2, Box 390, Morgan Hill, California.
20. Behavioral Research Laboratories, 42923 Isle Royal, Fremont, California.
21. STRANG, RUTH, and ROBERTS, RALPH: *Teen-Age Tales Series.* Burlingame, California, 1954.

Chapter 18

Michigan's Perceptual Development Program

Jean E. Lukens

T HE PERCEPTUAL DEVELOPMENT PROGRAM of the Oakland Schools, Michigan, is a public school program which is serving a small population of children in need of specialized instruction. The present status of the program and the procedures which have evolved to make the program operational may be of interest to those starting new programs or improving present programs.

Of greater interest to most of us will be the laboratory from which we learn — the children in the classroom. I would also like to share with you some knowledge gained from members of the diagnostic team, school administrators, teachers, parents and personnel from clinics offering ancillary services.

The Perceptual Development Program is a Special Education program for children with learning problems. The children are not mentally retarded, but they are academically retarded. On psychological test batteries they show deficiencies in certain areas, but they test within the normal range of intelligence — some test above average. In a regular class they have not learned by conventional procedures, they are frustrated children and they are frustrating to teach. They may be described as different learners rather than nonlearners.

Medical diagnosis indicates neurological immaturity or dysfunction, or sensory underdevelopment — minimal brain dysfunction.

Psychiatric evaluation indicates that the unusual behavior which the children sometimes exhibit can be attributed primarily to the neurological dysfunction and their reaction to failure, rather than to emotional maladjustment *per se*.

Educational assessment shows low achievement and uneveness in the development of skills needed for academic success. A reporting of behavior by the referring teacher includes some descriptions as follows: varied performance from day to day as well as from subject to subject; inability to follow directions; clumsiness; restlessness; much or very little verbal output; unfinished work, and poor copying from the blackboard. Problems in reading, spelling and writing are those most often reported although some children are said to read well but comprehend little.

Children are eligible to enter the program between six and ten years of age and to remain as long as they need the program and are progressing satisfactorily. The overall goal is to develop the child's skills for his return to regular elementary classrooms within a reasonable period of time. It is, therefore, imperative that children who have a favorable prognosis for meeting this goal are those found eligible and placed in the program. It is an interim program and not a total change of curriculum for the school years and for life planning. It is essential to have parent cooperation and understanding.

The name Perceptual Development was given to the program in an effort to identify specifically an area which is essential to school success and which can be developed. It is not meant to name the handicap, but rather the goal.

In Oakland County, Michigan, a pilot study was started in 1961 with four classes in local school districts. The purpose of the pilot program was to determine if an educational program could be planned and operated successfully in a public school setting for the population of children briefly described above. The program was based on the research of a committee appointed to study the problem, innovations have been made as indicated. Expansion has taken place and now twenty-three classes (as of January 1, 1968) are in sixteen school districts, and there are six modified class programs.

Nearly 250 children are enrolled in the program. Some have returned to regular classrooms after one year in the special class and a few have stayed four years. A follow-up study is being made in the local districts operating programs. Indications are that 90 to 95 per cent of those returning are doing average regular classroom work — a few are doing better — a few have not succeeded as yet. The modified-class teacher has functioned this year to help children return with success to the regular school program and to help children who need less than a full day of special teaching. The Perceptual Development Program is classified under "otherwise physically handicapped" — a presently defined category by the State of Michigan, Department of Education, Special Education. Two kinds of service are possible in this category — the special class and the modified class. As need is indicated by experience, suggestions for redefinition are being made.

The problems of the children referred for study are varied. Perception problems are evident and perhaps best described as presenting a variety of levels of function. Some children have motor problems, some have visual perception problems and some show auditory perception problems. Deficits in visual perception show that children cope with size, form, pattern and figure-ground poorly. It has been said that their organization is poor, recognition of differences and likenesses and other relationships are deficient. Some children see parts and not always the whole and make a judgment before all the data are gathered. They have an insufficient or incorrect perceptual pattern.

Some children show organizational and integration problems at the cognitive level. All of these differences in learning can be called deficits when they are described in relation to the normal range for a given age.

The language patterns of the children evidence differences in learning both from the auditory and the visual sense. The speech is often telegraphic, agrammatical or reversed just as the visual perception patterns are. Concept formation is poor and specific problems in language development are variously described as like dyslexia, aphasia, or dysgraphia.

Many of the children show poor understanding of directions, inability to name familiar objects, and other symptoms of behavior that indicate a real lack in the language areas. Problems in articulation are not more frequent than in the total population. Repeating correctly does not seem to be a problem of many of the children, but their understanding is lacking.

The amount of verbal output and the reaction of children to verbosity, their own or that of others, is evident. A general instability and lability of emotional control is seen in many of the children with learning problems.

Many of the children have difficulty in sustaining attention, they seem to be giving their attention to too many things. Perseveration is evidenced in their school work and in social behavior. They get stuck in a rut and need to continue an action long after it is appropriate.

Children vary considerably in motor coordination abilities. Some have good gross motor skills and very poor fine motor control. They swim well and write poorly. When discussing such skills as figure drawing and/or handwriting, of course, we are evaluating more than the motor problem — several perceptual skills are needed. The total task must be evaluated.

I have not described all of the problems of all of the children, but have endeavored to suggest some sample kinds of problems. You will note several things about the problems which might be summarized by saying the following:

1. Deficits are in some areas — usually not in all areas of performance.
2. Children show different kinds of problems and yet much can be attributed to deficits in perception.
3. Problems indicate a sort of general immaturity.
4. Many of the behaviors can be attributed to deficits that are not readily apparent.
5. The problems are more severe than can be attributed to lack of experience as is evidenced by recent studies with deprived children.

The Perceptual Development Program is one of many Special Education programs in Oakland County, which serves 250,000 school children in twenty-eight local school districts. The people of the county voted a special education tax, in the amount of one mill to provide reimbursement to local districts for facility and operational expense to supplement the funds reimbursed from the State of Michigan Special Education funds.

The costs involved in educational programming cover facility, equipment and operational expenses. The State of Michigan reimburses local districts for a part of the operational expenses of Special Education programs. The Intermediate School District, the corporate name of which is Oakland Schools, assumes responsibility for the reimbursement to local districts for the facility, equipment and a part of the operational cost as determined by formula.

In Michigan, Special Education is deemed to be a regional responsibility. Programs are operated by the local districts, but costs are totally reimbursed to them. Children may cross boundaries of school districts to the Special Education facility needed by them, as a matter of right and without cost or tuition.

Oakland Schools assists local schools in initiating programs, teacher orientation, consultation on individual case studies, building educational planning committees and the overall operation of programs.

The kind of program just briefly described is possible, then, because of complete services for more severely handicapped children, financial and legal feasibility and an administrative unit which encourages total programming for children with handicaps, as well as creative curriculum planning in General Education. It is unrealistic to expect that programming for children with lesser handicaps will receive service first.

In order for a program to be reimbursed by tax money, it must be accepted into a category of Special Education defined by the state. As has been mentioned, the present special class program has come under the category of "otherwise physically handicapped." This also means that eligibility criteria and diagnostic procedures must be consistent with the plan for the program. Although some of us would like to proceed from etiological categories for classification of children, we are willing to try programs within a narrow definition to provide the way for broader programming.

Children are declared eligible and placement is recommended by an Educational Planning Committee. All persons with a particular interest in the child's educational program are invited to participate in the action of the committtee. The referring teacher and principal, all persons having a part in the testing and reporting of diagnostic information, the local administrators concerned with the program, the special class and modified class teachers and the Oakland Schools representative of the Perceptual Development Program comprise a work group for the systematic recording and assessment of pertinent information. The responsibility of this body is to determine what the primary problems of the child are and in what educational setting he can best be helped. Referring teachers and principals of schools never go away from an educational planning session without better insight into the problem of the child and some concrete ideas for educational planning. This is true even if the child is not declared eligible for a special class program. This committee also convenes in evaluation sessions to determine readiness of the child for the next step in his education.

The multidisciplinary diagnosis of children has helped groups of professionals to work as a team. Members of the team have learned to read and evaluate the findings of the psychologist; to glean important facts from the medical reports; to judge the significance of social, developmental and health histories; to study the speech and language evaluations and the educational testing and to use this information for individual planning for each child. The diagnostic team is most effective when it is comprised of persons on the staff of the school district operating the program. In some school districts where personnel are limited in number and lack skill in diagnosis, meetings of the group have been organized to compile a list of the various clinic centers and other sources of diagnosis. Families are helped to learn about available resources and encouraged to confer with their family physician for direction in getting the required medical assessment. The professional team then becomes the core of the program with all disciplines of the professionals contributing to the process of gaining insight into the total problem and offering suggestions for help to the child and his family. Members have learned to ask the right questions of their colleagues to obtain pertinent information for educational planning.

The team has gained sophistication in understanding the child with minimal brain dysfunction and learning disabilties through current readings, discussions and workshops. The Oakland Schools Psychological Clinic and the Speech and Hearing Clinic have held seminars with local school psychologists and speech correctionists to present various instruments for testing and in delineating certain ways to observe and gather information.

Teachers for the Perceptual Development Program are chosen because they are good teachers of young children. Before university classes were available in the field of learning disabilities for children with minimal brain dysfunction, many training sessions were held for teachers. Developmental sequences were used as a basis for planning the educational diagnosis. Teachers, who are always good observers, were encouraged to try procedures the results of which showed deficits of children, and gave them points of articulation with other specialists on the team. Seminars are held one half day each month to keep teachers abreast of new findings in the field and promote discussions of problem areas.

Since one phase of investigation that must be squarely met is "how does this child learn?" various kinds of presentations were tried to help members of the team develop proficiency in investigating this question. The results of standardized measures alone do not seem to develop understanding, as well as learning all about the child's deficits and assets, charting them on a profile sheet and amassing all the test information. The teacher must learn for herself to ask the child how he does a process and then learn to listen to his answer. If the teacher can get to this level of functioning and is creative in planning the initial approach and initiating changes as needed, this teacher has developed from a user of methods and a remediator of skills into a clinical teacher of developmental skills — one who takes into account all aspects of behavior and finds out how the child learns.

I have mentioned briefly the articulation between disciplines. The ability of the teacher to report school behavior to parents, the social worker, the psychologist and the medical specialist involved in diagnosis and medical management is also very important. Discussions with teachers encourage them to seek help from other disciplines, to apply it to the educational setting and to stay within the educational framework. A teacher cannot be a psychiatrist, but she can use information given by the psychiatrist to understand behavior and to create a better educational plan. There can be some disastrous results when we try to play too many roles, even in the face of a shortage of personnel.

School administrators are often hard to convince of the necessity of different programming for children with problems. This is particularly true when there is unusual behavior in the child and excessive pressure from parents, the school and others outside the school. Those of us who work with teachers, children, parents and all members of the diagnostic team find it is especially important to present a good case for education. Documentation of all attempted procedures and the success or failure of these helps administrators to have reasons for change.

This overview of the Perceptual Development Program — its rationale and basic operational procedures — will furnish you with a background for looking at some of the children participating in the classroom instruction. The educational program is based on several premises, which have been helpful in understanding the educational structure and in initiating changes in instruction.

Learning has taken place when the following adaptations have been instituted:

1. Reducing detrimental stimuli and increasing proper stimuli for learning.
2. Providing a structure to allow for the prescribed educational procedures.

3. Individualizing the approach on the basis of need of the child as well as a developmental program for group participation. The needs of children indicate amount of adaptation required and timing for these changes.
4. Utilizing multi-sensory procedures whenever a deficit in one sensory modality needs training and/or reinforcement.
5. Building systematic sequential teaching procedures to insure the development of insight and success.
6. Fostering dependence of the child until he learns to take instruction and to develop his own organization pattern. Then groups are developed systematically and independent action on the part of the child is encouraged.
7. Returning to regular classrooms for short periods of the day in the area of greatest competency to prepare for total reintegration into the appropriate class.

SOME SUGGESTED CURRICULUM MODIFICATIONS FOR TEACHING

Many procedures and materials devised for the Perceptual Development Program can be adapted in the regular classroom to make learning easier for children with problems. In the educational planning, for any child with a learning problem, it is necessary to define the specific areas which are lagging according to his age and level of intelligence. The techniques used to help this child learn are based on the understanding of his particular problem and the application of certain principles of teaching and management which have proven helpful with other children presenting similar problems.

Specific materials or techniques are not the most essential element for teaching children with learning problems. The method is one of clinical teaching, where use of diagnostic information and continued evaluation points the way to the choice of techniques and materials. The method then is one of understanding all behavior of the child and setting the stage for his effective learning.

Some techniques have been found useful for several children and will be mentioned here in the hopes that the study of the individual child will suggest the proper place for these modifications:

1. Decreasing the amount of work expected of the child until he begins to experience success.
2. Increasing the focus on the part to be learned by underlining, color-cueing, using a marker or slot in a paper, using individual earphones and a tape recorder to pronounce words slowly and dis-

tinctly as the child reads or writes, or having the child face the wall or a screen with only his own reference charts in view, using a copy directly in front of the child instead of a blackboard some distance away and/or any creative way to help him see the part to be studied.

3. Giving direct and concise instructions verbally and by demonstration.

4. Choosing the remedial instruction needed by the child as the core of instruction rather than exposing him to all sequences of learning generally recommended for children with learning disabilities.

5. Providing a variety of materials and lessons directly related to his area of deficit and his learning method. This principle is involved when the child uses manipulative materials to sustain his attention and builds words from letters when his deficit is learning the organization and structure of words.

6. Keeping the child's level of intelligence and chronological age in mind when choosing materials. Puzzles are sometimes useful in helping the child see parts to whole, and form and shape. Map puzzles might be used for the older child rather than nursery rhyme puzzles which are used for young children.

7. Considering age and ability when talking to the child. A business-like attitude rather than the "fun and games" approach is often appreciated by children who want to learn. Praise is reinforcement when deserved.

8. Taking the child as quickly as possible through the concrete and gross steps and arriving at his level of abstraction and fine discrimination and/or motor performance — the learning level of the child.

9. Using materials such as lined or squared paper to help the child organize his work. Marking beginnings and direction with color, arrows, etc. to help the child develop insight into the problem before expecting him to remember. Simple adaptations often provide the structure.

10. Defining for the child the reason for the adaptation being used. This description should be concise and give a reason if the child is in need of this information.

Teachers are creative within this framework, in introducing developmental sequences to groups of children, and by using individual lessons for the child who needs more help at certain times. Classroom teachers are learning to observe behavior of children, in seeking clues for the modification of curriculum within a given classroom, to serve the child with fewer perceptual problems and to refer, for further study, children who do not respond to these modifications.

It should be remembered that the Perceptual Development Program is a very small part of the programming for children with problems in learning. Many changes in general education are taking place to eliminate the problems of children who can profit from better developmental sequences in the regular grades. Other services from both general and special education have been expanded or changed in view of new knowledge of the learning of children. Referrals for the Perceptual Development Program have been made earlier in the child's school life because of these new knowledges and services.

Our main interest is that all curricula shall be more concerned with the learning process. Many different kinds of service within the school as well as home and community services, which can be encouraged by parents and professionals, are needed to serve the child with learning disabilities.

Appendix

Organizations of Parents for Children with Learning Disabilities

THE FOLLOWING IS A list of many of the organizations to which parents belong for the purpose of helping their children with learning disabilities and each other. Since most of these organizations are run by volunteer parents without office help, the addresses tend to change and local chapters are founded or become inactive. It is therefore not possible to make a complete or up-to-date list. This list contains those organizations and local chapters which replied to a questionnaire mailed in October, 1967, and those listed in the ACLD Directory.

STATE AND LOCAL PARENT-ORGANIZED GROUPS CONCERNED WITH LEARNING DISABILITIES IN CHILDREN

Alabama

Alabama Assn. for the Education
of Brain Damaged Children
c/o Mrs. Beverly Branson
P.O. Box 835
Huntsville, Alabama 36601

Alabama ACLD
c/o Mrs. Hugh Lanier
2069 Montreat Circle
Birmingham, Alabama 35216

Alabama Foundation to Aid
Aphasoid Children
P.O. Box 3472
Birmingham, Alabama 35216

Aphasoid School
Parents' Group
3001 Montgomery Hwy.
Birmingham, Alabama 35233

ACLD Items of Interest
Mrs. Edna Thompson, Mgr.
912 S. 81st St.
Birmingham, Alabama 35206

Alaska

No Associations

Arizona

Arizona ACLD
c/o Mrs. William M. Bowling
5321 E. Calle del Medio
Phoenix, Arizona 85018

Arkansas

Arkansas Assn. for Children
with Learning Disabilities
Drawer A — Pulaski Heights Sta.
Little Rock, Arkansas 72205

Arkansas ACLD
c/o Dr. Edwin F. Mathis
4601 Woodlawn
Little Rock, Arkansas 72205

Arkansas ACLD Newsletter H.E.L.P.
Mr. R. P. Burnham, Jr., Editor
117 Winwood Road
Little Rock, Arkansas 72207

Note: This material is partly drawn from *A Directory of Organizations Concerned with Learning Disabilities.* Association for Children with Learning Disabilities, 2200 Brownsville Rd., Pittsburgh, Pa. 15210, March, 1968. Reprinted with permission.

Arkansas ACLD,
   Little Rock Council
c/o Mrs. Lois Dossett
6615 Sandpiper
Little Rock, Arkansas 72205

Arkansas ACLD,
   Monticello Council
c/o Mr. Charles Johnson
Monticello, Arkansas 71655

Arkansas ACLD,
   England Council
c/o Mr. Everett H. Watson
223 Maple
England, Arkansas 72046

Arkansas ACLD,
   Heber Springs Council
c/o Mr. Roy Rosin
Heber Springs, Arkansas 72543

Arkansas ACLD,
   Benton Council
c/o Mrs. Robert Brewster
Benton, Arkansas 72015

California

Calif. Assn. for Neurologically
   Handicapped Children
P.O. Box 604, Main Office
Los Angeles, California 90053

CANHC, Education and
   Information Committee
11291 McNab Street
Garden Grove, California 92640

CANHC MOVIE DISTRIBUTION
Mrs. Dorothy Jackson
6472 Will Rogers Street
Los Angeles, California 90045

CANHC LITERATURE
DISTRIBUTION
Mrs. Pat O'Betz, Director
1755 W. 245th St.
Lomita, California 90717

CANHC
Alameda North Chapter
P.O. Box 893
Berkeley, California 94701

CANHC
Contra Costa Chapter
P.O. Box 164
Orinda, California 94563

CANHC
East San Gabriel Valley Chapter
P.O. Box 773
West Covina, California 91790

CANHC
Fresno Chapter
P.O. Box 5119
Fresno, California 93755

CANHC
Hayward Chapter
P.O. Box 6023
Hayward, California 94545

CANHC
Imperial Chapter
391 West B
Brawley, California 92227

CANHC
Livermore-Amador Chapter
P.O. Box 1105
Livermore, California 94550

CANHC
Long Beach Chapter
P.O. Box 7634
Long Beach, California 90807

CANHC
Los Angeles Chapter
P.O. Box 45273
Los Angeles, California 90045

CANHC
Marin Chapter
P.O. Box 596
San Rafael, California 94901

CANHC
Merced Chapter
205 W. 26th St.
Merced, California 95340

CANHC
Napa Chapter
P.O. Box 2575
Napa, California 94558

CANHC
Orange Chapter
P.O. Box 1592
Santa Ana, California 92702

CANHC
Pomona Valley Chapter
P.O. Box 677
Pomona, California 91769

CANHC
Redlands-Yucaipa Chapter
524 Camino Real
Redlands, California 92373

CANHC
Riverside Chapter
8086 Sycamore Ave.
Riverside, California 92504

CANHC
Sacramento Chapter
P.O. Box 4565
Sacramento, California 95825

CANHC
San Bernardino Chapter
P.O. Box 95
San Bernardino, California 92402

CANHC
San Diego Chapter
P.O. Box 111
Escondido, California 92025

CANHC
San Fernando Valley Chapter
P.O. Box 2674
Van Nuys, California 91404

CANHC
San Francisco Chapter
P.O. Box 16380
San Francisco, California 94116

CANHC
San Mateo Chapter
P.O. Box 515
Belmont, California 94002

CANHC
Santa Clara Chapter
P.O. Box 6478
San Jose, California 95150

CANHC
Santa Cruz Chapter
P.O. Box 667
Aptos, California 95003

CANHC
Shasta Chapter
P.O. Box 3161, Enterprise Branch
Redding, California 96001

CANHC
South Solano Chapter
7825 Sereno Dr.
Vallejo, California 94590

CANHC
Stockton-San Joaquin Chapter
P.O. Box 4332
Stockton, California 95204

CANHC
Tuolomne Chapter
67 N. Stewart
Sonora, California 95370

CANHC
Vacaville Chapter
573 Cotton Wood St.
Vacaville, California 95688

CANHC
Ventura Chapter
1130 W. Devonshire Dr.
Oxnard, California 93030

CANHC
West Contra Costa Chapter
P.O. Box 515
San Pablo, California 94806

CANHC
Whittier Chapter
P.O. Box 67
La Habra, California 90631

CANHC
Woodland Chapter
117 Antelope St.
Woodland, California 95695

CANHC
Yuba-Sutter Chapter
P.O. Box 277
Sutter, California 95982

Colorado

Colorado Assn. for Children
with Learning Disabilities
P.O. Box 1506
Denver, Colorado 80201

Colorado ACLD
c/o Harry S. Grill
1937 Grape
Denver, Colorado 80220

Colorado ACLD
Boulder Chapter
c/o Mrs. Howard S. Cox
440 Japonica Way
Boulder, Colorado 80302

Colorado ACLD
Littleton Chapter
c/o Mrs. N. Bakarich
5911 S. Greenwood Circle
Littleton, Colorado 80120

Connecticut

Connecticut Assn. for Children
with Percept. Learning Disabil.
P.O. Box 2266 - Bishops Corner
West Hartford, Connecticut 06117

Connecticut Assn. for Children
with Percept. Learning Disabil.
c/o Wm. Fagan
253 Reservoir Rd.
Newington, Connecticut 06111

Southeastern Connecticut ACLD
P.O. Box 1111
New London, Connecticut 06320

S.E. Conn. ACLD
New London Chapter
c/o Mrs. Harvey Mallove
28 Mallove
New London, Connecticut 06320

Connecticut ACLD
Greater New Haven Chapter
P.O. Box 7362
New Haven, Connecticut 06519

Connecticut ACLD
Greater New Haven Chapter
c/o Mrs. Sydney Krass
255 Roydon Rd.
New Haven, Connecticut 06511

CACPLD, Bristol Town Com.
c/o Daniel Kervick
38 Henderson St.
Bristol, Connecticut 06010

CACPLD, Newington Town Com.
c/o John Deltano
107 Windmill Lane
Newington, Connecticut 06111

CACPLD, Vernon Town Com.
c/o Mrs. John Williamson
Gail Drive
Ellington, Connecticut 06029

CACPLD, West Hartford Town
Com.
c/o Mrs. Jerome Siegel
27 Brainard Rd.
West Hartford, Connecticut 06117

Connecticut Assn. for Children
with Learning Disabilities
P.O. Box 463
Norwalk, Connecticut 06852

Connecticut Assn. for Children
with Learning Disabilities
c/o Dr. Maximilian Trost
37 Douglas Dr.
Norwalk, Connecticut 06852

District of Columbia
No Associations

Delaware
No Associations

Florida

Dade Reading Foundation
Parent Group
c/o Mrs. B. R. Prentice, Sr.
7455 S.W. 118th St.
Miami, Florida 33143

Pompano Beach ACLD
c/o Mrs. Gary Du Bois
P.O. Box 211
Pompano Beach, Florida 33062

Georgia

Georgia Assn. for Children
with Learning Disabilities
c/o Rev. E. Eager Wood
403 Valley Brook Dr., N.E.
Atlanta, Georgia 30305

Georgia ACLD
P.O. Box 27507
Atlanta, Georgia 30327

Georgia ACLD
Atlanta Chapter
c/o Mrs. Frank P. Hudson
1425 West Paces Ferry Rd., N.W.
Atlanta, Georgia 30327

GACLD, Griffin Council
c/o Mrs. Ronald L. Ellison
314 Powell Ave.
Griffin, Georgia, 30223

GACLD, Marietta Council
c/o Mrs. H. M. Goldsworthy
P.O. Box 850
Marietta, Georgia 30060

Hawaii

Hawaii Assn. for Children
with Learning Disabilities
13A Slade Drive
Honolulu, Hawaii 96822

Idaho
No Associations

Illinois

ACLD Items of Interest
Randolph T. Snively, Editor
331 Branson Ave.
Glen Ellyn, Illinois 60137

Bureau County ACLD
c/o Ray L. Pollack
P.O. Box 333
Princeton, Illinois 61356

Chicago ACLD
c/o Mrs. Joseph Gleiter
8220 Washtenaw
Chicago, Illinois 60652

Chicago ACLD
P. H. Child — Box 4451
Chicago, Illinois 60680

DeKalb County ACLD
(Now being formed)
c/o James Tushaus
818 Sharon Dr.
DeKalb, Illinois 60115

Fund for Perceptually
Handicapped Children
P.O. Box 656
Evanston, Illinois 60201

Fund for Perceptually
Handicapped Children
c/o Howard J. Lurie
396 Orchard Lane
Highland Park, Illinois 60035

FPHC NEWSLETTER PERCEPTION
c/o Mrs. Charles R. Goldstein
9128 Karlov
Skokie, Illinois 60076

Illinois Council for Children
　with Learning Disabilities
c/o Bernard Kamin
8737 N. Trumbull
Skokie, Illinois 60076

Northwest Chicago ACLD
c/o Grace Lunde
6712 N. Olympia
Chicago, Illinois 60631

N. W. Suburban Council on Under-
　standing Learning Disabilities
(COULD) c/o Mr. Richard H. Stamm
1414 Redwood Dr.
Mount Prospect, Illinois 60056

Lake County ACLD
c/o Gerald Shaver
134 Sunset Dr.
Libertyville, Illinois 60048

South Suburban HELP
P.O. Box 104
Park Forest, Illinois 60466

South Suburban HELP
c/o Dr. Ronald Thompson
359 Westgate
Park Forest, Illinois 60466

West Suburban Assn.
　for the Other Child
c/o M/M W. Joseph Gartner
406 Hill Avenue
Glen Ellyn, Illinois 60137

West Suburban Assn. for the Other
　Child
354 Prospect Ave.
Glen Ellyn, Illinois 60137

Indiana

Indiana Assn. for Perceptually
　Handicapped Children
c/o Robert Yarman
R.2 Cable Trail
Fort Wayne, Indiana 46805

Bartholomew County ACLD
Now being formed
562 Cleveland St.
Columbus, Indiana 47201

JFK Assn. for Perceptually
　Handicapped Children
7 Hawthorne Dr.
Jeffersonville, Indiana 47130

Johnson County ACLD
c/o Mrs. Ralph Kidwell
506 Northgate Dr.
Greenwood, Indiana 46142

Marion County ACLD
c/o Frances X. Kenny
4611 Vera Dr.
Indianapolis, Indiana 46220

Iowa
　No Associations

Kansas
　No Associations

Kentucky

Kentucky Assn. for Children with
　Learning Disabilities
c/o Wm. H. McCann
R. 1, Bowmanmill Road
Lexington, Kentucky 40504

Kentucky ACLD
Box 7171
Louisville, Kentucky 40207

Louisville Fund for Perceptually
　Handicapped Children
c/o A. Hardy
P.O. Box 7234
Louisville, Kentucky 40207

Jefferson County Assn. for Perceptually
  Handicapped Children
c/o E. C. Grayson
9204 Tiverton Way
Louisville, Kentucky 40222

Louisiana

Louisiana ACLD
c/o Dr. David Clark
1552 Pressburg
New Orleans, Louisiana 70122

LACLD, Alexandria Council
c/o James Davis
530 Park Place
Alexandria, Louisiana 71301

LACLD, Baton Rouge Council
c/o Mr. Van M. Davidson
1208 Bel Air Dr.
Baton Rouge, La. 70806

LACLD, Lake Charles Chapter
c/o Philip Perry
1004 Cherry Hill
Lake Charles, Louisiana 70601

LACLD, New Orleans Council
c/o Glen L. Cowand
P.O. Box 24071
New Orleans, Louisiana 70124

LACLD, Shreveport Council
c/o Ed. Trickett
6135 Dillingham
Shreveport, Louisiana 71106

Maine
  No Associations

Maryland

Maryland Assn. for Children with
  Specific Learning Disabilities
Mrs. Helen Weintzweig
320 Md. Natl. Bank Bldg.
Baltimore, Maryland 21202

Ann Arundel County ACLD
c/o Mr. Donald Brunstetter
8 Wisler Ct.
Severna Park, Maryland 21146

Frederick County ACLD
c/o Mrs. Paul Mossburg
1515 Rosemont Ave.
Frederick, Maryland 21071

Harford County ACLD
c/o Mrs. Sharon Nahrgang
R.D. 2 Box 227A
Darlington, Maryland 21034

Howard County ACLD
c/o Hank Preiser
67 Carlinda Ave.
Ellicott City, Maryland 21043

Montgomery County Assn. for Children
  with Specific Learning Disabilities
Box 33
Kensington, Maryland 20795

Massachusetts

Massachusetts Assn. for Children
  with Learning Disabilities
c/o Mrs. Gertrude Webb
397 Moody Street
Waltham, Massachusetts 02154

Michigan

Michigan Assn. for Children with
  Learning Disabilities
Dr. Lee W. Haslinger
P.O. Box 743
Royal Oak, Michigan 48068

Michigan ACLD, Greater Detroit
  Chapter
c/o Mrs. Chas. Posen
14520 Bishop
Oak Park, Michigan 48237

Michigan ACLD, Pontiac-West Bloomfield
  Chapter
c/o Mrs. Robert Jones
5770 Arcadia
Orchard Lake, Michigan 48033

Michigan ACLD
c/o Mrs. Jack King
3119 Shenandoah Dr.
Royal Oak, Michigan 48073

Minnesota

Minnesota Assn. for Children with
  Learning Disabilities
Formerly MABI
P.O. Box 6391
Minneapolis, Minnesota 55423

Minnesota ACLD
c/o Geoffrey Rhodes
9625 Washburn Rd.
Minneapolis, Minnesota

MACLD Office, Newsletter Editor
320 16th Ave. So.
Minneapolis, Minnesota 55404

Mississippi

Hattiesburg Assn. for Perceptually
  Handicapped
P.O. Box 1787
Hattiesburg, Mississippi 39401

Missouri

Missouri Assn. for Children with
  Learning Disabilities
c/o Dr. and Mrs. Yates Trotter
1243 East Catalpa
Springfield, Missouri 65804

Montana

Great Falls Assn. for Children with
Box 2563
Great Falls, Montana 59401

Great Falls ACLD
Mrs. John England
630 Doris Drive
Great Falls, Montana 59401

Nebraska
No Associations

Nevada
No Associations

New Hampshire
No Associations

New Jersey

New Jersey Association
  for Brain-Injured Children
61 Lincoln St.
E. Orange, New Jersey 07017

NJABIC Newsletter Editor
c/o Mrs. Bernard Kahn
61 Lincoln St.
E. Orange, New Jersey 07017

NJABIC, Burlington Co. Section
c/o Mrs. Gerald Melman
319 High St., Box 512
Mt. Holly, New Jersey 08060

NJABIC, Central Section
c/o Mr. George Hoffman
120 North 3rd St.
Highland Park, New Jersey 08904

NJABIC, Essex-Union Section
c/o Mrs. Beatrice Antell
930 Ridgewood Rd.
Milburn, New Jersey 07041

NJABIC, Hudson Station
c/o Frank Monaco
237 Van Nostrand Ave.
Jersey City, New Jersey 07305

NJABIC, Monmouth Section
c/o Mrs. Charles Turner
32 Burki Place
Freehold, New Jersey 07728

NJABIC, Northern Section
c/o Mrs. Herman Struhs
53 Brewster Pl., Box 112
Bergenfield, New Jersey 07621

NJABIC, Ocean Section
c/o Robert Jersey
546 Vaughn Avenue
Jersey City, New Jersey 07305

NJABIC, Tri-County Section
c/o Mrs. Joseph Hogate
94 Sparks Ave.
Pennsville, New Jersey 08070

Inter-Agency Committee for the
  Education of the Handicapped
Attn.: Miss Tolomeo
60 South Fullerton Ave.
Montclair, New Jersey 07042

New Mexico
  No Organizations

New York

New York Assn. for Brain-Injured
  Children
Irving Zeitz, Exec. Dir.
305 Broadway
New York, New York 10007

NYABIC c/o Albert Hans
118 Montague
Brooklyn, New York 11201

NYABIC, Albany Chapter
c/o John Monty
615 Via Ponderosa
Schenectady, New York 12303

NYABIC, Binghamton Chapter
c/o Mr. Herbert Nickels
5 Norman Rd.
Binghamton, New York 13901

NYABIC, Bronx Chapter
c/o Fred Jentes
25 - 30 Independence Ave.
Riverdale, New York 10471

NYABIC, Brooklyn Chapter
c/o Mr. Dominic Castellano
531 East 31st St.
Brooklyn, New York 11203

NYABIC, Buffalo Chapter
c/o Donald Cobb
151 Pine St.
East Aurora, New York 14052

NYABIC, Duchess County Chapter
c/o Mrs. Russell Lock
4 Windover Dr.
Poughkeepsie, New York 12601

NYABIC, Manhattan Chapter
c/o Mrs. Michael Luce
350 Central Park West
New York, New York 10025

NYABIC, Nassau Chapter
c/o Gilbert Henoch
600 Hempsted Turnpike
West Hempstead, New York 11552

NYABIC, Niagara Unit
c/o Mr. Chas. Petrozzi
339 14th St.
Niagara Falls, New York 14303

NYABIC, Putnam County Chapter
c/o Mrs. Walter Osnoe
RFD No. 1
Brewster, New York 10509

NYABIC, Queens Chapter
c/o Mr. Saul Spindel
64-33 215th St.
Bayside, New York 11364

NYABIC, Rochester Chapter
c/o Mr. James Green Jr.
24 Coleman Ave.
Spencerport, New York 14559

NYABIC, Rockland County Chapter
c/o Mr. Wayne Simpson
11 Westminster Dr.
Pearl River, New York 10965

NYABIC, Staten Island Chapter
c/o Mr. Joseph Rubin
15 Leverett Ct.
Staten Island, New York 10308

NYABIC, Suffolk County Chapter
c/o Dr. Richard Abbett
14 Farmstead Rd.
Cowmack, New York 11725

NYABIC, Syracuse Chapter
c/o Mrs. Elizabeth Crossley
4548 Broad Rd.
Syracuse, New York 13215

NYABIC, Westchester County Chapter
c/o Mr. John Ritchie
14 Suzanne Lane
Pleasantville, New York 10570

The Foundation for Brain-Injured
    Children, Inc.
89-71 216th St.
Queens Village, New York 11427

North Carolina
    No Associations

North Dakota
    No Associations

Ohio
    (No State Association)

Akron ACLD
c/o Mr. Robert LaBate
251 Greenwood Ave.
Akron, Ohio 44313

Cleveland ACLD
c/o Dr. and Mrs. Arthur Blum
3042 Lincoln Blvd.
Cleveland Heights, Ohio 44110

Lucas County Assn. for Neur. Hand.
    Children
c/o Mrs. Henry Rumm
5143 West Bancroft
Toledo, Ohio 43615

Parents, Inc. (An Assn. for Neurologically
    Handicapped Children)
c/o Paul Shover
170 East Maynard Ave.
Columbus, Ohio 43202

Youngstown ACLD
c/o Mrs. Gerald Kessler
388 Cranberry Run Dr.
Youngstown, Ohio 44512

Oklahoma

Oklahoma Council for Children with
    Learning Disabilities
c/o Dr. George Truka
5341 East 33rd St.
Tulsa, Oklahoma 74135

OCCLD, Tulsa Council
c/o Mrs. Rex Short
6933 East 66th St.
Tulsa, Oklahoma 74135

OCCLD, Creek Capitol Council
c/o Mrs. William J. Imhoff
606 South Wilson
Okmulgee, Oklahoma 74447

OCCLD, Central Oklahoma Council
P.O. Box 1655
Oklahoma City, Oklahoma

OCCLD, Central Okla. Council
c/o Mrs. F. D. Asher
3420 N.W. 45 St.
Oklahoma City, Oklahoma 73112

OCCLD, East Central Okla. Council
c/o Mrs. Henry C. Williams
Route 5, Box 96E
Muskogee, Oklahoma 74401

Oregon
    No Associations

Pennsylvania

Pennsylvania Assn. for Children
    with Learning Disabilities
P.O. Box 664
Allentown, Pennsylvania 18105

PACLD, Allegheny Chapter
c/o Mrs. Katherine Tillotson
4728 Old Boston Rd.
Pittsburgh, Pennsylvania 15227

PACLD, Lehigh Valley Chapter
Mrs. Noreen DeLeon
Box 664
Allentown, Pennsylvania 18105

PACLD, Capitol Area Chapter
c/o Mrs. Doris Lock
Box 1404
Harrisburg, Pennsylvania 17105

PACLD, Delaware Valley Chapter
c/o Mrs. Barbara Stein
2829 Solly Ave.
Philadelphia, Pennsylvania 19152

PACLD, Erie Chapter
c/o Mrs. Mary Donovan
1331 West Eighth St.
Erie, Pennsylvania 16502

The Assn. for Specific Learning
   Disabilities
c/o Chancy E. Burtch
513 Maple Lane
Edgeworth, Pennsylvania 15225

Lancaster Assn. for Brain Injured
   Children
c/o Mrs. John Moeller (Marie)
13 Race Ave.
Lancaster, Pennsylvania 17603

Society for the Education of Brain
   Injured Children
c/o Vincent Paganon
230 Wilston Drive, Apt. C-88
Morrisville, Pennsylvania 19067

Rhode Island
   No Associations

South Carolina
   No Associations

South Dakota
   No Associations

Tennessee

Memphis Education Foundation
c/o Henry S. Hooker
P.O. Box 17034
Memphis, Tennessee 38117

The Nashville Foundation for Children
   with Psychoneurological Learning
   Disabilities
c/o Mrs. Daniel P. Mathews
827 Cammack Ct.
Nashville, Tennessee 37205

Texas

Texas Assn. for Children with
   Learning Disabilities
c/o Dr. Chester Gorton
Drawer E — TWU Station
Denton, Texas 72604

TACLD, Beaumont Council
c/o Mr. Henry Hilgemeier
2930 — 19th St.
Beaumont, Texas 77706

TACLD, Brady Council
c/o Mrs. J. H. Campbell
P.O. Box 544
Brady, Texas 76825

TACLD, Brazoport Council
c/o Chester D. Hall
Box 271
Lake Jackson, Texas 77566

TACLD, Fort Worth Council
c/o Mr. Wiley Dunken
7237 Robinhood Lane
Fort Worth, Texas 76112

TACLD, Houston Council
c/o Mrs. Everett Scogin (Alice)
3236 Ozark
Houston, Texas 77021

TACLD, Mid-Cities Council
c/o Mr. Joe Hall
804 Briarwood Blvd.
Arlington, Texas 76010

TACLD, Neches Council
c/o Ralph Gilmer
4000 Twin City Hwy.
Port Arthur, Texas 77640

TACLD, North Plains Council
c/o Mrs. J. Stanley Hale
P.O. Box 2010
Amarillo, Texas 79105

TACLD, Paris Council
c/o Royce L. Wagg
2905 Clarksville
Paris, Texas 75460

TACLD, South Texas Council
Mr. Carl Chandler
610 Dolphin Place
Corpus Christi, Texas 78411

TACLD, Tyler Council
c/o Mrs. J. M. Protas
3122 Cameron
Tyler, Texas 75701

TACLD, West Texas Council
c/o Mr. Guy Shaw
1150 Glenwood
Abilene, Texas 79605

Utah
No Associations

Vermont

Vermont Assn. for Children with
Learning Disabilities
c/o Ray Stowell
75 Hadley
So. Burlington, Vermont 05401

Virginia

Roanoke Valley Assn. for Children
with Learning Disabilities
P.O. Box 707
Roanoke, Virginia 24004

Washington
No Associations

West Virginia
No Associations

Wisconsin

Society for Brain Injured Children
c/o Mrs. Vivian Prudowski
5032 No. Ardmore Ave.
Milwaukee, Wisconsin 53127

Wyoming
No Associations

Australia

SPELD of New South Wales
c/o Mrs. Y. Stewart
16 Coronation Ave.
Mosman, 2088 Australia

Queensland Association for Children with
Learning Problems
c/o Mr. E. J. Garvey
34 Culgoola St.
Kedron, 4031
Queensland, Australia

Canada

Main and Provincial Offices
Canadian ACLD
Suite 318
88 Eglinton Ave. E
Toronto, Ontario, Canada

CACLD, Alberta Office
c/o Mrs. Irene Vetsch
1203 70th Ave. S. W.
Calgary, Alberta, Canada

Manitoba ACLD
c/o Mrs. Yude Henteleff
795 Lanark
Winnipeg 9, Manitoba, Canada

Ontario ACLD
Suite 318
88 Eglinton Ave. E
Toronto, Ontario, Canada

Quebec ACLD
c/o Mrs. Ellen Sabin
5572 Rosedale
Montreal 29, Quebec, Canada

Branch Offices
CACLD, Atlantic Provinces Br.
Mrs. B. Pelletier
9 Dunally St.
Dartmouth St.
Nova Scotia, Canada

CACLD, Kamloops, B. C. Branch
c/o Mrs. W. Lennant
2650 Thompson Dr.
Kamloops, British Columbia, Canada

OACLD, Brantford Branch
c/o Mrs. R. W. Moore
Box 105
St. George, Ontario, Canada

OACLD, Burlington Branch
c/o Mrs. O. A. Hileman
R. R. 1
Waterdown, Ontario, Canada

OACLD, Fort William Branch
c/o Dr. and Mrs. J. Augustine
416 Catherine St.
Fort William, Ontario, Canada

OACLD, Kingston Branch
c/o Mrs. P. Broadhurst
333 Norman Rogers Dr.
Kingston, Ontario, Canada

OACLD, Kitchener Branch
c/o Mrs. L. P. Breithaupt
570 Glasgow St.
Kitchener, Ontario, Canada

OACLD, London Branch
c/o Mrs. Barton Auld
Delaware, Ontario, Canada

OACLD, Markham Branch
c/o Mrs. J. A. Underwood
3 South Dill Dr.
Markham, Ontario, Canada

OACLD, Oshawa Branch
c/o Mrs. Bruce Affleck
795 Masson St.
Oshawa, Ontario, Canada

OACLD, Peterboro Branch
c/o Mrs. D. W. Kelly
Quaker Oats Co. of Can. Ltd.
Peterboro, Ontario, Canada

OACLD, Sarnia Branch
c/o Mrs. N. F. Anderson
1016 Edgewater Crescent
Sarnia, Ontario, Canada

OACLD, St. Catherines Branch
c/o Mrs. C. A. Pryer
17 Park Lane Crescent
St. Catherines, Ontario, Canada

OACLD, Sault Ste. Marie Branch
c/o Mrs. David Pond
743 Wellington Ave. E.
Sault Ste. Marie, Ontario, Canada

OACLD, Ottawa Branch
c/o Mrs. C. J. Davies
743 Eastbourne Ave.
Ottawa 7, Ontario, Canada

OACLD, Toronto Branch
Suite 318
88 Eglinton Ave. East
Toronto 12, Ontario, Canada

OACLD, Waterloo Branch
c/o Mrs. Grant Ely
R. R. #2
Waterloo, Ontario, Canada

OACLD, York County Branch
c/o Mrs. M. L. Smoke
48 Laverock Ave., Apt. 512
Richmond Hill, Ontario, Canada

Canada — nonaffiliated
Edmonton Aphasic Assn.
c/o Mrs. E. Unger
1141 — 111th Ave.
Edmonton, Alberta, Canada

Index To Authors of Works Cited

INDEX

DATE DUE

7 3 1 '80	
11 2 7 '80	

BRODART, INC.   Cat. No. 23-221